MORALITY, RULES, AND CONSEQUENCES

A Critical Reader

Edited by Brad Hooker,
Elinor Mason, and Dale E. Miller

EDINBURGH UNIVERSITY PRESS

© The Contributors, 2000

Edinburgh University Press Ltd
22 George Square, Edinburgh

Typeset in Fournier
by Hewer Text Ltd, Edinburgh, and
printed and bound in Great Britain by
MPG Books Ltd, Bodmin

A CIP record for this book is
available from the British Library

ISBN 0 7486 1128 2 (hardback)
ISBN 0 7486 1174 6 (paperback)

MORALITY, RULES, AND CONSEQUENCES

Contents

Introduction

Brad Hooker, Elinor Mason, and Dale E. Miller

What determines an action's moral standing, that is, whether it is right or wrong? While there is no comforting general consensus on an answer to this question, two ideas repeatedly bubble to the surface. The first is that a moral code ought to contain a number of rules that tell people how to behave and that are simple and few enough that the average person can learn and obey them. The second is that the consequences of actions matter, often more than anything else. It is clear that there is at least some tension between these ideas, since it seems unlikely that a relatively simple set of rules will always direct people to perform the actions which will result in the best state of affairs.

Rule consequentialism draws on each of these ideas. Very roughly put, rule consequentialists believe that whether an action is morally wrong depends on whether it is forbidden by the authoritative set of moral rules, and that the authoritative set of rules is the set the universal establishment of which would have the best consequences. Obviously this rough statement of the view can be interpreted in different ways. Rule consequentialists differ, for example, about how literally the notion of universal establishment should be taken, about precisely what it means to establish a set of rules, and about exactly what it means to say that one set of consequences is better than another. In any event, rule consequentialism is to be distinguished from act consequentialism, the view that an act is morally right if and only if no alternative act would have better consequences.

'Consequentialism' is a younger and broader term than 'utilitarianism'. All consequentialist theories accord some foundational role to the question of which states of affairs would be best. Utilitarian forms of consequentialism typically rank states of affairs in terms of nothing but the amount of well-being those states of affairs contain. Other consequentialist theories take other things to be valuable, for example justice, fairness, and equality.

Consequentialists face other questions about the basic components of their theory. One of these is the question of whether to require the best available state of affairs, or merely one that is in some sense 'good enough'.[1] Another is whether right and wrong should be defined with reference to what would in fact happen, or with reference to reasonable expectations.

But those questions, as well as the distinction between utilitarian and non-utilitarian brands of consequentialism, are not the main focus in this volume. The papers collected here concentrate instead on the distinction between act and rule versions of consequentialism.

The names 'act utilitarianism' and 'rule utilitarianism' were not introduced until R. B. Brandt's 1959 book, *Ethical Theory*.[2] But the theories are far older than the names. For example, George Berkeley was quite clearly a rule utilitarian in 1712.[3] John Austin was almost certainly a rule utilitarian.[4] And a number of John Stuart Mill's central claims seem strongly rule utilitarian, though some of his other claims point towards act utilitarianism.[5]

On the face of it, rule versions of utilitarianism and consequentialism are more complicated than act versions. The rule versions evaluate rules in terms of their consequences and then require conformity with optimal rules. The act versions evaluate acts directly in terms of their consequences. We could put the matter in another way. Act versions take only one rule to determine moral rightness – namely, the rule 'maximise the good'. Rule versions take moral rightness to depend on a variety of rules – such as 'don't physically attack others', 'don't steal', 'don't break your promises', 'don't lie', 'be loyal to your friends and family', and 'help the needy'.

Would aiming to follow always the simple rule 'maximise the good' result in as much good overall as the various rules endorsed by rule consequentialism? In the first chapter in this volume, William Shaw argues that, although G. E. Moore's criterion of right is firmly act consequentialist, Moore clearly saw the attraction of a plurality of familiar rules. Perhaps surprisingly, Moore attempted to defend *exceptionless* rules on consequentialist grounds. The number of exceptionless rules envisaged by Moore is small, and this, Shaw argues, makes a big difference to the plausibility of Moore's claims.

Sanford Levy's contribution considers practical differences between act and rule versions of utilitarianism. Levy argues that, since utilitarian theories can be self-effacing, what is important is what they recommend teaching, rather than their standard of rightness. Act utilitarianism tells us that the right act is the one that maximises utility, but can also say that the right code to teach people to believe in is something entirely different. Act utilitarianism recommends teaching whatever it would maximise utility to teach. Rule utilitarianism, according to Levy, tells us that the right code is the one it would maximise utility to teach. Thus there is one sense in which act utilitarianism and rule utilitarianism are educationally equivalent: the code of rules that, according to rule utilitarianism, determines what is morally right is the same code that, according to act utilitarianism, should be taught.

However, the situation is more complicated than this, according to Levy. He argues that just as act utilitarianism can be self-effacing, rule utilitarianism can be self-effacing. The code the teaching of which would maximise utility is not necessarily the same as the code that it would maximise utility to teach people to teach. Levy goes on to argue that, despite this, act utilitarianism and rule utilitarianism remain educationally equivalent for all practical purposes.

Jonathan Riley (acknowledging his debt to John Harsanyi[6]) also argues that a society will enjoy a higher level of aggregate well-being if its members follow rule utilitarianism. In a society of act utilitarians, the well-being of any person could be sacrificed whenever his or her loss would sufficiently be made up for by the gains to others. So, in a society of act-utilitarians, there would not be the general security of expectations made possible by a code that distributes fixed liberal rights. These rights guarantee not only valuable incentives to work and to invest but also valuable freedoms. The happiest society will be one whose members are committed to following a system of moral rules with a liberal content, even if complying with that system sometimes means performing suboptimal actions.

The emphasis on security of expectations and the value of personal freedom also animates David Haslett's contribution. Haslett first provides an account of moral justification leading to rule utilitarianism. Then, underlining the importance of clear expectations, he explains that from a rule-utilitarian perspective the duty to help others needs to be restricted in definite ways.

David Lyons's 1965 book *Forms and Limits of Utilitarianism* persuaded most philosophers that rule utilitarianism ends up requiring the very same actions as act utilitarianism requires. In his contribution to the present book, Lyons draws on the work of R. M. Adams and Peter Railton to argue that perhaps each of the familiar utilitarian theories is not entirely faithful to the 'guiding utilitarian idea' that what matters is that there is as much welfare as possible. What is the principle conformity to which would most effectively promote welfare? Lyons notes that utility is produced by a variety of different things: acts, motives, rules, laws, institutions, and so on. The principle most faithful to the guiding utilitarian idea must be able to combine assessments of these different aspects of our lives and instructions concerning them. This, Lyons claims, is practically impossible.

Lyons identifies further difficulties. First, should we be considering one principle for everyone, or more than one? Second, should we consider more than one principle for each person (after all, people change)? Third, should we be considering the welfare that would result from actual conformity, or the welfare that would result from (for example) acceptance of the principle? Lyons argues that utilitarianism itself has no way of answering these questions, and thus is indeterminate.

Shelly Kagan's paper takes up similar themes. Kagan distinguishes between imagining rules as being ideally embedded (that is to say imagining that everyone accepts and conforms to those rules) and imaging them as being realistically embedded (imagining that there is, at best, partial compliance with the rules). The rules that would be optimal given perfect compliance may not be optimal given partial compliance. Kagan examines the complications that arise from this, and concludes that whichever assumption we make about the level of compliance, insuperable problems arise, and thus rule consequentialism is implausible.

Kagan's suggestion is that consequentialists should have a plethora of evaluative focal points. Pettit and Smith argue along similar lines. They make a distinction between 'local consequentialism' and 'global consequentialism', and argue that all forms of local consequentialism (including rule consequentialism) are implausible. According to Pettit and Smith, there is no sensible ground of limiting consequentialist evaluation merely to rules or motives.

One reason for favouring rule consequentialism (a reason implicitly or explicitly invoked by Shaw, Levy, Riley, and Haslett) is that social acceptance of rule consequentialism will produce more good than social acceptance of act consequentialism. But the remaining chapters in the book instead accept Lyons's conclusion that we ought to be deciding between different utilitarian theories on the basis of how morally acceptable they are. If we accept one utilitarian or consequentialist theory over others because it is the most morally acceptable theory, have we not in effect swallowed a non-consequentialist argument for this theory? Indeed, Brad Hooker's recent attempt to defend rule consequentialism via John Rawls's method of reflective equilibrium is a kind of non-consequentialist defence of rule consequentialism.

Dale E. Miller, Alan Thomas, Phillip Montague, and Tim Mulgan attack this defence. Miller and Thomas both argue that Hooker seeks the wrong sort of reflective equilibrium. Phillip Montague picks out ambiguities in Hooker's formulations, and then argues that even the most charitable interpretation of Hooker's rule consequentialism leaves it unable to cohere with some of our considered moral convictions. In Montague's view, we believe there are certain facts that are necessarily significant morally, for example the fact that a certain promise was made. But he thinks rule consequentialism implies that such facts have only contingent moral significance. Mulgan explains how the obvious need to accommodate partial-compliance cases threatens to undermine Hooker's attempt to defend rule consequentialism. Another difficulty Mulgan raises is whether Hooker's cost–benefit analysis of the internalisation of a moral code is too speculative to be credible.

In his own contribution, Hooker elaborates his non-consequentialist defence of rule consequentialism. He acknowledges that his earlier arguments need amendment and supplementation. But he defends his interpretation of the method of reflective equilibrium, and tries to show that our ideas about moral contingency may fit with rule consequentialism in reflective equilibrium after all.

In the final contribution, Madison Powers investigates whether act consequentialism and rule consequentialism can do justice to some firmly held beliefs about the value of friendship. He argues that act consequentialism can assign high value to friendship, but has difficulty with its agent-relative aspect. Rule consequentialism, in contrast, can accommodate this aspect, according to Powers.

As this collection illustrates, there are different ways of developing rule consequentialism and different ways of defending it. There are also different ways of challenging it. We hope this collection pushes forward the discussion of the role of rules within consequentialism. But that role seems likely to remain controversial.

NOTES

1. See in particular Michael Slote, 'Satisficing Consequentialism Part I' and Philip Pettit, 'Satisficing Consequentialism Part II', both in *Proceedings of the Aristotelian Society*, Supplementary Volume 58 (1983), pp. 139–76.
2. Englewood Cliffs: Prentice-Hall.
3. Berkeley, *Passive Obedience, or the Christian Doctrine of Not Resisting the Supreme Power, Proved and Vindicated upon the Principles of the Law of Nature*. Reprinted in D. H. Monro (ed.), *A Guide to the British Moralists* (London: Fontana, 1972), pp. 217–27.
4. John Austin, *The Province of Jurisprudence* (1832).
5. J. O. Urmson, 'The Interpretation of the Philosophy of J. S. Mill', *Philosophical Quarterly*, 3 (1953), pp. 33–40; Roger Crisp, *Mill on Utilitarianism* (London: Routledge, 1997), pp. 102–24.
6. John Harsanyi, 'Rule Utilitarianism and Decision Theory', *Erkenntnis*, 11 (1977), pp. 25–53.

1

Between Act and Rule:
The Consequentialism of G. E. Moore

William H. Shaw

G. E. Moore's *Principia Ethica* played a leading role in shaping the analytic character of twentieth-century ethics and framing the metaethical disputes that engaged philosophers for several decades. Indeed, for nearly seventy years, no single work in ethics was to have repercussions as profound. It is hardly surprising, then, that Moore's contribution to ethics is generally seen as residing solely in his resistance to naturalism and in his thesis that 'good' names a simple, unanalysable property. However, Moore's objectives in *Principia Ethica* were not exclusively or even primarily metaethical, for he also wanted to address two substantive questions: what kinds of things are good in themselves, and what kinds of actions ought we to perform? In answering these questions, Moore broke fresh ground.

Moore criticised the hedonism of traditional utilitarianism and put forward a rival (albeit rather idiosyncratic) account of the things that are good. His doing this was not particularly novel, but Moore combined his non-hedonistic conception of good with a basically utilitarian normative theory. In recent years, moral philosophers have increasingly come to appreciate that utilitarianism is just one possible form of 'consequentialism'. In other words, while still retaining utilitarianism's characteristic normative structure, one can substitute for happiness a whole range of possible conceptions of the good. Moore pioneered this terrain by carefully elaborating a normative consequentialism emancipated from a hedonistic account of good and bad.

Moore's normative theory straddles act- and rule-consequentialist accounts of right in a creative way, and it is this aspect of his ethical thought that I shall be exploring. On the one hand, Moore argues that certain commonly recognised moral rules can be shown to be more socially useful than any conspicuous alternatives to them. These rules ought always to be obeyed. On the other hand, the domain of these rules is circumscribed. As a result, individuals will frequently encounter situations to which no relevant rule applies. Because of the difficulty in generalizing about the effects of actions, because of the great variety of circumstances people face, and because people's characters, dispositions, and temperaments differ, ethics can offer little in the way of general advice. With the aid of a few practical guidelines, individuals must simply determine as best they can which specific course of conduct will have the best outcome in the particular circumstances that confront them.

SECTION I: MOORE ON RULES

Moore defended an unequivocally act-consequentialist criterion of right, according to which it is one's duty to act so as to bring about as much good as possible. Indeed, in *Principia*, he stoutly maintains that asserting 'I am morally bound to perform this action' is equivalent to asserting 'This action will produce the greatest amount of good in the Universe.'[1] Although Moore believes that the rightness or wrongness of an action depends on the goodness or badness of its outcome as compared to the outcomes of alternative actions, he is so sceptical of our ability to foresee and compare the outcomes of actions that he doubts that we are ever fully justified in considering one action more right than another.

Nevertheless, if 'we confine ourselves to a search for actions which are *generally* better as means than any probable alternative', Moore maintains that it is 'possible to establish . . . most of the rules most universally recognised by Common Sense' (155–6). For consequentialists, if a rule is to be justified then it must be the case that better results come from people acting in accord with the rule than from their following some other rule or no rule at all. And this is what Moore hopes to establish with regard to most of the basic rules of everyday morality: 'if . . . we give the name of "duty" to actions which *generally* produce better total results', he writes, then we can 'prove that a few of the commonest rules of duty are true' (181).

The Rule against Murder

Although it occupies only a page of *Principia Ethica*, Moore's defence of the commonsense prohibition on murder is his most thorough discussion of any specific normative rule. The disutility of murder (and thus the utility of a moral rule against it) rests on two things. First, there are 'the immediate evils which murder generally produces' (156). Moore leaves these unelaborated, but presumably among the evils he has in mind are the loss of the goods that the deceased would have created and participated in had he or she lived, and the pain and other evils that his or her death causes other people.

Second, and this is the point Moore stresses, if murder were a common practice, then the insecurity it would breed would absorb time that might be spent to better purpose. 'So long as men desire to live as strongly as they do, and so long as it is certain that they will continue to do so, anything which hinders them from devoting their energy to the attainment of positive goods, seems plainly bad as a means' (157). Moore does not mean that murder is wrong because it thwarts people's desire to live. Rather, his central contention is that, given that people do strongly desire to live, if murder were permitted, then the threat of it would distract them from pursuing morally valuable aims.

Moore thus argues that 'it is generally wrong for any single person to commit murder', but his reasoning invites some questions and objections. In particular, the fact that if murder were a common practice then it would cause insecurity gives us a reason for thinking only that it would be bad for murder to be a common practice. It does not show that an isolated murder would be wrong or that a rule banning murder altogether is necessary. Here two points can be registered on Moore's behalf. First, Moore has probably understated his case. Contrary to what he implies, murder need not be 'a common practice' before human beings begin to feel insecure. A distant murder or two, or a certain probability of murder, may be all that is needed to induce people to take steps to make themselves feel more secure, thus diverting their energy from the attainment of important goods. Even those who are fortunate enough to feel safe from murder do so thanks in part to a criminal justice system that protects them. Although the threat of murder distracts them hardly at all from pursuit of the good, they owe their security to a protective apparatus that represents an expenditure of time and energy on the part of others – police officers, judges, and taxpayers, for instance – that could otherwise be devoted to things that are intrinsically valuable.

Second, Moore implicitly assumes that a society must either tolerate murder or ban it and that if murder is not proscribed, then it will be widespread. Both assumptions are plausible and may suffice to meet the objection that his argument does not show the wrongfulness of an isolated murder or justify a general rule against murder. Nevertheless, Moore's assumptions simplify the situation in some significant ways. For instance, our society tolerates, morally and legally, certain direct killings and overlooks altogether many failures to sustain the lives of others. It ranks those homicides it does not tolerate according to their perceived degree of wrongfulness and punishes killers in line with this. Consequentialists do not need simply to decide whether to permit murder (indeed, the very notion of a legal or morally permissible 'murder' borders on the oxymoronic). Rather, the significant task for them is to determine when, under what conditions, and to what extent killing people (as well as letting them die) is not to be tolerated and thus to determine, among other things, which homicides, of whom, and under what circumstances, are to be condemned as murders.

The Universal Core of Ordinary Morality

On almost any theory of the good, murder will typically produce more direct evil than it will good. But Moore anchors the case against murder on the disvalue of its indirect effects: murder and the threat of murder interfere with the ability of people to secure important goods. Like considerations, Moore argues, also support those rules 'most universally enforced by legal sanctions' (protection of property is his example) and some of the rules 'most commonly recognised by Common Sense' (he mentions industry, temperance, and the keeping of promises). Because people have an 'intense desire for property of some sort', a desire that seems to be universal, the rules that protect property 'serve greatly to facilitate the best possible expenditure of energy'. Likewise, industry, temperance, and the keeping of promises greatly assist us to acquire those things that are necessary for 'the further attainment of any great positive goods' (157).

These rules display two significant characteristics. First, 'in any known state of society, a *general* observance of them *would* be good as a means'. Their utility rests upon 'the tendency to preserve and propagate life and the desire of property', both of which are strong and widespread (157). Observance of these rules is an indispensable prerequisite for obtaining important moral goods, and in any case, Moore adds, it never makes a society worse off than non-observance would. Second, these rules can be defended independently of a correct view about what is intrinsically good because they are essential for the preservation of civilised society itself, which in turn 'is necessary for the existence, in any great degree, of anything which may be held to be good in itself' (158; cf. xxii).

Moore's first point rests on there being certain universal or very widespread human desires, 'so strong, that it would be impossible to remove them' (157). Given those desires, certain rules or certain kinds of rules are beneficial as means. Without these rules, people would have to spend more time and effort than they otherwise would in endeavouring to satisfy those basic desires – time and effort that could be better directed elsewhere. Moore does not argue that the core rules of ordinary morality, which facilitate the satisfaction of those elementary desires, are valuable because the desires they facilitate are valuable. Rather, they are good purely as means, valuable only because by addressing those desires they remove obstacles to our attaining those things in life that truly are intrinsically good.

Contrary to what Moore implies, his defence of these core rules does not really depend, at least in the abstract, on the desires for property and security being intense, relatively universal, and impossible to eradicate. Moore believes that because these desires are strong and widespread, human beings will, in the absence of rules that permit their satisfaction, inevitably occupy themselves with those elementary concerns to the detriment of more morally valuable pursuits. Yet, even if people did not strongly desire personal security or property, rules making these things possible might still be a prerequisite for attaining the more positive goods that interest Moore. Rules conducive to a civilised and secure social existence, one might plausibly hypothesise, would remain indispensable means to achieving those things that are inherently valuable even if we imagine that people did not long for security of life and possession per se. (By analogy, the settled existence made possible by agriculture is a social and historical prerequisite for the building of permanent dwellings and the goods those dwellings make possible, whether or not there is a strong and widespread desire among human beings to abandon hunting and gathering in favour of agriculture as soon as the opportunity presents itself.)

In any case, for Moore the important point is that these rules 'can be defended independently of correct views upon the primary ethical question of what is good in itself' (158). He does not argue that their defence is compatible with any notion of the good whatsoever. Perhaps certain conceptions of the good are sufficiently eccentric that their realisation would be thwarted by the rules that make possible civilised society. However, the rules in question facilitate the attaining of all (or almost all) the things people commonly and reasonably take to be good while hindering the realisation of none of them: 'There seems no reason', Moore writes, 'to think that their observance ever makes a society worse than one in which they are not observed' (157). Thus, these core rules can be vindicated without our knowing which philosophical conception of the good is ultimately correct.

Moore does not foreclose in principle one's vindicating certain commonsense moral rules 'by shewing their direct tendency to produce what is good in itself or to prevent what is bad' (165; cf. 160, 181). But he is sceptical of this approach, reminding us that 'a correct judgment of what things are good or bad in themselves . . . has never yet been offered by ethical writers' (181), and he does not pursue this strategy himself or suggest how one might develop it.[2] To vindicate the core rules of common morality, Moore prefers instead what he calls 'the ordinary method, which tries to shew in them a tendency to [the] preservation of society' (165). The parsimoniousness of this method is appealing, avoiding as it does reliance on possibly contestable judgements of good.

Unfortunately, however, Moore seems to overlook the possibility that alternative sets of rules might satisfy the strong and widespread desires he discusses. Different systems of property rules, for instance, might equally well fulfil whatever need people have for material possessions and provide them with the security necessary to turn their energies elsewhere. Moore writes as if the choice were simply between having rules and having no rules, where the former are implicitly the rules of his day. This fact lends a more conservative cast to his thinking than an ethical approach like his need have. That rules promoting security of property are necessary is an important truth, but consequentialists will inevitably be obliged to go beyond this elementary fact to survey and assess a range of alternative ways of providing that security. On Moore's behalf, though, it must be added that although he seeks to vindicate 'most of the rules most universally recognised by Common Sense', he writes that he does 'not propose to enter upon this defence in detail, but merely to point out what seem to be the chief distinct principles by the use of which it can be made' (156).

Rules Resting on Contingent Circumstances

So far Moore has argued that some of the most commonly recognised moral rules and most of the moral rules widely enforced by legal sanctions have two characteristics: first, their general observance would be good in any known state of society; second, these rules can be vindicated without a correct answer to the question what is good in itself. Moore recognises, however, that not all the rules of commonsense morality have these two characteristics. Arguments in favour of these other rules can prove their utility only 'so long as certain conditions, which may alter, remain the same: it cannot be claimed of the rules thus defended, that they would be good as a means in every state of society'. In particular, their utility hinges on conditions that cannot be 'assumed to be so universally necessary as the tendency to continue life and to desire property' (158).

For example, 'most of the rules comprehended under the name of Chastity' presuppose, for their vindication, conjugal jealousy and paternal affection. In societies where these sentiments are sufficiently strong and widespread, consequentialists can uphold the rules in question. But 'utilitarian writers or writers who assume as their end the conservation of society' err when they assume 'the necessary existence of such sentiments' (158). To the contrary, Moore writes, one can imagine a civilised society without those sentiments. To exonerate traditional sexual morality in such a society, consequentialist analysis would have to establish that violating these rules produces evil effects other than social disintegration. In particular, their vindication would require 'a correct view of what is good and bad in itself'.[3] A distinction therefore needs to be drawn, Moore writes, between rules whose utility depends on circumstances 'more or less likely to alter' and those whose utility seems certain under all possible conditions (158–9).

Among the circumstances that exist only in particular states of society and that are 'more or less likely to alter', Moore includes 'the sanctions of legal penalties, of social disapproval, and of private remorse' (159). These all involve important effects that must enter into consequentialist calculation. Although he believes that actions that are not independently wrong should be free of social penalties, Moore argues that where such sanctions do exist they are a chief part of the moral justification (and not merely the prudential motivation) for acting in certain ways. This is because 'the punishment [for a certain action] is in general itself a greater evil than would have been caused by the omission of the action punished'. Indeed, Moore maintains that the prospect of punishment can be an adequate reason 'for regarding an action as generally wrong, even though it has no other bad effects but even slightly good ones' (159).

This proposition might appear paradoxical. However, consequentialists must take into account all the likely results of their actions (and of the alternative actions open to them) even if those actions have the results they do only because of contingent social institutions or fortuitous social circumstances. 'The fact that an action will be punished', Moore writes, 'is a condition of exactly the same kind as others of more or less permanence, which must be taken into account in discussing the general utility or disutility of an action in a particular state of society' (159). For this reason, it can be wrong on consequentialist grounds for an individual to violate a moral rule, even though the rule itself lacks utility.

There's a problem with Moore's reasoning, though. He introduced discussion of social sanctions in the context of an argument intended to show that certain moral rules may be justified because of the results they produce in particular states of society – in the context, that is, of examining, not whether an individual should follow a given rule, but whether society is justified on consequentialist grounds in having that rule in the first place. True, Moore does suggest that actions that would not be independently wrong should be free of sanctions. Yet he also states, as we have seen, that the existence of a punishment can make an action generally wrong even though it has no other bad effects.

To designate an action as being generally wrong or having general disutility because it will be punished is perilously close to circular reasoning: for one cannot cogently appeal to the existing structure of legal penalties and social disapproval to defend society's having the rules that give rise to that structure in the first place. This circularity may only be apparent. If individual actions rather than moral rules are the intended referent of 'generally wrong' or 'general utility' in the above passages, then there would be no circularity. But while this interpretation would preserve Moore against this charge, it would imply that he had lost the thread of his argument, prematurely and inadvertently shifting the topic from the justification of moral rules to individual moral decision-making.

On the other hand, because Moore explicitly identifies 'the so-called *sanctions*' as being among the temporary conditions that justify certain rules as useful means to the preservation of society (xxii), it is hard to escape the impression that the great disutility of social disapproval and legal penalties led him to believe that current moral rules have at least some of the utility they do simply because society already observes and enforces them. If this interpretation is correct, it would account for his reference to 'moral rules generally recognised and practised, and which, therefore, we may assume to be generally useful' (163). It would also help to explain why

Moore so confidently believes that it is 'possible to prove a definite utility in most of those [rules] which are in general both recognised and practised' (160) and that 'the general utility of an action most commonly depends upon the fact that it is generally practised' (164).

Rules Not Generally Observed

Moore believes that consequentialist analysis can vindicate most of the common-sense moral rules that are generally recognised and followed in society. By contrast, he thinks that such analysis cannot justify rules that are advocated but not normally observed. Although 'a great part of ordinary moral exhortation and social discussion consists in the advocating of rules, which are *not* generally practised', these rules commonly suffer from at least one of three possible defects. These defects make it unlikely that one can establish the general utility of the recommended rules (160).

The first defect is that the actions required by the rule are 'impossible for most individuals to perform by any volition'. Yet, says Moore, we do not regard something as a moral rule unless almost everyone can perform the required action, if he or she only wills to do so. The second defect is that the conditions necessary for the actions required by the rule to have good effects do not exist. 'A rule, of which the observance would produce good effects, if human nature were in other respects different from what it is, is advocated as if its general observance would produce the same effects now and at once' (160). The third defect is that the usefulness of the rule rests on conditions that are likely to alter or on conditions that it would be easier or more desirable to change than it would be to observe the proposed rule.

The absence of concrete examples makes it difficult to assess Moore's claim that these three defects effectively undercut the utility of any rules that are not now generally observed. At the very least, complicated empirical issues are at stake, and consequentialists should not be too quick to decide from their armchairs which rules are useful to promulgate and which are not. For his own part, Moore believes that one or more of these three defects generally militate against 'proposed changes in social custom, advocated as being better rules to follow than those now actually followed'. Accordingly, he concludes that 'it seems doubtful whether Ethics can establish the utility of any rules other than those generally practised' (161). This is certainly Moore at his most conservative.

Moore endeavours to palliate his conservative conclusion by reflecting that the inability of ethics to establish the utility of new rules 'is fortunately of little practical moment'. The reason is that even if a new rule would have greater utility, this fact would have no impact on individual conduct: 'The question whether the general observance of a rule not generally observed, would or would not be desirable, cannot much affect the question how any individual ought to act' (161). This is because (1) the individual cannot bring about general observance of the rule and (2) the fact that its general observance would be useful gives no reason to conclude that, absent that general observance, the rule ought to be obeyed.

Moore is certainly right to doubt that an individual's acting in accord with a rule that is not currently followed will cause other people to adhere to it. Except in the most fanciful of circumstances, there is indeed 'a large probability that he will not, by any means, be able to bring about its general observance' (161). Yet this fact leaves the question of utility open. Even though an individual's action cannot bring about general observance of a rule, it may nevertheless encourage to some extent future observance of the rule both by others and by the agent himself. Even if modest, this effect might be significant enough to make the action the right one for the agent to do. As we shall see later, Moore emphasises the harm one can do by a bad example, but here he ignores the benefits that may flow from a good example.

Moore's second argument is that the usefulness of a rule's general observance does not, in the absence of such observance, give the moral agent any reason to follow it. Now there clearly are cases where obeying a rule will have no utility unless or until a certain level of compliance is reached. Suppose, for instance, that scientific study reveals that driving on the left-hand side of the road results in fewer traffic accidents than driving on the right-hand side. In a society where right-side driving is the norm, the superior utility of left-side driving would not give an individual a reason to drive on the left-hand side. In this case the current practice, though suboptimal, is still superior to a situation in which only a few individuals follow the rules associated with the optimal practice, while others adhere to the older practice. Nor is the validity of Moore's point restricted to situations where the status quo is governed by formally institutionalised rules. For example, a tourist has no moral reason to queue outside a government office she needs to visit in a foreign country where queues are ignored and everyone else is elbowing his or her way to the front.

Moore's argument, however, erroneously presupposes that examples like these are representative of all instances of observing rules that are not generally practised. Contrary to this supposition, an individual might in fact do some good by following a new and superior rule, in the absence of some other general rule or even in the teeth of current practice, because his or her actions have beneficial results regardless of what people do generally. There can be circumstances in which it is reasonable on consequentialist grounds for the tourist to queue and to tell others to fall into line, or for a working wife to refuse to do more than half the housework, or for a professor to write evaluations of her job-seeking students that are free of artificially inflated praise, even if none of these actions accords with usual practice. Following a new rule by doing these things may have good results even if others do not generally follow the rule. In addition, doing so may help establish a new and superior practice.

The true and insightful kernel of Moore's argument that the hypothetical utility of a currently unobserved rule will have no impact on how an individual ought to act is that consequentialists appropriately treat as irrelevant to moral deliberation the good results that would come from observing a proposed rule when these results are premised on counterfactual suppositions about how other people are likely to act. Moore accurately discerns that there are good reasons for viewing sceptically the advocacy of moral rules that people do not now follow. But these reasons are less conclusive than he thinks, and his brusque dismissal of such rules is, at best, premature. This is especially so because Moore himself allows, at least in principle, that 'an independent investigation of what things are good or bad in themselves' could establish the case for a 'proposed change in social custom' (xxiii; cf. 165).

SECTION 2: INDIVIDUAL MORAL CHOICE

Moore holds that we can establish the utility of some of the basic rules of commonsense morality, but what does this imply for individual moral agents? What role should rules play in their decision-making? We turn now to Moore's answers to these questions, examining first situations where there is a generally reliable rule to guide individuals and then situations where there is no such rule.

No Exceptions

Even if a rule is generally useful, following it will not always produce the best results, so that 'in some cases the neglect of an established rule will probably be the best course of action possible' (162). This conclusion suggests that consequentialists should be prepared to violate a generally useful rule whenever doing so will maximise good. In line with this, act utilitarians have long argued against rule utilitarianism that it is fetishistic to stick to rules that generally conduce to the greatest good in cases where doing so would produce suboptimal results. After all, they contend, rules are only general guides to the good, and what is the point of following such a guide when you know in a particular case that it is pointed in the wrong direction?

Moore, however, maintains to the contrary that 'the individual can . . . be confidently recommended *always* to conform to rules which are both generally useful and generally practised' (164). Now, strictly speaking, what consequentialists should recommend to a moral agent and what the agent should do are not extensionally equivalent. What one is obliged to recommend and what the agent is obliged to do can sometimes diverge. But Moore is not seeking to exploit this potential gap. He straightforwardly asserts that the individual is never 'justified in assuming that his is one of these exceptional cases' in which neglecting a generally useful rule will bring more good than obeying it (162).

Moore provides three reasons in support of this proposition. First, if it is certain that observing the rule is useful in most cases, then there is a large probability that breaking it in the present case will be wrong. Second, because we can predict only poorly the consequences of our actions, it is doubtful that an individual's judgement that violating a rule will have good results can outweigh the general probability that actions of that kind will prove wrong. Third, any such judgement will generally be biased. Thus, 'with regard to any rule which is *generally* useful, we may assert that it ought *always* to be observed' because in any particular case the probability of its being useful to do so is greater than the probability of our deciding correctly that an exception is called for. 'In short, though we may be sure that there are cases where the rule should be broken, we can never know which those cases are, and ought, therefore, never to break it' (162–3).

Moore's first reason lends credence to his conclusion, but fails to prove it. If one knows that the superior utility of people following rule R in circumstances C has been established, and if one knows nothing else, then it is a tautology to assert that following R is probably the best thing to do. In the pertinent case, however, the moral agent is claiming to know something further about the situation that makes it reasonable to believe that better results would come from ignoring rule R than following it. Ex hypothesi, the agent believes that the present circumstances are such that what is usually the case is not now the case. Moore's first point simply does not come to terms with that supposition.

What Moore says, though, should give any conscientious consequentialist pause. The stronger the evidence we have, say, that telling the truth produces more good than lying and the more cases we know in which lying misfired or had poor results, then the less willing we should be to conclude that lying would be preferable to telling the truth in the present case. But while Moore's point counsels caution, it does not show that we are bound to be mistaken whenever we determine, on the basis of careful reflection, that making an exception to a justified rule will bring about more good than sticking to it.

Moore's second reason, however, leads him to think otherwise. 'The uncertainty of our knowledge both of effects and of their value, in particular cases, is so great', he writes, 'that it seems doubtful whether the individual's judgment that the effects will probably be good in his case can ever be set against the general probability that that kind of action is wrong' (162). Against this proposition, one might object that the difficulty of knowing the full consequences of our actions cuts two ways: both against the claim that sticking to the rule will have good results and against the claim that violating it will. Moore, it might be argued, does not demonstrate that one's judgement that breaking a rule would be useful will invariably be less certain than one's judgement that the rule is generally good or that following it in the present circumstances would have superior results.

Is it harder to know the consequences of individual actions in particular cases than it is to know the typical consequences of actions of that sort? One reason for doubting that it is harder is simply this: the knowledge that following rule R has good results in general seems to rest on knowledge of the benefits of following R in particular cases. If we cannot discern that a given lie will produce more or less good than the truth, how can we know whether truth telling in general is better or worse than lying? In defence of Moore, however, one can plausibly rejoin that even though we are unable (as he thinks) to foresee accurately the likely consequences of the courses of action we must now choose between, we can nevertheless know what happened when different choices, analogous to those now before us, were made in similar situations in the past. Human beings, for example, have extensive knowledge of the past effects of truth telling and lying and, thus, have grounds for predicting in general what the comparative benefits of the two are likely to be. What Moore probably has in mind, then, is that in adhering to the rule, I rely on the knowledge and experience of many people before me, but in breaking it I proceed on my own without any such assurance. This point is well taken even if Moore exaggerates the epistemic superiority of socially based knowledge claims in comparison with individually derived knowledge claims.[4]

The third reason Moore offers in support of his 'no exceptions' position might be thought to supply what is missing from his first two arguments. This is the supposition that our judgement that an exception is warranted will 'generally be biased by the fact that we strongly desire one of the results which we hope to obtain by breaking the rule' (162). Moore's point has merit. Too frequently people are prepared to exempt their own actions from the generally accepted principles of morally correct conduct, and there are few, if any, evils that someone, somewhere, has not at some time rationalised as a legitimate exception to a justified and established moral principle. These elementary facts should worry any moralist. There is indeed a real danger that when one decides one is justified in making an exception to a valid moral rule, self-interest or personal preference will have distorted one's judgement. This danger is easy to appreciate in the abstract but – self-deception being what it is – often hard to recognise in one's own case. Does it follow from this that one should, as Moore believes, always follow the rule?

Moore implicitly assumes that one cannot or will not identify the circumstances in which one may be prone to bias and then take adequate measures to guard against partiality in decision-making. Yet, one's doing so does not seem impossible. Suppose that although I cannot identify any errors in my own reasoning, I know that people tend to be biased in decision-making circumstances like those in which I now find myself; accordingly, I take certain precautions to prevent bias infecting my delibera-tions. One might respond on Moore's behalf that the best precaution to take would be simply to cleave to the established rule. This is likely to be sound advice in cases where self-interest would favour my breaking the rule. But contrary to what Moore implies, not every case in which someone contemplates making an exception to a general rule is a case where the individual would personally prefer breaking the rule to upholding it.

Like an administrator asked by a student to make an exception to some university rule, the individual may have no personal interest in the decision.[5]

Bad Examples

Moore offers a further and distinct consideration in favour of his no-exceptions thesis. This is that even if one knew that in some particular situation breaking a generally useful rule would be better than adhering to it, one's doing so would set a bad example. 'So far as our example has any effect at all in encouraging similar action', Moore writes, 'it will certainly tend to encourage breaches of the rule which are not advantageous' (163). In fact, 'we may confidently assume that' what will be impressed upon the imagination of others is not the circumstances that justify our action as exceptional, but 'the points in which it resembles other actions that are really criminal'.[6] The effect of an exceptional right action, Moore reasons, will generally be to encourage wrong ones. Moreover, it will exercise this effect not only on other persons, but also on the individual. Having once approved of a generally wrong action, one will be more likely to do so under circumstances other than those that justified it in the original case.

Notice, first, that Moore's initial phrasing of his argument is conditional ('so far as our example has any effect at all in encouraging similar action') and thus implicitly acknowledges the possibility that our example may in fact have no such effect. Other people, for instance, may be unaware of what I have done or not perceive that it violates an established rule.[7] Obviously, if one's action does not have 'any effect at all in encouraging similar action' on the part of others, then it is immune to the objection that it will have the effect of encouraging wrongful conduct on their part. Although this point is sound, its scope is limited, first, because our actions do sometimes influence others and, second, because our making an exception to a rule also sets a precedent for ourselves, increasing the likelihood, as Moore says, that in the future we will make a morally unjustified exception to the rules.

Moore holds that making an exception to a sound rule will have an untoward effect on one's future decisions because 'it is impossible for any one to keep his intellect and sentiments so clear, but that, if he has once approved of a generally wrong action, he will be more likely to approve of it also under other circumstances than those which justified it in the first instance' (163). The implication, of course, is that the agent would not be justified in making an exception to the rule in those 'other circumstances'. But consider two situations. In the first, Rita Reckless performs an action that is morally justifiable although contrary to an established rule, but her decision to do so was so marred by bias and lack of evidence that it was only a matter of luck that she did what was right. In the second case, Justine Judicious performs the same, morally justified action but on the basis of a fully informed, impartial, and accurate moral calculation.

Moore's point surely tells against Rita. It can reasonably be supposed that her behaviour in this case will embolden her in the future to act in ways that will breach the established rules but with results that are adverse, rather than fortunate. Does Moore's point have equal force against Justine? Let us grant that her following her considered judgement that an exception was called for will make it more likely that in analogous future circumstances she will do the same rather than defer to the established moral rule. However, if we assume that Justine is conscientious and reasonably intelligent, we have no reason for suspecting that in the future when she makes an exception to a rule she will be acting incorrectly. To the contrary, we now have some small inductive evidence that her future judgements are likely to be well grounded.

But what about the effect of Justine's example on others? Moore's 'bad example' argument assumes that other people (or at least a significant number of them) will prove less judicious than Justine and will thus fail to appreciate the distinctive features of her situation. They will be so struck by the fact that Justine is doing something that is not normally permitted that they will be blinded to those aspects of the situation that justify her conduct. Having seen a rule broken, but unable to discern the reason for it, such people will have greater difficulty in the future keeping themselves within the confines of the rule. Unfortunately, these suppositions seem too speculative to carry the necessary argumentative weight. On Moore's behalf, one might instead argue that once average people know that one can justifiably breach a moral rule, they will be more likely to attempt this feat themselves despite the fact that it is enormously difficult to accurately identify those situations in which neglecting an established rule would be justified. In other words, Justine's example will only tempt them to try to do something that they probably will not succeed in doing, however honourable their intentions. Here, though, the 'bad example' argument falls back on Moore's earlier, epistemic line of argument, about which doubts have already been raised.

Despite these difficulties in his argument, Moore is so wary of bad examples that he advocates universal enforcement of the moral rules. That is, he defends punishing someone who has violated a generally useful rule even though it was the right thing for the person to have done in that particular case:

> It is undoubtedly well to punish a man, who has done an action, right in his case but generally wrong, even if his example would not be likely to have a dangerous effect. For sanctions have, in general, much more influence upon conduct than example; so that the effect of relaxing them in an exceptional case will almost certainly be an encouragement of similar action in cases which are not exceptional. (164)

Moore glides into this argument without noticing that he has changed the topic. His 'bad example' argument, like the earlier considerations of bias and lack of knowledge, was intended to buttress the contention that one should never violate a valid moral rule. Moore is now upholding punishment of rule-violators, regardless of whether what they did was justified in consequentialist terms, because of the bad effects that are likely to come from tolerating a violation of the established rules. But whether society is right to punish an action leaves open the question whether it was right for the individual to have done it in the first place. For consequentialists, these are distinct issues.

Beyond Rules

Although Moore believes that individuals should always conform to rules that are generally useful and generally followed, the practical implications of his position are less conservative than they might appear to be. This is because there are not many such rules. Not all rules that are generally observed can be shown to have utility, and we are unlikely to establish the utility of any rule not already generally observed. As a result, much of our conduct and many of the decisions we make will fall outside the scope of any binding rule. Moore probably insisted so confidently that one must always obey certain core rules just because those rules are few and their domain of jurisdiction restricted. By contrast, when we consider proffered 'rules of which the general observance *would* be useful but does not exist, or . . . rules which are generally practised but which are not useful', the situation is entirely different, and 'no such universal recommendations [of obedience] can be made' (164).

In the case of rules that lack utility but are nonetheless generally recognised and practised, the fact that punishment may greet one's failure to conform to them can be a decisive reason for compliance. Moreover, there is, Moore asserts, 'a strong probability in favour of adherence to an existing custom, even if it be a bad one'. This is because the fact that society generally follows a certain rule may give conforming actions a utility, and non-conforming actions a disutility, they would not otherwise have. The current rule and accompanying social practices may have so structured individual expectations that little, if any, good will come from not honouring the rule. Moreover, because even harmful rules can form part of the fabric of a stable society, one ought to be careful about breaking them.[8]

However, if we assume that 'the rule which [the individual] proposes to follow, *would* be better than that which he proposes to break, *if* it were generally observed', then 'the effect of his example, so far as it tends to break down the existing custom, will here be for the good' (164). Moore neglects the fact that one need not be acting on a better rule for one's actions to do good by helping to undermine a bad rule. And one could be justified in neglecting a bad rule even if one's conduct had no effect on whether others observe that rule (and thus no tendency to subvert it). This is simply because ignoring the rule might have good results all by itself.

Moore may have been envisioning situations where the current rule is suboptimal but superior to having no settled rule at all. In such cases, simply abandoning the rule will not maximise utility; a better rule must replace it. Moore reminds us that 'cases, where another rule would certainly be better than that generally observed, are . . . very rare' (164). Yet if ex hypothesi we know that the existing rule is not just suboptimal but bad, then it may not be that difficult for an individual to establish the superiority of observing either another rule or no general rule at all.

Principia's discussion of rules that are socially observed but lack utility segues into an examination of what an individual should do in situations not covered by 'rules which are both generally practiced and strongly sanctioned among us'. In these situations, Moore again emphasises, it is extremely improbable that 'any general rule with regard to the utility of an action will be correct' (165). This extreme improbability he describes as 'the chief principle' to be taken into account when discussing the considerations that should guide one's ethical choices.

Moralists have proposed various and often conflicting rules for our conduct, but those that are not socially established are of only limited value. 'The most that can be said for the contradictory principles which are urged on us by moralists of different schools as universal duties', Moore writes, is that 'they point out actions which, for persons of a particular character and in particular circumstances, would and do lead to a balance of good' (165). Even if one succeeds in identifying the particular dispositions and circumstances that would render certain kinds of actions generally advisable for certain kinds of people, Moore argues, this 'would not give us, what moral laws are usually supposed to be – rules which it would be desirable for every one, or even for most people, to follow'.

How, then, should one act when no useful, generally observed rule governs the situation? Moore's answer to this larger question is perfectly straightforward: the agent should simply 'guide his choice by a direct consideration of the intrinsic value or vileness of the effects which his action may produce'.[9] In other words, where there is no useful, generally practised moral rule, the individual must decide what to do on the basis of a direct act-consequentialist evaluation of the alternatives. Moore maintains, however, that three practical principles should guide the individual.

SECTION, 3: MOORES THREE PRINCIPLES

When weighing and comparing rival courses of action, a consequentialist must consider not only the relative goodness of their consequences but also the relative probability of those consequences being achieved. Moore stresses, in particular, that if the difference in probability is sufficient, a lesser but more likely good will be a worthier target than a greater though less probable good. This fact, he argues, underwrites 'the general truth' of the following three practical principles: (1) an agent does better to aim at a lesser good for which he has a strong preference than at a greater good 'which he is unable to appreciate'. This is because 'natural inclination renders it immensely more easy to attain that for which such inclination is felt' (166). (2) One should aim at goods affecting oneself and those in whom one has a strong personal interest rather than 'attempt a more extended beneficence'. This is because one is far more likely to secure such goods. (3) Goods in the present are to be preferred to those in the future, which 'are, for that reason, far less certain of attainment' (167). Let us examine these principles in turn.

First Principle

Moore's first practical principle advises us to aim at those goods for which we have a strong preference rather than at objectively greater goods that move us less. The reason is simple. Because of our stronger attachment to the lesser good, we are more likely to attain it than we are to achieve any greater good. Given this fact and assuming that the lesser good is a genuine good 'and not an evil', it follows that we will usually accomplish more good by aiming at it than by more lethargically pursuing a greater good.

A critic might object that Moore's first principle incorrectly treats the actor's own inclinations as a given, as a brute fact outside his or her control. It views them as if they were an external factor like the weather which shapes, independently of one's will, the decision situation one faces. In response to this argument consequentialists like Moore can certainly concede that one can act contrary to one's inclinations and preferences (or at least to one's immediate and first-order inclinations and preferences). But they will insist that in deciding how to act, one cannot turn a blind eye to any features of the world (including one's own inclinations) that will affect the likely results of rival courses of action.

Our character is not entirely beyond our control, however, and our present choices and actions can and do influence our future desires and inclinations. Consequentialists will want to formulate policies and recommend practical guidelines that acknowledge these elementary facts. The question, then, is whether Moore's first principle will foster complacency about our own characters and too great a readiness to acquiesce in our present inclinations and motivations. If promulgating Moore's principle leads people to settle too quickly for lesser goods instead of rising above their current dispositions and striving for worthier goals, it would fail to maximise utility.

This issue is not easy to resolve, but we can see more than a kernel of truth in Moore's first principle if we connect it to his comment that with regard to 'actions or habits of actions, usually recognised as duties or virtues, it is [not] desirable that every one should be alike' (166). Some people are better equipped and more inclined to promote the good in certain ways than in others. Acknowledging this diversity will do more to advance total good than will regimentation of purpose and goal.

Second Principle

Moore's concern with the effects of one's inclinations on the success of one's pursuit of the good carries over into his second principle that one ought in general to aim at 'goods affecting himself and those in whom he has a strong personal interest, than to attempt a more extended beneficence' (166–7). In elaborating this principle, Moore states that 'Egoism is undoubtedly superior to Altruism as a doctrine of means.'[10] By 'egoism' Moore presumably has in mind the pursuit both of purely self-regarding concerns (narrow egoism) and of concerns for others – like one's children, friends, colleagues, and neighbours – with whom one has some special connection (extended egoism or self-referential altruism[11]). But narrow egoism and self-referential altruism represent quite different policies, and Moore does not say what the optimal balance between them is.

In searching for that balance and in recommending principles to guide our conduct, consequentialists must not slight our purely self-regarding concerns. Self-interest, after all, is a strong and enduring motivation, and to preach an abstract altruism that ignores this basic fact may prove futile. Although no invisible hand guides the moral world, permitting people, at least in the first instance, to pursue the goods that affect them personally may be an efficacious route to overall good. Still, this point should not be overstated. Consequentialists will worry that promulgating egoism as a practical principle of conduct will encourage the pursuit of self-interest in circumstances where more altruistic motivation would bring greater good into the world. Unless checked and circumscribed, narrow egoism – that is, the policy of focusing on purely self-regarding goods – seems likely to produce less total good than a policy that takes some direct cognisance of goods involving other people.

From a consequentialist perspective, a policy of encouraging people to pursue self-referentially altruistic concerns is probably superior to encouraging them to pursue narrowly egoistic concerns. But is it also superior to a policy that advocates altruistic conduct of a more general sort? Moore evidently believes so, and there are some reasons for thinking he is right. People's personal attachments are inevitably limited, and the circle of those for whom we can genuinely care, and with whom we can share the goods of deep personal affection, is restricted. Consequentialists have long acknowledged, in addition, that pragmatic considerations strongly favour concentrating our energies on goods that affect those nearby, whom we know and whose participation in various goods we are well placed to assist.

However, our conduct can affect others who are outside our network of colleagues, friends, family, and neighbours. For this reason, consequentialist considerations favour expanding our circle of concern beyond those intimates for whom we already care and with whom our lives are already intertwined. For one thing, the world has changed greatly since Moore's day. Rapid worldwide communication and increased international ties mean that many of us can now have an impact on the lives of distant strangers, whose circumstances we could not, in previous decades and centuries, have known of, still less affected.

Third Principle

Moore's third principle is that we should prefer goods that are present here and now to future and therefore less certain goods. If one assumes that the goods in question are of roughly equal value, then this principle is surely sound. Because the right is only that which is a means to good, 'a thing that is really good it itself, if it exist[s] now, has precisely the same value as a thing which may be caused to exist in the future' (167). Moore thinks we are likely to overlook this elementary fact.[12]

The rules of morality, Moore reminds us, do not directly produce positive goods; rather, they provide the framework or social prerequisites necessary for the existence of such goods. And he warns elsewhere against the 'danger of confusion between the degree in which the actual lives lived [by people] are really intrinsically better, and the degree in which there is improvement merely in the *means* for living a good life'.[13] For these reasons and because so much of our time and effort are directed towards 'securing the continuance of what is thus a mere means', including 'the claims of industry and attention to health', Moore urges that 'in cases where choice is open, the certain attainment of a present good will in general have the strongest claims upon us' (167). We should not spend our lives so absorbed with the preconditions for enjoying the goods that make life worth living that – like the man who scrimps his whole life for a leisurely retirement he never lives to see – we never actually attain those goods.

Moore's third principle poses the question whether people are more prone to neglect present goods than they are to ignore future goods. People who sacrifice important future goods to lesser goods of the moment or concentrate on present enjoyments at the expense of constructing a life of greater overall value (perhaps, with greater accomplishments and self-realisation but fewer immediate pleasures) are guilty of erroneously discounting the future. Are these tendencies more or less worrisome than that against which the third principle warns us? This question is hard, and any answer to it must draw on one's theory of the good and on various psychological speculations.

All three of Moore's principles raise intriguing and important issues, but one must remember that they are only practical guidelines, which we might choose to revise. They are not themselves moral rules. Moore advances his principles to counteract the misleading influence and emphases of other normative ethical theories rather than to impose additional moral requirements on how we act. However, his principles are not exactly like the 'rules of thumb' that act utilitarians often recommend. Rules of thumb – for example, 'Always be as frank as you can with a student about his or her prospective grade' – are supposed to provide a convenient and reasonably reliable substitute for doing utility calculations anew in routine situations. They are intended to point us towards the action with the optimal outcome. By contrast, Moore's three principles are not intended to help us quickly identify and follow the course of action that would have the best results, were we to succeed in doing it. Rather, they highlight certain factors that may stand between our attempting to undertake the course of action that really would have the best outcome and our actually achieving that outcome.

For Moore, of course, the morally right course of action for the individual in cases where there is no relevant, generally useful rule remains the same: it is the course of action that results in more overall, net good than any alternative. But Moore did not acknowledge as explicitly as he should have that his theory implies that we may be in situations where the decision-making principles it is wise for us to follow will instruct us not to attempt to do the thing that (were we actually to do it) would be the right thing for us to have done. Because he held that we can only dimly foresee the results of our actions, Moore probably believed that we rarely if ever know ourselves to be in such a situation. Nevertheless, his normative theory does imply that there can be such situations; indeed, it is to the credit of his theory that it permits us to distinguish the consequentialist criterion of right from the decision-making principles that consequentialists should follow.

The contrast between these two is even more striking in the case of rules. As we have seen, Moore argues against making exceptions to generally useful rules as firmly as any rule utilitarian could, yet he nevertheless adheres to an act-consequentialist criterion of right and wrong. Moore's normative theory fruitfully blends elements of both act and rule consequentialism, while avoiding the difficulties that arise from adhering to either a purely act-oriented or an entirely rule-based approach. His theory appreciates the advantages of firm adherence to established, utility-maximising rules. But because valid moral rules must be socially recognised and practised, and not merely hypothetical, Moore avoids some standard criticisms of rule consequentialism.[14] And because the valid rules are few in number, his theory retains much of the flexibility of a purely act-consequentialist approach.[15]

NOTES

1. G. E. Moore, *Principia Ethica* (Cambridge: Cambridge University Press, 1986 [1903]), p. 147. See also pp. xxi, 25, 101, 150, and Moore, *Ethics* (New York: Oxford University Press, 1965 [1912]), pp. 26, 100. All page references in the text are to *Principia Ethica*.
2. In fact, Moore's discussion of moral rules in *Principia Ethica* precedes his account of the things that are intrinsically good and bad, an account that he reserves for the final chapter.
3. *Principia Ethica*, p. 158. Some writers exaggerate the radicalness of Moore's stance. For example, Baldwin writes that Moore 'explicitly questions conventional sexual morality' ('Review of Tom Regan, *Bloomsbury's Prophet*, and G. E. Moore, *The Early Essays*', *Mind*, 97, no. 385 (January 1988), p. 131). What Moore explicitly questions, though, is only whether conventional sexual morality is universally valid. And his questioning this is perfectly compatible with his believing it fully valid for the society in which he lived.

4. Russell Hardin, *Morality within the Limits of Reason* (Chicago: University of Chicago Press, 1988), p. 16.
5. Note that one may be biased or have a personal interest in favour, not of making an exception to, but rather of upholding, a general rule. Consider the administrator who takes satisfaction in adhering rigidly to rules and enjoys turning down student requests or whose self-interest within the institution is advanced by having a reputation for being a stickler.
6. *Principia Ethica*, p. 163. See also Bertrand Russell, 'The Elements of Ethics', in Wilfred Sellars and John Hospers (eds), *Readings in Ethical Theory* (New York: Appleton-Century-Crofts, 1952), p. 12.
7. Moore acknowledged this point in *The Elements of Ethics*, ed. Tom Regan (Philadelphia: Temple University Press, 1991), p. 172.
8. Jonathan Harrison, 'Rule Utilitarianism and Cumulative-Effect Utilitarianism', *Canadian Journal of Philosophy*, suppl. vol. 5 (1979), p. 24.
9. *Principia Ethica*, p. 166. J. J. C. Smart is thus incorrect to assert that 'Moore argued on act-utilitarian grounds that one should never in concrete cases think as an act-utilitarian' (J. J. C. Smart and Bernard Williams, *Utilitarianism: For and Against* (Cambridge: Cambridge University Press, 1973), pp. 43-4). Bernard Williams acquiesces in Smart's interpretation at p. 125.
10. *Principia Ethica*, p. 167. The qualification 'as a doctrine of means' is important because Moore firmly rejects egoism as a normative theory – that is, as an account of what makes right actions right.
11. J. L. Mackie, *Ethics: Inventing Right and Wrong* (Harmondsworth: Penguin, 1977), p. 132.
12. As did Russell, who called it 'the moralist's fallacy' ('The Elements of Ethics', pp. 28–9).
13. 'The Nature of Moral Philosophy', in G. E. Moore, *Philosophical Studies* (Paterson, NJ: Littlefield, Adams, and Company, 1959), p. 328.
14. See, for example, Peter Railton, 'Alienation, Consequentialism, and the Demands of Morality', *Philosophy and Public Affairs*, 13 (1984), pp. 156–7.
15. This essay draws on Chapters 5 and 6 of my book, *Moore on Right and Wrong: The Normative Ethics of G. E. Moore* (Dordrecht: Kluwer, 1995), which discusses further many of the issues raised here.

2

The Educational Equivalence of Act and Rule Utilitarianism

Sanford S. Levy

On most formulations, act utilitarianism and rule utilitarianism yield different lists of right and wrong actions. This would seem to make the choice between them of practical significance, where the significance lies in the difference between the lists. If we follow act utilitarianism, we will perform actions that we will not perform if we follow rule utilitarianism.

However, in this chapter, I will show that often, the practical significance of the choice between what I will call 'analogous forms' of act and rule utilitarianism is less than the difference between their lists of right and wrong actions would make it seem; and in some cases, there is no practical significance at all. For the practical significance of the choice between two moral theories lies not in the difference between their lists, but rather in the difference between their theories of moral education. I will show that even while differing greatly in their lists, analogous forms of act and rule utilitarianism are quite similar, and sometimes even identical, in their theories of moral education.

By a 'theory of moral education' I mean prescriptions about what we should teach people about right and wrong. I will assume this takes the form of a system of moral rules, which I will call the moral theory's 'educational code'. What is a moral theory's correct educational code and how does it relate to the moral theory itself? There are several possibilities, but I will assume the following. Suppose we have a moral theory, M. First, the correct educational code for M is the one that M says it is right to teach. Second, teaching a code consists of acts, teaching-acts, and the rightness of teaching-acts is determined by the same standard that M brings to bear on any issue, whatever that standard may be.

This answer, though innocent on its face, has a significant consequence. Many moral theories say it is right to teach themselves. But it is possible for a moral theory to recommend teaching something other than itself. This has long been recognised for act utilitarianism since it might maximise utility to teach something besides the principle of utility. Act utilitarianism might recommend teaching itself plus something more, as Hare's act utilitarianism recommends teaching an intuitive level of thought on top of an act-utilitarian critical level. Or it could recommend effacing itself altogether.[1] What is not always recognised is that the same is true for other forms of utilitarianism, and in particular, for rule utilitarianism. So given how I define 'educational code', a moral theory's correct educational code might not match its list of right and wrong actions.

When I say that the practical significance of the choice between two moral theories lies not in the difference between their lists of right and wrong actions, but rather in the difference between their theories of moral education, what I mean is this. Suppose a group is making a choice between various moral theories. The practical significance of the choice is given by the impact this choice has on the world in the long run. When moral theories recommend teaching themselves, the practical significance of the choice between them is given more or less by the differences in their lists of right and wrong actions. (I say 'more or less' because we cannot assume people will successfully learn or follow all of a moral theory's requirements.) But, when moral theories recommend teaching something other than themselves, as could happen with utilitarianism, in the long run it is the educational code, rather than our original moral theory, that will guide people's actions. The worlds created by our students will be a reflection of the educational code we teach them rather than being a direct reflection of our own moral theory itself. If a moral theory, M, recommends teaching something else, M', then our acceptance of M will lead us to teach M' which will, in the long run, yield what might be called an 'M'-world' rather than an 'M-world'.

My claim, then, is that the practical significance of the choice between analogous forms of act and rule utilitarianism is less than it might seem, and is sometimes even non-existent, because their theories of moral education are quite similar, and sometimes identical. In this chapter, I will define the conditions under which various kinds and degrees of educational equivalence obtain for these forms. And I will argue that even when full educational equivalence does not obtain, these analogous forms are educationally sufficiently similar so as to greatly reduce the practical significance of the choice between them.

Note, this educational equivalence thesis should not be confused with the extensional equivalence thesis discussed some years back.[2] Indeed, I have chosen to work with forms of act and rule utilitarianism that pretty clearly are not extensionally equivalent.

I begin with basic definitions of act and rule utilitarianism, though I will also distinguish several variants later. Act utilitarianism says that an act is right if and only if it maximises utility. It applies the 'test of utility' directly to individual acts. Rule utilitarianism says that an act is right if and only if it is recommended by the ideal code. Several interpretations of the ideal code are possible. For example it could be defined as the code it would maximise utility for everyone to follow successfully. Or it could be the one it would maximise utility for everyone to accept, which does not imply that people always successfully follow it. I, however, take it to be the one it would maximise utility to teach. Since discussions of these and other variants have been common in the literature over the years, I will not go into more detail here.[3] In particular, I will not go into what I mean by 'teach' except for one point. I assume that teaching a code involves inculcating various dispositions to act and feel, for example the disposition to perform certain actions and to feel guilty if one does not.

As a first step in the consideration of educational equivalence, I will argue that

(1) Act utilitarianism's educational code is rule utilitarianism's ideal code.

At first this is a surprising thesis. For it says act utilitarianism recommends teaching the student to believe something is right if and only if rule utilitarianism says it is right! But note two things. First, this does not make rule utilitarianism and act utilitarianism extensionally equivalent in the sense of saying the same acts are right and wrong. Act utilitarianism does not say that what is really right is what rule utilitarianism's ideal code recommends. It only says that we should teach the student to believe rule utilitarianism's ideal code.

Second, thesis (1) leaves open just what will be included in rule utilitarianism's ideal code and hence what will be included in act utilitarianism's educational code. Will it consist of, or in some way contain, the act-utilitarian principle? If not, then act utilitarianism will recommend effacing itself. Will the ideal code include what might be called 'the rule-utilitarian principle' according to which an act is right if and only if it is in accord with the ideal code? If so, then act utilitarianism will not only recommend effacing itself, but will also recommend teaching students to be fully-fledged rule utilitarians. Fortunately, we need not resolve the nature of rule utilitarianism's ideal code here as my argument will not turn on exactly what is in that code.[4]

The basic argument for thesis (1) is this. Rule utilitarianism needs a code of rules, its ideal code, which specifies right and wrong. As I am interpreting rule utilitarianism, this is the code it maximises utility to teach. Now, act utilitarianism does not need such a code since it defines right and wrong directly. But it does need an educational code, a code to teach students. What is the correct educational code for act utilitarianism? As I explained, I make two assumptions. First, the correct educational code for any moral theory, including act utilitarianism, is the one that that theory says it is right to teach. Second, teaching a code consists of teaching-acts, and the question of rightness for teaching-acts must be answered just as it is for any other acts. For act utilitarianism, the test for the rightness of any act is whether or not it maximises utility. So the correct educational code for act utilitarianism is the code it maximises utility to teach. Hence, the test for rule utilitarianism's ideal code and the test for act utilitarianism's educational code are the same: what it maximises utility to teach. So rule utilitarianism's ideal code is the same as act utilitarianism's educational code. This establishes thesis (1).

This argument requires three comments, two brief and one extensive. First, it is a simplification to speak of teaching a code as an act. Rather, it involves a course of action. Indeed, it often involves numerous courses of action undertaken by many people. My argument therefore treats courses of action as if they were actions for purposes of act-utilitarian evaluation. And I will later do the same thing in the context of rule utilitarianism. I cannot here go into potential problems with this approach.[5]

Second, strictly speaking, act utilitarianism does not ask what the right teaching-act is on any occasion. Rather, it just asks what the right *act* is, whether or not it is a teaching act. And it is possible that, on any given occasion, the best act will not be a teaching-act at all. However, I do not think there is anything wrong with separating out a subclass of acts for evaluation. Given that we are going to teach an educational code, we can reasonably ask which one is best from the point of view of our chosen moral theory. And in any event, given the significance of teaching, teaching-acts will often win over other acts by the act-utilitarian standard, and when they do, the best teaching-act is the one that maximises utility.

A third comment requires much more space. An elaboration of thesis (1) is important in itself and to help avoid confusion throughout this chapter. There are several versions of rule utilitarianism, even when we restrict ourselves to 'teaching' formulations of the ideal code as I am. And there are also several forms of act utilitarianism, as well as several educational questions a single form of act utilitarianism can ask. These forms of act utilitarianism and rule utilitarianism are not, perhaps, all equally plausible and interesting. But it is worth seeing how they tie together with respect to thesis (1). It turns out that (1) only holds for what I will call 'analogous forms' of act and rule utilitarianism.

First, I will distinguish four versions of rule utilitarianism based on four under-standings of how to define the ideal code. Rule utilitarianism says that the ideal code is the one it would maximise utility to teach. But who teaches and who is taught? Probably the most common approach makes society both teacher and student. Thus,

(A) *Group–Group Rule Utilitarianism*: The ideal code is the one it would maximise utility for society to teach to itself.

The interpretation of this form of rule utilitarianism is as follows. The ideal code is the one it would maximise utility for large numbers of people in a society to habitually teach to large numbers of people in the society, where teachers and students overlap. The teaching can be formal or informal. It can involve parents and their children, professional teachers and their students, clergy and their flocks, as well as people without any special status as teachers or students.

A rule utilitarian can also say that society should teach different codes to different students. For rule utilitarianism can be 'situationalistic' in its definition of the ideal code just as act utilitarianism is situationalistic in everything. What maximises utility depends on the situation. And the code it maximises utility to teach one student might not be the same as the code it maximises utility to teach another student. Thus,

> (B) *Group–Individual Rule Utilitarianism*: The ideal code for a particular student, S, is the one it would maximise utility for society to teach S.

Next, depending on how one comes to one's rule utilitarianism, it is not unnatural to ask what code it would maximise utility for a particular teacher, T, to teach. This is another side of a possible rule-utilitarian situationalism. For a variety of reasons it might maximise utility for me to teach one thing and for you to teach another. Thus, we have

> (C) *Individual–Group Rule Utilitarianism*: The ideal code for a particular teacher, T, is the one it would maximise utility for T to teach to society.[6]

And combining the two kinds of situationalism involved in (B) and (C), we have a fourth form of rule utilitarianism:

> (D) *Individual–Individual Rule Utilitarianism*: The ideal code for T/S (a teacher/student pair) is the one it would maximise utility for T to teach to S.[7]

I will now distinguish two (not four) forms of act utilitarianism. But each form can ask two different educational questions, so there are four possible act utilitarian ways to define the correct educational code. The first form of act utilitarianism is the more usual one: it focuses on the acts of individual agents and says that an act is right for an individual if and only if it maximises utility. From this point of view, there are two natural act-utilitarian educational questions with links to rule utilitarianism's ideal code as defined under (C) and (D). The act utilitarian can ask:

> (c) What moral code should T teach to society?
> (d) What moral code should T teach S?

The act-utilitarian answer to (c) is the ideal code defined in (C). The act-utilitarian answer to (d) is the ideal code defined in (D).

There are also act-utilitarian educational questions for which the ideal codes as defined in (A) and (B) are the answers, if we allow an expansion on how we understand act utilitarianism. When act utilitarianism says that an act is right for an agent if and only if it maximises utility, it generally assumes the agent to be an individual. But act utilitarianism can include collective agents such as society as a whole, just as we recognise corporations as agents in the law. I will call this sort of view 'collective act utilitarianism'.[8] Assuming the agent is society as a whole, the ideal codes as defined in (A) and (B) will be, respectively, answers to the following collective act-utilitarian questions about moral education:

    (a) What moral code should the collective teach itself?
    (b) What moral code should the collective teach S?

When I say that act utilitarianism will recommend teaching rule utilitarianism's ideal code in thesis (1), and when I speak of educational equivalence, I will mean these things for analogous forms of rule and act utilitarianism, combined with particular act-utilitarian educational questions. For example, if we are dealing with group–group rule utilitarianism, I focus on a collective act utilitarianism which asks 'What should society teach itself?' Similarly, if we are dealing with an individual–individual rule utilitarianism, I focus on an individual act utilitarianism asking 'What should T teach S?' So long as this is kept in mind, it will not hurt sometimes to leave the qualification 'analogous' implicit. Note, I will not ask whether thesis (1) and educational equivalence hold for other, non-analogous forms of act and rule utilitarianism. But I suspect that even many non-analogous forms, including ones not discussed here, will have at least similar educational recommendations, far more similar than would appear from the differences between the moral theories themselves and from the differences in their lists of right and wrong actions.

Thesis (1) takes us some way towards educational equivalence. But it is not educational equivalence itself. I will now state the simple condition that must be satisfied for educational equivalence to obtain. However, I will then go on to explain that simple as it is, this condition might not be satisfied so that full educational equivalence might fail.

Thesis (1) says that act utilitarianism recommends teaching rule utilitarianism's ideal code. Given this, the condition for what I will call 'full educational equivalence' is:

    (2) There is full educational equivalence if and only if rule utilitarianism's ideal code is identical to its proper educational code.

So, if we knew that rule utilitarianism did recommend teaching its own code, we would have educational equivalence.

Now, at first glance, someone might believe that not only is (2) true, but it is trivially true. For as I have defined terms, rule utilitarianism's correct educational code is the one it will recommend teaching, and surely it will recommend teaching the code it maximises utility to teach, that is, its own ideal code. However, this reasoning involves a mistake. I next argue for a thesis which to some extent pulls us away from educational equivalence and hence makes it more interesting and more challenging to establish.[9]

(3) Rule utilitarianism's test for the ideal code is not the same as its test for its educational code, so its ideal code might be different from its educational code.

This is important. For given that act utilitarianism's test for the correct educational code is rule utilitarianism's test for the ideal code, (3) gives us:

(4) Act utilitarianism's test for the correct educational code is not the same as rule utilitarianism's test for the correct educational code, so rule utilitarianism's correct educational code might be different from act utilitarianism's correct educational code.

So, given (3), full educational equivalence does not follow from (1).

Thesis (3) is rather surprising. Rule utilitarianism's ideal code is the one it would maximise utility to teach. One could justly wonder how rule utilitarianism's test for the proper educational code could possibly be different. And it would seem particularly odd that, according to (1), act utilitarianism will recommend teaching rule utilitarianism's ideal code, while we are now being told that rule utilitarianism might not recommend teaching its own ideal code!

But, though this sounds odd, it is simply a version of the point that a utilitarian theory could recommend effacing itself. This point applies as much to rule utilitarianism as to act utilitarianism. Indeed, the argument for (3) parallels the argument showing that act utilitarianism's correct educational code might not be act utilitarianism itself. Both arguments turn on the same assumptions. First, we identify a moral theory's correct educational code with the code the moral theory says it is right to teach. Second, the question of what it is right to teach is answered, as any other question of rightness is for a moral theory, by applying the theory's usual standard. In the case of act utilitarianism, the argument is completed quickly and easily: it is obvious, for the standard reasons, that act utilitarianism might not recommend teaching itself. The matter is more complex for rule utilitarianism and it is worth spending some time seeing why the same result applies there.

We can argue for (3) as follows. The correct educational code for rule utilitarianism is the one it is right to teach according to rule utilitarian lights. Now for rule utilitarianism, an act is right if and only if recommended by the ideal code. So a teaching-act is right if and only if recommended by the ideal code. Since teaching a code is a teaching-act, it follows that the correct educational code is the one the teaching of which is recommended by the ideal code.

Thus, the rule-utilitarian ideal code is the one it maximises utility to teach, while the proper rule-utilitarian educational code is the one the teaching of which is recommended by the ideal code. These tests are different. But at a glance, it might not be clear that they are, in fact, different tests rather than confusingly different verbal formulations of the same test. And if they are different tests, it is not yet clear what the difference comes to or how significant it is. This requires further investigation.

We can see that they are different tests, and can sometimes diverge, as follows. What I will do is take rule utilitarianism's test for the correct educational code and put it through a series of largely verbal transformations. I am not sure that they are all merely verbal or that I end up with an exact equivalence to where I began. But it is close, and the resulting transformation allows a comparison of the test for the correct educational code with the test for the ideal code.

For our purposes, rule utilitarianism's test for the correct educational code can be put: we should teach the code that it would maximise utility to teach people to teach. That this formulation works can be seen as follows. According to rule utilitarianism, we should do act A if and only if A is recommended by the ideal code. But the ideal code is the code it would maximise utility to teach. So, we should do A if and only if A is recommended by the code it maximises utility to teach. Now, it seems harmless to put this as, we should do A if and only if it maximises utility to teach people to do A, so long as we keep in mind that the test is of an entire code and not of the rule 'Do A' in isolation. Next, since this last statement is general and applies to teaching-acts as well as others, we have that we should perform teaching-act X if and only if it maximizes utility to teach people to perform teaching-act X. And if the teaching-act we are concerned with is the teaching of a moral code, we get the formulation I want: we should teach a particular code if and only if it maximises utility to teach people to teach that code.

This formulation makes clearer the difference between rule utilitarianism's test for the ideal code and its test for the correct educational code. The ideal code is the one it maximises utility to teach. The correct educational code, given the argument of the last paragraph, is the one it maximises utility to teach people to teach. And these tests are genuinely different. They can diverge.

That they can diverge can be seen as follows. Suppose I am an educator and that I can teach X, Y, or Z. Suppose further that because of my own teaching skills, it is possible for me to teach people X and that it would maximise utility for me to do so. However, when it comes time to educate other would-be educators, I might find that I cannot teach them to teach X effectively since teaching X requires a knack which I have and others lack. It might be hideously expensive, or downright impossible, for me to communicate this knack. So, it might be best for me to teach them to teach Y. In itself, Y is second best, and it would be second best for me to teach Y. But it might be best for me to teach others to teach Y. This is, indeed, a common occurrence in education and often undermines the value of teaching experiments dealing with all kinds of subjects from mathematics to morality. We seek to improve education by trying to discover what has worked elsewhere, only to find that successful programmes frequently do not export well. Often, the reason has to do with the nature of the teacher involved in the original experiment, something that cannot always be taught to others. Thus, rule utilitarianism's test for its ideal code (what it maximises utility to teach) and its test for its educational code (what it maximises utility to teach people to teach) can diverge.

To recapitulate briefly, according to thesis (2), full educational equivalence between analogous forms of act and rule utilitarianism turns on whether or not rule utilitarianism will recommend teaching its own ideal code. And this cannot be assumed, according to (3). Just as act utilitarianism might judge certain acts right and yet recommend teaching something else, so might rule utilitarianism. That is, rule utilitarianism might recommend teaching something other than its own ideal code. The argument for this is more complex than it is for act utilitarianism, but the same point holds. If we identify the correct educational code for a theory with what that theory says it is right to teach, and if we evaluate the rightness of teaching-acts by the same test as we evaluate any other acts, it follows that rule utilitarianism's ideal code is not necessarily its correct educational code.

But this only means that the test for rule utilitarianism's ideal code can diverge in principle from the test for its educational code. Will it diverge in fact? Will rule utilitarianism really recommend teaching something other than its own ideal code? I have no general proof one way or the other. But one thing seems clear. The explanation for possible divergence just given is in terms of one person's having a knack for teaching something that another person lacks. And this point applies most strongly to some versions of rule utilitarianism and much less strongly, if at all, to other versions. It applies most strongly to versions like individual–group rule utilitarianism. Here, the ideal code is the one it would maximise utility for a particular teacher, T, to teach. Since T might have the knack for teaching a particular code while others lack this knack, it might maximise utility for T to teach that code while teaching others to teach something else. On the other hand, the knack problem seems much less significant, and possibly of no significance, for versions like group–group rule utilitarianism. Suppose it maximises utility for the group to teach its members a particular code. The group does this through parents teaching children, schools teaching students, adults exhorting other adults, and so on. Now if it in fact maximises utility for society to teach the code, the relevant knack must be wide spread through society. Hence, the cited reason for possible divergence no longer applies.

The knack problem is the main reason I can think of that rule utilitarianism's ideal code might diverge from its proper educational code. Since it does not seem to apply to versions of rule utilitarianism like group–group rule utilitarianism, this suggests educational equivalence for those forms of rule utilitarianism and their act-utilitarian analogues. And since the problem does apply to versions like individual–group rule utilitarianism, full educational equivalence is much less likely for those versions and their analogues.

Our next question is this. When a particular version of rule utilitarianism is not fully educationally equivalent to its act-utilitarian analogue, how much educational similarity is there likely to be? How great is the practical significance of the choice between rule utilitarianism and act utilitarianism in those cases? We can still argue that even without full educational equivalence, there will be a great deal of similarity and that there is relatively little practical significance in the choice.

First, although rule utilitarianism and act utilitarianism have different tests for the proper educational code, their tests are not all that different. So even if they do yield different educational codes, probably the difference will not be large. It will correspond to the difference between what it maximises utility to teach and what it maximises utility to teach people to teach. For example, those without the relevant knack might teach a simplified version of the more difficult to teach code.

Second, we can define two kinds of partial educational equivalence: lag equivalence and end-point equivalence. The former will, and the latter may, obtain even when full equivalence does not. This further reduces the practical significance of the choice between act utilitarianism and rule utilitarianism.

To understand these partial forms of educational equivalence, we first need two notions: a moral theory's n-generational educational code and educational progression. It is possible for a moral code, C, to recommend effacing itself and to recommend teaching C''. But it is also possible for C' to recommend teaching something other than itself, C'. And so on. This is educational progression. It might lead in a circle back to C, or it might be linear. If linear, it might lead to any degree of variation, great or small. And it might lead to a final educational code where change ends, that is, to a code that does not recommend effacing itself. Suppose we have educational progression and that C recommends teaching C', C' recommends teaching C'', and so on. I will call C' the 'first generational educational' code of C; C'' will be the second generational educational code of C, and so on.

We can now introduce lag equivalence and then end-point equivalence. Suppose that rule utilitarianism does not require teaching its own ideal code so that rule utilitarianism's recommended educational code is different from act utilitarianism's. Nevertheless, there will be a kind of partial equivalence. Rule utilitarianism's first generational educational code is identical to act utilitarianism's second generational educational code. And, in general,

(5) Rule utilitarianism's n-generational educational code is identical to act utilitarianism's n+1-generational educational code.

I call this 'lag equivalence' since act utilitarianism's educational code lags one generation behind rule utilitarianism's in an educational progression.

Thesis (5) is straightforward. According to rule utilitarianism, the best educational code is the one that its ideal code recommends we teach. Call this educational code 'E'. E is rule utilitarianism's first generational educational code. But, as already argued, act utilitarianism's first generational educational code is rule utilitarianism's ideal code. So, the student taught by act utilitarians to accept rule utilitarianism's ideal code will believe that the best form of education is the one recommended by that code. Again this is E. Hence, E is not only rule utilitarianism's first generational educational code, but is also act utilitarianism's second generational educational code. This relationship is extended through the generations. If there is educational progression, rule utilitarianism's n-generational educational code is always act utilitarianism's n+1-generational code. This is lag equivalence.

Lag equivalence does much to bring the practical effects of adopting act utilitarianism and rule utilitarianism together, even when full educational equivalence is lacking. And we can go one step further. If progression ends at some point, then act utilitarianism's sequence of educational codes will catch up with rule utilitarianism's. In this case, there is a further kind of educational equivalence for rule utilitarianism and act utilitarianism at the point where the progression ends, end-point equivalence. Thus,

(6) Rule utilitarianism and act utilitarianism have end-point educational equivalence if and only if one of the educational codes in the rule-utilitarian/act-utilitarian educational progression does not recommend effacing itself.

I will now summarise our results and their significance. First, rule utilitarianism might recommend teaching its own ideal code, in which case we have full educational equivalence (for analogous forms) since act utilitarianism also recommends teaching rule utilitarianism's ideal code. This seems more likely for some forms of rule utilitarianism, though less likely for others. Second, suppose rule utilitarianism does not recommend teaching its own ideal code. This starts an educational progression. Nevertheless there is a kind of educational equivalence, lag equivalence. Rule utilitarianism's n-generational educational code is act utilitarianism's n+1-generational educational code. Third, given that educational progression has started, there are two possibilities. This progression may end at some generation, in which case act utilitarianism's educational code catches up with rule utilitarianism's. This is end-point equivalence. Or the progression might not end. If this happens we still have lag equivalence, but not end-point equivalence.

All this does much to lessen the practical significance of the choice between analogous forms of act and rule utilitarianism. If rule utilitarianism recommends teaching its own ideal code so that we have full educational equivalence, then there is no practical significance in the choice even though act and rule utilitarianism are different moral theories and say different things are right and wrong. Students will be taught the same codes and will create the same worlds. And if we do not have full educational equivalence, there might nevertheless be relatively little practical difference. For lag equivalence guarantees that act utilitarianism is always only one generation behind rule utilitarianism in the educational progression, which, over time, will make relatively little difference, particularly if progression ends and we have end-point equivalence. And in any event, it is hard to believe that the difference between act- and rule-utilitarian n-generational educational codes will be very great even if progression takes place. For example, act utilitarianism's first generational educational code is what it maximises utility to teach; but rule utilitarianism's first generational educational code is what it maximises utility to teach people to teach. It is unlikely that what it maximises utility to teach is generally all that different from what it maximises utility to teach people to teach. Thus, as long as we restrict ourselves to 'teaching' formulations of rule utilitarianism, and keep in mind that we are talking about analogous forms of act and rule utilitarianism, the choice between them loses all or much of its practical significance.

NOTES

1. For Hare's view, see *Moral Thinking: Its Levels, Method and Point* (Oxford: Clarendon Press, 1981). For the idea that a moral theory might recommend effacing itself, see Derek Parfit, *Reasons and Persons* (Oxford: Clarendon Press, 1984). The possibility that a moral theory might recommend effacing itself raises a number of issues. For example, it is linked to the issue of publicity. Perhaps the most important proponent of a publicity requirement has been John Rawls. For his recent views on the topic see *Political Liberalism* (New York: Columbia University Press, 1993).
2. See David Lyons, *Forms and Limits of Utilitarianism* (Oxford: Clarendon Press, 1965).
3. See Lyons, *Forms and Limits of Utilitarianism*, for a discussion of various forms of rule utilitarianism. Also, see various articles by Richard Brandt, e.g., 'Some Merits of One Form of Rule-Utilitarianism', reprinted in *Morality, Utilitarianism, and Rights* (Cambridge: Cambridge University Press, 1992). Note, it is more common for rule utilitarians to define the ideal code in terms of acceptance-utility rather than teaching-utility. And I admit that I chose the formulation in terms of teaching because it makes educational equivalence more likely. But there are three points in defence of my choice. First, teaching formulations are, in fact, not uncommon. For example, in 'The Concept of a Moral Right and its Function' (reprinted in *Morality, Utilitarianism, and Rights*), rule-utilitarian Brandt says that a moral code is justified for a society if and only if 'A fully rational and informed person who expected to live in that society would support bringing about and keeping in place that certain moral code' pp. 182–3. Presumably, 'bringing about and keeping in place' means 'teaching'. This is a form of rule utilitarianism if we assume that the right act is the one recommended by the justified code and that a fully rational and informed person will appeal to the test of utility in choosing codes. Second, even when rule utilitarianism's ideal code is defined in terms of teaching-utility, the educational equivalence thesis is far from obvious and there is much to learn by investigating the conditions under which it holds. Third, if I am right about educational equivalence for the teaching formulation of rule utilitarianism, I suspect an argument can also be developed for near educational equivalence for other forms of rule and act utilitarianism, even if the equivalence is not quite as close as with the teaching formulation.

4. Though I do not want to push the point, and nothing in this chapter turns on it, I do not believe the rule-utilitarian ideal code will contain the rule-utilitarian principle itself. First, we might assume that the ideal code will just include rules telling us what to do or not do, for example, rules like 'Do not steal'. But the rule utilitarian principle is not a rule telling us what to do so much as a rule for selecting rules telling us what to do. Second, and more importantly, including the rule-utilitarian principle in the ideal code would be odd since the principle only comes into effect if the system is flawed, and there seems to be no room for a 'how-to-fix-a-flawed-system' rule in what is supposed to be an ideal code. On the other hand, there might be a place for it in rule utilitarianism's educational code. Since, in the real world, no rules we come up with are likely to be truly ideal, it is worth teaching how-to-fix-it rules. Still, even this cannot be assumed, just as it cannot be assumed that act utilitarianism will recommend teaching itself.

5. For a few words about the application of the test of utility to courses of action as opposed to individual acts, see my 'Utilitarian Alternatives to Act Utilitarianism', *Pacific Philosophical Quarterly*, 78:1 (March 1997), pp. 93–112.

6. When I speak of an individual's teaching a code to society, I cannot assume that the individual has enough control to really determine what society as a whole believes. So, if 'teach' implies obtaining significant compliance, individuals cannot generally teach society. But I will not assume significant compliance need occur for teaching to count as teaching. And in any event, the ability of an individual to affect society is different only in degree from the ability of society to affect the individual. Perfect compliance is not possible in either case.

7. There are interesting questions about these forms of rule utilitarianism. For example, the ideal code defines the right act. But for whom? The teacher? The student? Both? Consider, for example, version (D), which says that the ideal code for T/S is the one it would maximise utility for T to teach S. It will not do to say that this code defines the right for both teacher and student. For suppose Sue were my teacher and that the code it maximised utility for her to teach me were C, but that the code it maximises utility for me to teach John is different, C'. Then, where C and C' differ, an act will be both right and wrong for me. Perhaps the rules define the right for the student. But this leads to trouble too if John has two teachers and the rules it maximises utility for me to teach him are different from the ones it would maximise utility for Sue to teach him. Fortunately, we do not have to deal with this and other tricky issues here.

8. Collective act utilitarianism is not a form of rule utilitarianism. Collective act utilitarianism merely modifies what counts as an agent. It does not give an indirect definition of rightness. Further, we can develop versions of rule utilitarianism that allow collective agents as well as the ordinary versions which assume individual agents. The more forms of rule and act utilitarianism we distinguish, the more possible educational equivalence theses we have. But the idea is clear enough without drawing more distinctions than I already do, so I leave these additional complexities aside.

9. There may be an argument available that rule utilitarianism's educational code will differ from its ideal code on at least one item. The argument turns on a point made in note 4. The 'rule-utilitarian principle' says that an act is right if and only if in accord with the ideal code. As I pointed out in note 4, this principle will probably not appear in the list of ideal rules. But it very well might appear in rule utilitarianism's educational code. If it does, then the ideal code and the educational code will be different in at least this one way. However, since I do not wish here to get into the content of rule utilitarianism's ideal and educational codes, I put this point aside. The argument of the main text does not turn on judgements about what is likely to be in these codes.

3

Defending Rule Utilitarianism

Jonathan Riley

Rules are necessary, because mankind would have no *security* for any of the things which they value, for anything which gives them pleasure or shields them from pain, unless they could rely on one another for doing, and in particular for abstaining from, certain acts. And it is true, that man could not be conceived 'as man', that is, with the average human intelligence, if he were unable to perceive so obvious an utility [as security].

(J. S. Mill[1])

SECTION I: ACTS OR RULES?

Act consequentialism says that a moral agent is generally obligated to choose from a given set of feasible acts one that has the best overall consequences for a given set of individuals. Perhaps the most familiar brand of this moral view is act utilitarianism, which combines act consequentialism with welfarism – the claim that the only consequences which count for moral assessment are those reflected in the set of individual utilities or welfares –, and summing or averaging of the relevant individual welfares.[2] According to act utilitarianism, a moral agent is required to choose a feasible act that maximises the general welfare, where general welfare is conceived in terms of aggregate or average welfare.[3]

Act utilitarianism is typically viewed as pure maximising utilitarianism. Agents who seek to maximise the general welfare can do no better, it is widely believed, than to invariably perform those acts with the best consequences for general welfare. Even Shelly Kagan apparently takes this view.[4] Despite his assertions that foundational utilitarians might opt to maximise general welfare by focusing not on acts but on rules or virtues or institutions or some other objects, he also seems to believe that these other evaluative focal points lose their appeal for utilitarian maximisers in what may be termed the ideal case, namely, the case in which all agents can be assumed to have developed the capacities of intellect, will, and empathy for others required to identify and perform optimal acts. Thus, when considering rule utilitarianism, for example, where the basic idea is that the right thing to do is to conform to an optimal code of rules, he suggests that an optimal code must be extensionally equivalent to act utilitarianism in the ideal case: 'But what rule could possibly lead to better results than . . . the rule which commands us to do the act with the best results!' he exclaims. 'Obviously enough, if people were to obey this rule, if they did perform the acts with the very best results overall, then the results would have to be better than they would be were people to obey some alternative rule which gave different instructions.'[5] Similarly, given the assumptions about agents' capacities in the ideal case, an optimal set of character traits must consist in the capacities and dispositions required to implement act utilitarianism, an optimal array of social institutions must reduce to policies and directives that mimic act-utilitarian reasoning, and so on.

At the same time, act utilitarianism is clearly an extremist view from the commonsense perspective of 'ordinary morality', which consists of the intuitions which most people in our social context share about right and wrong acts. On the one hand, act utilitarianism is overly permissive because it doesn't recognise ordinary moral constraints against doing or allowing serious harm (including death) to others. Because it doesn't recognise these constraints, it denies that individuals have corresponding fixed rights not to be harmed. To save the lives of five patients who need different organ transplants, for example, a surgeon will be permitted to seize and chop up the innocent Chuck to harvest his healthy heart, liver, lungs and so on, if these organs happen to be matches for the respective patients. 'After all, if everyone counts equally, then it is simply a matter of five versus one. Obviously, it is a horrible result that Chuck will end up dead; but it would be an even worse result if *five* people end up dead. So the right thing to do – according to [act] utilitarianism – is to kill Chuck.'[6] There isn't any thought that Chuck has a 'deontological right' not to be killed for his organs.[7]

On the other hand, act utilitarianism is also overly demanding because it doesn't recognise ordinary moral options to choose suboptimal acts. Because it doesn't recognise these options, it denies that individuals have any freedom to deviate from their act-utilitarian obligations. An agent is generally obligated to sacrifice even his own life if by doing so he can promote the greater good of others. Thus, if you are Chuck in the organ-transplant situation, 'you must *volunteer* for the operation, sacrificing your own life to save the lives of the five other patients'.[8] There isn't any thought that Chuck has an option not to volunteer so that he can pursue his own interests. His act of self-sacrifice is morally required. Act utilitarianism finds no room for the ordinary moral category of supererogatory acts whose performance may merit praise but is not obligatory.

Evidently, pure maximising utilitarians have a lot of explaining to do if they are necessarily committed to moral extremism of this sort. It's hard to take act utilitarianism seriously just because of its general contempt for the ordinary moral constraints and options accepted by most people in our relatively advanced civil societies. Indeed, it seems reasonable to conclude that pure maximising utilitarianism is an absurd doctrine if the focus on optimal acts is essential to its meaning. To escape this conclusion, reasons must be supplied for thinking that a focus on rules or virtues or some other objects can serve to generate a higher level of general welfare than can be generated by a focus on acts. If it can be shown that more general welfare can be produced by conforming to an optimal code which is not extensionally equivalent to act utilitarianism than by invariably relying on act-utilitarian reasoning, for example, pure maximising utilitarianism would become tied to a focus on optimal rules rather than optimal acts. Moreover, if rule utilitarianism provides support for ordinary moral constraints and options, pure utilitarianism might break free of the charges of extremism and absurdity which commonly surround it.

One way to proceed is to insist that human beings are not ideal act-utilitarian agents: our limited intellectual, imaginative, and volitional capacities will inevitably prevent us from performing or even identifying optimal acts. An act-utilitarian code is suboptimal for people like us because we are generally incapable of framing and complying with such a code. Since an act-utilitarian code isn't really feasible for agents with our imperfect natures, better overall results may be achieved under a relatively simple and undemanding rule-utilitarian code which can easily be learned by most people with all their frailties in the given social context. As Kagan admits, this more 'realistic' version of rule utilitarianism might justify something akin to commonsense deontology.[9] After all, ordinary moral codes with their constraints and options are by definition those which are accepted by actual majorities.

Although this familiar route to rule utilitarianism has much to recommend it, it does carry a danger of rationalising existing moral conventions — those which happen to prevail among the majority — as the best possible. It apparently takes for granted that ineluctable human weaknesses block any possibility of radical improvement in our existing moral rules. Without further argument, however, there seems no reason to insist that humans are so limited. Perhaps we are capable of significantly improving our moral capacities, even to a point at which an act-utilitarian code would become feasible. If so, it may be that we are morally required to transform our characters accordingly. Indeed, some extraordinary individuals may already display the capacities for self-sacrifice required of act-utilitarian saints. What this seems to boil down to is that our ordinary moral rules shouldn't be viewed as anything but 'starting points', likely to be far short of what more developed humans are capable of achieving. Rule utilitarianism shouldn't foreclose the possibility of moral progress and reform, however gradual.

Another difficulty stems from the fact that 'realistic' rule utilitarianism would collapse into act utilitarianism in the ideal case. The approach doesn't pretend to tell us why highly developed agents capable of implementing act utilitarianism should nevertheless conform to an optimal code that is not extensionally equivalent to act utilitarianism. But the problem is not merely that rule utilitarianism is thereby confined to non-ideal cases in which most people are too ignorant or self-oriented to make act utilitarianism feasible. More generally, even people of our limited capacities must be able at times to identify and perform acts which, though impermissible under optimal rules, would bring better overall results than any permissible act. If we know that harvesting Chuck's organs would maximise the general welfare, for example, why should we comply with any moral rule against murder in this situation? Any obligation to comply seems rooted in 'rule worship' as opposed to a concern for the general good. This problem of 'rule worship' seems to persist whether agents are assumed to have limited capacities like ours or highly developed ones like act-utilitarian saints. Opportunities will inevitably arise to bring about better overall results by deviating from the rules.

A different way to proceed, which I shall pursue, is to confront the problem of 'rule worship' directly by arguing that pure maximising utilitarianism implies a focus on rules rather than acts, even if humans are assumed to be capable of implementing act utilitarianism. Needless to add, such an approach will be condemned as heresy by many philosophers. As Brad Hooker remarks, '[m]any philosophers seem convinced that defending rule consequentialism is a lost cause once one accepts that what ultimately matters is maximization of the good'.[10] In my view, however, there is no warrant for the claim that an optimal code would collapse into act utilitarianism in the ideal case where all can be expected to comply perfectly with the rules. Even if everyone is capable of identifying and performing those acts which of all feasible acts have the best overall effects, there is good reason to believe that a higher level of general welfare could be generated by conforming to an optimal code that is not extensionally equivalent to act utilitarianism. Rational agents who seek to maximise the general welfare can do better by agreeing to cooperate with each other rather than by refusing to cooperate in accord with such a code, even if the refusal to cooperate is prompted by act-utilitarian considerations. As odd as it may sound, performing an optimal act in violation of an optimal code doesn't produce the best overall results in terms of a proper cooperative conception of general welfare.[11]

A key claim underlying my way of defending rule utilitarianism is that any particular act typically has 'negligible effects' on other people's expectations.[12] It is simply not the case that any rational person forms fixed beliefs about how another agent will behave on the basis of a single isolated act. Rather, expectations are the product of habitual interactions and other signs of mutual cooperation which together are symbolised by an optimal code of rules. Thus, as I use the term, an 'optimal act' is a feasible act with overall effects that are at least as good if not better than any other feasible act, keeping in mind that any particular act typically has negligible expectation effects. Similarly, by the phrase 'maximising the general welfare in act-utilitarian terms', I shall mean performing an optimal act.

It follows that act utilitarianism cannot adequately take account of certain aspects of general welfare which are consequences of optimal codes that are not extensionally equivalent to act utilitarianism. More specifically, act utilitarianism cannot properly appreciate the valuable coordination of different persons' activities made possible by an optimal code. As well, it cannot appreciate the general security of expectations made possible by a code that distributes fixed liberal rights and correlative obligations, nor the valuable freedom to choose and the valuable incentives to work and invest which are inseparably associated with that security. Security, freedom, and productive efficiency are effects of liberal codes not of particular acts. Act utilitarianism focuses on the consequences of acts per se in order to prescribe acts with the best overall results of all feasible acts. It thus fails to properly appreciate the valuable effects of optimal liberal codes that cannot be reduced to any array of optimal acts.

Rule utilitarianism as I conceive it prescribes particular suboptimal acts (including omissions) for at least a couple of reasons. First, it recognises that the overall effect of a combination of acts (that is, an *interaction*) may not reduce to a mechanical sum of the overall effects of the particular acts comprising the combination. A combination of optimal acts performed by different persons may result in less overall good than a combination of suboptimal acts because of interactions among the effects of particular acts: the effects of different optimal acts might interfere with each other whereas the effects of suboptimal acts don't. This point is exemplified by a version of the Prisoners' Dilemma (PD) in which act-utilitarian agents have incentives to refuse to cooperate.

Second, it claims that certain special ingredients of general welfare (for example, freedom of choice, security of expectations) are made possible by an optimal liberal code's implicit limitation of permissible interactions. Of all the possible combinations of acts by different persons, the code permits only some restricted number. Thus, suboptimal acts may also be prescribed because they are components of permissible interactions which give rise to the special ingredients of general welfare not adequately captured in the effects of optimal acts. When considered in conjunction with the overall effects of particular acts, these distinct forms of welfare made possible by the rules more than compensate for the loss of welfare associated with failure to perform optimal acts.

Any suboptimal act prescribed by a rule-utilitarian code is a component of a larger 'package', namely, a 'permissible (and perhaps obligatory) act – strictly speaking, interaction – under optimal rules'. For example, a permissible interaction might consist of a suboptimal act that is freely chosen by an agent in accord with his fixed rights distributed under a liberal code, rights that his fellows are obligated to respect. If we look solely at the consequences of particular acts, the act included in the interaction is not one with the best possible consequences. But when we consider the valuable freedom made possible by the rules in addition to the consequences of acts per se, then a suboptimal act that is freely chosen under the rules can produce better overall results than an optimal act that is not freely chosen.

What is distinctive about rule utilitarianism, in my view, is that it focuses on an optimal liberal code as a symbol of certain permissible interactions which rational people who seek to maximise the general welfare jointly commit themselves to perform repeatedly as different types of choice situations arise over and over again. It is by virtue of their continuing commitment to mutual cooperation in terms of the rules that rule-utilitarian agents are able to create and maximise such valuable overall effects as security of expectations, freedom of choice, and productive efficiency. The rules themselves mark certain permissible acts which these co-operative agents can rely on each other to *indefinitely repeat* as they find themselves again and again in the relevant circumstances. These remarks may require a bit of unpacking, to clarify where the contrast with act utilitarianism lies.

If we are act utilitarians who look solely at the consequences of particular acts, a PD situation can arise such that act-utilitarian reasoning leads to a suboptimal overall result. In this PD, agents who are motivated to maximise the general welfare in act-utilitarian terms have incentives to refuse to cooperate even though cooperation would produce the best overall outcome. Optimal acts are non-cooperative ones. But rule utilitarianism recognises that better overall consequences can be achieved if the agents agree to interact by each performing a suboptimal act. To achieve their ultimate purpose, therefore, utilitarian agents must agree to coordinate their activities by following optimal rules rather than perform optimal acts outside the rules. They must be rule utilitarians rather than act utilitarians. From a rule-utilitarian perspective, act-utilitarian agents have incentives to deviate from optimal rules which, if all utilitarians obey them, will generate a higher level of general welfare than if all perform optimal acts.

Now, act utilitarians might aim to avoid this version of the PD problem by insisting on an indefinitely repeated game framework in which act-utilitarian agents are uncertain about when the game ends and, say, impartial between present and future welfare (that is, zero discount rate). In such a framework, these act-utilitarian agents might achieve an optimal outcome. As is well known, mutual cooperation becomes a Nash equilibrium under such conditions. But, in the first place, it isn't obvious that this repeated game framework is essential to act-utilitarian reasoning. Why should we assume that act-utilitarian agents are always uncertain about how often their interactions will be repeated and always impartial between present and future benefits? More importantly, even if we accept the relevant assumptions, they don't allow act utilitarians to entirely escape the PD problem. As is also well known, suboptimal non-cooperative Nash equilibria remain: there is no guarantee that the relevant agents will choose to cooperate. Cooperation is merely a possibility.

In my view, rule utilitarianism properly avoids this sort of PD problem by generally obligating utilitarian agents to coordinate their activities in terms of an optimal liberal code. The focus on rules serves to guarantee that mutual cooperation is required by utilitarianism. The general obligation always to comply with the rules is justified by taking account of security of expectations, freedom of choice and productive efficiency as aspects of general welfare which are not adequately appreciated by a focus on acts. Because of these valuable effects of an optimal code, there is invariably a higher level of general welfare associated with mutual cooperation under optimal rules than is reflected in the utility payoffs which comprise the act-utilitarian result of coordinated action in a PD situation. PDs arise under act utilitarianism because of its failure to properly appreciate the overall benefits of cooperation under rules. But to create the valuable freedom, assurance, and productive incentives associated with an optimal code, utilitarian agents must jointly agree to accept the rules as binding constraints on their conduct. By agreeing to invariably obey the rules, these agents agree in effect to interact indefinitely in ways (and only in ways) permitted by the rules. Thus, they agree to adopt a long-run perspective that transforms any one-shot choice situation – including a one-shot PD situation – into an indefinitely repeated game such that mutual cooperation becomes a Nash equilibrium. More than this, they agree to rely on one another to create the security, freedom and economic efficiency which can only emerge under an optimal liberal code that is not extensionally equivalent to act utilitarianism. Security emerges, for example, because rule utilitarians predict and believe that their fellows will continue to act in accord with the code as the same choice situations are repeated indefinitely – fixed liberal rights and duties will be respected, and so on. The code (including rules for reforming the rules) manifests the continuing shared commitment to work together in these ways to maximise the general welfare.

If this is right, pure maximising utilitarianism doesn't properly focus on particular acts. Rather, the utilitarian calculus applies at the level of codes. Given an optimal code, any act of deviation from its rules must be viewed as an element of an indefinitely repeated series of such deviations, the effect of which would be to destroy the relevant rules and their valuable consequences for general welfare.

1. Some Objections

Despite what has been said, it might be objected that the special effects which I am attributing to optimal codes are included among the effects of optimal acts. An act's consequences include the effects on people's expectations, some may claim, as well as the concatenating effects of these possibly altered expectations. Indeed, rules of behaviour themselves are surely the products of acts. As mentioned earlier, however, I think Harsanyi is right that any particular act typically has 'negligible effects' on others' expectations (ignoring extraordinary cases where a catastrophic act destroys or threatens to destroy a given society and its moral code). Anyone who disputes this point seems to fly in the face of the evidence about how expectations are formed. Moreover, rules of behaviour are not internalised or accepted as binding by the relevant group of people as a result of any optimal act or acts, a point to which I shall return in due course (Section 3). Thus, I don't see how act utilitarians can adequately recognise the importance of coordination, security, freedom, or productive incentives by focusing exclusively on particular *acts*.

It might also be objected, however, that act utilitarianism can be stretched to recognise that *rules* have these valuable consequences. Although the details of the stretching exercise are not always clear, there seem to be at least two possibilities. First, act utilitarians might take Hare's type of route and prescribe rules as devices that in effect substitute for act utilitarian reasoning in ordinary everyday moral situations.[13] 'Proles' without the time or capacities to be fully-fledged act-utilitarian 'archangels' can still generally produce act-utilitarian outcomes by following these 'secondary' rules (which may be more than mere rules of thumb). The rules are part of a two-level act-utilitarian scheme of morality. Such rules are not too complex or demanding for people like us, nor is it too costly in principle to inculcate dispositions to abandon the rules in novel or hard situations where they don't apply in favour of fully-fledged act-utilitarian reasoning.

Actually, Hare's own inclination seems to be to reject as 'unrealistic' any examples in which act-utilitarian reasoning departs too far from our commonsense deontology. Perhaps he is right about this. If so, any hypothetical case, in which acts that violate some basic liberal rights and duties are said to have the best overall results, is based on a false view of what the world is like. Given the world as we know it, in other words, act utilitarianism largely reproduces our commonsense deontology: optimal acts rarely if ever diverge from acts permitted or required by a conventional liberal code. If this is Hare's approach, I don't dispute its appeal. But I think such an approach implicitly restricts act utilitarianism; in other words, some effects on general welfare are dismissed as 'unrealistic' or 'not feasible in the real world' if they are attributed to this or that particular act. If an act of torturing the innocent is assumed to produce better overall effects than an act of respect for their persons in some unusual circumstances, for example, the example is generally rejected as a distortion of the real world as we know it. In my view, then, Hare and his followers seem to be restricting act utilitarianism to include a certain liberal content. They aren't working with a pure unrestricted version of the doctrine in which particular acts can be matched to any conceivable level of general welfare given the right circumstances.

Now, a pure act-utilitarian code cannot produce the effects of an optimal liberal code that is not extensionally equivalent to act utilitarianism. Even if act-utilitarian reasoning happens to give some support to existing conventions as 'secondary rules', these rules are not adapted to myriad novel and hard choice situations which can arise – many complicated exceptions to the rules and to any rights and obligations associated with them may be prescribed. Thus, not only is there no freedom to depart from act-utilitarian obligations but also there is no limitation of permissible interactions, no security of expectations and no stable incentives of the sorts associated with fixed liberal rights and obligations distributed by an optimal code. Ultimately, the expectation effects of particular acts are all that matter for act-utilitarianism, and these are typically trivial. A pure act utilitarian code seems unable to secure basic liberal rights, for example, in situations where acts in violation of such rights have better consequences for general welfare than do acts respecting them.

The second possibility open to act utilitarians is to recognise the valuable effects of rules which happen to prevail, even though the rules cannot be *prescribed* by act utilitarianism. It is certainly true that act utilitarians can take account of existing conventions of private property, for example, and prescribe as optimal certain acts of production which take for granted such background conventions. Act utilitarianism might stipulate that, given the actual structure of conventional beliefs, a particular act of producing corn is associated with the producer's expectation of owning his production (including selling it on the market if he likes) and also with others' expectations that they will be/should be punished if they don't respect his property. If agents interact as they ought under the given structure, every particular act has the effect (however trivial) of reaffirming that structure of expectations. If a particular act of deviation occurs and goes unpunished, the consequences may include some slight damage to the prevailing system of conventions. Moreover, act utilitarianism can recognise that valuable acts of production under the rules might not be valuable at all in the absence of those rules of private property. For example, it makes no sense to produce corn if your selfish and/or needy neighbour can legitimately take whatever you produce for his or her own consumption.

But the point remains that act utilitarianism doesn't focus on the consequences of those prevailing rules. Its focus is on optimal acts in the context of the given conventions. Although it can take account of the existing rules as constraints on how people may currently be expected to act, it cannot *prescribe* those rules as optimal if particular acts that breach the rules have better overall consequences than acts permitted by the rules. It cannot defend rules when acts in violation of them have better overall consequences than acts in conformity to them. From an act-utilitarian perspective, any such defence of the rules amounts to 'rule worship'. So, again, I don't see that pure act utilitarianism can adequately deal with the valuable effects of an optimal liberal code, given that such a code is not extensionally equivalent to act utilitarianism.

If rule utilitarianism prescribes a given code as optimal, however, and if that code happens to prevail, act utilitarianism can replicate rule utilitarianism by restricting attention to acts permitted or required by the rules. Such a restricted version of act utilitarianism effectively ignores acts that violate the rules even though such impermissible acts may have better overall consequences than any permissible ones. As I've already suggested, Hare seems to adopt this sort of restricted act-utilitarian approach. Act utilitarianism thus modified implicitly accepts the relevant liberal rules as given and prescribes as optimal those acts which are components of permissible (including obligatory) interactions under the optimal rules. But this is not pure unrestricted act utilitarianism. It is act utilitarianism made to yield rule-utilitarian outcomes. The underlying reasoning is rule-utilitarian in form.

Under rule utilitarianism, the focus is on rules to which acts must generally conform unless the optimal code is destroyed by, say, civil war. The focus is not on optimal acts which secondary rules may help to locate in everyday circumstances. The optimal rules have a certain rigidity about them. They aren't anything like flexible rules of thumb that permit myriad acts of deviation whenever the relevant act has better overall consequences than any act permitted by the rules. This doesn't mean that an optimal code is frozen or static, since the rules may include rules for altering the code. But it does mean that the rules (including rules for reforming the rules) must invariably be obeyed by utilitarian agents seeking to maximise general welfare.

As well, these optimal rules are not merely conventions which should prevail because most people in a given social context have actually learned to guide their actions in accord with them. Majority acceptance of a code may be a necessary condition but it isn't a sufficient one for the code's optimality. The code must also be reasonable in some sense. In other words, its rules must be of suitable content to create and maximise certain aspects of general welfare which can be created and maximised in no other way, to wit, freedom, security, and productive efficiency. For example, the code should not interfere unduly with any minimally rational person's control over certain personal aspects of her life: its rules must distribute and suitably enforce certain rights to be left alone. In short, the code must be a liberal one, I suggest, involving (among other things) a system of equal rights and correlative obligations designed to promote a reasonable balance among such social goals as community safety, personal freedom from interference, some threshold of material prosperity, and some fair distribution of wealth and income.[14]

2. The Conception of General Welfare

This focus on a liberal code is tied, of course, to a rule-based conception of general welfare. According to the conception, those who seek to maximise general welfare can do no better so far as we can tell than to jointly commit to an optimal code which symbolises their shared intention to interact indefinitely in the relevant ways and, to that end, distributes certain equal rights and correlative obligations, obligations that don't correlate to rights, permissions that don't correlate to obligations, and so on. These various rights, obligations and liberties (together with their due recognition and enforcement by majorities) are viewed as essential to maximisation of general welfare. Indeed, these things create the equal freedom, security and economic incentives which are such valuable effects of liberal codes.

Foundational maximising utilitarians must focus on rules, therefore, because rule utilitarianism is superior to act utilitarianism for achieving the ultimate utilitarian purpose. Of course, the various rights and liberties distributed by an optimal code permit options to act-utilitarian obligations.[15] But these options to select suboptimal acts are not options to refrain from maximising the general welfare. Rather, the options are part of what it means to maximise general welfare properly understood in rule-utilitarian terms. Similarly, the various obligations (including the general obligation to obey the rules) distributed by the code impose constraints against performing optimal acts that unduly harm other people.[16] But these constraints are not constraints against maximising overall good. Rather, they are part of what it means to maximise it. Optimal acts which are impermissible under the optimal rules don't really maximise general welfare properly conceived. Even though an optimal act has better overall consequences than any acts permitted by the code if we look solely to the consequences of acts, more general welfare can be attained by performing a permissible suboptimal act once the valuable effects made possible by obedience to the rules are considered along with the effects of acts per se. All of this needs to be suitably qualified to the extent that an optimal code ceases to be optimal and requires reform with advances in the state of knowledge. But the reforms always lead to a new optimal code that distributes new rights, liberties and obligations – some such code is essential to maximisation of general welfare under rule utilitarianism.

I shall attempt next to clarify at least some of the valuable effects of optimal liberal codes which only a rule-based conception of general welfare can adequately appreciate. For the moment, I shall assume the ideal case in which all members of society are fully capable of complying with *any* code (including an act-utilitarian code), since my claim is that rational utilitarian agents would even then choose to conform to an optimal liberal code that is not extensionally equivalent to act utilitarianism.

3. Freedom of Choice

An adequate conception of general welfare must recognise the permanent value of personal freedom of choice for human beings capable of rational persuasion. On some accounts, the special value of freedom is tied to the bias displayed by most people in favour of their own narrow interests and those of their families and friends. The psychic cost of suppressing the bias in order to act with strict impartiality towards the interests of everyone is said to be prohibitive for the average person, from which it follows that act-utilitarian morality is simply too demanding for ordinary humans as opposed to gods or saints. Act utilitarianism recognises no overall good in the freedom to deviate from its requirements – such deviant acts are condemned as violations of moral obligations. Rule utilitarianism can promote more overall good for humans by recognising the importance of the freedom to pursue personal interests contrary to the demands of act utilitarianism. An optimal code that distributes and sanctions equal rights and liberties to choose suboptimal acts becomes privileged over act utilitarianism for people like us.

Such accounts of the overall value of freedom are vulnerable to the objection that the observed bias is a contingent feature of human nature which can and should be removed by education (however long the process takes). Other accounts are possible, however, which aren't vulnerable to the objection. In particular, the special importance of freedom can be tied to any human's continuing need to develop and maintain for himself the intellectual and moral capacities required to appreciate and act upon a warranted idea of the general welfare. The agent's interest in self-improvement of this sort evidently doesn't involve any bias against maximisation of the general good. Promotion of the one doesn't hinder promotion of the other. Rather, the two interests – personal and general – can and must be pursued in harmony. As fallible beings, we can never know with certainty what the general welfare looks like in detail or how best to achieve it. The only way to improve our limited capacities of understanding and cooperation is to experiment freely with different ideas, lifestyles, modes of production and exchange, and so on. Moreover, even as we became capable of the most enlightened understanding and of the most stringent impartiality possible for humans, the special value of freedom would remain. Humans would still be fallible beings, and some equal rights and liberties to choose suboptimal acts would still be essential to *maintain* the highly developed capacities – even if further improvement of them proved impossible. It is surely not plausible that people could eventually become infallible beings with some magical power to maintain their capacities without freedom of choice.

According to this second account, then, even if our common bias could be expected to disappear as society approaches an ideal state of education, the superiority of rule utilitarianism over act utilitarianism would remain. A focus on acts cannot bring about the best possible overall results. Rather, a focus on rules is needed to capture the valuable freedom of choice made possible by an optimal liberal code. Since freedom remains essential for the maintenance of our capacities, its value does not diminish if our capacities undergo indefinite improvement. Thus, even if we lose our inclinations to choose in favour of our own narrow interests, an optimal code must give the individual agent options to choose among some permissible set of acts, by distributing certain equal rights and liberties. We may not be able from our present vantage points to fix in complete detail what those rights and liberties should look like for ideal utilitarian agents with highly developed capacities. Given our limited capacities, in other words, we may be unable to foresee precisely how our more developed fellows will follow the rules to alter the code. Thus, we may not be able to specify the precise content of an ideal right to freedom of expression, for example, or to decide whether property rights or rights to participate in self-managed socialist enterprises would be accepted by ideal agents. But we do have warrant to believe that these agents would include *some* liberal system of equal rights and liberties in their code, given the special value of freedom for beings of our nature.[17]

On this second account, freedom is a permanent aspect of human well-being. Unlike act utilitarianism, which focuses on the overall effects of particular acts, a liberal rule utilitarianism can recognise that freedom of choice has what Harsanyi calls a 'procedural utility' such that this procedural value is added to the act-utilitarian value of any act which is freely chosen by an agent and not otherwise forbidden by the rules.[18] By assigning the procedural value to whichever act the agent freely chooses from some permissible set of acts (including the act required by act utilitarianism), an optimal code can bring about a higher level of general welfare than act utilitarianism can. Reconsider the case of Chuck, who has a moral duty under act utilitarianism to volunteer his organs to save the lives of five other people. If the overall value of freedom to pursue one's own interests (including a broad interest in self-development) is sufficiently large, Chuck can bring about even more overall good by performing a suboptimal act permitted by fixed rights or liberties distributed by an optimal liberal code. To see this, suppose that the contribution of freedom of choice to general welfare is sufficiently great that, when added to the act-utilitarian value of a suboptimal act of refusal to allow one's organs to be harvested, the result is that freely choosing to refuse the operation has better overall consequences than the optimal act of undergoing the operation. By permitting anybody in Chuck's position to choose suboptimal acts which, if freely chosen, would produce more general welfare than is produced by an optimal act per se, and then assigning the value of free choice to any act which is actually chosen by the agent from the relevant permissible set, an optimal liberal code can produce more general good than act utilitarianism can.

It should be emphasised that any act which is freely chosen from the permissible set will maximize the general welfare in rule-utilitarian terms. Only an act which is freely chosen is associated with the value of free choice. The unchosen acts in the permissible set remain at their respective act-utilitarian values, which are each by assumption less than the rule-utilitarian value assigned to the freely chosen act. In this way, rule utilitarianism is able to reconcile pure maximising utilitarianism with options to choose suboptimal acts. Moreover, rule utilitarianism can thereby recognise what act utilitarianism cannot, namely, 'the traditional, and intuitively very appealing, distinction between merely doing one's duty and performing a supererogatory action going beyond the call of duty'.[19] Chuck fulfils his duty to maximise the general welfare if he freely chooses any act in the set permitted by his rights and liberties, given that the value of free choice will be superimposed on to the act-utilitarian value of whatever permissible act he chooses. But he performs a supererogatory action by freely choosing to undergo the operation, sacrificing himself for others as act utilitarianism *requires*.

4. Security and Productive Efficiency

An optimal code doesn't rely entirely on the special value of free choice to justify rights and liberties – the permissible sets of acts that can be freely chosen by the individual agent. There are other aspects of general welfare which can only be created by a liberal code, namely, general security of expectations as well as productive efficiency. An agent may be permitted and perhaps obligated to choose suboptimal acts not merely because of the special value of freedom but also because of the special values of security and efficiency which a focus on acts cannot properly appreciate.

An optimal liberal code can create valuable security for individuals by protecting certain 'vital human interests' as rights.[20] Obligations correlative to the rights are crucial elements in the creation of this security.[21] Such obligations constrain others from coercively interfering with the right-holder's choices, where coercive inter-ference can include not only forcing him to do something else but also failing to act on his behalf as well as refusing to provide services which he needs to act. These constraints do prohibit others from choosing to act so as to seriously harm the right-holder by damaging his vital interests. But they are not constraints on the maximisation of general welfare. Rather, they are essential elements in the maximisation exercise.[22]

Strictly speaking, since rights are correlative to obligations, the security that flows from others' recognition of their obligations is merely another name for the freedom of choice enjoyed by the agent in virtue of his or her rights. In Chuck's case, for example, the special value of security is also the value of freedom which attaches to any permissible act which Chuck freely chooses in accord with his rights. By considering the value of security from harm produced for him by others' respect for his rights, we can say that his suboptimal act of refusing to undergo the operation is nevertheless associated with a higher level of general welfare than any optimal act which he is coerced to perform, whether by the surgeon or anyone else.[23]

At the same time, an optimal code can create valuable incentives, partly by distributing obligations whose recognition prevents or at least reduces the likelihood of certain harmful consequences of suboptimal acts, including acts of material production, and partly by permitting different agents to compete.[24] By assuring the agent that the beneficial consequences for him of a suboptimal act are very likely to be realised whereas its harmful consequences for him are very likely to be frustrated, a liberal system of rights and correlative obligations creates incentives to choose that protected act rather than an optimal one. The special value of security artificially enhances the relative appeal of the protected act for the agent. An act of material production looks more attractive relative to an optimal act of idleness, given that the latter isn't associated with harmful reactions from other people anyway since there is no valuable product to steal or otherwise appropriate. By encouraging people to choose the suboptimal acts of production and allowing them to interact competitively by exchanging their products, the liberal code can generate a higher level of general welfare than if everyone remained idle. In short, by assuring agents of the competitive market fruits of their labour, saving, investment, and entrepreneurship, a liberal code can promote economic efficiency since agents have far more powerful incentives to perform these socially valuable activities than otherwise would be the case.

Even if rules of private property and market exchange would cease to be optimal with improvements in our intellectual and moral capacities, highly developed utilitarian agents will continue to include some liberal system of equal rights and correlative obligations in an optimal code, I suggested earlier, if only because of the special value of freedom of choice for people with our natures. It can now be added that, although different systems would create different patterns of expectations depending on the precise natures of the rights and obligations distributed, some system of equal rights and obligations will also be essential to maximise the special values of security of expectations and productive efficiency for humans who, after all, have vital interests not only in freedom of choice and self-development but also in sound bodies, nourishment, and other scarce resources.

5. Against the Enforcement Thesis

Before closing this section, it is also worth emphasis that rule utilitarianism as I conceive it is not committed to the thesis that an optimal act is a moral obligation if and only if society finds it generally expedient to impose external sanctions – legal penalties, for example – to suitably compel performance of the act by agents who stand to gain more personal utility by choosing a suboptimal act. The idea behind this enforcement thesis, which Hart attributed to Mill, seems to be that if the external sanctions required to motivate selfish agents to perform an optimal act would reduce the general welfare below the level associated with leaving the agents alone, then the optimal act ceases to be an obligation.[25] As Kagan argues against Waldron, however, such an idea appears to have little if any appeal.[26] It seems to carry some odd implications, to wit, obligations cease to exist if they can't be effectively enforced by external means; and the more agents stand to personally gain by choosing a suboptimal act, the less likely it is that a moral obligation exists to do anything else.

In my view, rule utilitarianism is committed to the distinct thesis that a sub-optimal act is obligatory if and only if it is an obligation distributed by an optimal liberal code as, for example, restraining oneself from violating another's rights is, in which case there is an optimal rule of conscience compelling performance of that act of restraint. True, any person's failure to perform such a compulsory act entails some form of punishment for him or her – everybody must be encouraged to satisfy their obligations under the rules. But the optimal means of enforcing any optimal rule of conscience remains a separate issue. Depending on the circumstances, the general welfare might be maximised by social enforcement of the rule as a law or custom, in which case rule-breakers can expect to meet with, respectively, legal penalties and social stigma or merely stigma. Or the general good might instead be maximised by a social policy of laissez-faire, that is, leaving individual agents alone to observe the rule as a common dictate of conscience, in which case rule-breakers should experience internal sanctions of guilt or shame but no legal penalties or stigma. Rule utilitarians must assume that individual agents have developed a conscience – which Mill equated with 'a desire to do right' – to some degree, and I am supposing that any agents who have done so will experience spontaneous feelings of guilt and shame if they violate its dictates.[27] Indeed, if individuals develop their capacities near to the point of human perfection, it seems possible that an optimal code might be able to dispense with legal penalties and social stigma altogether, as individuals will voluntarily satisfy their obligations without being coerced by external sanctions.

It emerges that, given an adequate conception of human welfare that is sensitive to our vital interests in freedom, security and productivity, rule-utilitarianism is superior to act utilitarianism for utilitarian purposes: a higher level of general welfare can be generated by conforming to an optimal liberal code that distributes equal rights and obligations than by deviating from the rules to perform optimal acts. Deviating from the rules for any reason erodes rather than promotes the overall good. Such deviations are incompatible with rule-utilitarian reasoning, which refuses to consider the effects of any particular act and instead looks to the consequences of indefinitely repeated acts. Indefinitely repeated acts of deviation would evidently destroy the rules as well as their valuable effects in terms of general welfare. Thus, foundational utilitarians must eschew a focus on acts because such a focus can't properly appreciate these special overall benefits of codes.

Of course, act utilitarians may well continue to insist that they can capture the importance of freedom, security, and productive efficiency through a focus on acts. No doubt the individuation of acts is a difficult matter. But we can in principle identify a feasible set of acts in any choice situation independently of whether those acts are or are not freely chosen by the agent, and of whether they are or are not tied to other acts through the actual expectations of some group of people. The effects of acts per se can thus be distinguished from the freedom, security and productivity that are the effects of liberal codes. Still, it might be objected such a distinction is unnecessary. For example, act utilitarians might treat 'act x freely chosen by agent i' and 'act x performed by agent i under coercion' as two distinct acts and invariably recommend the freely chosen act as the one with the better overall consequences, thereby replicating a liberal rule utilitarianism. Similarly, act utilitarians might differentiate between 'act y by person i which calls forth act z by person j because of expectations created by prevailing rules' and 'act y by person i which doesn't provoke act z because the relevant rules and expectations don't exist' and invariably prescribe the act with the expectations as the one with the better overall results. As I've indicated earlier, however, this is not pure act utilitarianism but rather a restricted act utilitarianism that mimics rule-utilitarian reasoning.

SECTION 3: A DYNAMIC OPTIMAL CODE

Act utilitarians may press on to insist that an optimal code is created by acts so that the overall effects of the code can be ascribed to the acts that created it. If the act with the best overall consequences is one that founds an optimal code, for example, then act utilitarianism really prescribes a sacrifice of its form of reasoning in favour of rule utilitarianism. In this case, act-utilitarian agents would be required to transform themselves by a single act into rule-utilitarian cooperators. But this is absurd. Act utilitarianism cannot properly imply its self-destruction, just as freedom cannot mean the freedom to become a slave. An optimal code is *not* the product of any optimal act or even of any combination of optimal acts. Even if an optimal code could be framed and made fully binding on all agents by a single founding act, for example, that founding act wouldn't be optimal because occasions must subsequently arise when particular acts of deviation have better overall consequences in act-utilitarian terms than acts of conformity to the rules.

In any case, the ideal scenario in which a society of highly developed utilitarian agents is assumed, by a single binding act of agreement, to select an optimal code and commit themselves to comply with its rules is merely a heuristic device.[28] It is a useful tool for illustrating that what is distinctive about rule utilitarianism is the idea of a joint commitment by utilitarians to limit themselves forever to certain patterns of acts – permissible interactions under the rules, including rules to amend the rules – as situations arise over and over again. To perform a permissible interaction, the relevant agents may each be allowed and perhaps required to choose a suboptimal act. The patterns of suboptimal acts under the rules maximise the general welfare, despite the feasibility of patterns of optimal acts. The latter patterns may lack the crucial element of coordination which is essential to bring about the best overall results.

The ideal case is evidently not 'realistic'. Moreover, no attempt is made to explain how the relevant agents have developed the requisite capacities to identify and comply with an optimal code. For heuristic purposes, it is simply assumed that the agents already possess the formidable capacities required to predict the permissible interactions (strictly speaking, the equilibria of the non-cooperative games) which arise when rational people pursue their personal interests in accord with the rules of each of the alternative possible codes; identify an optimal code whose rules yield the permissible interactions with the best overall effects; and comply with the optimal rules. But people of our limited abilities generally can't predict how different persons will interact under myriad alternative codes; we can't imagine much more than the broadly liberal outline of any optimal code that might be accepted by people of highly developed capacities; and most of us wouldn't comply with the rules of such an ideal code anyway.

Clearly, if it aims to be a complete theory, rule utilitarianism must go beyond the ideal case to, first, specify an optimal code which would be accepted by rational utilitarians with limited capacities like ours, and, second, connect that 'realistic' optimal code to an 'idealistic' one which would be accepted by ideal utilitarian agents with far more developed capacities of intellect, empathy, and will than ours. A *dynamic* rule utilitarianism is needed, one which shows how a realistic optimal code is reformed in accord with optimal rules for changing the rules such that it can in principle be transformed into an ideal liberal code as moral progress occurs. The ideal case remains important in this dynamic theory. Ultimately, an optimal code must be one that ideal utilitarian agents who may be expected to comply perfectly with its rules accept for maximising the general welfare, a code whose liberal outlines, I have suggested, we can only dimly see from our imperfect vantage points. But the doctrine must also have its more realistic side that speaks to people like us.

The dynamic theory which I propose owes much to Mill. Very briefly, it goes as follows. We start with the observation that actual majorities in advanced societies like ours do comply with some set of more or less liberal moral conventions, to wit, our commonsense deontology. Indeed, there is considerable social pressure on the individual to conform. This empirical fact requires explanation. Perhaps most people in our societies are sufficiently educated to see that general compliance with a somewhat liberal (or quasi-liberal) code brings about better overall results than the alternatives, for example, or perhaps most simply tend to blindly imitate how majorities are said to have habitually acted from time immemorial in the given social context. But I don't need to offer any particular explanation for present purposes.

The next step is to claim that so far as utilitarians of our limited abilities can tell, the common moral code which has been internalised by most people in our advanced society is in the neighbourhood of an optimal code for the given state of mass education. In particular, the existing rules accepted by majorities for regulating harmful other-regarding acts are most likely to be optimal rules. This doesn't mean that the existing rules of other-regarding conduct should be viewed as permanent fixtures. Evidently, as most people develop their capacities so that the state of moral education improves, these rules may cease to be optimal, requiring reform of the code in accord with its optimal rules of amendment (including rules for employing the political process to enact new legislation, and so on). With that caveat, however, actual majority sentiment as reflected in the existing rules may be accepted by utilitarians as a reasonable test of which other-regarding rules are most likely to have the best overall results. Given the capacities of the average person in the relevant social context, this majority opinion is a fairly reliable indicator of how best to regulate harm to others in this society because each person is assessing harmful effects which he or someone he cares about can reasonably expect to experience if the relevant acts are left unregulated.

In contrast, the existing rules accepted by majorities for regulating purely self-regarding acts are more likely than not to be suboptimal. The problem is that these rules attempt to manage *every* person's personal affairs even though each member of the majority can in principle only have information that pertains to her own case (since other people's self-regarding acts cause her no perceptible damage against her wishes). Following Mill, the optimal rule for regulating these personal acts is arguably no rule whatsoever: complete individual liberty to do as one pleases should be protected by right. The relevant individual's own judgement and desires should be accepted by utilitarians as the test of which purely self-regarding acts are likely to have the best overall results. This sort of personal freedom is essential to the further self-development which most people in our societies must undergo if majorities are to be persuaded to reform existing rules in the direction of an ideal liberal code.

Rule utilitarian agents with limited capacities like ours can accept the other-regarding portion of existing majoritarian conventions as optimal, while at the same time arguing for rights to self-regarding liberty, including the liberty to issue opinions that may be critical of the existing rules. Moreover, to discourage non-compliance, such 'realistic' rule utilitarians can prescribe generally expedient means of enforcing those existing rules that are designed to prevent serious harm to others. In this regard, the form of enforcement with the best overall effects may vary from rule to rule, depending on the overall costs of the form of enforcement weighed against the overall benefits of preventing the relevant harmful other-regarding acts. Legal penalties for non-compliance may be optimal in the case of some optimal rules, for example, whereas social stigma or even laissez-faire might be optimal in the case of others.

The remaining steps are to spell out optimal rules for reforming the existing moral rules to bring about higher and higher levels of general welfare as majorities develop their capacities and the state of moral education improves. Given the importance of general security of expectations associated with moral rights and correlative obligations which are recognised under an existing optimal code, for example, any reform that alters or abrogates those existing rights in the course of establishing a new optimal code must include fair compensation to the right-holders. Fair compensation is essential if security is to be maximised under the new liberal system of rights and duties distributed by the reformed code. Indeed, without fair compensation, reform must tend to erode even the existing level of security since right-holders have reason to fear that their rights are meaningless. Thus, obligations to provide fair compensation can be determined by rules which are elements both of an existing code that has ceased to be optimal and of a reformed code that has become optimal in the improved state of education.[29]

It may be helpful to make this picture of dynamic rule utilitarianism somewhat more explicit. Denote by M* an 'idealistic' optimal code which would be accepted by ideal utilitarian agents, a code that distributes some ideal liberal system of equal rights, permissions and duties which fosters substantial material equality with plenty of wealth and leisure for all. This idealistic code is not yet feasible in any society, however, because nobody with our limited capacities knows what its rules look like in detail. Much ambiguity surrounds the rights, liberties, and obligations which it would assign. Even if it could be well defined from our vantage point, utilitarians might not recognise M* as optimal because few if any have the capacities to judge correctly its overall consequences relative to those of alternative codes. In any case, most people in the present state of moral education lack the self-control and empathy for others required to comply with its rules. Moreover, there is no prospect of remedying common incapacities overnight, through some form of revolution. Until a long and gradual process of mass education is carried out, even people who are interested in maximising the general welfare can't be expected to commit jointly to M*.

In the meantime, rule utilitarians have little choice but to accept some more 'realistic' optimal code M_t in the present state of mass education at time t. Given the common human frailties which are characteristic of the present state of education, this 'realistic' optimal code can be assumed to overlap with existing conventions accepted by actual majorities for regulating harmful other-regarding conduct. But M_t will reject any existing conventions for regulating purely self-regarding conduct, and instead give the individual a Millian right to liberty. Actual majorities can be expected to comply with the optimal rules of other-regarding conduct, even if they meddle unduly with the individual's right to be left alone in his or her personal affairs. Moreover, the means accepted by majorities for coercing uncooperative agents to comply with the existing other-regarding rules can also be accepted as optimal, where the means might be legal penalties, social stigma or simply the internal dictates of individual conscience as specified by rules of enforcement included in M_t.

The optimal code M_t may be viewed as a best approximation to M^* at time t, given the imperfect state of education at t. In any advanced social context, M_t is assumed to involve some liberal system of equal rights (including the Millian right to liberty of self-regarding action) and correlative obligations, even if significant inequality of wealth is also permitted and some members of society are mired in poverty. Suppose that the existing state of moral education improves at a later time t+1, however, by virtue of the self-development made possible by individual exercise of rights to liberty. Rule-utilitarian agents now understand that acting in conformity to M_t doesn't maximise the general good. Rather, with the improved state of education at t+1, the set of feasible codes has expanded to include another element, M_{t+1}, which is recognised to yield a higher level of general welfare than M_t does. Rule utilitarians thus have good reason to prescribe reform of M_t according to its optimal rules for changing the rules to bring about the new 'realistic' optimal code M_{t+1} at t+1.

The new optimal code M_{t+1} can be viewed as a best approximation to M^* at time t+1, given the improved state of education at t+1. Another improvement in the state of education at t+2 may lead rule utilitarians to prescribe reform of M_{t+1} to establish a distinct 'realistic' optimal code M_{t+2} at t+2, and so on. In general, if education improves, rule utilitarianism thus conceived involves an indefinite series of 'realistic' optimal codes M_t, M_{t+1}, M_{t+2}, M_{t+3}, and so on, one code for each distinct state of education, tending towards an 'idealistic' optimal code M^*, with the caveat that M^* may never actually become a feasible alternative. It's worth remarking that differences between states of education can be made as fine as we like, such that the distinct optimal codes corresponding to two distinct states of education may differ only with respect to a single rule. Needless to add, education might deteriorate rather than improve in a given society, in which case the direction of movement between 'realistic' optimal codes would be reversed as time goes on.

It seems that many of the stock objections to rule utilitarianism have no bite against this dynamic conception. There is no significant problem of non-compliance, for example, since actual majorities can be reasonably expected to comply with the optimal rules at any state of education and to enforce compliance by the recalcitrant. Indeed, the more serious problem is likely to be an excessive conformity to existing rules, including non-optimal rules that regulate self-regarding acts rather than leaving them free from interference. Of course, there is no problem of non-compliance in the ideal case, where everyone by assumption has the capacities to obey the rules of the ideal liberal code M*.

Another familiar objection that loses force is the objection stated by Kagan that rule utilitarianism 'seems to be conflating, without justification, social norms and individual morality'. In his view, 'the two-level approach assumes that once we know what set of norms it would be best to have taught in a society we also know the complete set of moral considerations relevant to an individual agent's actions; morality is exhaustively captured by the optimal set of social norms'. But that assumption is unwarranted, he argues, because 'there might be morally relevant considerations that would not be fully and precisely captured by the set of moral rules whose promulgation would be optimal'.[30] In addition to presupposing without argument that a focus on acts is superior to a focus on rules for utilitarian purposes, this sort of objection appears to rest on a crudely static conception of rule-utilitarian morality. Rule utilitarianism seems to be viewed in terms of a fixed optimal code, frozen over time, which vainly tries to embody all morally relevant considerations for judging acts despite our fallibility and other common human shortcomings.

Under the dynamic conception of rule utilitarianism, however, no assumption is made that the set of norms embodied in an optimal code at any time is the complete set of moral considerations relevant to an individual agent's actions. Morality may well be incompletely captured by the code whose promulgation is optimal at t, although the extent of the incompleteness is not known at t. If it is subsequently learned at t+1 that some existing rules are no longer optimal, rule utilitarians can recognise that the individual should violate some rule of M_t to maximise the general welfare. Unlike the act utilitarian who merely recognises an obligation to act in violation of the existing rule, however, the rule utilitarian recommends suitable reform of M_t to establish a new optimal code M_{t+1} that reflects the improved state of knowledge at t+1. As already indicated, 'suitable reform' includes fair compensation to recognised right-holders under M_t, given the importance of security of expectations associated with recognised rights.

It's important to stress that, as conceived, this dynamic rule utilitarianism never reduces to act utilitarianism. Unlike act utilitarianism, which focuses on whether a particular act in violation of an optimal rule has better overall effects than an act of conformity to the rule, rule utilitarianism focuses on whether indefinitely repeated acts of violation of the kind in question would have better overall effects than indefinitely repeated acts of conformity. If an affirmative answer is given to that latter question, then the existing rule has ceased to be optimal and must be reformed to maximise general welfare taking into account the valuable effects of optimal codes which aren't properly appreciated by act utilitarians. After reform, the suboptimal rule will have been suitably transformed into an optimal one, generally by the addition of exceptional clauses that grant permission to any person to ignore the old rule in such and such circumstances. The new rule modifies the old one by carving out a class of exceptions to it. Repeated modifications of this sort may transform a fairly simple optimal code into a more complex one. But they don't imply that the optimal code must eventually become extensionally equivalent to act utilitarianism as the state of education improves. The optimal code may continue to evolve indefinitely towards an ideal liberal code M* that remains more or less ambiguous in certain respects.

SECTION 4: CAN'T WE DO BETTER?

But this defence of rule utilitarianism as pure maximising utilitarianism may leave some (perhaps many!) unpersuaded. They may object that even if a focus on rules is superior to a focus on acts for maximising general welfare, why should maximising utilitarians limit themselves to just these two focal points? Perhaps even more overall good can be achieved by a focus on character traits or institutions, for example, or by focusing simultaneously on multiple points. I shall largely leave this important question open.[31] One suggestion which I shall argue against, however, is that general welfare might be maximised by focusing directly on acts and rules at the same time. The suggestion is that a mixture of act utilitarianism and rule utilitarianism can produce a higher level of general good than either of the two alone.[32] In particular, given that an optimal liberal code has been established, why not permit *secret* act-utilitarian deviations from that code – deviations that violate optimal rights and obligations – when those particular deviations would promote more overall good in act-utilitarian terms than conforming to the rules? Let the optimal code remain authoritative for the vast majority, for example, but permit some individuals or groups to break the rules to do more good when this can be done without fear of detection.

Consider the following elaboration of Chuck's case. Alice, the surgeon, has power of attorney for Chuck, her husband, who enjoys good health and is fervently committed to following the existing optimal rules (as are most of his compatriots). By assumption, that prevailing liberal code gives Chuck a deontological right to keep his own healthy organs, a right which Alice is obligated to respect. Super-erogatory acts of donating one's organs are deemed praiseworthy but are not required under the rules.[33] But Alice feels obligated to do as much overall good as possible without damaging the valuable effects of the optimal code. She realises that she can harvest her husband's organs without him or anyone else ever finding out what is going on. She can persuade Chuck that he needs some routine surgery, administer potent drugs the night before that will take effect during the operation to kill him without damaging his organs or leaving a trace, and then use her power of attorney to authorise the harvest of his organs. In her view, she has a duty to perform these extraordinary acts of deviation from the rules, even though Chuck will die as a result.[34] By assumption, saving the lives of the five other people who need his organs results in a higher level of general welfare than saving his single life. Isn't it obvious for maximising utilitarians that Alice ought to secretly violate Chuck's rights rather than stick to the code?

There is no denial in this case that the prevailing liberal code really is an optimal code in the given state of education. If we learned that the code were suboptimal, of course, rule utilitarianism itself would recommend suitable reforms to establish a new optimal code. For example, perhaps more overall good could be promoted by a new code which gives anyone in Alice's circumstances an obligation to secretly harvest the organs of anyone in Chuck's circumstances, an obligation that supersedes Chuck's rights in the relevant class of situations. If so, a new optimal code adapted to the improved state of knowledge would contain exceptional rules to override the general rules pertaining to personal safety, medical practice, marriage, and so on, in those situations. But, in this case, Alice wouldn't be acting counter to her obligations under optimal rules. Rather, she ought to act in secrecy to harvest Chuck's organs since such acts are permissible and indeed required under the optimal code. In our example, however, there isn't any doubt that the existing code is optimal. So far as most people in that social context can tell, no other code would promote a higher level of general welfare.

Given that the existing rules of other-regarding conduct are optimal, the suggestion that Alice can do even more overall good by secretly deviating from the optimal code to harvest her husband's organs is unpersuasive. Alice is unwilling to openly endorse a rule of conscience to the effect that anyone in her position should act as she is acting. After all, if she is willing to do that and most agree with her, then there can't be any objection to rule utilitarianism. By implication, Alice knows that she is a non-cooperative agent and that her particular act of deviation, if performed repeatedly by others in like circumstances, would destroy the existing optimal code and its valuable effects of freedom, security, and so on. Moreover, as a moral agent seeking to maximise general welfare, she must admit that rational utilitarians like herself will infer that, in the present state of education, even moral agents – let alone purely selfish agents – may try to secretly deviate from the rules in these circumstances. Since this can be assumed to be common knowledge, utilitarians can further infer that such deviations will take place repeatedly unless appropriate measures have been taken to prevent them. Even if – what seems highly unlikely – none of the many deviations would ever be detected in the absence of the appropriate measures, the warranted fear that they are occurring would be sufficient to destroy the existing liberal code and its expectation effects.

The point is that Alice, as well as any other maximising utilitarian who imagines herself in like circumstances, can infer from her own intention to secretly deviate from the rules how other moral agents in the present state of education can reasonably be expected to behave in such circumstances. Since these agents know that repeated attempts to secretly breach the code will be made by people like themselves, they know that the code itself must include optimal rules for enforcing its provisions. It must include various measures to assure people like Chuck that people like Alice have little if any incentive to secretly harvest a patient's organs for redistribution to other patients. In short, if it really is optimal in the given state of education, the existing code must include rules that provide suitable checks and balances on Alice's behaviour. For example, spouses might be prohibited from operating on each other, medical panels might be required to frequently monitor and review a surgeon's operations and other medical practices, and so on. Otherwise, everyone knows that even moral agents can't be reasonably expected to fulfil their obligations under the code, which in that case must be viewed as suboptimal in the present state of education.

This is not to argue that an optimal code could never dispense with rules providing such checks and balances. As already suggested, it seems plausible that, with great improvements in our intellectual and moral capacities, utilitarian agents could be counted on to comply voluntarily with an ideal liberal code, without any need for people to check each other's activities and apply external sanctions if required. But utilitarians of limited capacities like Alice must accept that in a society of people like themselves – people who know that they and their fellows are capable of indefinitely repeated secret act-utilitarian deviations which would destroy the existing optimal rules – a 'realistic' optimal code must contain suitable provisions to check such deviant acts. Otherwise, these utilitarians will validly fear that the optimal rules are not binding for all. Such fears are incompatible with the given assumption that an optimal code has been accepted in the given state of education.

Undoubtedly, more examples can be put forward to challenge the superiority of an exclusive focus on rules. Unless utilitarian agents are assumed to make errors about the capacities of their fellows in the given state of education, however, it seems incorrect to think that general welfare could be maximised by a simultaneous focus on rules and acts.

SECTION 5: RECONSIDERING ORDINARY MORALITY

The received view among philosophers that general welfare maximisation requires a focus on acts is misplaced. This view has led to much confusion in the literature.

Because act utilitarianism is widely seen as the archetype of pure maximising utilitarianism, pure utilitarianism is usually depicted as an extremist doctrine deeply at odds with ordinary moral intuitions. Even Kagan, who suggests that a foundational commitment to maximising utilitarianism doesn't dictate the choice of a focal point, seems nonetheless to take for granted that maximising utilitarians can do no better than to focus exclusively on acts if they can be reasonably sure that the acts will be performed. '[F]oundational consequentialists – even maximizing foundational consequentialists – need not pick *acts* as the primary evaluative focal point', he says, 'they could pick something else instead . . . [T]he choice of maximizing consequentialism at the foundational level does not in and of itself commit you one way or another as far as the choice of focal point is concerned.'[35] But he also suggests that 'if perfect conformity is indeed the appropriate embedding condition for testing the various competing rules, then it certainly looks as though no set of rules that diverges from [the rule to always perform the acts with the best consequences of all feasible acts] could be truly optimal'.[36]

Against the received view, I have argued that a foundational commitment to pure maximising utilitarianism *does* require an evaluative focus on rules rather than acts. Rule utilitarianism is superior to act utilitarianism for utilitarian purposes since act utilitarianism can't properly appreciate the valuable overall effects made possible by optimal codes. If this is right, Kagan is incorrect to assert that maximising utilitarians can opt to focus on acts or rules. Rather, maximising utilitarians are obligated by their own foundational commitment to focus on rules instead of acts, even if for the sake of argument we leave open the possibility that a focus on virtues or institutions will prove even better than the focus on rules.

At the same time, I have argued that, for people of our limited capacities, 'realistic' optimal codes overlap with existing majoritarian codes in important respects, namely, with respect to rules regulating harmful other-regarding conduct. By implication, pure maximising utilitarianism supports something akin to commonsense liberal deontology, with the important caveat that Millian rights to liberty ought to replace any existing rules that meddle with purely self-regarding acts. Given our limited capacities, it is rarely an easy matter to decide if existing other-regarding rules continue to be optimal or if majorities are now ready to reform them. Because Millian rights to liberty are invariably distributed by an optimal code in any given state of education, however, rational utilitarians are always free to criticise the existing rules as suboptimal and to propose new rules for adoption by majorities.

By way of conclusion, I wish to point to some ordinary moral rules which may well be optimal rules so far as we can tell, contrary to received philosophical opinion. I shall also re-emphasise where ordinary morality seems in one respect to fall far short of an optimal code in social contexts like ours, a failing that is not adequately emphasised in the literature.

Consider the ordinary moral rule that prohibits killing of innocent human beings like Chuck. Is it really so obvious that this is a constraint that prohibits the maximisation of general welfare? Many philosophers apparently think so. Thus, Kagan, for example, often takes for granted that the general good might be promoted by murdering an innocent victim if that act is essential to prevent the deaths of some greater number of innocents. But any such intuition is highly contestable. It seems plausible to insist that an act of murdering any innocent person (including oneself) has *infinitely* bad overall effects just as an act of saving one has *infinitely* good effects, if for no other reason than that each innocent person's life has indefinite positive value. In that case, the act of chopping up Chuck to save five others doesn't have *better* overall consequences than the act of allowing the five to die by refusing to kill Chuck. Both acts have neutral consequences overall: infinite good offsets infinite bad as a result of either. It follows that a focus on acts is indeterminate here. Act utilitarianism thus restricted becomes indifferent between Chuck having the operation or refusing to undergo it and between the surgeon harvesting Chuck's organs or refusing to operate. Everything seems permissible.[37]

But it is absurd to think that general welfare could be maximised by this sort of moral free-for-all. Rather than a focus on the effects of particular 'life and death' acts, a focus on the effects of liberal codes is required. Since each innocent person's life is assumed to have indefinite positive value, it seems reasonable – at least so far as people of our limited capacities can tell – to include in an optimal code a general rule that distributes equal obligations to refrain from the killing of innocents for any reason. Innocents have a corresponding deontological right not to be murdered. Such rights and obligations seem essential to maximisation of general security. Similarly, it seems reasonable to include a general rule that gives equal permission to agents to sacrifice voluntarily their lives for others if the act of sacrifice is an optimal act, without any obligation to do so. Such liberties seem essential to maximise freedom of choice without compromising the maximisation of security. If such a network of equal rights, liberties and obligations can be accepted as part of a 'realistic' optimal code for the present state of education, pure maximising utilitarianism supports ordinary moral intuitions in these difficult 'life and death' cases.[38]

Now let's consider another ordinary moral rule, namely, the one that obligates us to give away some proportion of our wealth to help to support the needy but doesn't obligate us to reduce ourselves to bare subsistence or worse as act utilitarianism may require. Again, is it really so obvious that ordinary morality imposes a constraint against maximisation of general welfare in this case? An affirmative answer supposes, among other things, that the value of freedom to pursue our own interests (including the interest in self-development) can never justify denying the claims of others for our resources when needed for bare physical survival. But even that supposition is contestable. I shall mention only a couple of considerations, without pretending to deal adequately with the issue here. First, if it is plausible to think that every innocent human life has infinite positive value, then no innocent person has an obligation to sacrifice his own life so that the lives of others (even a zillion others) may be saved. Each life is equally valuable and each is as valuable as all the rest together. From an act-utilitarian perspective thus restricted, every person is permitted to act to save his or her own life at the expense of others' lives or to sacrifice his or her life to save the lives of others. Again, these acts both have neutral overall consequences. Considerations other than the effects of such acts per se must decide what is right for any agent to do. The equal freedom to live our lives or sacrifice them for other people seems to be a paramount consideration.

Second, it's clear that unrestrained redistribution of wealth can encourage overpopulation and thus ever-increasing demands for more redistribution in the present state of education. Indeed, population density might grow so high that the effect of additional human beings on freedom, security, and other valuable effects of an optimal code turns negative. A rule-utilitarian case can be made, therefore, that any obligation to redistribute wealth must be made conditional on recipients' acceptance of suitable birth-control measures. This opens up a whole can of worms, to wit, what is a utilitarian population policy? Although that question is an important one for utilitarianism, however, any attempt at a reasonable answer must await another occasion. For present purposes, the point is merely that an obligation to redistribute wealth to needy others tends to drive us towards larger populations with lower levels of freedom, security, and so on, unless rules are devised to duly limit the obligation by requiring recipients of transfers to meet prevailing standards of education, by prohibiting recipients from bearing more children until they can afford to raise them at some reasonable standard of living, and so on.

Up to now, I have been suggesting that some ordinary moral rules may be optimal rules so far as we can tell, given our intellectual and moral disabilities. But I wish to close by repeating that ordinary morality is notably suboptimal in at least one respect, namely, its failure to distribute equal rights and correlative obligations to all adults assuring absolute liberty of choice with respect to purely self-regarding acts. As Mill suggested, the ordinary rules accepted by the majority may often be in the vicinity of optimal rules for a given state of education, in so far as those rules govern acts whose immediate consequences involve harm to other people in the broad sense of any perceptible damage to them against their wishes. The majority's rules governing purely self-regarding acts, whose direct consequences involve no harm to others even in the broad sense, continue to be unduly meddlesome in our societies, however, and should be abandoned to make way for the freedom of choice that is essential for self-development and ever higher levels of general welfare.[39]

NOTES

1. J. S. Mill, 'Whewell on Moral Philosophy', in J. M. Robson (gen. ed.), *Collected Works of J. S. Mill*, Vol. 10 (London and Toronto: Routledge & Kegan Paul and University of Toronto Press, 1969), p. 192.

2. See A. K. Sen, 'Utilitarianism and Welfarism', *Journal of Philosophy*, 76 (1979), pp. 463–89. I shall treat 'utility' and 'welfare' as synonymous terms. But they are often distinguished within modern decision theory, where 'utility' refers merely to the value of a mathematical function used to represent a decision-maker's preferences. Preferences may embody welfare judgements but often the two things will be distinct.

3. As is well known, the directives of aggregate utility can conflict with those of average utility if the choice is between populations of different sizes. Aggregate utility maximisation may lead to the 'repugnant conclusion' that a large population of individuals each with near-zero utility is better than a smaller population of individuals each with substantial positive utility, whereas average utility maximisation may lead to another repugnant conclusion that relatively unhappy individuals should be killed off to make way for a relatively well-off elite. For leading discussions, see C. Blackorby, W. Bossert, and D. Donaldson, 'Intertemporal Population Ethics: Critical-Level Utilitarian Principles', *Econometrica*, 63 (1995), pp. 1303–20; Blackorby, Bossert, and Donaldson, 'Intertemporally Consistent Population Ethics: Classical Utilitarian Principles', in K. J. Arrow, A. Sen and K. Suzumura (eds), *Social Choice Re-examined*, II (London: Macmillan, 1996), pp. 137–62; Blackorby, Bossert, Donaldson, and M. Fleurbaey, 'Critical Levels and the (Reverse) Repugnant Conclusion', *Journal of Economics*, 67 (1998), pp. 1–15; and T. Cowen, 'What Do We Learn From the Repugnant Conclusion?', *Ethics*, 106 (1996), pp. 754–75. But I shall ignore the population problem for present purposes.

4. S. Kagan, *Normative Ethics* (Boulder: Westview Press, 1998), pp. 212–39.

5. Ibid., p. 226. In fairness, Kagan (ibid., pp. 229–35) does say that even if perfect compliance can be assumed, rule utilitarianism need not collapse into act utilitarianism because the optimal rules accepted under this assumption might prescribe suboptimal acts for situations where some people do not comply with the rules. But since we are by assumption never in those situations, this difference is of little interest. Either perfect compliance is the relevant assumption or it isn't. If it isn't, there is no sense in speaking of optimal codes predicated on perfect compliance! Any code predicated on the assumption should surely be viewed as irrelevant if such situations arose. I shall return to these matters in due course.

6. Ibid., p. 71; emphasis in original.

7. Ibid., pp. 172–3.

8. Ibid., p. 157; emphasis in original.

9. Ibid., pp. 227–30.

10. B. Hooker, 'Rule-consequentialism, Incoherence, and Fairness', *Proceedings of the Aristotelian Society*, 95 (1995), pp. 19–35, at p. 28. Hooker himself avoids defending rule utilitarianism as the best way for foundational utilitarians to satisfy their commitment to maximise general welfare. He is 'interested in an argument for rule consequentialism that is *not* founded on an overarching commitment to maximize the good', to wit, the argument that 'it does a better job than its rivals of matching and tying together our moral intuitions' (ibid., pp. 28–9). See also B. Hooker, 'Ross-style Pluralism versus Rule-consequentialism', *Mind* 105 (1996), pp. 531–52.

11. As Kagan (*Normative Ethics*, pp. 230–35) suggests, a problem of 'rule worship' arises if rule-utilitarian agents are obligated to comply with optimal rules when interacting with people who have no intention of complying themselves. The importance of this problem of non-compliance or 'partial compliance' is emphasised by many. See, e.g., B. Hooker, 'Rule-consequentialism', *Mind*, 99 (1990), pp. 67–77; and Hooker, 'Rule-consequentialism, Incoherence, and Fairness', pp. 19–27. It could indeed be disastrous if rule-utilitarian cooperators were required to follow rules predicated on the assumption that all people will comply when in fact most do not comply. As Hooker points out, such rules could place absurd demands on the cooperators. But this sort of problem doesn't arise under the dynamic version of rule utilitarianism which I defend later in the text. In my view, in addition to rules which are 'realistic' in terms of the limited intellectual and moral capacities of most people in a given social context, an optimal code must include special rules for dealing with noncooperative agents who refuse to comply with its provisions (including provisions that obligate us to help others). Rational utilitarian cooperators cannot be required to cooperate with non-cooperative agents motivated by selfish concerns or act-utilitarian ones. The special rules would include rules for exercising coercion, meting out punishment, and so on. They are special in the sense that they are optimal rules for *enforcement* of the optimal code of which they are a part in a given state

of moral education. Such rules would become redundant in the ideal case, of course, where perfect compliance can be assumed.

12. Harsanyi emphasises this point. See J. C. Harsanyi, 'Game and Decision Theoretic Models in Ethics', in R. J. Aumann and S. Hart (eds), *Handbook of Game Theory*, I (Amsterdam: Elsevier, 1992), pp. 669–707, at p. 690.

13. R. M. Hare, *Moral Thinking* (Oxford: Clarendon Press, 1981).

14. Following Mill (whom I regard as a type of rule utilitarian), I think the relevant test of 'reasonableness' in any advanced social context may be broken into two parts. One part relates to other-regarding acts that pose a credible threat of perceptible damage to other people against their wishes: the test for this class of acts is whatever the given majority habitually accepts as reasonable since each person is judging something which potentially harms his or her own interests. The other part relates to purely self-regarding acts that pose no such credible threat to others: the test here is whatever the individual agent wants and judges to be reasonable for him- or herself.

15. As I understand it, a 'right' is roughly a claim to choose any element of a permissible set of acts without coercive interference by other people and, under special conditions (past promises, for example, or family relationships), with their active assistance. Others have correlative obligations not to interfere with the agent's chosen action and, in special cases, to act on his or her behalf. They are prohibited from forcing him or her to suffer another act, permissible or otherwise. This idea is similar to Kagan's idea of a 'full' (negative or positive) right, with the caveat that a right-holder may lack authority to personally enforce others' obligations. Kagan himself thinks, however, that the idea of a right at 'the heart of most rights-talk' is a 'thin' right that involves constraints but not options to choose suboptimal acts. A thin right gives the right-holder an injunction that prohibits others from coercively interfering with his or her choices. But it doesn't give him or her permission to choose an act if the act would fail to maximise the general welfare. Nor does it give him or her a right to enforce the injunction. See S. Kagan, *The Limits of Morality* (Oxford: Clarendon Press, 1989), pp. 219–30.

   In contrast, a 'liberty' is a claim to choose any element of a permissible set of acts subject to competition from other people. Others don't have correlative obligations not to interfere with the agent's choice. They can force him or her to choose another element of the permissible set.

16. A 'perfect obligation' is a duty to choose particular permissible acts, including refraining from coercive interference with another's acts, as required by another's right. The duty-holder is prohibited from coercively interfering with the right-holder's chosen acts and, if special relationships obtain, he or she must actively assist the right-holder to make his or her choice. 'Imperfect obligations' of charity don't correlate to others' rights. But they may be ignored for present purposes.

17. As is well known, Mill argues that equal rights to absolute liberty of purely self-regarding conduct must be distributed in any civil society, however far development proceeds. I have defended Mill's view elsewhere. See J. Riley, *Routledge Philosophy GuideBook to Mill on Liberty* (London: Routledge, 1998); and Riley, *Mill's Radical Liberalism: An Essay in Retrieval* (London: Routledge, 2000).

18. Harsanyi, 'Game and Decision Theoretic Models in Ethics', p. 689.

19. Ibid., p. 689.

20. As I have argued elsewhere, classical utilitarians like Mill seem to equate liberal justice with maximisation of general security in terms of equal rights and correlative obligations. See J. Riley, 'Mill on Justice', in D. Boucher and P. Kelly, (eds), *Social Justice: From Hume to Walzer* (London: Routledge, 1998), pp. 45–66. For a similar interpretation of Bentham, see, e.g., P. Kelly, *Utilitarianism and Distributive Justice* (Oxford: Clarendon Press, 1990).

21. In contrast to rights, liberties as I understand them don't figure prominently in the creation of security because they don't have correlative obligations. The same is true of imperfect obligations of charity which don't correlate to rights. An agent has discretion in fulfilling his imperfect obligations – he isn't required to give charity to everyone who asks. But he is required in every instance to meet his 'perfect obligations' of justice, which correlate to others' rights.

22. Nevertheless, there are no constraints against harming in some broad empirical sense. Rather, the conception of 'serious harm' involved is a normative conception, merely a way of redescribing what happens if somebody fails to meet his moral obligations and thereby violates another's rights. This normative conception of harm could be extended to include failures to satisfy imperfect obligations.

23. Harsanyi might wish to distinguish between the value of freedom and the value of assurance in a slightly different way. He refers to freedom as a positive 'implementation effect' of a liberal code because he apparently conceives freedom in terms of liberties or permissions that don't have correlative obligations, whereas he refers to assurance as a positive 'expectation effect' because it flows from our expectations that others' will satisfy their obligations (including obligations correlative to claim-rights) under the rules. See Harsanyi, 'Game and Decision Theoretic Models in Ethics', pp. 689–94. Like the classical utilitarians, I use the term 'assurance' or 'security' as another name for the portion of freedom associated with rights. The freedom associated with mere

liberties or permissions is not secure because others can legitimately compete against the agent, that is, others have no obligations to respect the agent's choices.

24. Again, by assigning one person a liberty to compete, the code doesn't forgo assigning others permission to compete for the same thing. A moral permission to compete for the same job, for example, is not nearly so strong a claim as a moral right not to be murdered or enslaved. The agent may not get what he or she wants in the one case whereas he or she is guaranteed not to be interfered with in the second. Unfortunately, the idea of a 'right' is often applied indiscriminately to both cases, especially in legal terminology.

25. See H. L. A. Hart, 'Natural Rights: Bentham and J. S. Mill', in Hart, *Essays on Bentham* (Oxford: Clarendon Press, 1982), pp. 79–104.

26. S. Kagan, 'Defending Options', *Ethics*, 104 (1994), pp. 333–51, at pp. 339–46; and J. Waldron, 'Kagan on Requirements: Mill on Sanctions', *Ethics*, 104 (1994), pp. 310–24. Like Hart, Waldron attributes a version of the enforcement thesis to Mill. Kagan agrees to call it 'Mill's thesis' without conceding that Mill actually subscribed to it. My own view is that Mill subscribed to the distinct rule-utilitarian thesis sketched in the main body of the text.

27. Waldron also seems to allow that 'the experiencing of guilt and shame [is] surely the natural concomitant of any moral judgment' ('Kagan on Requirements', p. 322). If so, it isn't clear why such an experience is 'a distinct event' from a judgement that one has violated dictates of one's own conscience. The failure to do what one is obligated to do under optimal rules seems to be inseparable from the appearance of guilt feelings in a person who has developed a conscience that urges him or her to do what the rules require (which may be to perform a suboptimal act).

28. Following Harsanyi, I have employed this heuristic device myself at times. See, e.g., Riley, 'Mill on Justice', pp. 51–4; and Harsanyi, 'Game and Decision Theoretic Models in Ethics', pp. 692–4.

29. For further discussion of fair compensation and of other obligations arising during this process of reforming the rules, see Riley, 'Mill on Justice', pp. 57–61.

30. Kagan, *The Limits of Morality*, p. 37.

31. I'm inclined to ignore possible differences between rule utilitarianism and other indirect approaches such as disposition utilitarianism or virtue utilitarianism, however. Optimal dispositions and virtues are plausibly viewed as habits of acting in accord with optimal rules, where the rules may be nothing more than internal dictates of conscience which may be amended with advances in the state of knowledge.

32. This is a move towards a version of what Kagan calls 'direct consequentialism', which would 'evaluate *all* focal points directly'. 'Thus, instead of evaluating acts indirectly, in terms of conformity to the best rules, or evaluating rules indirectly, in terms of promotion of the best acts (not to mention even more elaborate possibilities, such as evaluating acts in terms of conformity to the rules promulgated by the best institutions), we might simply evaluate acts, rules, motives, institutions, virtues, and so on, all of them directly in terms of the evaluative standpoint provided by the foundational theory' (*Normative Ethics*, pp. 238–9). But, for him, presumably, direct utilitarianism cannot be superior to act utilitarianism for maximising general welfare.

33. To avoid needless complications, I ignore the possibility of 'imperfect' charitable obligations to donate one's organs. For example, if one is terminally ill, one might have an imperfect obligation to allow one's organs to be harvested before they are severely damaged by the illness.

34. The assumption that nobody will ever discover Alice's secret activities strains credibility, of course, but it isn't inconceivable.

35. Kagan, *Normative Ethics*, pp. 223–4.

36. Ibid., p. 228. But see note 5 above.

37. It might be suggested that act utilitarianism is not indifferent but rather incapable of evaluating, or choosing between, acts with these sets of infinitely good and infinitely bad consequences. Perhaps infinite good cannot be compared to infinite bad, in which case we cannot even in principle calculate the overall values of the acts in question. But a refusal to prescribe any choice would certainly not save act utilitarianism in these situations. Indeed, such a refusal seems tantamount to indifference when some choice must be made for practical purposes.

38. Mill seems to see maximising utilitarianism as supporting commonsense deontology in these 'life and death' cases. See, e.g., his letter dated 17 April 1863, to William Thomas Thornton, reprinted as Letter 606, in J. Robson (gen. ed.), *Collected Works of J. S. Mill*, Vol. 15 (Toronto and London: University of Toronto Press & Routledge & Kegan Paul, 1963–91), pp. 853–54. In the letter, he discusses the case where the Roman senate demanded that the Carthaginians must surrender up Hannibal to save themselves and their city from destruction by the legions. Mill's view appears to be that Hannibal has a deontological right not to be given up and that the Carthaginians should mutually cooperate by fighting against the Romans to the death if need be.

39. I am particularly grateful to Brad Hooker, Dale Miller, and John Skorupski for helpful comments and discussion. None of them is likely to agree with the views expressed in this paper. Responsibility is mine alone.

4

Values, Obligations, and Saving Lives

D. W. Haslett

Every day thousands of children throughout the world die from easily treatable diseases, malnutrition, and bad drinking water. By sending a relatively small amount of money to legitimate life-saving organisations, such as UNICEF and OXFAM, you can save one of these lives. Are you morally obligated to do so?[1] Peter Unger, in a challenging book entitled *Living High and Letting Die*, argues that are you are obligated to send not only this small amount of money, but much more as well.[2] You are obligated, he argues, 'to send to the likes of UNICEF and OXFAM, about as promptly as possible, nearly all your worldly wealth'.[3] In what follows, I shall argue that, on the contrary, you are not obligated to send anything. I shall conclude that, aside from two rather limited exceptions, you do not have, and should not have, any obligation at all to help others.[4] This conclusion may appear to be cruel and heartless, but I shall try to show that, on the contrary, this conclusion is justified in terms of the overall well-being of people in general, including even that of the needy themselves.

SECTION I: UNGER'S PUZZLE

Unger's book is, essentially, an attempt at solving a puzzle generated by two hypothetical cases concerning those in dire need. The first case, 'The Vintage Sedan', he sets out as follows.

> Not truly rich, your one luxury in life is a vintage Mercedes sedan that, with much time, attention and money, you've restored to mint condition. In particular, you're pleased by the auto's fine leather seating. One day, you stop at the intersection of two small country roads, both lightly traveled. Hearing a

voice screaming for help, you get out and see a man who's wounded and covered with a lot of his blood. Assuring you that his wound's confined to one of his legs, the man also informs you that he was a medical student for two full years. And . . . he's knowledgeably tied his shirt near the wound so as to stop the flow. So, there's no urgent danger of losing his life, you're informed, but there's great danger of losing his limb. This can be prevented, however, if you drive him to a rural hospital fifty miles away. 'How did the wound occur?' you ask. An avid bird-watcher, he admits that he trespassed on a nearby field and, in carelessly leaving, cut himself on rusty barbed wire. Now, if you'd aid this trespasser, you must lay him across your fine back seat. But, then, your fine upholstery will be soaked through with blood, and restoring the car will cost over five thousand dollars. So, you drive away. Picked up the next day by another driver, he survives but loses the wounded leg.[5]

Unger points out, correctly I think, that most people's intuitive reaction to your refusing to help this wounded man is that your behaviour was 'very seriously wrong'.

Unger sets out the second hypothetical case, 'The Envelope', as follows.

In your mailbox, there's something from (the U.S. Committee for) UNICEF. After reading it through, you correctly believe that, unless you soon send in a check for $100, then, instead of each living many more years, over thirty more children will die soon. But, you throw the material in your trash basket, including the convenient return envelope provided, you send nothing, and, instead of living many years, over thirty more children soon die than would have had you sent in the requested $100.[6]

Contrary to their reaction to Sedan, most people's intuitive reaction to this case, Unger reports, is that your behaviour was 'not even mildly wrong'. Most people, although they will not, of course, view your failure to contribute in Envelope to be praiseworthy, will not consider it to be blameworthy either.

Here then is the puzzle. Why do people intuitively believe that failing to help is wrong in Sedan but not in Envelope, even though, for the following five reasons, it seems that it should be the other way around? First, the cost to the agent of helping is over fifty times *less* in Envelope than in Sedan. Second, without the agent's help in Sedan, only *one* person will suffer a serious loss, while, without the agent's help in Envelope, over *thirty* people will. Third, without the agent's help in Sedan, the loss suffered by the man will be merely that of his *leg*, while, without the agent's help in Envelope, the loss suffered by the thirty children will be that of their *very lives*. Fourth, in Sedan the person needing help is largely responsible for the fact that he needs help, while, in Envelope, the children needing help are not. Fifth, in Sedan the man needing help needs it as a result of his objectionable trespassing behaviour, while the children needing help in Envelope need it through no fault of their own.[7] So how then can failing to help in Sedan be morally wrong without its being *at least* as wrong to fail to help in Envelope?

Unger claims that the solution to this puzzle is that human beings are subject to certain psychological dispositions that prevent them, in certain cases such as Envelope, from getting in touch with their true moral commitment to helping others. The most important of these misleading, psychological dispositions, he says, is 'futility thinking'. Futility thinking is the trick our minds play on us in cases, such as Envelope, in which the overall problem, such as mass starvation, is so great that no matter how much we may contribute personally towards its solution, our contribution will remain just a drop in the bucket since vast numbers of people will still remain in dire need of help. In such cases, Unger suggests, the obvious futility of any contribution by us for solving the *whole* problem tends, in our minds, to become generalised, so that we therefore tend to think, fallaciously, that any contribution by us would be *altogether* futile. So intuitively, he says, we view not contributing as permissible.[8] But our intuitions, he claims, must be wrong. Since it is morally obligatory to help the person in need in Sedan, and since the need for help is even greater in Envelope and can be given at less sacrifice, it must therefore, Unger concludes, also be obligatory to help the children in Envelope, by donating the $100 to UNICEF.

Finally, there seems to be little relevant difference between, say, giving an initial $100 to UNICEF or some other life-saving charity, and giving a second $100. For most people, a second $100 will not be at any appreciably greater sacrifice for them, and will do just as much good. Likewise, there seems to be little relevant difference between giving a second $100 and giving a third, and so on. In short, it seems that, once we admit that giving the initial $100 to the charity is obligatory, we will be on a 'slippery slope' that will not end until we admit that giving nearly *all* of our wealth to the charity is obligatory, which, as we have seen, is exactly what Unger tells us we are morally obligated to do. I shall argue that, on the contrary, we are not obligated to give anything to charity, and I shall try to provide a more plausible explanation than Unger's for what appears to be the inconsistency in our intuitive reactions to Sedan and Envelope.

SECTION 2: MORAL JUSTIFICATION

Let me begin by explaining, briefly, that approach to moral justification that my argument presupposes. This approach follows from two premises. The first premise – the 'point-of-morality' premise – is that, viewed in the most abstract sense possible, the point, purpose, or function of morality is our well-being. Societies have morality – that is, a code of morality – rather than none at all, simply because, with morality, things go 'better' for us; without morality life will tend to be, as Hobbes said, nastier, more brutish and shorter. The second premise – the 'equal-considera-tion' premise – is this. For calculating which, from alternative rules, or entire codes, of morality are most successful at achieving well-being, *equal degrees* of well-being are to be given *equal weight*, no matter whose well-being it may be. In other words, for purposes of this calculation, the well-being of everyone, everywhere, is to be taken as equally important.[9] Putting these two premises together, we get the following: the purpose of morality is well-being, taking everyone's well-being to be equally important. This purpose may be referred to simply as 'overall well-being'.

Now if things of a certain kind have a purpose, then it makes sense to evaluate alternatives of that kind in terms of how successful they are at achieving that purpose. For example, if knives have the purpose of cutting, then it makes sense to evaluate alternative knives in terms of how successful they are at cutting. Likewise, if the purpose of morality is overall well-being, then it makes sense to evaluate alterative rules, or entire codes, of morality in terms of how successful they are at achieving overall well-being; it makes sense, in other words, to *justify* them in these terms. In the literature, this approach to moral justification is given various names, among them being 'rule consequentialism', 'rule utilitarianism', and 'indirect utilitarianism'.

I do not know whether Unger agrees with this approach to moral justification. It is a weakness of his book that it does not touch upon theoretical questions such as this at all. But I would think that Unger at least agrees with the point-of-morality premise. The point-of-morality premise entails that, other things being equal, a morality that is more successful at achieving human well-being is superior to one that is less successful at doing so. Unger is obviously a compassionate person, deeply concerned about human well-being. So I would be surprised if he did not consider the morality that was more successful at achieving it to be superior. He could, of course, claim that morality had no point at all. But then if he thought that, why would he bother to write a book about it?

Whether Unger agrees with the second premise – the equal-consideration premise – is perhaps more problematic. But this premise, I suggest, follows directly from the principle of universalisation, which tells us to treat cases the same, unless there is a relevant difference between them. I do not know how one could show that, *for purposes of justifying moral codes*, there was a relevant difference between the well-being of any one person and that of any other. But this is exactly what Unger would have to show if he did not agree with the equal-consideration premise. On the other hand, if Unger does agree with the equal-consideration premise, as well as the point-of-morality premise, then he does implicitly hold a rule-consequentialist approach to moral justification, perhaps in spite of himself.[10] In any case, that is the approach I am presupposing here.

Rule consequentialism comes, of course, in a number of different versions, depending upon how one unpacks what it means for a moral rule, or code, to be the one that is most successful at achieving well-being – or, more generally, depending upon how one unpacks what it means for the rule, or code, to be the one with the best consequences. I favour unpacking this in terms of whether, very roughly speaking, the rule, or code, is the one with the best consequences if backed by the sort of social pressure that moral rules, or codes, *typically* command. This very rough formulation will not be sufficient for all purposes, since the consequences of a society's backing a rule, or code, with social pressure may at times depend largely upon the *degree* of social pressure with which it is backed; that is, upon the social pressure's intensity, form, and scope. The greater the degree of social pressure, the greater the social-pressure *costs* are likely to be, negative consequences which, in any complete evaluation, must be taken into account also. Thus, for evaluating alternative rules, or codes, it will not always be sufficient to calculate their consequences assuming that each alternative is to be backed by the *same* degree of social pressure – namely, that degree which is 'typical'. But it is sufficient for my purposes here.[11]

To uncover what follows from the rule-consequentialist approach to moral justification that I am presupposing here, let us perform a kind of 'thought experiment'. Let us suppose that we are charged with designing, from scratch, a code of morality. In designing this code, we are to concentrate not upon its details, but upon its basic components and how they are related to each other. In other words, we are to concentrate upon what we may refer to as this code's general 'taxonomy'. And we are to assume that whatever code we design will actually be *adopted* by our society – that is, adopted to the extent that it is not already current in our society. By a moral code's being 'adopted' by a society, I mean that the code becomes the one that, to a greater extent than any other moral code, is *backed by social pressure* in that society. If a moral code is adopted by some society, this does not mean, of course, that people in that society will always comply with it. It means only that people in that society will *tend* to criticise deviations from it, will *tend* to teach it to their children, and so on. And, as already pointed out, we are assuming here that the degree of these tendencies will be that which is 'typical'. Our goal in this thought experiment is to be that of designing a code which, once it is adopted, *will bring about more overall well-being than would any other*. For convenience I shall, throughout, be referring to such a code simply as a 'well-designed' code.

SECTION 3: MORAL TAXONOMY

What then are the general features of a *well-designed* code of morality, a code which, once it is adopted, will bring about more overall well-being than would any other code had it been adopted instead? Let us begin with basics. The first feature of a well-designed moral code will, I submit, be this. It will leave people with ample freedom from moral constraints so that they may pursue their *own* well-being. And, of course, people's pursuit of their 'own' well-being is to be understood as involving, as well, their pursuit of the well-being of loved ones, and of personal 'projects' of various sorts. The importance of a code's leaving people ample freedom to pursue their own well-being seems often to be overlooked by moral philosophers, especially act utilitarians, but was not overlooked by John Stuart Mill. As Mill explained, although there are, of course, exceptions, generally speaking people *know* more about themselves (and their loved ones), and thus what will be most conducive to their *own* well-being, than they know about others in general, or than others in general know about them.[12] So if morality leaves people with ample freedom to pursue their own well-being, more overall well-being is likely to result than if people instead are required by morality always to pursue the well-being of others in general, or have their well-being decided for them by others. And more often than not, people who are left free to pursue their own well-being will, even without intending to do so, end up contributing to the well-being of others as well. The person who, in the pursuit of his own well-being, builds himself a house has built something that, after he has finished with it, others are likely to benefit from as well. The person who, in pursuit of her own well-being, starts a business will be contributing to the well-being of others by providing the community with important goods or services. The person who, in the pursuit of his own well-being, invests his wealth wisely, will be benefitting others by contributing to economic growth and creating jobs for people. And so on.

But, of course, not all ways of pursuing one's own well-being are likely to increase overall well-being. Some ways, such as by killing, rape, theft, deceit, and the like, are counter-productive in that, as a general rule, pursuing one's well-being by these means will, through the harm they do to others, and ultimately perhaps even to oneself, generally *decrease* overall well-being. Thus the second feature of a well-designed code will be that it will contain moral principles prohibiting such behaviour (or requiring certain other behaviour), principles such as 'Do not kill', 'Do not rape', 'Do not take what does not belong to you', 'Do not deceive', 'Do not cheat', 'Pay your debts', and 'Keep your promises'. Such principles delineate *moral obligations*. Those obligations that prohibit us from doing something *to* others, such as raping them, are referred to as 'negative' obligations, and those that require us to do something *for* others, such as keep our promises, are referred to as 'positive' obligations.[13]

Obligations delineate the *minimum* that is morally acceptable. Their function is to generate a certain 'comfort zone' in which people can pursue their own well-being with a reasonable degree of security and trust in others. This comfort zone will exist, of course, only if we can count upon people generally *adhering* to their moral obligations. And we can count upon people generally adhering to their moral obligations only if morality requires people to adhere to them even in those cases in which they think the best overall consequences result from not adhering to them. Thus, in a well-designed code, no exceptions to obligations will be tolerated for doing what (one thinks) will have the best overall consequences.[14] But this does not mean that no exceptions at all will be tolerated. A limited number of exceptions should indeed be 'built into' moral obligations, thereby softening their rigidity somewhat. So as not to undermine this comfort zone, however, these exceptions must be rather clear-cut and relatively limited in scope, such as, in the case of the obligation not to kill, an exception for self-defence.

Some of these exceptions will be 'across-the-board', ones built into all, or almost all, obligations, such as an exception for consent, and an exception for urgent need. The exception for urgent need, to be discussed in Section 7 below, serves to soften the rigidity of obligations considerably. Another exception that all the moral obligations within a well-designed code will have built into them is, I suggest, an exception for cases in which (1) adhering to what they normally prescribe conflicts with adhering to what another obligation normally prescribes, and (2) according to the 'rules of priority' of the code, the other obligation is to be given priority.[15] For example, what our obligation to tell the truth normally prescribes is that we tell the truth, and what our obligation to keep our promises normally prescribes is that we keep our promises. But, to use a well-known illustration, say that we promise to hide our friend, Sam, in our basement from Bill, who is looking for him with a gun, and Bill comes knocking at our door asking if we know where Sam is. In this case, what the obligation to keep our promises normally prescribes should, I assume, be given priority over what the obligation to tell the truth normally prescribes. The importance of this across-the-board exception for conflicts is that, as a result of this exception, we need *never* violate any moral obligation within a well-designed code, even in cases in which the obligation conflicts with another obligation that has priority over it. In such cases, rather than our having to violate the obligation, we are, instead, *excused*, by means of this exception, from doing what the obligation normally prescribes.

The third feature of a well-designed code that I want to emphasise is that the lines which the moral obligations of this code draw between the permissible and impermissible will, for the most part, be clear in both theory and practice. These lines are clear *in theory* if they can be stated without significant ambiguity, and these lines are clear *in practice* if they are such that, typically, people will have enough *factual* information to know right off whether their current behaviour is in conformity with their obligations or not. Obligations such as, for example, an obligation to keep promises, an obligation to not to kill, and an obligation not to rape satisfy these conditions. Aside from a few well-known problems, there is relatively little conceptual ambiguity about what counts as 'keeping a promise', 'killing', and 'raping', and, typically, people have more than enough factual information to know right off whether or not they are keeping a promise, killing a person, or raping someone. Of course nothing in morality can be made so clear that there will never be borderline cases. Moreover, there is certainly room for debate about what exceptions to these obligations should be recognised; whether, for example, to recognise an exception to the obligation not to kill for euthanasia, for capital punishment, and so on. But the point of moral obligations is, as we have seen, to provide people with a certain 'comfort zone' within which they can pursue their own well-being with reasonable security and trust in others. To the extent that obligations are unclear, people will be unable to adhere to them and, to the extent that people are unable to adhere to them, this comfort zone will be undermined. So for obligations to meet a rather high standard of clarity is crucial. And for them to be clear is only fair as well, in that failing to meet our obligations may subject us to serious censure. Thus, in a well-designed code, what is obligatory will be clear enough so that, *in the great majority of cases*, people can be confident about whether they, or others, are adhering to their obligations.

The fourth feature of a well-designed code that I want to emphasise is that the moral obligations of this code will not be so contrary to *human nature* that the social pressure which a society's morality typically commands cannot motivate general compliance with them. Moral obligations with which people cannot be motivated to comply are obviously of little practical value.[16]

Finally, I want to emphasise that for every obligation within a well-designed code there will be a right correlated with it, a right that the obligation be performed. For example, correlated with our obligation to pay our debts will be a right that others have that our debts to them be paid, correlated with our obligation not to rape will be a right that others have that we not rape them, correlated with our obligation to keep our promises will be a right that others have that our promises to them be kept, and so on for every obligation. Rights without anyone's being obligated to fulfil them are of little value to people, and obligations without anyone's having a right to their fulfilment are too easily avoided.[17]

So far we have been investigating only one fundamental branch of moral taxonomy: moral obligations. The taxonomy of a well-designed code, however, will have a second branch that is equally fundamental: moral values. Every *good* value delineated by a code of morality comes correlated with its contrary, a *bad* value, and every *bad* value comes correlated with its contrary, a *good* value. Examples of good values, along with their contrary bad values, are 'kindness / unkindness', 'unselfishness / selfishness', 'friendliness / unfriendliness', 'compassion / callousness', 'courage / cowardliness', 'gratefulness / ungratefulness', 'wisdom / foolishness', 'graciousness / offensiveness', 'thoughtfulness / thoughtlessness', and 'generosity / greed'.[18]

To understand the status of helping others in a well-designed code, it will be useful for us to examine how, exactly, values differ from obligations. Let me just list, without extended argument, eight interrelated ways. Although this list reflects, so I submit, how moral values are to be distinguished from moral obligations in a *well-designed* code of morality, I do not think most people will find these distinctions between obligations and values to be especially controversial, for I think that, generally speaking, they are found in current morality as well.

1. Good and bad values delineate those kinds of acts that are *good* and *bad* to do (or not do), whereas obligations delineate those kinds of acts that are *wrong* to do (or not do).

2. Good and bad values admit of degrees (i.e., there are degrees of kindness and unkindness, of generosity and greed, and the like) whereas obligations generally do not admit of degrees (e.g., either you have fulfilled your obligation not to rape or you have not, just as either you are pregnant or you are not). This follows from (1) above, in that 'goodness' and 'badness' admit of degrees, whereas 'wrongness' does not; something is either wrong or it is not.[19]

3. Good values have contraries that delineate what is blameworthy (e.g., the contrary of kindness is unkindness, which is blameworthy); whereas bad values have contraries that delineate what is praiseworthy (e.g., the contrary of thoughtlessness is thoughtfulness, which is praiseworthy). Typically, not exemplifying a good value (e.g., kindness) will not be equivalent to exemplifying its contrary bad value (unkindness) and thus will not be blameworthy, but will instead be morally neutral. And, typically, not exemplifying a bad value (e.g., unkindness) will not be equivalent to exemplifying its contrary good value (kindness) and thus will not be praiseworthy, but will instead be morally neutral as well. The contraries of *obligations*, on the other hand, are acts that are *permissible*. Permissible acts may, but need not, be either blameworthy or praiseworthy. And since obligations delineate the minimum that is morally acceptable, we are normally not praiseworthy merely for adhering to an obligation, but are blameworthy for failing to adhere to it.[20]

4. Good and bad values can be used as criteria for judging either an *act* of a person, or the person *in general*. For example, if Jones makes fun of a person's deformity, we can say either that Jones' act was 'unkind', or (if Jones often does such things) we can say *of Jones* that he is, in general, an 'unkind' person. When used to judge a person, good values are often referred to as 'virtues', and bad values are referred to as 'vices'. Obligations, on the other hand, can only be used as criteria for evaluating acts.

For example, we can say that Jones' *act* of forcing sex upon Mary violated the obligation 'Do not rape', but this is not a criterion for judging Jones in general as distinct from a particular act of Jones' (although, of course, Jones is blameworthy for violating this obligation and, as a result of doing so, may be thought of as a 'bad' person in general).

5. Good and bad values do not have moral rights correlated with them (e.g., we have no *right* to be treated generously by another, or not to be treated in a way that exemplifies greed), whereas obligations do always have rights correlated with them (e.g., we do have a right that others pay their debts to us, or not rape us).

6. In a conflict between refraining from exemplifying a good value (or not exemplifying a bad value) and fulfilling an obligation, the obligation always has priority (although this priority rule is tempered by the exception for extreme need set out in Section 7).[21]

7. It is always morally permissible to determine whether to exemplify a good or bad value merely by considering the overall consequences of doing so. For example, it is permissible to determine whether, generously, to donate a large sum to the Cancer Fund (good values) by considering the overall consequences of doing so as compared with not doing so. But it is not permissible to determine whether to adhere to an obligation merely by considering the overall consequences of doing so.

8. Whether to exemplify a good or bad value is, morally speaking, discretionary; whether to fulfil an obligation never is discretionary.[22]

The sort of behaviour that, so I claim, is morally obligatory, as distinct from exemplifying good or bad values, is just the sort of behavior that is typically made *legally* obligatory as well; that is, there are moral as well as legal obligations to pay debts, keep contracts, not steal, not murder, not rape, and the like. But good and bad *values* typically are not made into legal obligations. That is to say, there are no legal obligations not to be selfish, not to be unkind, not to be callous, not to be ungrateful, not to be unfriendly, and the like. Nor are there any legal obligations to be generous, kind, grateful, thoughtful, and the like. Good and bad values are too vague to require or prohibit legally.[23] Moreover, doing so would diminish people's flexibility of behaviour too much. Consider how much it would constrict our behaviour if we were legally obligated always to be generous, kind, friendly, thoughtful, and the like. For largely the same reasons, good and bad values are not *moral* obligations either.

Moreover, to turn exemplifying (or not exemplifying) values into obligations would, unwisely, foreclose any consideration of overall consequences in determining whether to exemplify them. As we saw earlier, morality must foreclose consideration of overall consequences in deciding whether to adhere to obligations; otherwise, obligations cannot generate that 'comfort zone' necessary for pursuing our interests with reasonable security and trust in others. But it is not wise to foreclose consideration of overall consequences in deciding whether to exemplify good and bad values. Without a consideration of overall consequences, we may not even know, in a given case, which from alternative acts *constitutes* exemplifying a good or bad value. Indeed, the obligation/value distinction represents, I suggest, a useful compromise between two main opposing viewpoints throughout the history of moral philosophy – deontology and teleology. For those acts and omissions that fall within the category of obligations – not murdering, not raping, paying our debts, and the like – deontologists are correct; we must do, or refrain from doing, them regardless of the consequences. But for those kinds of acts and omissions that fall within the category of good and bad values – 'generosity', 'unkindness', 'friendliness', and the like – teleologists are correct; in determining whether to exemplify them, or even what constitutes exemplifying them, we *should* take overall consequences into account.

So, to summarise, the taxonomy of a well-designed code of morality – or, rather, that part relevant to us – will, so I submit, look like Figure 4.1.:

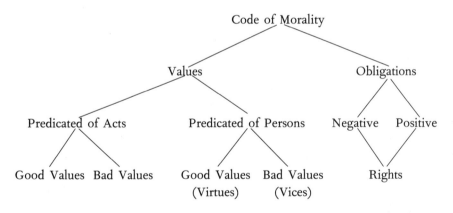

Figure 4.1 Taxonomy of a well-designed code of morality.

This brief sketch of moral taxonomy has been necessary for understanding that account of the moral status of helping others which is to follow. On the other hand, that account which is to follow is necessary for a full appreciation of this brief sketch of moral taxonomy. So, although much about this sketch is, of course, controversial, I recommend reserving final judgement until the account is complete.

SECTION 4: THE MORAL STATUS OF HELPING OTHERS

Helping others should not have the moral status of being obligatory; rather, the moral status of helping others should be that it exemplifies good values, ones such as generosity, unselfishness, and compassion. Let me try to explain why. Consider, first, a code that contains what we may refer to as a 'general' obligation to help others, one that is not qualified in any way, such as by limiting *to whom* help is obligatory, the *times* during which help is obligatory, or the *amount* of help that is obligatory. Since, during every moment of our lives, there are always innumerable people in need of help of *some* sort that we could be helping in *some* way, a moral obligation to help others as general as this would require that we do virtually nothing our entire lives other than help others. Or, to be more exact, it would require that we do nothing other than this except, perhaps, for adhering to other moral obligations that we may have. But an obligation as stringent as this is unacceptable. First of all, such an obligation will leave no room whatever just for pursuing one's own well-being. Thus a code that contains this obligation fails to exemplify the very first feature of a well-designed code. Moreover, such an obligation is surely beyond what, given human nature, people can be motivated to do. Thus such a code also fails to exemplify the fourth feature, emphasised above, of a well-designed code.

But what about there being, instead, a 'qualified' obligation to help others, one that is qualified is some way such as by being limited to 'what one feels one can do', or 'what one can do without significant personal sacrifice'? Qualifications as thoroughly vague as these simply will not do. As we have seen, the third feature of a well-designed code is that the obligations imposed by the code must be clear enough so that people are at least able to determine, in the great majority of cases, whether they and others are fulfilling these obligations or not. But who can know whether a person really has helped others to the extent that he 'feels' he can? If, on the other hand, *whatever* a person did were to count as what he 'felt' he could do, then the obligation would be meaningless. And how far must a person's help extend in order for the person's sacrifice to be 'significant'? These questions do not come even close to having adequately clear answers. Obligations stake out the morally impermissible from the permissible and, to do this job properly, obligations need to be delineated by relatively clear-cut lines. Values, on the other hand, delineate that which is such that the *more* of it or (in the case of bad values) the *less* of it, the *better*. In other words, values, but not obligations, always admit of degrees. Thus values, by admitting of degrees, cannot be, and are not, delineated by the relatively clear lines that must be drawn for obligations. Finally, a code of morality with obligations as vague as the above fails to exemplify the fifth feature of a well-designed code as well – namely, that every obligation be correlated with a right. For with obligations this vague, who exactly can be said to have the right that they be fulfilled?

There is, of course, the possibility that an obligation to help others can be qualified not in some vague way like the above, but in a way *specific* enough to make the obligation clear. The problem here is that any such specific qualification will be largely arbitrary and, through eliminating donor flexibility along with any consideration of consequences, is likely to do more harm than good. Say, for example, we were to try to qualify an obligation to help others by specifying *to whom* help must be provided. Should we, for example, qualify the obligation by making it obligatory to help the *starving* with, say, donations to OXFAM rather than helping the *sick* with, say, donations to the Cancer Fund? This, or any other such qualification, hardly seems desirable, since it will eliminate people's flexibility to decide for themselves whom to help, thereby leaving some worthy causes with perhaps more than needed, and others, perhaps, with hardly anything at all. Moreover, if we were morally *obligated* to help, say, the starving, then, given that every obligation has a right correlated with it, this would mean the starving had a *right* to our help. But recognising such a right might give rise to additional problems. It could, for example, reduce the incentive of those in poor countries to work towards self-sufficiency, for why, they might wonder, should they make whatever sacrifices might be necessary for self-sufficiency if they have a *right* to the rest of us coming to their rescue without their making these sacrifices? In deciding whether to help, potential *consequences,* such as the effect of the help on people's incentives to help themselves, should be something that morality allows us to take into account. But in making the help obligatory, rather than good values, any such consideration of consequences is ruled out from the start. Or say that, instead, the obligation to help others were qualified by limiting the *times* during which one was obligated to help others through charitable donations and the like. But then what if, at whatever times were designated as those during which one was obligated to help others, one needed one's funds instead to put oneself, or one's child, through medical school? Or what if one needed one's funds instead to start a business that not only would be of great benefit to the community, but would enable the total of one's overall lifetime donations to be far greater than if one had been forced to donate at the designated times? And, of course, the same sorts of arguments can be made against qualifying an obligation to help others by specifically limiting, in some way, the *amount* of help one is obligated to give.

In short, helping others is just not the sort of behaviour appropriate for making obligatory. It should instead represent good values. Only if, *as a general rule,* helping others represents good values rather than being be obligatory will a moral code allow people that degree of flexibility, and consideration of consequences, which is important when it comes to helping others. There should be, I grant, two exceptions to this general rule. First, helping others should obligatory if we have wrongly put them into a position of needing our help. If, for example, in teasing our nervous friend by rocking the rowboat in which we are fishing, we go too far and negligently knock him overboard, this should obligate us to do what we can to save him from drowning. Second, helping others should be obligatory to the extent that our help is a normal expectation of a 'special relationship' we have voluntarily entered into with them. For example, the doctor/patient relationship, lawyer/client relationship, parent/child relationship, and promisor/promisee relationship should create, on the part of the doctor, lawyer, parent, and promisor, an obligation to do, for the patient, client, child, or promisee, whatever necessary to fulfil the normal expectations brought about by the special relationship.[24]

But, aside from just these two exceptions, helping others is not, for the reasons we have seen, the sort of behaviour appropriate for making obligatory. And if, as a general rule, it is not the sort of behaviour appropriate for making obligatory, then it should not be made obligatory in the hypothetical, well-designed code of morality that, in our thought experiment, we are charged with designing. Moreover, if helping others should not be made obligatory in a *well-designed* code, then it should not be made obligatory in our society's *current* code of morality either. And, aside from the above two exceptions of course, I do not think that helping others is, in fact, normally viewed by most people as obligatory. If most people did view helping others as *obligatory*, then, since rights are normally correlated with obligations, we would expect them also to view those in need of the help as having a *right* to it. That obligations, but not values, are correlated with rights is, it will be recalled, one of the eight ways listed above in which values differ from obligations (difference no. 5). Yet virtually no one views the starving children that, in Envelope, will be helped by a $100 donation as having a *right* to this donation, and even in those cases, such as Sedan, in which most people view failure to help as blameworthy, few will view the recipient of the help as having a *right* to it.[25] Indeed, that most people view helping others to be a matter of values rather than obligation can be further substantiated in terms of other differences between values and obligations. That most people view helping others to be a matter of values is, for example, further substantiated by the fact that most people view helping others as praiseworthy, whereas if it were a matter of obligation instead, doing so would not be praiseworthy, but merely what was expected (difference no. 3). And it is substantiated still further by the fact that most people view helping others as admitting of degrees (difference no. 2); by the fact that most people think that, except for certain cases of extreme need (see Section 7 below), anything which clearly *is* an obligation, such as paying one's debts, always has *priority* over helping others (difference no. 6); and by the fact that, for any given case, most people consider it appropriate to determine whether or not to help others by taking into account the *overall consequences* of doing so in that particular case (difference no. 7). Moreover, most people view helping others to be, in most cases at least, discretionary (difference no. 8).[26]

Consider, finally, how radically different most people's intuitive reaction to Envelope is from their intuitive reaction to the following hypothetical case, which we may call Poisoned Cake. In Poisoned Cake, a person *kills* thirty starving people, just for the fun of it, by sending them a large cake laced with cyanide. Most people, of course, view this as being about as morally heinous as anything can be. Yet, just as Unger reports, most people view failing to save thirty lives in Envelope by donating $100 to be not blameworthy, but morally neutral instead. The radical difference in most people's intuitive reactions to Envelope and Poisoned Cake cannot be explained by a difference in consequences since, in both cases, the consequences are that thirty people die who otherwise may well have lived. It can be explained, so I submit, only if most people view failing to save thirty lives in Envelope not as a violation of an *obligation*, as is killing thirty people in Poisoned Cake, but as a *failure to exemplify good values*. Typically, a failure to exemplify good values is not equivalent to exemplifying bad values, but is morally neutral (difference no. 3). So if most people view failing to save the lives in Envelope as failing to exemplify good values, and if, typically, failing to exemplify good values is morally neutral, then this explains why most people – contrary to how they view killing in Poisoned Cake – view failing to save lives in Envelope to be morally neutral and, thus, not blameworthy.

But why, it might now be asked, should failing to exemplify good values be, typically, morally neutral rather than blameworthy? And why, typically, should it also be morally neutral *not* to exemplify *bad* values, rather than being praiseworthy? Let me try to explain why. If, instead, failing to exemplify good values was always blameworthy, then, for any given good value (for example, thoughtfulness, friendliness, and kindness), every moment we were not exemplifying it we would be blameworthy. And if not exemplifying bad values was always praiseworthy, then, for any given bad value (for example, thoughtlessness, unfriendliness, and unkindness), every moment we were not exemplifying it we would be praiseworthy. Since, at any given moment in our lives, there would then be innumerable good and bad values we were not exemplifying, it would follow that everything we did, or omitted doing, at every moment of our lives would be both praiseworthy and blameworthy in innumerable different ways at once. Merely by sitting by myself watching TV, for example, I would be praiseworthy for not, at that moment, exemplifying greed, unfriendliness, cowardliness, ingratitude, and so on for most bad values, while, at the same time, I would be blameworthy for not, at that moment, exemplifying generosity, friendliness, courage, gratitude, and so on for most good values. But surely this would be to make a mockery of praise and blame. With such an abundance of praiseworthiness and blameworthiness for doing so little, none of it would mean very much to anyone anymore. So it makes perfectly good sense for not exemplifying good values to be morally neutral, typically, rather than blameworthy, and for not exemplifying bad values to be morally neutral, typically, rather than praiseworthy. Accordingly, the fact that, in Envelope, most people view failing to donate $100 – thereby failing to exemplify good values – not as blameworthy, but as morally neutral, should not be surprising.

In sum: that helping others is, and should be, a matter of good values, not an obligation, explains a lot, including the difference in our intuitive reactions to Envelope and Poisoned Cake. But one glaring matter remains unexplained – namely, the difference in our intuitive reactions to Envelope and Sedan. Although, as we might expect, we do not view failing to help as blameworthy in Envelope, we do indeed view failing to help as blameworthy in Sedan. Why should this be so, especially since the consequences of failing to help in Envelope (thirty children dying) are so much worse than the consequences of failing to help in Sedan (one person losing a leg)? To make sense of this difference in our intuitive reactions, we must, in Section 5, work out our hypothetical, well-designed code a little more fully.

SECTION 5: THE NEED / SACRIFICE STANDARD

Notice that, curiously enough, most people view driving the injured person to the hospital in Sedan not as morally neutral, but as exemplifying good values and thus praiseworthy. So for most people at least, although providing help exemplifies *good* values in both Envelope and Sedan, failing to provide help exemplifies *bad* values *only* in Sedan. This is, I think, exactly as it should be. Praise for doing something, as opposed to blame for failing to do it, does not impose any significant moral constraints upon our freedom to do as we choose. Thus there is nothing to lose, and something to gain, for a code of morality to encourage, by counting them praiseworthy, *all* acts of helping others that are not already obligatory. Only in certain cases, however, does failing to help others count as *blameworthy*, in most cases, such as in Envelope, it counts as morally neutral. But then which cases should be which, and why? As before, it will be helpful, I think, to approach this as a question about how the cases will be sorted out in a well-designed code. Thus let us phrase the question before us as follows. How, in a well-designed code, will cases in which failing to help others counts as morally neutral be distinguished from cases in which it instead counts as bad values and is blameworthy?

Perhaps the distinction will be drawn somewhat as follows. Let N equal the extent of the *need* for the agent's help, 'need' in a sense broad enough for any *increase* in well-being, or the *prevention* of any *decrease*, to count as needed. And let S equal the extent of the *sacrifice* the agent must make if he is to help satisfy the need. Perhaps, in a well-designed code, failing to help others will count as bad values, and be blameworthy, only if N relative to S is extremely great. Let us refer to drawing the distinction in this way as drawing it in terms of the 'need/sacrifice' standard. In the most extreme cases of all, such as where a child can be saved from drowning merely by kicking her out of a puddle, or where a person can be prevented from walking off a cliff on a foggy night merely by yelling a warning, need relative to sacrifice is so great that failing to help will, according to this standard, be not just selfish and callous, but absolutely despicable. In these 'limiting' cases, failing to help, although not murder, nevertheless will be about as blameworthy as murder.[27] On the other hand, where need relative to sacrifice is not extremely great, such as where the sacrifice takes the form of, say, giving up one's own life by running in front of a truck to save the lives of two people, failure to do so, according to this standard, will not be blameworthy, although doing so will, of course, be praiseworthy, indeed saintly.

The rationale for requiring that need relative to sacrifice be *extremely* great before failing to help others counts as bad values is related to need for a well-designed code to leave people with ample freedom to pursue their own well-being. At every moment of our lives, there are people somewhere whom we could be helping in some way. So if we were subject to being blamed for all, or almost all, failures of ours to help others, this would leave us with little or no freedom from the constraints of blameworthiness to pursue our own well-being, thereby greatly restricting our personal autonomy. This would be true even though here the blame would be not for violating an obligation, but for exemplifying bad values. But if, as called for by the need/sacrifice standard, blameworthiness for failing to help others is reserved only for those cases in which need relative to sacrifice is extremely great, so great that we are likely to be confronted with such cases only occasionally, then relatively little personal freedom and autonomy will be lost. So the key to preserving personal freedom and autonomy is that the 'threshold for blameworthiness' be made high enough so that we are likely to be confronted only occasionally with cases in which failing to help others counts as blameworthy.

Although I think the need/sacrifice standard as formulated so far succeeds in capturing most people's moral intuitions about most kinds of cases, it fails to do so in one kind of case: namely, a case such as Superbowl. In Superbowl, an insane person bursts into television headquarters an hour before kickoff and, holding the technicians at gunpoint, says that either you must agree to have your leg amputated immediately or else he will destroy the equipment necessary for televising the Superbowl. As great a sacrifice as your losing your leg will be, the aggregate 'need' satisfied by this sacrifice – many millions of people's enjoyment of the Superbowl – may well be so enormous that need relative to sacrifice in this case is at least as great as in Sedan. But if it is at least as great as in Sedan, then failing to sacrifice your leg in this case is, according to the need/ sacrifice standard as formulated so far, at least as blameworthy as failing to help in Sedan. According to most people's moral intuitions, however, failing to sacrifice your leg in this case should not count as blameworthy at all. Perhaps this is because certain sacrifices, such as severe bodily mutilation, are simply so immense that failing to make them should not count as bad values no matter how great the need. Do not misunderstand me; sacrifices this immense are, to be sure, immensely praiseworthy, often saintly. I am suggesting only that there may be good reasons for a code of morality not to *condemn* those *failing* to make them. These reasons include ones similar to those already set out in justification of the need/sacrifice standard as formulated so far. But the most important reason may be this. For a code of morality not to hold failure to make such immense sacrifices to be blameworthy makes it absolutely clear (as any code should) that, in cases such as Transplant, in which five vital organs are needed from Jones in order to save the lives of five people in desperate need of a transplant, Jones is not exemplifying bad values by refusing to donate his organs. And, as a bonus, this also makes it clear that, in Superbowl, you are not exemplifying bad values by refusing to sacrifice your leg. A code of morality must, after all, provide people with a certain comfort zone against severe harm not only from other people, but from the 'demands' of morality itself, a comfort zone that may be invaded only by obligations arising from special relationships voluntarily undertaken. If then, as I suspect, a well-designed code of morality will not hold failure to make such immense sacrifices to be blameworthy, then the need/sacrifice standard as formulated so far is incomplete. A more complete formulation of this standard will be something like the following.

> A person's failure to help others will count as bad values, and thus be blameworthy, only if (1) the need for the person's help relative to how much the person will have to sacrifice is extremely great, and (2) the sacrifice required is not so immense as to involve death or severe bodily harm.

The need/sacrifice standard is formulated as a necessary, but not sufficient, condition for blameworthiness since other factors are relevant for determining whether failure to help is blameworthy, factors such as the extent to which those in need of the help brought on their need themselves by wrongful behaviour. And remember that the standard is meant to be applicable only to those in need of help whom the agent is not *obligated* to help – that is, obligated as a result of either having wrongfully put them in need of help or having voluntarily undertaken a special relationship, such as that between parent and child or doctor and patient. Special-relationship obligations may, of course, require that we help others even when need relative to sacrifice is not extremely great and, in the case of soldiers, rescue workers, bodyguards, and the like, even when the sacrifice is indeed immense.

SECTION 6: A SOLUTION TO UNGER'S PUZZLE

The solution to Unger's puzzle – that is, the reason why we view failing to help as blameworthy in Sedan but not in Envelope – is, I shall now argue, that need relative to sacrifice is actually greater in Sedan than in Envelope, or at least may reasonably appear to be so. But to see why, we must first examine exactly what must be taken into account in determining the *extent* to which a given agent's help is needed. The most important thing to realise is that the extent to which a given agent's help is needed is not merely a function of the extent to which overall well-being will be increased (or not decreased) if the agent's help leads to a satisfaction of the need. Two other factors, both related to probability, must be part of the equation as well.

The first additional factor that must be taken into account in determining how much a given agent's help is needed is how probable it is that the need will be successfully satisfied if the agent does help. The greater the probability of success if the agent does help, the greater the need for the agent's help. If, for example, John, a closer friend of Mary's than Sam, is *more likely* than Sam to be successful in persuading Mary to stop smoking heavily, then it makes sense to say that Mary 'needs' John's advice on smoking more than she needs Sam's. And there are two dimensions to this probability factor. The first is how probable it is that the agent's *own* part in satisfying the need will be successful. The second is how probable it is that the *other* necessary parts of the overall combination of acts required for satisfying the need will be successful. For example, in Envelope the agent's donation is only one part of what is necessary for the need to be satisfied; other necessary parts include that of the officials at UNICEF and of the country where these needy children live turning the agent's donation into life-saving food or whatever else may be necessary. Now the probability of being successful in donating money if one attempts to do so may be very close to 100 per cent. To be sure, the donation can be lost or stolen in the mail before reaching its destination, but that is improbable. But if, in Envelope, the officials charged with turning the agent's donation into food are so corrupt that the donation is much more likely to end up in their pockets instead, then the probability of the other necessary parts being successful will be low. The *overall* probability of an agent's help being successful is some combination of (1) the probability of the agent's *own* part in the necessary combination of acts being successful and (2) the probability of the *other* necessary parts being successful.

The second additional factor that must be taken into account in determining how much a given agent's help is needed is how probable it is that the need will be successfully satisfied if the agent does *not* help. The greater the probability of success if the agent does not help, the *less* the agent's help is needed. And the probability of success if the agent does not help is, in turn, largely a function of two additional, not unrelated, factors: urgency and other potential benefactors. Say, for example, that, while you are between two swimming pools, each of them a hundred yards away, you hear a drowning stranger cry for help from each pool. The first pool has no one around it, while the second pool has hundreds of people around it. With hundreds of people around the second pool, many potential benefactors other than you can save the person drowning in that pool, while only you can save the person drowning in the first pool. It, therefore, makes sense to say that the person in the first pool needs your help more.[28]

All of this can be put more precisely as follows. Let N be the need for the agent's help; let W be the extent to which well-being will increase (or not decrease) if the need for help is successfully satisfied; let p^a be the probability of the need being successfully satisfied if the agent helps; and let p^o be the probability of the need being successfully satisfied if the agent does not help. The extent to which an agent's help is needed is:

$$N = W \times (p^a - p^o)$$

In other words, the need for an agent's help equals the increase in overall well-being if the need is successfully satisfied times the probability of success if the agent helps minus the probability of success if the agent does not help.

Consider, for example, the following case. Say that the agent and Jones are the only two people by a pool in which Smith is drowning. Since helping Smith by jumping into the pool and attempting to save him is a one-person job, either the agent *or* Jones may attempt to save Smith, but not both the agent *and* Jones. We cannot, of course, very well quantify the degree to which well-being will be increased (or not decreased) if a need for help, such as Smith's, is satisfied. This is especially true if the increase in well-being is that resulting from a person's life being saved, since we are far from knowing how to place a numerical value on a person's life. But, merely for the sake of illustration, assume that we can do this, and that if Smith's need to be helped is successfully satisfied (that is, if his life is saved) then overall well-being (his and his family's) will increase (or not decrease) by 1,000,000 units. We can then determine the need for the agent's help using the above formula as follows. First assume that, since the agent is not a very good swimmer, if the agent attempts to help Smith then, although the agent will be in no danger himself, he has only a fifty-fifty chance of succeeding, but if he does not attempt to help Smith, then Smith will drown for certain since Jones, who hates Smith, will not, under any circumstances, attempt to help Smith. Given this scenario, the need for the agent's help is equivalent to 500,000 units of expected well-being (or 'expected utility'), calculated as follows: 1,000,000 x (.50 - 0) = 500,000. Second, assume once again that, if the agent attempts to help Smith, he has only a fifty-fifty chance of succeeding, but if the agent does not attempt to help Smith, then Jones will attempt to do so, and Jones, who also is not a very good swimmer, also has only a fifty-fifty chance of succeeding. In other words, if the agent does not help, it is certain that someone else will, and with exactly the same probability of succeeding. Given this scenario, there is no need at all for the agent's help, calculated as follows: 1,000,000 x (.50 - .50) = 0. Third, assume now that the agent is an extremely good swimmer, and that if he attempts to help Smith, he has a 100 per cent chance of succeeding, but if he does not attempt to help Smith, then Jones will attempt to do so, but Jones has only a fifty-fifty chance of succeeding. Given this scenario, the need for the agent's help is 500,000 units of expected well-being, calculated as follows: 1,000,000 x (1 - .50) = 500,000. Finally, assume, once again, that the agent is not a very good swimmer and has only a fifty-fifty chance of saving Smith if he attempts to help, but that Jones is an extremely good swimmer with a 100 per cent chance of saving Smith if he attempts to help, and assume, furthermore, that Jones will attempt to help if and only if the agent does not. Given this scenario, not only does Smith not need the agent's help, but Smith needs the agent *not* to help – that is, the agent's help has *negative* expected well-being, calculated as follows: 1,000,000 x (.50 - 1) = -500,000.

In reality, of course, we cannot plug into the above formula the figures that are necessary for grinding out answers as precise as the ones above. But we can normally arrive at approximations that will serve well enough for most practical purposes. The basic idea, once again, is that the extent of the need for an agent's help is not just a function of (1) the extent to which overall well-being will increase (or not decrease) if the need is satisfied, but is also a function of (2) the probability of the need being satisfied if the agent helps, and (3) the probability of its being satisfied if the agent does not help. With this in mind, we can begin to see why it is not unreasonable to view the failure to help in Sedan as exemplifying bad values and blameworthy, but not in Envelope. To be sure, the extent to which overall well-being will increase if help succeeds is much less in Sedan than in Envelope – if help succeeds in Sedan a man's *leg* will be saved, while if help succeeds in Envelope children's *lives* will be saved. The difference between Sedan and Envelope in the extent to which well-being will increase may not be quite as great as it appears, however. If commentators such as Garrett Hardin are correct, saving the lives of people in poverty-stricken countries now will only cause the population in these countries to increase so that, in the next generation, there will be many more such people suffering and in need of help.[29] So, if Hardin is correct, donations will, in the long run, actually decrease overall well-being. Unger, on the other hand, claims that keeping children alive in poor countries is much more likely to *stabilise* population than cause it to increase since, as child mortality goes down, people no longer need to have as many children as before just in order for a few to survive.[30] I think Unger is correct about this. Thus I will grant that, for determining in which case, as between Sedan and Envelope, need is greater, factor (1) above clearly favours Envelope. But each of the other two factors clearly favour Sedan. Let me explain.

First, let us compare Sedan and Envelope with respect to how probable it is that the need will be satisfied if the agent does help. In Sedan, the agent will *personally* escort the injured man to the hospital. Thus he can be virtually sure that his help will indeed successfully place the injured man in the hands of physicians, and can reasonably assume that the physicians, for their part, will then succeed in saving his leg. Since there is very little that is likely to go wrong, the probability of the agent's help successfully leading to the satisfaction of the need is close to 100 per cent. Envelope, on the other hand, is a different story. The chances are that the donation itself will be successfully completed. But thereafter the probabilities go down. First of all, even if the donation saves the children's lives for the moment, conditions in these countries are such that, at the next moment, these lives may still be lost. And, of course, everyone has heard the stories about corruption within charitable organisations, and how people's donations end up being used more to make the managers of these organisations rich than to make the needy better off. Moreover, everyone has also heard the stories about how corrupt governmental officials in poor countries channel donations more into their own pockets than into the necessary aid. And so on. It is no wonder that people will feel far less confident about the probability of charitable donations leading to success than about the probability of personally escorting an injured man to a hospital leading to success.

To this Unger might reply that, according to Envelope, the agent's contribution will be successful *by hypothesis*. This reply, however, would not be entirely satisfactory. No matter how much Unger may stipulate to the contrary, donations to charitable organisations, by their very nature, cannot be as certain of leading to success as is driving an injured man to a hospital. Even granting that reservations based on corruption are not well founded with respect to reputable organisations such as UNICEF and OXFAM (and I think this should be granted), with charitable donations there still remain, in reality, more ways than with driving an injured person to a hospital in which the help may fail to lead to success. And people's intuitive reactions to Envelope will, in spite of any stipulation of Unger's to the contrary, tend to be based upon this reality.

Next, let us compare Sedan and Envelope with respect to how probable it is that the need will be satisfied if the agent does not help. As I suggested above, this probability is, in part, normally a function of how *urgent* the need for help is. Obviously the more urgent the need, the less probable it is that, if the agent does not help, help will come from some other source. In Sedan, a seriously injured man is suffering by the side of the road in great pain and, in addition, without help within 24 hours will lose his leg, Clearly his need for help is urgent, urgent enough, in fact, for this to count as an 'emergency'. In Envelope, on the other hand, it is not at all clear how urgent the need for the agent's help is. But it is fair to say that, generally speaking, the children in need of aid, in Envelope, are not going to die within the next 24 hours, the next month, or perhaps, in many cases, not even within the next 24 months. Indeed, since, as Unger points out, a donation today will take a month to process before it will help any children, we know that, in Envelope, any children capable of being helped by our donation today will not die for *at least* a month. So perhaps it is fair to say that, in Envelope, the agent is not, as in Sedan, faced with need that is urgent enough to qualify the situation as an 'emergency'.

Unger, on the other hand, argues that there is plenty of urgency in Envelope as well as in Sedan.[31] Simply for the sake of argument, let us grant Unger this point since, for determining the probability of success if the agent does not help in this case, there is, I think, a much more important factor than urgency – namely, the extent to which other potential benefactors exist. Let us now compare Sedan and Envelope with respect to this factor. Since, in Sedan, the injured man is at a lonely spot where it is highly unlikely that anyone else will drive by in time to save his leg, it is thus highly likely that the agent in Sedan is the *only* potential benefactor. In Envelope, on the other hand, there are literally many *millions* of potential benefactors, in the sense that there are literally millions of people who are perfectly able to donate money to UNICEF, and are thus in approximately as good a position to help the children as the agent. To this Unger will reply that, although millions of people have the *capacity* to donate money, far fewer have the *willingness* to do so, and we must calculate how scarce the number of potential benefactors are by taking into account both capacity and willingness.[32] I agree. Yet even taking into account the number of potential benefactors throughout the world with both capacity and willingness, the number will still be quite large. But then, Unger might point out, it would seem that we must take into account still another factor: namely, the number of potential benefactors relative to the number of people who need the help. I agree that this factor is relevant as well. In Envelope, even though there may be millions of people able and willing to donate money to UNICEF, we know that the number of children in need of help in the form of a monetary donation will far exceed the number that will be given this help. Nevertheless, other potential benefactors are still much more prevalent in Envelope than in Sedan. Let me try to explain why.

Consider first a rather unrealistic, yet instructive, hypothetical variation of Sedan, which we may refer to as 'City Sedan.' In City Sedan, not just one person with an injured leg needs a ride to a hospital. Rather, *innumerable* people with injured legs need a ride to the hospital. Imagine, if you can, that, in cities throughout the world, they are found every few yards beside every road. Although these people are able to crawl to the hospital themselves in time to save their life, doing so does not enable them to get there in time to prevent their injured leg from being amputated. But, fortunately, a great many passing motorists stop from time to time to give one of them a leg-saving ride to the hospital, even though doing so is always at great expense and inconvenience since, for one thing, it means getting the interiors of their cars all bloody. In fact, were it not for this help from passing motorists, twice as many of these injured people would end up losing their legs. Nevertheless, just as soon as one of these injured people gets a ride to the hospital, another one takes his place, so that, in spite of help from passing motorists, which reduces the overall number who end up losing a leg by 50 per cent, there is still no full solution to the problem in sight. Finally, you live in one of these cities and are among the many passing motorists who, from time to time, stop to provide a leg-saving ride to the hospital – doing so about as often as well-off people in our society donate money to life-saving charities – and you intend to continue doing so, from time to time, in the future. But today you happen to drive to work and back without giving any of them a ride. I suspect that the intuitive reaction that most of us will have to this case is that, by not giving any of them a ride today, you did not exemplify bad values any more than you did in failing to contribute today in Envelope. In both cases help would be praiseworthy, rather than failing to help being blameworthy.

Incidentally, it must always be kept in mind, of course, that in viewing a failure to give a ride, or donate money to UNICEF, to be not blameworthy, what people are holding to be not blameworthy is failing to do so *today*. Almost everyone, I suppose, will hold it to be blameworthy for a well-off person *never* to provide any such help. But in talking about its being blameworthy never to help, notice that we are no longer talking about the evaluation of a person's *act*, but have switched to talking about the evaluation of the person *in general*, which is a different dimension of evaluation altogether. It is important that these different dimensions of evaluation not be confused with one another.

Compare now City Sedan with the original Sedan case. Why do we tend to consider refusal to help in the original Sedan case to be blameworthy, but not in City Sedan? The answer, I think, is that, in the original Sedan case, the *need* for the agent's help is significantly greater than in City Sedan. With respect to the increase in well-being if help is successful and the probability of success if the agent does help, both cases are identical. But with respect to the third factor that must be taken into account in determining the extent of need – namely, the probability of success if the agent does not help – the two cases are far from equal. We hypothesised that 50 per cent of the injured people beside city roads are indeed given rides to the hospital in time to save their leg. So for any one of these injured people, if the agent does not help her, the chances that she will be helped by another benefactor are 50 per cent. In the original Sedan case, on the other hand, the agent comes across the injured person on a lonely country road where it is highly unlikely that anyone else will drive by in time to help. So if the agent does not help this injured person, the probability of his urgent need for help being successfully satisfied is virtually zero. And, other things being equal, the less the probability of success if the agent does not help, the greater the need for the agent's help. Finally, other things being equal, the greater the need for the agent's help, the greater the need *relative* to sacrifice. Since, as between City Sedan and (original) Sedan, things are indeed equal other than the significant difference between them in the probability of success if the agent does not help, it is this probability factor, so I claim, that accounts for why need relative to sacrifice is great enough in the original Sedan case to make failure to help blameworthy, but not in City Sedan. Moreover, it is precisely this that, perhaps more than any other factor, accounts for why we take failure to help in (original) Sedan to be blameworthy, but not in Envelope. In Sedan, if the agent does not help the injured person, his chances of being helped in time by another benefactor are close to zero. In Envelope, on the other hand, even if as few as one child in two can be expected to receive the necessary help, nevertheless each child's chances of receiving this help from a benefactor other than the agent will then be 50 per cent. And, for all that most people know, the chances will be significantly greater than 50 per cent. In other words, in Envelope other potential benefactors are not extremely scarce.

So let us now take stock. The question we have been addressing is: what, in a well-designed code, will be the difference between that help which we are not blameworthy for failing to provide and that which we are blameworthy for failing to provide? Although there will not be any clear line between the two, I suggested that failure to help passes from merely being not praiseworthy into being blameworthy as need relative to sacrifice increases. Moreover, I suggested that the extent of need for help from a given agent should be viewed as a function of three factors: (1) the increase in well-being if the need for help is successfully satisfied; (2) the probability of success if the agent helps; and (3) the probability of success if the agent does not help. For determining which, as between Envelope and Sedan, presents the greater need, we have seen that factor (1) favours Envelope, but factors (2) and (3) favour Sedan. Now whether this is sufficient for us to conclude that need is greater in Sedan is hardly a matter capable of being calculated precisely. *Values are not, and need not be, as sharply defined as obligations.* But I will say this much. To conclude, as I suspect most people do, that, because of factors (2) and (3), need is indeed significantly greater in Sedan is not unreasonable. Perhaps a fuller understanding of certain facts would change many people's minds. I do not know. But given the facts as I think most people understand them to be, it is not, so I claim, unreasonable to view need as significantly greater in Sedan than in Envelope, greater enough, in fact, for need relative to sacrifice to be classified as 'extremely great' in Sedan, but not in Envelope. In other words, although both Sedan and Envelope *may* meet the need/sacrifice standard for blameworthiness, only in Sedan is it *clear* that this standard is met. Accordingly, it is not unreasonable to conclude that not helping is blameworthy in Sedan, but not in Envelope.

I have argued that, in terms of the need/sacrifice standard, failure to donate the money to UNICEF may reasonably be viewed as morally neutral, while failing to give the injured man a ride to the hospital is blameworthy. Unger might object to all of this by claiming the 'bar' that separates the morally neutral from the blameworthy should be put higher than the need/sacrifice standard puts it, high enough so that failing to help clearly counts as blameworthy in both cases. In fact Unger's mentor,

Peter Singer, argues as if he wants to put the bar so high that your failure to help those in need is blameworthy just as long as what you will have to sacrifice is even just a *little* less than what will be gained from your help. As Singer puts it, 'if we can prevent something bad without sacrificing anything of comparable significance, we ought to do it'.[33] Thus, according to this standard, your failing to help those in need is blameworthy unless by helping you will actually be sacrificing *as much or more* than they gain. Such a high standard does indeed demand that, as Unger puts it, you 'send to the likes of UNICEF and OXFAM, about as promptly as possible, nearly all your worldly wealth'.[34] If failing to adhere to this extremely high standard for helping others were not to count as blameworthy by way of violating an *obligation* then, Unger and Singer would no doubt say, it should at least count as blameworthy by way of exemplifying *bad values*.

Perhaps, in a well-designed code, the bar separating the neutral from the blameworthy should be put at least somewhat higher than our current code of morality puts it. But I think it is a mistake to put it nearly as high as people such as Unger and Singer seem to want to put it. Helping others through charitable work and donations is clearly one of the most worthwhile uses to which people can put their time and money. But there are, after all, many other very worthwhile uses to which people can put their time and money as well – going to medical school, starting a business, and the like. In fact, many of the innovations, both technological and cultural, that make life most worthwhile for both rich *and* poor have come about, and will continue to come about, only in response to pressures generated by personal consumption far above bare necessities. Thus, in the overall scheme of things, even a certain amount of personal consumption above bare necessities is socially important. For morality to compromise too severely people's freedom to put time and money towards these other worthwhile or, in the overall scheme of things, socially important uses would be a grave mistake.

And we must remember that there will probably be no permanent solution to the problem of need and poverty until there is more wealth *overall* throughout the world. But more wealth does not just come about magically from nowhere. And, as beneficial as well-conceived charitable and governmental welfare programmes may be, more wealth does not come about mainly by giving money away either. Rather, more wealth is created from existing wealth, in poor as well as rich countries, mainly, and most effectively, by increasing capital accumulation through private savings and investment. But increasing capital accumulation through private savings and investment requires that people be given far more latitude in how they use their wealth than they are given by a standard for helping others as inflexible as the one Unger and Singer seem to advocate, a standard so inflexible that it even leaves people subject to being blamed if, rather than giving 'nearly all' of their wealth away, they use it to create more wealth overall. A standard as inflexible as this will end up doing more harm than good. Indeed, by thus discouraging savings and investment and other economic initiatives, such an extreme standard, if taken seriously, will tend to prevent overall wealth from even being maintained at its current level, much less increased. And a world with less wealth overall is also a world with less wealth available for helping others. Thus, ironically enough, such an inflexible standard will, so I submit, end up hurting even the very people it is designed to help – the needy.

SECTION 7: THE EXCEPTION FOR URGENT NEED

But there is still another good reason not to 'raise the bar' as high as Unger and Singer advocate. To explain what this reason is, however, I must first try to fill in one final part of our hypothetical, well-designed code – namely, an exception for urgent need that is to be built into all moral obligations.

First, let us see why such an exception is needed. Unger, in his book, presents us with many other moral puzzles besides that of how to reconcile the case of Envelope with Sedan. One of the most interesting is how to reconcile the case of 'Yacht' with that of 'Account'.[35] A consideration of these two cases shows why a well-designed code needs an exception for urgent need. In Yacht, you are asked to envisage yourself employed by a billionaire to take care of his waterfront estate. Through binoculars you see a woman who is floundering far out in the water and will soon drown. You can save her only if you take the billionaire's yacht, without his permission, and rush out to get her. In doing so, however, you will be forced, by weather conditions, to return by way of a narrow channel that will result in over a million dollars of uninsured damage to his yacht. Nevertheless you take his yacht and manage to save the woman just before she drowns. Unger points out that most people consider this to be morally good behaviour, even though it costs the billionaire over a million dollars. In the second case, Account, you are to envisage yourself as, instead, the billionaire's accountant. As his accountant, you are in a position to embezzle a million dollars from him without anyone ever knowing, and donate it to a life-saving charity. You do so, thereby saving the lives of 10,000 starving people. But, Unger reports, most consider this to be wrong. The puzzle raised by this pair of cases is this. Why do we consider it morally permissible to make the billionaire at least one million dollars poorer, without his permission, to save just *one* person in Yacht, while, in Account, we consider making him one million dollars poorer to save *10,000* people to be morally wrong?

As before, Unger resolves this puzzle by reference to alleged 'tricks' that our minds play upon us that, in cases like Account, prevent us from getting into touch with our alleged, true moral commitment to helping those in need. And, as before, he apparently interprets our 'true commitment' to helping others as that of doing so whenever we can prevent more harm from occurring than we sacrifice by helping.

So, he concludes, not only is it morally good to take the yacht without permission in Yacht, but it is also morally good to embezzle the money in Account.

This conclusion is, of course, outrageous. If, merely to prevent greater harms, not doing what obligations normally prescribe really were, as Unger claims, always permissible, then we might as well remove obligations altogether from our morality, for they would no longer be meaningful enough to provide the security, and trust in others, that they are supposed to provide. No one would place any importance upon a person's obligation to pay his or her debts, to keep his or her promises, to not steal, to not kill, and the rest, if it were permissible to do these things just as long as doing them prevented greater harm; rationalising virtually *anything* in terms of its preventing greater harm would then be all too easy. A better way to resolve the puzzle raised by Yacht and Account is to soften the rigidity of obligations by building into them an exception for certain kinds of urgent need, such as that in the case of Yacht.

The problem, however, is how to formulate this exception judiciously, so that it does not allow violations of what obligations normally prescribe too liberally. In other words, we need to formulate the exception so that it allows us to take boats to save drowning girls, as in cases such as Yacht, but does not allow us to embezzle money to save starving people, as in cases such as Account. And we need to formulate this exception so that it does not allow us to do such things as kill a healthy person against his will to save five people who are in desperate need of having the healthy person's organs transplanted into them, as in the case of Transplant. It is, to be sure, important for a code of morality to soften, somewhat, the rigidity of moral obligations by building into them an exception for urgent need. But in formulating this exception for that hypothetical code that we are, as a thought experiment, designing, we must keep in mind the very point of there being moral obligations in the first place, which is to provide people with a certain 'comfort zone' within which they can pursue their own well-being with reasonable security and trust in others. Moral obligations would provide us relatively little 'comfort' if they did not protect us from, at any moment, having our money embezzled, being stripped of our vital organs, and the like.

With this in mind, I propose that the exception for urgent need be formulated as follows. To prevent harm or bring about benefit, an agent may do what an obligation normally prohibits (or fail to do what it normally requires) if

1. doing what the obligation normally prohibits (or failing to do what it normally requires) is very likely the only way to prevent the harm or bring about the benefit;

2. either (a) the agent has no way of determining, without losing the opportunity to prevent the harm or bring about the benefit, whether

the person to whom this obligation is owed is willing to relinquish the right to its performance, or (b) the harm to be prevented is severe bodily harm or death; and

3. the person to whom the obligation is owed would, by refusing to relinquish the right to its performance, be exemplifying bad values.

This exception allows us to act contrary to what an obligation normally requires in two, and only two, kinds of cases. The first kind of case is that in which it cannot be determined whether the person to whom the obligation is owed is willing to relinquish the right to its performance. The second kind of case is that in which acting contrary to what the obligation normally prescribes is necessary for preventing severe bodily harm or death. But the key to this exception – that which keeps it from allowing us to do *too much* that is contrary to what obligations normally prescribe – is that this exception does not apply unless the person to whom the obligation is owed would, by refusing to relinquish the right to its performance, be *exemplifying bad values*.

To illustrate how this exception works, take the case of 'Flight'. Say that your friend, Sue, has to catch an important flight to Europe, but, at the last minute, her ride to the airport unexpectedly falls through, and the only way she can now possibly get to the airport in time is for you to drop everything and give her a ride. But say, also, that you had promised to play tennis during this time with John, another friend, and there is simply no time to get John's consent to postponing the match. Thus you can drive Sue to the airport only by failing to keep your promise to John. But, surely, for John to refuse, in these circumstances, to relinquish his right to your keeping this promise would exemplify bad values. So your driving Sue to the airport falls squarely within this exception and, therefore, in doing so you are excused from your obligation to keep your promise to John. Similarly, for the billionaire, in Yacht, not to relinquish his right to your not taking his boat, so that you could save the drowning girl, would exemplify bad values. So taking his boat to save her also falls within this exception. And in this case, incidentally, clauses (a) and (b) of condition (2) are *both* met. On the other hand, taking the billionaire's money to save the poor, as in Account, and taking a person's vital organs to save five others, as in Transplant, do not fall within the scope of this exception since, in neither case, is condition (3) met. As the cases of Flight, Yacht, Account, and Transplant suggest, this exception probably succeeds in capturing most people's moral intuitions about which cases of urgent need justify doing what obligations normally prohibit, and which cases do not.

But what is more important than its capturing most people's moral intuitions is that this exception will not undermine the very point of there being moral obligations in the first place, which, once again, is to provide a certain 'comfort zone' within which people can pursue their own well-being with reasonable security and trust in others. Most of us normally do not want to exemplify bad values and, given a free choice, normally will choose not to do so, especially if our exemplifying bad values will result in severe bodily harm to someone, or death. And since the exception for urgent need only kicks in for those kinds of cases specified by condition (2), which include cases in which severe bodily harm or death would indeed be the result of exemplifying bad values, this exception will not, for most of us, result in our suffering any harm that we would not have freely chosen to suffer anyway, had we been in a position to make a choice. Thus, with this exception, the comfort zone we derive from obligations owed to us remains intact.

To be more exact, this comfort zone remains intact provided that the bar separating failure to help that merely fails to exemplify good values from that which exemplifies bad values is not put as high as Unger and Singer apparently think it should be put. As we have seen, Unger and Singer apparently think the bar should be so high that your failure to help others exemplifies bad values just as long as what you will sacrifice is even just a *little* less than what will be gained by your helping. If the bar were put this high, then there would be no telling what sorts of things the exception for urgent need would allow. Consider, again, the cases of Account and Transplant. If the bar were put this high, then this exception would allow the accountant to take the billionaire's money, and allow us to kill a healthy person for his vital organs, after all. And if the exception did allow such things as this, then it would indeed undermine the comfort zone which obligations are supposed to provide. This then is still another reason why the bar should not be put this high.

Let me conclude where I began, with the fact that, every day, thousands of children throughout the world die from easily treatable diseases, malnutrition, and bad drinking water. Unger claims that for us not to make the sacrifices necessary for saving these children violates an obligation or, at the very least, exemplifies very bad values. I disagree. For it to count either as violating an obligation or as very bad values would take, so I have argued, a radical change in the taxonomy of our society's current code of morality. I have also argued that such a radical change would be unwise; it would do more harm than good, even for those in need. But about the most important point of all, Unger and I agree: the deaths of these children is an ongoing tragedy of inconceivable proportions, a tragedy that will justify almost any sacrifices to bring to an end. If, as I have argued, we are not, and should not be, 'forced' by morality to make these sacrifices, then let us somehow find the resources to do so from good will, wisdom, and compassion.

NOTES

1. I have profited much from ongoing discussions about this topic with Mike Rae, along with extensive comments from him, Jeff Jordan, and David Silver on an earlier draft of this chapter. I also appreciate the helpful comments I received from Brad Hooker and Dale Miller.
2. Peter Unger, *Living High and Letting Die: Our Illusion of Innocence* (Oxford: Oxford University Press, 1996).

3. Ibid., p. 143.

4. In an interesting exchange of views, Tim Mulgan argues that rule consequentialism cannot account for the moral obligation (or 'requirement') to help the needy, while Brad Hooker argues that it can. See Tim Mulgan, 'Rule Consequentialism and Famine', *Analysis*, 54 (1994), pp. 187–92; 'One False Virtue of Rule-Consequentialism and One New Vice', *Pacific Philosophical Quarterly*, 77 (1997), pp. 62–79; and Brad Hooker, 'Rule-consequentialism and Obligations To the Needy', *Pacific Philosophical Quarterly*, 79 (1998), pp. 19–31. Although, as a rule consequentialist myself, I tend to agree with much of what I find in Hooker's paper, nevertheless I think that, ultimately, both Mulgan and Hooker are mistaken. From my perspective, it is as if Mulgan argues that the present king of France is bald (i.e., the obligation to help the needy cannot be grounded in rule consequentialism), and Hooker argues that he is not bald (i.e., this obligation can be grounded in rule consequentialism), while I argue that there is no present king of France (i.e., there is not, and should not be, any such obligation).

5. Unger, *Living High and Letting Die*, pp. 24–5

6. Ibid., p. 25. In real life, incidentally, we cannot save 30 children's lives by contributing a mere $100. Unger estimates, on p. 148, that, in real life, it takes about *$200* to save *one* child. So, in real life, to save 30 children would require about $6,000.

7. Ibid., pp. 26–7.

8. Ibid., pp. 75–7

9. So as to avoid any possible misunderstanding, perhaps I should emphasise one point. According to the equal-consideration premise, everyone's interests are to be taken as equally important – that is, given equal consideration – not for determining *what act to perform*, but for determining *what code of morality is most justified*. For reasons that I cannot pursue here, that code which is most justified certainly will not require that, in all cases, we give everyone's interests equal consideration for determining what *act* to perform. This code will permit us, in many cases, to give the interests of our own children priority over the interests of other children, and to give the interests of decent people priority over the interests of, say, serial killers.

10. I say 'in spite of himself', since, in footnotes on pp. 171–2 of *Living High and Letting Die*, Unger appears adamant about distancing himself from rule utilitarianism. But since he never addresses moral theory directly, it is difficult to know exactly what he thinks about these matters.

11. The most satisfactory way to formulate rule consequentialism more exactly is, I suggest, in terms of an entire social-pressure system. A 'social-pressure system' is an all-inclusive, worldwide system of 'informal' social norms and values – not just *moral* norms and values, but any other social norms and values as well, such as norms of aesthetics and norms of etiquette. Each of the norms and values within a social-pressure system is to be thought of as (hypothetically speaking) coming already conjoined with informal social pressure of a certain intensity, form, and scope in support of it, along with, of course, any costs which such social pressure brings with it in reality. According to this version of rule consequentialism, the most justified social-pressure system is the one which has the best consequences. Within the same, overall social-pressure system, incidentally, norms and values with scopes that differ from one another can contradict one another, and, in the most justified system, probably will indeed do so, at least within areas such as aesthetics and etiquette. Now take, for a given society, some moral code, *M*, made up of moral norms and values, along with, for each of them, social pressure of a certain intensity, form, and scope. Let us consider *M* in relation to social-pressure system *S*, of which *M* is supposed to be a part. According to this version of rule consequentialism, *M* is more justified than any alternative to *M* if and only if *S* with *M* has better consequences than S with any alternative to *M*. Finally, take a moral norm (or value) *N*, conjoined with social pressure of a certain intensity, form, and scope. Let us consider *N* in relation to some (current or hypothetical) moral code, *M*, of which *N* is supposed to be a part. According to this version of rule consequentialism, *N* is more justified than any alternative to *N* if and only if *M* with *N* has better consequences than *M* with any alternative to *N*. And, of course, for determining the overall consequences of an alternative, its consequences in the form of social-pressure *costs* must always be balanced against any benefits. I explain and defend this version of rule consequentialism in D. W. Haslett, *Capitalism with Morality* (Oxford: Clarendon Press, 1994), ch. 1, and *Equal Consideration: A Theory of Moral Justification* (Newark, DE: University of Delaware Press; London and Toronto: Associated University Presses, 1987).

12. John Stuart Mill, *On Liberty*, 1859, many editions. Cf. Thomas Nagel, *The View from Nowhere* (New York: Oxford University Press, 1986), ch. 10; R. M. Hare, *Moral Thinking* (Oxford: Clarendon Press, 1981), sec. 11.7.

13. I am, obviously, using the word 'obligation' here to refer to a moral requirement, as opposed to something that we perhaps ought, morally, to do, such as treat people in a friendly, or a kind, manner, but which is not, strictly speaking, morally *required*. Some philosophers use the word 'obligation' more narrowly than this, to refer only to moral requirements arising from specific undertakings. See, for example, T. M. Scanlon, *What We Owe to Each Other* (Cambridge, MA: Harvard University Press, 1999), p. 6–7. According to this more narrow use of

'obligation', we are obligated to keep a promise we have made (since this moral requirement arises from a specific undertaking by us) but we are not obligated to refrain from raping people (since the moral requirement that we not rape does not arise from a specific undertaking by us, but exists independently of any specific undertaking). I do not find this narrow use of 'obligation' to be especially enlightening. It is, I think, more compatible with most ordinary usage to use moral 'obligation' as I am using it here, to refer to any moral requirement, be it one arising from a specific undertaking or not. And the distinction I make here between 'positive' and 'negative' obligations is, I think, more useful, philosophically, than a distinction between moral obligations in the narrow sense and other moral requirements. But I have no deep quarrel with those who insist on using 'obligation' in this narrow sense; they may, throughout this discussion, simply substitute for 'obligation' the word 'duty', or 'requirement', or any other word that may please them, provided only that, by their preferred word, they mean anything *required* by morality.

14. Anyone for whom this is not obvious might profit from reading G. J. Warnock, *The Object of Morality* (London: Methuen, 1971).

15. A well-designed code will, of course, have certain 'priority rules' for determining which of two conflicting obligations is to be given priority. One of the most important of these priority rules will be that 'negative' obligations have priority over 'positive' obligations. Moreover, all of the obligations in such a code will, I submit, be prima facie only, not *absolute*. An 'absolute' obligation is one that always has priority over every other obligation, no matter what, whereas a 'prima facie' obligation (as I am defining it at least) is an obligation which is such that what it *normally* prescribes is subject to being overridden by what another obligation normally prescribes, if there is a conflict between the two. We need not, however, pursue these details here.

16. This motivation feature presupposes, of course, that we are able to distinguish between aspects of human psychology that are alterable through social pressure and those that, being 'human nature', are not, or are alterable only by doing more harm than good. Although we may not always be able to make these distinctions with absolute precision, we can do so precisely enough for most practical purposes, and can, in any case, become ever more precise through trial and error.

17. The thesis that, in a well-designed code, every obligation will have a right correlated with it and vice versa needs to be worked out and defended more fully than I am able to do here. For example, assuming, as I think we should, that we have a moral obligation not to torture animals, and a moral obligation, with certain exceptions, to obey the law, who then, it may be asked, has the correlated rights? In the case of animals, I, myself, have no more qualms about attributing rights to animals than I do to infants or severely retarded people, all or whom are equally incapable of understanding what moral rights and obligations mean. In the case of the obligation to obey the law, the question of who has the correlated moral right becomes a little complex. Two possibilities are as follows: (1) everyone within the jurisdiction to which the law applies has a moral right that everyone else not be 'free riders', but rather do their part in supporting the law by obeying it; (2) the state (a 'group' which represents the people as a whole) has a moral (as well as legal) right that its laws be obeyed, just as it has a moral right that debts to it be paid. But we need not try to work out details such as these here.

18. Rather than saying that any given value has *a* contrary, it is more accurate to say it has a number of contraries that are synonymous or closely related. For example, the contraries of 'graciousness' include, I suppose, not just 'offensiveness', but 'clumsiness', 'discourteousness', 'uncouthness', 'brashness', 'coarseness', and many others.

19. It always exemplifies bad values not to adhere to obligations; if nothing else, it exemplifies the bad value of 'lack of integrity'. Likewise, adhering to an obligation may well exemplify a good value, such as 'integrity', 'honesty', or the like. But this does not mean obligations are somehow subsumed under values in any way that threatens the distinction between them. Nor does it mean that obligations must admit of degrees. It may, for example, exemplify bad values for an unmarried teenager deliberately to get pregnant, but this does not mean that, therefore, *pregnancy* must admit of degrees. And, of course, some wrongdoings – that is, violations of obligations – are worse than others (that is, they exemplify bad values to a greater extent). But, once again, this does not mean that wrongness, and obligations, admit of degrees. Some teenage pregnancies are worse than others; that is, some exemplify bad values to a greater extent than others. But this does not mean that pregnancies admit of degrees. One obligation that does appear to admit of degrees, however, is the obligation to pay our debts.

20. Acts can indeed be praiseworthy and blameworthy even though, of course, we do not praise and blame the acts themselves, but the people who perform them. Accordingly, to say that an *act* is 'praiseworthy' is to say something like this: the act is such that the person performing it is deserving of praise for having performed it. Phillip Montague has a sensible discussion of this matter in *In the Interests of Others: An Essay in Moral Philosophy* (Dordrecht: Kluwer Academic Publishers, 1992), ch. 2. Any blameworthiness, or praiseworthiness, presupposes, of course, that the agent meets certain standards of mental competence.

21. It is, I think, sometimes assumed that, since obligations always have priority over values in cases of conflict between them, violating obligations must therefore always be more blameworthy than exemplifying bad values,

even *absent* any conflict between them. This assumption is, of course, mistaken. Violating our obligation to pay Mary back the quarter we borrowed from her for a parking meter is, and surely should be, far *less* blameworthy than is exemplifying the bad values of selfishness and callousness by failing to help the injured man in Sedan. Indeed, in certain extreme circumstances, exemplifying bad values is, and should be, be just as heinous, and thus blameworthy, as violating the obligation not to kill a person. James Rachels illustrates this with his well-known Bathtub case in which Jones can save a small child from drowning merely by lifting the child's head out of a few inches of bath water in which the child has fallen, bumped his head, and is laying face down unconscious. Although not murder, it is as heinous as murder for Jones to exemplify extreme selfishness and callousness by refusing to lift a finger to rescue the child. James Rachels, 'Active and Passive Euthanasia', *The New England Journal of Medicine*, vol. 292 (1073), pp. 78–80; reprinted, among many other places, in *Killing and Letting Die*, 2nd edn, edited by Bonnie Steinbock and Alastair Norcross (New York: Fordam University Press, 1994). I discuss this case in some detail in 'Moral Taxonomy and Rachels' Thesis', *Public Affairs Quarterly*, 10 (October 1996), pp. 291–306, a paper that is closely related to the topic under discussion here.

22. The sense of 'discretion' relevant here is relative to certain standards, or type of standards, *S*; a person, *P*, has discretion to do something, *X*, if *P*s doing *X* is not prohibited by *S*. Ronald Dworkin calls this the 'strong' sense of discretion. *Taking Rights Seriously* (Cambridge, MA: Harvard University Press, 1977), pp. 32–3. As Dworkin goes on to point out, 'discretion' in this sense is not tantamount to licence, and does not exclude criticism or blame. Perhaps an analogy from basketball will help. Jones is a good three-point shooter, but Smith is not. So coach Brown makes it a *rule* for Smith that he is never, under any circumstances, to take three-point shots, but applies no such rule to Jones. Smith thus has no discretion with respect to taking three-point shots, just as we have no discretion with respect to doing what obligations prohibit. Jones, to whom no such rule applies, does have discretion with respect to taking three-point shots, just as we have discretion with respect to values, but Jones is still subject, from the perspective of what is good for the team, to being blamed or praised for how he uses this discretion, just as we are subject, from a perspective of what is good overall, to being blamed or praised for how we use our discretion with respect to values.

23. The closest to a legal requirement that we exemplify good values is a legal requirement in many European countries – but not in the United States and most common-law jurisdictions – that, in certain circumstances, we aid those in need. Even though such laws are written to be applicable in only a limited number of circumstances that are clearly specified, the wisdom of having any such 'good-Samaritan' laws remains highly controversial. See, for example, A. D. Woozley, 'A Duty to Rescue: Some Thoughts on Criminal Liability', *Virginia Law Review*, 69 (1983), and *The Good Samaritan and the Law* (New York: Anchor Books, 1966).

24. This chapter examines *personal* morality only; not *political* morality. Political morality – that part of morality applicable to the behaviour of not persons, but political units, like governments and nations – is another matter. Although my views about personal morality – especially about there being no general obligation to help others – may be somewhat compatible with the views of many libertarians, any compatibility between my views and libertarian views does not carry over to political morality at all. I explain my views on political morality, and then go on to work out, in detail, the governmental programmes and overall economic system I believe follow from these views, in *Capitalism with Morality*.

25. Of course those who insist that, even though not correlated with any rights, helping others nevertheless is obligatory can always fall back on the position that these so-called obligations (or duties) are 'imperfect' ones. Yet if we press them to tell us exactly what *imperfect* obligations are, imperfect obligations may begin to look suspiciously like values. And if values are indeed what they really mean by 'imperfect obligations', then their 'imperfect-obligation' terminology has no merit; ordinary language already contains a perfectly good, and less confusing, word for what they mean – namely, 'values'. If, on the other hand, values are not what they mean by 'imperfect obligations', then, so I suggest, their view on the moral status of helping others may have less support from current morality than they think.

26. In some cases, to be sure, people view failing to help as highly blameworthy, especially in cases of 'easy rescue'. I suspect, however, that, if pressed, many of these people will reveal that they view failing to help in these cases as highly blameworthy not, strictly speaking, because they view it as violating an *obligation*, but because they view it as exemplifying *extremely bad values*.

27. Given that exemplifying bad values can, in the right circumstances, be just as morally heinous, and thus blameworthy, as the most heinous of obligation violations, there is little need, it seems to me, for going to great lengths, as does Phillip Montague, ibid., to try to show that rescues, or easy ones at least, are, somehow, obligatory.

28. One might object, as follows, to the relevance of other potential benefactors. If other potential benefactors are to be taken as relevant for determining need, so the objection might go, it will provide people with too easy an excuse for not helping others, as we can see from the infamous Kitty Genovese case. Kitty Genovese, it will be

recalled, was a young woman who, over a period of 30 minutes screaming all the while, was stabbed to death at 3a.m. at a New York City apartment building, while 38 people watched from their windows, none of whom even bothered to call the police. Obviously, by not even calling the police, all these people exemplified terrible values, and were deserving of great censure. But, according to this objection, if we allow scarcity of other potential benefactors to be a factor in determining need, then this will mean that these people did not exemplify bad values after all since, for each, Kitty Genovese's need for that person's help will have been 'diluted' by the presence of the 37 other potential benefactors. The answer to this objection is that the presence of the 37 other potential benefactors did, for each of these people, somewhat dilute Kitty Genovese's need for that person's help. But this is far from enabling us to conclude that, therefore, none of these people were exemplifying bad values by not helping since, after all, 'other potential benefactors' is only one factor relevant for determining need – other factors strongly point towards the need, in this case, being extreme. Moreover, the sacrifice of merely lifting the phone and dialing 911 for help was so minor that need relative to sacrifice was extremely great in spite of the other potential benefactors.

29. See, for example, Garrett Hardin, *The Limits of Altruism* (Bloomington, IN: University of Indiana Press, 1977).
30. Unger, *Living High and Letting Die*, pp. 38–9.
31. Ibid., pp. 45–8.
32. Ibid., pp. 39–40. This is, in fact, Unger's *only* reply to the argument that, with respect to the important 'other-potential-providers-of-help' factor, need is far greater in Sedan than in Envelope. But since I concede Unger's point, his reply does not touch my argument.
33. Peter Singer, *Practical Ethics*, 2nd edn. (Cambridge: Cambridge University Press, 1993), p. 230. Singer does qualify this high standard of aid by modifying 'significance' with the word 'moral' so that it becomes the following: one should always prevent something bad from happening if one can do so without sacrificing anything of comparable *moral* significance (p. 229). Apparently the idea behind this qualification is to make the standard more acceptable to non-consequentialists, who are concerned about 'sacrifices' other than those in the form of well-being. But for Singer himself, who is, essentially, an act consequentialist, this qualification does no more than direct us to evaluate sacrifices and needs not from a personal perspective in which one's own well-being has unique importance, but from an impersonal perspective in which everyone's well-being has equal importance. Others, besides Unger, who have defended a Singer-like standard include Shelley Kagan, *The Limits of Morality* (Oxford: Clarendon Press, 1989), and Garrett Cullity, 'International Aid and the Scope of Kindness', *Ethics* 105 (1994) pp. 99–127.
34. Unger, *Living High and Letting Die*, p. 143.
35. Ibid., pp. 63–4.

5

The Moral Opacity of Utilitarianism[1]

David Lyons

SECTION I: THE PROBLEM

Utilitarians sometimes suggest that their moral theory has an advantage over competing theories in basing moral judgements on the consequences of conduct. As its dictates are determined by empirically determinable facts, it offers a procedure for settling moral controversies on objective grounds. One need not appeal, for example, to the dubious authority of 'moral intuitions'.[2]

Claims like these are subject to familiar objections at various levels. I shall mention a representative sample and then focus on more serious difficulties stemming from aspects of utilitarianism that I believe have not been fully enough explored.

The claim made on behalf of utilitarianism seems premature. First, the suggested contrast between utilitarianism and its competitors obscures a more fundamental similarity. For we have no reason to believe that a utilitarian conception of right conduct could be established as sound solely by reference to empirically confirmable facts. Second, suppose we assume a consequentialist framework. The question what consequences have value does not present itself as an ordinary empirical issue. Third, suppose we take for granted that utilitarianism concerns itself specifically with the welfare or well-being of individuals. This is a standard reading of utilitarianism and by no means an ungenerous interpretation. Questions about the nature or constituents of individual welfare do not seem decidable by ordinary empirical means.[3]

Each of the considerations so far mentioned suggests that value judgements are required for determining the utilitarian criterion of right conduct. Until the criterion is identified, we do not have a theory that is available for application.

I turn now to complications of a different kind: they assume there are solutions to the foregoing problems and initially concern the application of a utilitarian standard.

Determining the utilitarian difference it makes to act one way rather than any other is at best extremely difficult. No more than one of the alternative courses of conduct that are available in a given situation can be initiated, for example, and some of its potentially relevant consequences will always remain unrealised. In practice, furthermore, judgements of marginal utility are subject to bias and wishful thinking. So a utilitarian principle may not provide a very reliable decision procedure.

I want now to suggest a closely related but much more serious set of problems for utilitarianism. The discussion so far assumes, in effect, that utilitarianism either is or in principle grounds a single, determinate moral theory – one criterion of right conduct. Moral theorists already recognise that, in one sense at least, this is not so. For it is commonplace to distinguish act and rule utilitarianisms and more generally direct and indirect forms of the theory. We have not yet, I think, fully appreciated how deep the potential ambiguity may go.

In this chapter I shall explain, first, why the moral implications of utilitarianism are at best *opaque* – practically impossible to determine – because the utilitarian criterion of right conduct is itself practically impossible to determine. That sort of indeterminacy can obtain even if, in the final analysis, utilitarianism determines one and only one criterion of right conduct. Second, I shall suggest that utilitarianism does not determine one unique criterion of right conduct; that is, no single criterion of right conduct best represents utilitarianism. If that is in fact the case, then utilitarianism is not just morally opaque but is morally *ambiguous* – lacking determinate implications for conduct.

SECTION 2: ACT UTILITARIANISM

For much of the twentieth century, utilitarianism has been understood as preferring the approach to morality that requires individuals to act so as to promote welfare as much as possible; that is, to maximise utility. In other words, the utilitarian approach to morality has been equated with (some form of) act utilitarianism. This understanding may be less common today than it was a couple of generations ago, but I think it remains commonplace.

Act utilitarianism applies directly to particular acts as performed by particular individuals on particular occasions. It directly evaluates conduct, and only conduct, from a moral point of view. It does not directly evaluate other things that are also subjected to moral appraisal, such as laws, character traits, or moral attitudes, even though these are usually assumed to have utilities. Act utilitarianism takes account of those other utilities indirectly, by considering the effects of conduct on laws, traits, and attitudes and the effects of laws, traits, and attitudes on conduct.

The act-utilitarian appraisal of acts does not seem to entail or to be entailed by utilitarian moral appraisals of other things, such as laws. Because acts that affect what laws we have possess other consequences as well, we cannot assume that optimific acts bring about optimific laws or that acts which bring about optimific laws are themselves optimific. This suggests that evaluations of conduct that primarily focus on acts or laws, respectively, do not necessarily converge. I'll return to this point presently.

In the recent past, other kinds of utilitarian moral principles have been developed, the most familiar being rule utilitarianism. The latter requires of individual acts, not that they maximise welfare, but that they conform to rules that maximise welfare.

Rule utilitarianism was developed, at least in part, so as to accommodate moral objections to act utilitarianism. It may therefore be regarded as a compromise between utilitarian and nonutilitarian ideas about morality. Partly for that reason, act utilitarianism is still seen by many theorists as the most faithful moral expression of what Peter Railton calls 'the guiding utilitarian idea . . . that the final ground of moral assessment . . . must lie in effects on people's well-being'.[4]

I will return later to the guiding utilitarian idea and the distinction between it and utilitarian moral principles. For the sake of argument now, I assume that the guiding utilitarian idea calls for welfare to be promoted as much as possible. For, if the realisation of an increment of welfare is assumed to have positive value and to provide a reason for any course of conduct that brings it about, it would seem that the very same theory favours both maximising welfare and any course of conduct that does so.

It is natural to suppose that act utilitarianism is the most faithful moral expression of the guiding utilitarian idea, so understood. For act utilitarianism requires one to promote welfare as much as possible. In other words, it is natural to suppose that perfect conformity with a principle that requires one to maximise welfare would, on any and all occasions, maximise welfare.

But we have reason to doubt that assumption. We have reason to believe that conforming our behaviour to act utilitarianism does not guarantee that we shall maximise welfare. If that seemingly paradoxical claim is true, the question arises whether there is a better interpretation of utilitarianism – a better representative within moral theory of the guiding utilitarian idea.

I shall now review briefly some reasons for thinking that act utilitarianism may not be the best moral interpretation of the guiding utilitarian idea. Then I shall explore the possibility of an alternative.

To simplify matters, I will consider only theories which require that welfare actually be maximised (actual-consequence utilitarianism). Perfect compliance with a probable-consequence version of act utilitarianism, which requires conduct that is most likely to maximise welfare, can fail to maximise welfare. This is possible because a justified estimate of consequences can be mistaken. No such complication prevents conformity to actual-consequence act utilitarianism from maximising welfare. As the very formulation of act utilitarianism seems to guarantee, it is natural to suppose that welfare is promoted as much as possible on any occasion when actual-consequence act utilitarianism is followed perfectly.

If that assumption is mistaken, it would seem to mark a *utilitarian* shortcoming of act utilitarianism. The assumption seems mistaken.

SECTION 3: ACCESSIBLE BUT UNREALISED INCREMENTS OF VALUE

The first problem is this. The acts of two or more people might each conform perfectly to act utilitarianism without promoting welfare as much as it would be possible for them collectively to do, in the same surrounding circumstances, by means of a different pattern of conduct.

The following example suggests why. Suppose that Alice and Barbara sing together and improvise as they perform. They harmonise well, so it is better when they harmonise than when they merely sing together. The musical results are good when Barbara sings high and Alice sings low, but they are best when Alice sings high and Barbara sings low. If Alice sings high, then (other things equal[5]) act utilitarianism requires Barbara to sing low, and if Barbara sings low, then it requires Alice to sing high. In that case, all of the (directly relevant) benefits that they might collectively realise through their singing will be realised. Suppose, however, that Barbara sings high: then act utilitarianism requires Alice to sing low; and if Alice should sing low, then it requires Barbara to sing high. In the latter two cases, some benefits which Alice and Barbara *might* realise through their conduct will *not* be realised.[6]

How much welfare is promoted depends not just on what Alice and Barbara do but also on the relations between their acts. Different patterns of conduct can result in different degrees to which welfare is promoted. Alice and Barbara might each maximise welfare and conform perfectly to act utilitarianism, given what the other does. But, in some cases, Alice and Barbara might collectively promote welfare to a greater degree if they both acted differently. Because of this, some available increments of welfare may *not* be realised by conduct that conforms *perfectly* to act utilitarianism.

So, while perfect conformity to act utilitarianism guarantees that the conduct of one or more individuals promotes welfare as much as it can in their respective circumstances, perfect conformity to that principle does not guarantee that welfare will be promoted as much as it might be by all of those individuals in their joint circumstances. This should lead us to wonder whether perfect conformity to a different principle would promote welfare more effectively.[7]

SECTION 4: AVAILABLE BUT INACCESSIBLE VALUE

Here's another problem. Some available increments of welfare may not be accessible at all to conduct that conforms perfectly to act utilitarianism. This problem derives from the fact that utility can be assigned to many things besides acts.[8]

Appreciation of this fact has given rise to novel variants of utilitarianism. We have already noted the development of rule utilitarianism. Another variant is motive utilitarianism, which concerns behavioural dispositions such as character traits and subjective interests. As Robert Adams defines it, motive utilitarianism holds 'that one pattern of motivation is morally better than another to the extent that the former has more utility than the latter'.[9]

Adams explains motive utilitarianism by using an example with the following structure. Jack has interests, pursuit of which realises benefits that presuppose those interests. His interests lead him to some acts that fail to maximise value in their circumstances and accordingly violate act utilitarianism. The important claim is this: If Jack lacked those interests, his conduct could conform to act utilitarianism, but he would also realise a lower level of benefits in the long run than he would by pursuing those interests.

Railton observes that 'certain goods are readily attainable – or attainable at all – only if people have well-developed characters'.[10] He argues that 'loving relationships, friendships, group loyalties, and spontaneous actions are among the most important contributors to whatever it is that makes life worthwhile'.[11] These factors may be so useful overall that a 'sophisticated' utilitarian would generally favour their possession and nurturance, even though they may result in violations of act utilitarianism.[12]

The relevant point is that very useful dispositions may generate some acts that do *not* promote the general welfare as much as it is possible for the individual to do in the circumstances; but it may nevertheless be *more* useful in the long run to be led by those dispositions sometimes to violate act-utilitarian dictates than to lack the dispositions and conform perfectly to act utilitarianism.

Here's an example. Honesty is a useful trait of character – so useful, indeed, that in the long run welfare may be better served when people are honest, act in character, and as a consequence do not always act so as to maximise welfare, than it would be served if people conformed perfectly to act utilitarianism. If that is so, it is presumably because consistent manifestations of honesty in conduct encourage and facilitate cooperative projects that promote welfare. In short, firm honesty of character, manifested in conduct that is sometimes suboptimific, can have benefits that exceed its costs.

The point I take from these examples is that some available increments of welfare may not be accessible to act-utilitarian conduct. Perfect conformity to act utilitarianism may be causally incompatible with the realisation of those benefits. Most important, welfare may be promoted to a greater degree if act utilitarianism is violated and those increments of welfare are realised.

For this possibility to be realised, another condition must be satisfied. It must not be possible for the relevant behavioural dispositions to be brought about by welfare-maximising conduct. If that were possible, then the relevant increments of welfare might be accessible to act-utilitarian conduct indirectly.[13]

The implications of the Adams and Railton examples, therefore, should not be exaggerated. They establish only the *possibility* that welfare is better promoted when conduct reflects useful behavioural dispositions that lead to violations of act utilitarianism than if it conforms perfectly to act utilitarianism. The examples do not show that all the relevant factual conditions are satisfied in the real world.

So we cannot infer from the examples that act utilitarianism is not the most faithful moral expression of the guiding utilitarian idea. But we cannot reasonably assume the contrary, either.

I am going to suppose that the examples are not misleading, and that act utilitarianism *may not be* the most faithful moral expression of the guiding utilitarian idea. That leaves us with the question, '*What sort of utilitarian principle might best express the guiding utilitarian idea?*'

SECTION 5: GENERIC UTILITARIAN REASONING

It is time to draw attention to some features of my argument so far. They concern a little-noticed aspect of theorising about utilitarian moral principles, which I shall call *generic* utilitarian reasoning.

Consider the familiar claim that using act utilitarianism as a practical guide to the morality of conduct is counter-productive because estimates of consequences are unreliable and more accurate guides to optimific conduct are available.

That argument can be understood in two different ways. It might mean that there are more dependable methods of complying with the requirements of act utilitarianism than by consciously and deliberately trying to follow that principle. On this reading, the claim is that using act utilitarianism as a decision procedure is counter-productive from an act-utilitarian point of view.

But the argument is usually understood differently. Then it means that there are *better methods of promoting welfare* than by consciously and deliberately trying to follow act utilitarianism. Using act-utilitarianism as a decision procedure is counter-productive, not from a specifically act utilitarian perspective, but from a generic utilitarian point of view.

The theoretical literature contains other examples of generic utilitarian reasoning about utilitarian moral principles. Consider a standard version of rule utilitarianism.

It requires that we follow rules, general conformity to which would maximise utility. It is sometimes said, however, that one person's compliance with that rule utilitarian principle can be counter-productive because following some rules is useful only when many are following them. A standard example is resistance to an oppressive regime. Isolated resistance may have worse consequences than no resistance at all. In many circumstances, to be effective, resistance must be widespread.

Thus, small-scale compliance with utilitarian moral principles can be harmful rather than beneficial overall. This is a *utilitarian* argument against the rule-utilitarian principle itself. It is another example of generic utilitarian reasoning about a utilitarian moral principle. It concerns whether or not conformity to the principle would promote welfare.

I shall not evaluate the factual claims made in generic utilitarian arguments. What is important for present purposes is not their soundness but that they assume a distinction between the guiding utilitarian idea and utilitarian moral principles. The guiding idea is not formulated in moral terms; nor does it entail any particular moral standard. It assumes that individuals' welfare has basic value and implies that more welfare is better than less. It holds that moral worth is relative to the promotion of welfare. But no premise of that sort entails a specific moral principle, such as one claiming that an act is morally wrong unless it maximises welfare.[14] The differences between the guiding utilitarian idea and utilitarian moral principles help to explain how a number of different principles can be counted as utilitarian.

I have assumed here that any standard using the criterion of maximising welfare as the basis for moral evaluation counts as a utilitarian moral principle. The resulting class includes principles that appraise acts (more or less directly) by reference to their utilities, principles that appraise character traits by reference to their utilities, principles that appraise laws by reference to their utilities, and so on.[15]

I have assumed, further, that a commitment to the value of welfare implies a commitment to maximising utility. So, in asking what moral principle most faithfully represents the guiding utilitarian idea, I have understood this as the question, '*Can we identify a moral principle, conformity to which would most effectively promote welfare?*'[16]

SECTION 6: VALORIC UTILITARIANISM

In grappling with the question I just posed, I have consulted others' attempts to address related problems. Peter Railton, for example, imagines the construction of a complex theory which he dubs 'valoric utilitarianism'.[17] The first step in constructing it is to apply the criterion of maximising utility to all objects of moral appraisal. Character traits, persons, acts, rules, institutions, and resource allocations, for example, would each be ranked, on *generic* utilitarian grounds, as 'more or less morally fortunate'. In the relevant version of this theory, such utilitarian rankings would not be confused with ordinary moral appraisals; for such an account of moral rightness would be implausible: there is a conceptual mismatch between scalar utilitarian rankings and binary moral appraisals like right or wrong. To achieve a valoric utilitarian account of right action, another step is needed:

> [O]nce the valoric utilitarian moves beyond judgments of what is more or less morally fortunate, about which he is relentlessly direct,[18] he is free to become indirect. Indirect and intricate . . . any plausible account of, say, moral rightness can be expected to be quite elaborate, involving not only questions about rules or principles, but also about motivations, dispositions to feel guilt or attribute blame, and so on.[19]

The challenge for valoric utilitarianism is to integrate these diverse elements, each of which is based on generic utilitarian calculations, in order to arrive at a plausible utilitarian account of right conduct. A valoric utilitarian account of rightness would be influenced by utilitarian assessments of (for example) the attitudes accompanying actions as well as by utilitarian assessments of the behaviour itself.

A familiar example will suggest why, and will also help to relate Railton's project to our problem. Suppose that shortages of food, fuel, or water threaten the general welfare, but that we have access to adequate shares of such necessities because of general compliance with rationing restrictions. Suppose that I am in a position to take more than my share without endangering the rationing arrangement or risking detection. My doing so may be condemned as 'free-riding'.

Familiar utilitarian moral theories appear inadequate to account for the relevant moral judgements. Actual-consequence act utilitarianism implies that, in the circumstances imagined, I should take advantage of others' compliance with the rationing arrangement by free-riding. Probabilistic act utilitarianism might argue either way, depending on the circumstances. If it recommends free-riding, it faces the moral objection that was just levelled against actual-consequence act utilitarianism. If it counsels compliance, it does so for reasons that may be considered morally inadequate, such as the risk of undermining the rationing regime. That factor accounts for part, but only part, of the relevant moral concerns.

That it accounts for only part of the moral concerns can be explained by reference to the possibility that taking more than my share is not wrong. When taking more would not endanger the rationing regime, for example, the morality of my doing so depends on my reasons – whether I take more because I think I can do so with impunity or because I know that the extra goods are urgently needed by someone (either myself or another person). It may be morally permissible for me to take more than my share in order to meet someone's urgent need. In fact, taking more for that reason in those circumstances would not even count as 'free-riding'.[20]

The rationing example is interesting because we can imagine a generic utilitarian account of at least some of the various moral considerations which must somehow be combined in order to construct a valoric utilitarian account of right conduct. An overall valoric utilitarian appraisal of my action would be based on the utility of my attitudes as well as the utility of my taking more than my share. Some of the relevant utilitarian considerations are familiar. On the one hand, it is generally useful for us to comply with necessary rationing restrictions, but it can be even more useful to take extra benefits in special circumstances in order to meet urgent needs that are not addressed by the restrictions. On the other hand, it is useful for people to have a moral disposition to condemn free-riding and value fair play. That is because the temptation to ride free can be both strong and harmful, and a firm moral aversion is needed to prevent counter-productive free-riding, which by force of example can undermine useful cooperation. However, the most useful aversion would presumably be flexible enough to take due account of urgent needs which are not reflected in the rationing restrictions.

The challenge for valoric utilitarianism is to integrate such diverse considerations. A moral judgement of my action would be determined by a complex principle that appropriately combines a generic utilitarian appraisal of behaviour with, for example, a generic utilitarian appraisal of the relevant states of mind.

This incomplete sketch of valoric utilitarianism begins to suggest what the utilitarian moral principle I am seeking might be like. It is important to see, however, that valoric utilitarianism is not that principle.

Railton does *not* ask what kind of utilitarian moral principle most faithfully represents the guiding utilitarian idea. He imagines a utilitarian moral theory that might 'overcome some of the difficulties facing' the more familiar utilitarian moral theories.[21] His concern is the possibility of constructing a morally adequate version of utilitarianism. That project is different from mine, as I shall now explain.

Consider the idea that candidate moral theories should be subjected to a process like the one that is supposed to result in what John Rawls has termed 'reflective equilibrium'.[22] The process is believed to give reasons for preferring the moral conceptions that emerge from it to those that enter it. We begin with a select set of moral principles and moral judgements at various levels as well as other relevant information. We try to reconcile them all, as far as possible, perhaps modifying some principles or judgements, perhaps rejecting some entirely. The aim is to come up with a set of more defensible principles and judgements.

Imagine that among the moral principles fed into this process is one that best, most faithfully represents the guiding utilitarian idea. The principle may be modified in the process so as to make it a more defensible moral theory. Now we can compare Railton's concerns with ours.

Railton is concerned with a principle that might enjoy reflective equilibrium with other considered moral judgements rather than a principle that would be fed into the equilibrating process. He assumes that utilitarian moral theories can take a variety of forms. Partly to accommodate moral objections to familiar utilitarian principles, he imagines the construction of a complex theory that would integrate various utilitarian factors.

Whereas Railton is concerned with the *output* of the equilibrating process, my concern here is with the *input*. My question is, in effect, '*What moral principle should initially represent utilitarianism – prior, that is, to possibly modifying it so as to bring the theory into reflective equilibrium with other considered moral judgements?*'

SECTION 7: MULTIPLE-INFLUENCE PRINCIPLES

An answer to that question is suggested by Amartya Sen. In discussing the basic elements of utilitarianism, Sen identifies a principle which he regards as common to 'all variants' of the theory.[23] He names the principle 'outcome utilitarianism' and formulates it as follows:

> Any state of affairs x is at least as good as an alternative state of affairs y if and only if the sum total of individual utilities in x is at least as large as the sum total of individual utilities in y.[24]

Sen claims that 'A utilitarian moral structure consists of the central element of outcome utilitarianism combined with some consequentialist method of translating judgments of outcomes into judgments of actions.'[25] He depicts act utilitarianism as the result of combining outcome utilitarianism with act consequentialism, which he understands as follows:

> An action α is right if and only if the state of affairs x resulting from α is at least as good as each of the alternative states of affairs that would have resulted respectively from each of the alternative acts.[26]

Sen calls acts and rules 'influencing variables'. He calls theories such as act utilitarianism and rule utilitarianism 'single-influence' utilitarianisms. He distinguishes single-influence from multiple-influence theories, and makes the following claim. He asserts that any single-influence utilitarianism 'fails to achieve the best outcome that could have resulted from a comprehensive structure'.[27]

I understand this as the generic utilitarian claim that conformity to some (as yet unspecified) utilitarian moral principle, which refers directly to more than one factor – which refers to, say, rules and behavioural dispositions as well as acts – would promote welfare better than would conformity to any utilitarian moral principle that refers only to a single factor. For Sen also asserts that

The most comprehensive consequentialist structure would require that the combination of all influencing variables be so chosen that the result is the best feasible state of affairs according to outcome utilitarianism.[28]

Although Sen's argument does not require him to elaborate on that claim, he points in the general direction of what I am seeking.

Railton imagines a moral principle that *least controversially* represents utilitarianism in the moral sphere – a principle calculated to meet objections against utilitarian moral theories. Sen imagines a moral principle that *most faithfully* represents utilitarianism in the moral sphere – a principle designed to ensure that conformity to it maximises welfare.

SECTION 8: THE MORAL OPACITY OF UTILITARIANISM

What might such a principle be like? Although I am not confident about this, I shall assume that there is a principled basis for determining one way of specifying each of the various factors that must be incorporated in a comprehensive utilitarian moral principle for appraising conduct (each of what Sen calls 'influencing variables').

Consider the case of rules. We might select them on the basis of their actual or their predictable consequences. Consequences of either type might be attributed to rules on the basis of perfect conformity or some more realistic criterion. For the guiding utilitarian idea to have a best moral representative, the principle's reference to rules (as well as to other variables) must be unambiguous. Perhaps the selection criteria for the rules should be determined so as to maximise the utility of the resulting principle.

Another thing that is unclear is how such a principle integrates the various factors so as to generate authoritative utilitarian moral appraisals of particular actions. Call this the combination problem.[29] This problem indicates that utilitarianism is morally opaque. There may be a unique principle of right conduct that best represents utilitarianism in the moral sphere, but we have no idea what it might be like.[30]

The combination problem may be explained informally as follows. It is unclear how much of our efforts should be dedicated to producing the best consequences by our actions and how much should be diverted (when a choice seems needed) to promoting useful institutions, laws, social rules and practices, character and personality traits, and so on, and how much one's personal division of labour should vary with circumstances and how such a division of labour should vary from one individual to another.

The free-riding example might appear to suggest at least a partial solution to the combination problem. As I have interpreted ordinary moral judgement, it implies that the morality of taking more than one's fair share is determined largely by the agent's attitudes. This suggests a generalisation, namely, that the natural expressions in conduct of useful dispositions should take precedence over alternative courses of action with greater marginal utility.

But we cannot generalise in that way if we wish to construct a utilitarian moral principle that best represents the guiding utilitarian idea. The suggested precedence derives from a considered moral judgement rather than generic utilitarian reasoning. To solve the combination problem, we need a principle conformity to which would maximise welfare, and we cannot assume that such a principle would agree with our considered moral judgements and thus would generally condemn free-riding or favour the natural expressions in conduct of useful dispositions over alternative courses of action with greater marginal utility.

To get a rough idea of the sort of principle we seek as well as the difficulties involved, we might begin with an artificially simple principle that takes into account the utility of rules as well as acts. Generic utilitarianism would seem to argue for a principle that calls for compliance with useful rules, except when welfare would be promoted better in the long run by deviation from them, and to call for conduct that maximises welfare, except when it would be more useful in the long run for conduct to comply with the useful rules.

Application of such a principle must determine when it is useful to promote useful rules, what useful rules should be promoted in what circumstances, what effort to expend on that project, what effort to expend on promoting compliance with actual rules, and what effort to expend on promoting compliance with possible rules. As this incomplete catalogue of questions implies, both the identification and the application of such a principle are complicated by the fact that various rules, with varying degrees of utility, actually exist within the various social groups whose rules apply to one's conduct, and that such rules are actually complied with to a greater or lesser degree.

There might very well be a determinate answer to such questions, at least in theory. But as the relevant facts are largely unknowable, we seem bound to remain ignorant of how to frame such a principle. We have no reason to expect it ever to become available for use as a criterion of right conduct or as the basis of a decision procedure.

As we have seen, there are generic utilitarian reasons for the principle we are seeking to include direct consideration of other factors, such as useful dispositions. Incorporating them can be expected to complicate matters further.

I'll now suggest what a principle with this third factor added would involve. Generic utilitarianism would seem to argue for a principle that calls for conduct that maximises welfare, except when it would be more useful in the long run for conduct to express useful dispositions or to comply with useful rules. The principle would not permit useful conduct to undermine dispositions or rules that it would be more useful in the long run to maintain, though the latter would presumably vary with circumstances. It would require that conduct promote useful dispositions and useful rules, but only when it would be more useful in the long run to do so.

I assume that we can theoretically state the implications for action of behavioural dispositions as readily as we can for useful rules. Rules proclaim their requirements for conduct. Behavioural dispositions have natural expressions in conduct. We sometimes act at variance with our stable dispositions, and utility might sometimes be maximised by so acting. It will be the task of the principle we seek to take account of that complication.

Application of such a principle must determine not only when it is useful to promote useful dispositions, but also what dispositions they might be, what effort to expend on that project, and when we should promote useful rules, useful dispositions, or more directly useful actions. This will be made somewhat more complex by the fact that individuals at any time have various dispositions, with varying degrees of utility, and varying degrees of firmness.

Some of the problems that accrue to identifying useful rules, for the purpose of applying the principle, accrue as well to identifying useful behavioural dispositions. The utility of behavioural dispositions, like that of rules, varies with circumstances. A complicating factor is that we must consider among the circumstances other characteristics of the individuals whose dispositions they are, for dispositions are likely to interact.

I do not believe we are at all likely to have reliable information that would make possible a more practically helpful formulation of such a principle. This means that such a principle will not be available for use as a criterion of right conduct or as the basis of a decision procedure.

The combination problem suggests that, if there is a most faithful moral representative of utilitarianism, it has implications for conduct that are practically unknowable. I have assumed that the variables that must be incorporated into a comprehensive utilitarian moral principle have determinate values that are fixed somehow by the guiding utilitarian idea. I am not confident that this is the case. If it is not the case, then my argument suggests that there is no best moral interpretation of the guiding utilitarian idea.

SECTION 9: MORAL AMBIGUITY

I come finally to the representation problem. This concerns the criteria for determining what moral principle most faithfully represents utilitarianism. My argument so far has taken for granted that this is no problem at all. It has assumed that a moral principle most faithfully represents the guiding utilitarian idea if conformity to it would most effectively promote welfare. I shall now question that assumption.

We can raise at least three questions about the test which I have supposed is implied by the guiding utilitarian idea: (1) one principle for everyone, or more than one? (2) one principle for each person, or more than one? and (3) what constitutes the relevant kind of conformity?

(1) The first question is whether, in comparing the effects of conformity to different principles, we are simply to compare the effects of conformity to each principle, in turn, by everyone. For there is an alternative, which is to compare the effects of conformity to different principles by different individuals. It would seem advisable to contemplate this possibility because it is conceivable that welfare would be better promoted if different individuals conformed to different principles.[31] Utilitarianism would seem to provide no way of deciding between these two different ways of comparing utilitarian moral principles.[32]

(2) The second question is whether, in comparing the effects of conformity to different principles, we are simply to compare the effects of continuing conformity to each principle in turn. There is an alternative, however, which is to compare the effects of conformity to a succession of different principles. It would seem advisable to contemplate this possibility because it is conceivable that persons or circumstances might change over time in such a way that welfare would be better promoted if the principles people conformed to varied over time.[33] Once again, utilitarianism would seem to provide no way of deciding between these two different ways of comparing utilitarian moral principles.[34]

(3) My argument has so far assumed that conformity to a principle is to be understood as doing only what the principle permits. Instead of considering the effects of simple conformity to a principle, however, we might consider the effects of its acceptance by individuals. Acceptance involves consistent, conscientious effort to follow a principle but also allows for some deviation from the principle on occasion.[35] It is conceivable that the possible disutility of divergence from a presumably useful principle can sometimes be outweighed by some special utility that might attach to the relaxation of attitudes that acceptance without perfect conformity involves.[36]

The representation problem, then, is this. If generic utilitarianism determines one single set of criteria for identifying its most faithful representative in the moral sphere, we might reasonably assume that one and only one moral principle best satisfies those criteria. If, however, there are alternative possible ways of identifying utilitarianism's moral representative, we have that much less reason to assume there is just one such principle. In that case, utilitarianism may well be morally ambiguous: substantively different principles of right conduct might equally well qualify for the position of utilitarianism's moral representative, and different principles can be presumed to have differing implications for right conduct.[37]

If, for any reason, such as the reasons I have suggested, the guiding utilitarian idea fails to determine a unique criterion of right action, it is possible that it might do so with the aid of substantive moral judgements that we are prepared to make without the conscious deployment of utilitarian ideas. To shape a utilitarian moral principle on that basis, however, would be to discard the project of discovering the most faithful moral interpretation of utilitarianism itself and to seek instead a *morally acceptable* version of utilitarianism. In that case, and to that extent, utilitarian moral theory would be driven by external factors rather than by its own guiding utilitarian idea.

NOTES

1. Ancestors of this paper were presented at Boston University, Carleton University (Ottawa), SUNY Albany, SUNY Geneseo, the University of Colorado, the University of Texas, and the International Society for Utilitarian Studies. I am grateful to discussants on those occasions, and especially to Alan Fuchs, Thaddeus Metz, William Nelson, Martino Traxler, and Henry West.

2. The problems which I shall later discuss concern both criteria of right conduct and practical procedures for deciding what conduct is morally permissible, so I shall generally ignore that important distinction.

3. Nor does the question how to take account of the welfare of non-human animals seem an ordinary empirical one either.

4. Peter Railton, 'How Thinking about Character and Utilitarianism Might Lead to Rethinking the Character of Utilitarianism', *Midwest Studies in Philosophy*, 13 (1988), pp. 398–416, at p. 398.

5. This qualification will be understood but not stated hereafter.

6. In Allan Gibbard's original example, the best outcome results from both persons doing X, the next best from their both doing Y, and their acting differently is neutral. (Allan Gibbard, 'Rule Utilitarianism: Merely an illusory Alternative?', *Journal of Philosophy* 43, 1965, pp. 211–21.) My variation on Gibbard's example makes the point that the relevant coordination patterns need not involve everyone's doing the same thing.

7. Donald Regan's 'cooperative utilitarianism' is designed to address this problem (Regan, *Utilitarianism and Co-operation* (New York: Oxford University Press, 1980)). Regan's principle requires an individual to coordinate with others optimally whenever possible. It is unclear whether perfect conformity to that principle would in fact promote welfare better than would perfect conformity to act utilitarianism. We may never have adequate grounds for a confident answer to this complex question. In any case, cooperative utilitarianism does not attempt to address the next problem.

8. This point was appreciated by Jeremy Bentham and John Stuart Mill. Both writers judged various objects of moral appraisal, aside from acts, such as laws, character traits, and moral attitudes, directly by reference to their respective utilities. From a twentieth-century perspective, this might seem to show that, in their hands, utilitarian moral theory had not yet matured. That judgement need not be disrespectful. It would not disparage either writer to suggest that later theorists were enabled by their predecessors' work to develop a more refined moral interpretation of the guiding utilitarian idea. We should withhold judgement, however: Bentham and Mill might have understood utilitarianism better than their act-utilitarian successors.

9. Adams, 'Motive Utilitarianism', *Journal of Philosophy*, 73 (1976), pp. 467–81, at p. 470.

10. Railton, 'Alienation, Consequentialism and the Demands of Morality', *Philosophy and Public Affairs* 13 (1984), pp. 134–71, at p. 158.

11. Ibid., p. 139.

12. Ibid.', p. 153. I have paraphrased part of Railton's argument so that it refers to utilitarianism. He initially makes his points relative to a broader consequentialism ('Alienation, Consequentialism and the Demands of Morality', pp. 149ff.). The difference between consequentialism and utilitarianism does not matter for present purposes.

13. One reason to doubt this is that the inculcation of behavioural dispositions requires extended patterns of conduct, the utility of early stages of which depends on continuation of such training.

14. That an act would maximise value may provide a reason for performing it. We cannot assume, however, that the implied reason is or entails a moral prescription.

15. It does not matter how we define the class of utilitarian moral principles. The point is members of that class are distinct from the guiding utilitarian idea.

16. I shall have some more to say about these assumptions later.

17. See Railton, 'How Thinking about Character', pp. 409–13.

18. This suggests that the initial stage of appraisal ranks particular items in each class much the way act

utilitarianism ranks particular acts. When acts alone are ranked, however, all other conditions are given. It is unclear how to rank all of these particular items when the other conditions that affect a particular item's utility include particular items in other classes whose members are likewise to be ranked and for that reason would not seem to be regarded as given.

19. Railton, 'How Thinking about Character', p. 41f.

20. Note that my comments on this example are not purely utilitarian. For the aim of valoric utilitarianism is not to maximise utility but to use generic-utilitarian elements in the construction of a defensible criterion of right conduct. I'll get back to this point in a moment.

21. Railton, 'How Thinking about Character', p. 410.

22. Rawls, *A Theory of Justice* (Cambridge, MA: Harvard University Press, 1971), p. 48.

23. Amartya Sen, 'Utilitarianism and Welfarism', *Journal of Philosophy*, 76 (1979), pp. 463–89, at 463.

24. Ibid., p. 464.

25. Ibid., p. 466. Sen's 'utilitarian moral structures' support moral appraisals of acts only, although outcome utilitarianism would not seem to imply any such restriction and utilitarian moral appraisals would seem possible of things other than acts.

26. Ibid., p. 464.

27. Ibid., pp. 463–89, at p. 466. Although Sen refers to an argument establishing this point (p. 466, n. 8), I have not found it.

28. Ibid., p. 466.

29. We could avoid this problem by applying the influencing variables and balancing them in an 'intuitionistic' manner. This would not yield a determinate principle, but it suggests a model for utilitarian reasoning in practice.

30. I think it is also unclear how to determine whether a principle best or most faithfully expresses the guiding utilitarian idea. Call that the representation problem. I'll come back to it in the next section.

31. Here's a further complication. The range of principles that we imagine different individuals conforming to might be limited to ones that are recognisably utilitarian; alternatively, we might include within the range of principles some that are not recognisably utilitarian.

32. It might be objected that morality requires its principles to apply universally. The alternative criterion does not deny this. It accords with the possibility of fundamental moral disagreement, which the concept of morality does not deny.

33. The previous complication might apply here. The range of principles that we imagine individuals conforming to might either be limited to ones that are recognisably utilitarian or might include some that are not recognisably utilitarian.

34. It might be objected that morality requires its principles to apply constantly. The alternative criterion does not deny this. It accords with the possibility that individuals change their basic moral commitments over time, which the concept of morality does not deny.

35. Because acceptance involves certain moral attitudes, whereas simple conformity does not, acceptance may also involve further distinguishing consequences.

36. This alternative test would also seem to reflect a more realistic notion of the role we might ideally expect moral principles to play in our lives than perfect conformity does.

37. It is also conceivable that some neutral factor, such as the concept of morality or of rationality, would, when added to generic utilitarianism, somehow disqualify all but one potential moral representative of the guiding utilitarian idea and would thus save utilitarianism from moral ambiguity. But I see no reason to assume this.

6

Global Consequentialism

Philip Pettit and Michael Smith

SECTION I: GLOBAL VS LOCAL CONSEQUENTIALISM

Global consequentialism identifies the right x, for any x in the category of evaluands – be the evaluands acts, motives, rules, or whatever – as the best x, where the best x, in turn, is that which maximises value. Value may be actual or expected, of course, but we shall ignore that complication here. So, for example, according to global consequentialism, the right act for someone to perform is the act that has greater value than any of the acts that might have been performed instead; the right motive-set for someone to have is that motive-set whose possession has greater value than any of the motive-sets that might have been possessed instead; the right set of rules for someone to have internalised is that set of rules which has greater value than any of the sets of rules that they might have internalised instead, and so on.[1]

The best-known statement and defence of global consequentialism is to be found in Derek Parfit's *Reasons and Persons*. Here is what Parfit has to say:

> There are different versions of *Consequentialism*, or *C*. *C*'s *central claim* is
>
> (C1) There is one ultimate moral aim: that outcomes be as good as possible
>
> C applies to everything. Applied to acts, C claims . . .
>
> (C2) What each of us ought to do is whatever would make the outcome best
>
> . . . Consequentialism covers, not just acts and outcomes, but also desires, dispositions, beliefs, emotions, the color of our eyes, the climate, and everything else. More exactly, C covers anything that could make outcomes better or worse. According to C, the best possible climate is the one that would

make outcomes best. I shall use 'motives' to cover both desires and dispositions. C claims

>   (C5)   The best possible motives are those of which it is true that if we have
>   them, the outcome will be best.[2]

Thus, according to Parfit, C tells us not just which acts are the right ones to
perform, but also which desires, beliefs, and emotions are the right ones to have,
whether it is right to have this colour eyes or that, whether it is right for it to be
rainy or cloudy or sunny, and so on and so forth. This is global consequentialism if
anything is.[3]

As Parfit's remarks make clear, the crucial feature of global consequentialism is
that it does not privilege any category of evaluand. In particular, it does not
privilege the category of acts that has often been privileged, by default, in much
consequentialist writing. It does not say, for example, that the right motive-set for
someone to have, or the right set of rules for someone to have internalised, is that set
which would promote the choice of the right acts. This is important, as someone's
possession of certain motives, or his or her having internalised certain rules, may
have consequences that are not mediated by any act to which those motives or rules
give rise.[4] Your clear benevolence towards me, and mine towards you, can provide
each of us with a sense of warmth and reassurance independently of any acts that it
occasions. And the mere knowledge that you have internalised a rule of promise-
keeping provides me, well in advance of any contract we enter into, with a rich sense
of the arrangements we may form.

Global consequentialism thus contrasts with any form of consequentialism that
privileges one or another category of evaluand, and which is therefore *local*. The
sort of consequentialism just described – the sort that privileges acts – is a local *act*
consequentialism. It privileges the category of acts, defining right acts as those
which maximise value – in this it agrees with global consequentialism – but it then
goes on to identify right motive-sets, right sets of rules, and so on, as the sets that
promote the choice of right acts. Other forms of local consequentialism are
distinguished from global in so far as they privilege some non-act category of
evaluand.

Consider, for example, the version of rule utilitarianism described by J. J. C.
Smart:

>   Rule utilitarianism is the view that the rightness or wrongness of an action is
>   to be judged by the goodness or the badness of the consequences of a rule that
>   everyone should perform the action in like circumstances.[5]

This form of rule utilitarianism privileges rules, and then defines right acts in terms
of the right rules. It is therefore local, in the sense that contrasts with global.[6]

The version of rule consequentialism Brad Hooker defends is similarly local. According to Hooker,

> An act is wrong if and only if it is forbidden by the code of rules whose internalization by the overwhelming majority of everyone everywhere in new generations has the highest expected value. The evaluation of a code is to count all the costs involved in getting it internalized.[7]

Hooker's version of rule utilitarianism thus also privileges rules, and defines right acts in terms of the right rules.

Robert Merrihew Adams recommends that motive consequentialists embrace a form of local consequentialism.

> This position – that we have a moral duty to do an act, if and only if it would be demanded of us by the most useful kind of conscience we could have – may be called 'conscience utilitiarianism', and is a very natural position for a motive utilitarian to take in the ethics of actions.[8]

Conscience utilitarianism thus privileges consciences, and defines right acts in terms of the conscience it would be best for us to have.

Finally, and more generally, the various forms of indirect utilitarianism described by Simon Blackburn are all local theories that privilege non-act evaluands.

> The doctrine that applies utilitarianism to actions directly, so that an individual action is right if it increases happiness more than any alternative, is known as direct or act utilitarianism. Indirect versions apply in the first place to such things as institutions, systems of rules of conduct, or human characters: these are best if they maximize happiness, and actions are judged only in so far as they are those ordained by the institutions or systems of rules, or are those that would be performed by the person of optimal character.[9]

Thus, according to Blackburn, indirect utilitarianisms quite generally privilege some non-act category of evaluand – institutions, rules of conduct, human characters, or whatever – and then go on to define right actions in terms of the right things in the privileged category.

The form of local consequentialism that privileges acts has been justly criticised in the literature by consequentialists themselves.[10] Their objection has been that by ignoring the non-act mediated consequences of motives, rules, and the like, local-act consequentialism fails to pay due regard to the fact that these things are the significant sources of value that they so plainly are. Strikingly, however, consequentialists have said little or nothing about the corresponding failings of the various forms of local consequentialism that privilege some *non-act* category of evaluand. Indeed, as we have seen, some have even gone on to defend their own versions of local consequentialism.[11]

In our view, this oversight is unjustified. Consequentialists should think that those forms of local consequentialism that privilege some non-act category of evaluand, and redefine rightness in such terms, are just as bad as those that privilege acts. These forms of local consequentialism also fail to pay due regard to a significant source of value. In this case, however, the significant source of value is *acts*.[12]

SECTION 2: A PROBLEM AND OUR STRATEGY FOR OVERCOMING IT

There is a problem to be overcome in mounting an argument against local consequentialism, however. What, after all, does it mean to privilege a particular category of evaluand in the definition of right acts? Unfortunately, because different answers can be given to this question, local consequentialism is difficult to formulate in a definitive way. The upshot is thus that even if we could provide a decisive refutation of some version of the theory, a committed local consequentialist could with some justification insist that the refuted theory isn't the best version. We will illustrate this problem with two examples.

Consider local motive consequentialism. According to this theory, the right motive-set for someone to have is that motive-set whose possession has greater value than any of the motive-sets that might have been possessed instead. In this respect local motive consequentialism agrees with global consequentialism. But how does local motive consequentialism go on to privilege the category of motives in defining right acts? There are various possibilities. It might go on to define right acts to be those which are caused by the right motives; or it might define them to be those which would have been caused by possession of the right motives; or it might define them to be those which would have been caused by the motives that it would be best for someone to try to have; or it might define right acts in some yet further way.

Or consider local rule consequentialism. According to this theory, the right rules for someone to have internalised is that set of rules adherence to which has greater value than any of the sets of rules that the person might have internalised instead. Again, in this respect it accords with global consequentialism. But how does local rule consequentialism then go on to define the right acts? It might define them to be those which are caused by having internalised the right rules; or it might define them to be those which would have been performed by someone who had internalised the right rules; or it might define them to be those which would have been performed by someone who had internalised the rules that it would be best for someone to try to internalise; or it might define right acts in some yet further way. Again, there is a variety of possibilities.

Our strategy, in order to overcome this problem, is to argue inductively against all versions of local consequentialism at once. We begin by considering the various versions of local motive consequentialism just described. We note that they are liable to a similar pattern of objection. In our view, every form of local consequentialism will be liable to that same pattern of objection, and we attempt to prove that this is so by indicating the way in which the objections apply to the various versions of local rule consequentialism just described. Once one sees how the pattern of objection applies in one case, we think it is hard not to conclude that all forms of local consequentialism will fall to that same pattern of objection. As with any inductive argument we may, of course, be wrong. However we leave it to the defenders of local consequentialism to prove that that is so.

SECTION 3: LOCAL MOTIVE CONSEQUENTIALISM: FIRST VERSION

Consider the version of local motive consequentialism which holds that the right acts are those which are caused by the right motives. We have two related objections to this theory. The first is that it is absurd to hold, as this theory does, that only acts which are caused by the right motives are right. The second is that it is equally absurd to hold, as this theory also does, that every act which is caused by the right motives is right.

Why hold that only acts which are caused by the right motives are right? After all, those people who do not have the right motives – and hence those whose acts cannot be caused by the right motives – are still able to act in ways that contribute more or less value to the world. For example, they are able to perform, or not to perform, those acts, of the acts available to them, that produce the best consequences, and they are also presumably able to perform, or not to perform, those acts, of the acts available to them, that would have been performed by people who did have the right motives. Given that the acts available to these people contribute different amounts of value to the world it surely follows that some of them are to be recommended over others, on consequentialist grounds. But once this point is conceded we must ask what merit there is in insisting, as the first version of local consequentialism insists, that the act thus recommended is still not the right act for these people to perform. It seems unnecessarily ad hoc to invent a new word to characterise the acts which are to be recommended to those who do not have the right motives.

The second objection is that it is equally absurd to suppose that every act which is caused by the right motives is a right act. Focus on a particular case in order to see why. Imagine that, in a certain situation, the best consequences will flow from someone's having a set of motives that includes a strong desire to provide benefits, no matter how small, for his children, and only a weak motive to provide benefits, no matter how large, for strangers. Moreover, imagine that this person has these motives, and that he faces a particular choice situation in which he can provide either a smaller benefit for his children or a larger benefit for some strangers. Finally, let's suppose that in these particular circumstances, providing the larger benefit for the strangers will have better consequences than giving the smaller benefit to his children. Which is the right act for him to perform?

According to the first version of local motive consequentialism the right act for this person to perform is giving the smaller benefit to his children. But why? Let's agree that the person we are imagining *will* act so as to give the smaller benefit to his children, provided he functions properly psychologically. So much follows from the fact that his desire to give them the smaller benefit is stronger than his desire to give the larger benefit to the strangers. But the fact that he *will not* give the larger benefit to the strangers is neither here nor there in deciding whether his giving the strangers that larger benefit is the right thing for him to do.

Nor is the fact that, given that he has the motives that it is right for him to have and functions properly psychologically, the act of giving the larger benefit to the strangers is only available to him by grace of the possibility of a psychological malfunction or anomaly. The value or disvalue associated with psychological malfunction is, after all, to be decided by a consequentialist on consequentialist grounds, and, in the circumstances that we are imagining, giving the larger benefit to the strangers has the best consequences, notwithstanding the fact that it would involve psychological malfunction. A consequentialist should surely think that there is therefore much to rejoice about, and little to regret, if the person we are imagining manages to give the larger benefit to the strangers.

The latter point needs emphasising. We think that one main attraction of the view that it is always right to act on the motives that it is right to have is the implicit assumption that failing to act on these motives will somehow undermine possession of them. But this thought is multiply confused. For one thing, it is implausible to suppose that the occasional occurrence of a psychological malfunction which causes someone to act contrary to the motivations that he has will undermine his possession of these motives. Patterns of motivation are more robust than that. For another, if, as we are supposing, giving the larger benefit to the strangers has the best consequences then, even if it does undermine the agent's possession of the motives that it is currently right for him to have, by hypothesis the benefits of his so acting clearly outweigh that cost. It is thus hard to see why a consequentialist should be worried by the fact that the agent undermines his possession of the motives that it is currently right for him to have if, as we have supposed, the possible world in which he no longer has these motives contains more value than the world in which he retains them.[13]

But, in that case, we must surely ask what reason there is for supposing that it is always right for a person to act on the motives that it is right for him to have. The only defence of the suggestion left, as far as we can see, is that the acts which are deemed to be right, on such a definition of rightness, accord more closely with our pre-theoretical intuitions about which acts are right and which are wrong than do the acts which are deemed to be right by a direct application of the consequentialist principle itself. But it seems to us that someone could think this only if she forgets about a whole range of possible cases in which people have and act upon the motives that it is right for them to have.

Consider, for example, the possible world in which there is a mad scientist who will make millions of people miserable if certain individuals don't have malignant motives, but who couldn't care less which acts these individuals perform. In such a world consequentialists will very plausibly suppose that it is right for these individuals to have malignant motives. But does it accord well with our pre-theoretical views about which acts are right and wrong to suppose that their acting on these malignant motives is right in that world? Not at all. If there is an act available to these individuals that produces greater value than that produced by acting on their malignant motives, then it surely accords much better with our pre-theoretical intuitions to suppose that the right act for them to perform in that possible world is the one that produces greater value.

The upshot, in our view, is thus that though consequentialists are right to concern themselves with the intuitive plausibility of their theory, the intuitions that should matter to them are the basic intuitions about what is valuable and what isn't. Those who find themselves reluctant to believe that right acts are those which maximise value should therefore reassess their entire commitment to a consequentialist way of thinking, rather than attempt to redefine rightness in the manner recommended by the first version of local motive consequentialism. Such a redefinition can be given no clear rationale.

SECTION 4: LOCAL MOTIVE CONSEQUENTIALISM: SECOND VERSION

Consider next the version of local motive consequentialism which holds that right acts are those which would have been caused by possession of the right motives, rather than those that are actually so caused. This version of the theory differs from the first version because it explicitly allows that people who do not have the right motives might nonetheless act rightly.

Thus, if we once again imagine that the right set of motives for people to have includes a stronger desire to give a small benefit to their children and a weaker desire to give a large benefit to strangers, then the main difference with the first version of local motive consequentialism is that, according to this second version, those who don't have this pattern of motivation are still able to act rightly just so long as they are able to give their children that smaller benefit. Of course, given that they have a much stronger desire to give a larger benefit to strangers it follows that they could only do so if they were to act out of an even stronger desire to be a decent parent, or to avoid the criticism of other family members, or perhaps by acting on the basis of some psychological malfunction or anomaly. But, whatever the cause of their so acting, so long as they succeed in giving their children that smaller benefit they do at least succeed in acting rightly, according to this second version of local motive consequentialism. The real question facing this version, however, is the same as the question that arose in our discussion of the first version. What is the consequentialist case supposed to be for the claim that someone who acts as if they had the right motives always acts rightly?

Note, to begin, that since the person who acts as if they had the right motives may not actually have the right motives, there need not be the same non-act mediated benefits associated with their action as would have been in place if they did have the right motives. There may be some overlap – pretending to be a friend might have some of the good consequences of being a friend – but this is bound to be only partial and, in any case, highly contingent. There is thus little room on this front for making a consequentialist case for someone's acting as if they had the right motives.

Perhaps the thought is that acting as if you had the right motives will generally produce the right motives; that therein lies the motive consequentialist case for so acting. But this thought is confused. There are three points to be made against it. The first is that acting as if you had the right motives might not bring it about that you have the right motives. Indeed, the right motives might not be motives that you could bring about by any act available to you. Perhaps the only way to have acquired these motives is by having had a different childhood. The second is that if the right act is the act that the right motives would cause, then it is in any case not clear why it is right for anyone to try to bring about the right motives. After all, the act of trying to bring about the right motives is not one that the right motives would cause; the presence of the right motives would make the act of trying to bring about the right motives unnecessary. And the third point is that, among the motives that you could bring about in yourself, the motives that would be brought about by acting as if you had the right motives might be manifestly inferior to some other set of motives that you could have brought about by acting differently. Perhaps the best motives will be brought about by engaging in a course of psychotherapy, something that someone who had the right motives would never do.

If these points are not obvious then that may be because of a tendency to conflate the claim that certain motives are the right ones to have with the quite different claim that certain motives are the right ones *to try* to have: the right ones to try to inculcate or maintain in oneself. In estimating which motives it is best to have we must ignore the costs of inculcating or maintaining them: the evaluand is the *having of the motives*, not the *act* of getting to have them or keep them. However in estimating which motives it is best to try to have or keep we factor in such transition costs: the evaluand is the *act* of getting to have or keep the motives, not just the *having of them*. The distinction is on a par with that to which Dr Johnson drew attention when he remarked that, yes, the Giant's Causeway was worth seeing – but that it was hardly worth going to see.

The only defence of the suggestion left, as far as we can see, is once again that the acts which are deemed to be right, on such a definition of rightness, accord more closely with our pre-theoretical intuitions about which acts are right and which are wrong than do the acts which are deemed to be right if we appeal directly to the consequentialist principle. But, once again, it seems to us that this requires that we forget about a whole range of possible cases in which people have the motives that it is right for them to have.

Consider, once again, the possible world in which there is a mad scientist who will make millions of people miserable if certain individuals don't have malignant motives, but who couldn't care less which acts these individuals perform. The malignant motives are, let's assume, the right motives for them to have in this possible world. Suppose that in this case, however, these individuals do not have these motives. It certainly doesn't accord with our pre-theoretical intuitions to suppose that the right way for them to act in this world is as if they had these malignant motives. Acting as if they had malignant motives will simply add to the disvalue that will be brought into the world by the mad scientist. It is much more plausible to suppose that they act rightly if they maximise value. The right thing for them to do is thus surely to act so as to acquire the malignant motives as quickly as possible, rather than acting as if they already had them.

The upshot, in our view, is thus once again that consequentialists who find themselves reluctant to believe that right acts are those which maximise value should reassess their entire commitment to a consequentialist way of thinking, not simply attempt to redefine rightness in the manner recommended by the second version of local motive consequentialism. For the idea that the right act for someone to perform is that act, of the acts available to them, which they would have performed if they had the right motives, unlike the idea that the right act is that which maximises value, is one which can be given no clear consequentialist rationale.

SECTION 5: LOCAL MOTIVE CONSEQUENTIALISM: THIRD VERSION

Consider finally the version of local motive consequentialism which holds that the right acts are those which would have been caused by the motives that it would be best for someone to try to inculcate. The main objection to this version, as in the last case, is that it is difficult to see what the consequentialist case could be for so acting.

Once again, note that there need not be the same non-act mediated benefits attached to actions that would have been caused by the motives it is best to try to inculcate as attach to actions that actually spring from such motives. The thought must therefore be, as with the second version of local motive consequentialism, that acting as if you had the motives that it would be best for you to try to inculcate will generally produce or sustain those motives; that therein lies the local motive consequentialist case for so acting.

But this thought is once again confused. There are three relevant points. The first is that acting as if you had these motives might not in itself help you to inculcate them. The second is that if the right act is the act that the motives it is best to try to inculcate would cause, then it is not clear why it is right for anyone to try to inculcate them; the presence of the motives it is best to try to inculcate would not cause anyone, unnecessarily, to try to inculcate them. And the third is that the motives that you would inculcate in yourself by so acting might be manifestly inferior to others that you could have inculcated instead.

Nor is it plausible to suppose that this theory delivers a more intuitive conception of right action either. Consider the possible world in which there is a mad scientist who will make millions of people miserable if certain individuals don't have malignant motives in the future, but who couldn't care less which acts they perform now. Let it be agreed that it would therefore be best for them to try to have malignant motives. Yet it is surely quite implausible to suppose that these people act rightly, here and now, if they act as if they had these motives already. Once again, it is far more intuitive to suppose that they act rightly, here and now, if they act so as to maximise value; far more intuitive to suppose that it is right for them here and now to try to acquire the malignant motives, rather than acting as if they already had them.

It is therefore once again difficult to see what the consequentialist justification is supposed to be for performing the act which would have been caused by the motives that it would be best for someone to try to inculcate. The upshot is, again, that those consequentialists who find themselves reluctant to believe that right acts are those which maximise value should reassess their entire commitment to a consequentialist way of thinking rather than simply attempting to redefine rightness in the manner recommended by the third version of local motive consequentialism.

SECTION 6: GENERALISING THE ARGUMENT

We are now in a position to generalise our argument. Local rule consequentialism parallels fairly closely the sort of doctrine we have been describing as local motive consequentialism. Rules may refer to personal policies or to social practices and so local rule consequentialism may direct us to a local consequentialism at the individual or the collective level. But in either case the doctrine may assume any of the three forms described, and in either case it is subject to the same sorts of problems raised with local motive consequentialism.

Clearly, however rules are understood, local rule consequentialism may hold that the right act is that which is caused by having internalised the rules it is best to have internalised; or that the right act is that which would be caused by having internalised the rules it is best for someone to have internalised; or that the right act is that which would be caused by having internalised the rules it is best for someone to try to internalise; or something of the kind. And clearly, so we maintain, familiar problems are going to arise for each of these versions of local rule consequentialism.

The first version has the absurd consequence that those who have not internalised the rules which it is best for them to have internalised cannot act rightly. But it is difficult to see what the consequentialist rationale might be for this claim when, among the acts available to them, some produce better consequences than others. The theory is also vulnerable on another score as well. For no consequentialist rationale can be given for the claim that those who have internalised the right rules always act rightly when their acts are caused by their internalisation of those rules. So long as there really is an alternative act available to an agent which produces more value, it is hard to see what there could be for a consequentialist to regret in the performance of such an act.

The idea that the first version of local rule consequentialism delivers a more intuitive conception of right action than that delivered by a direct evaluation acts in terms of the consequentialist principle is also refuted by a variation on the mad-scientist examples. Imagine a possible world in which there is a mad scientist who will make millions suffer if people don't internalise callous rules of conduct, but who couldn't care less which acts the people perform. Suppose that people all internalise these callous rules. Is it intuitive to suppose that these people act rightly when they act on their internalisation of these callous rules? Not at all. It is far more intuitive to suppose that they act rightly if they maximise value.

The second and third versions give rise to the same difficulty that plagued the second and third versions of local motive consequentialism. The question, again, is what the consequentialist case is supposed to be for redefining rightness in the ways proposed. Acting as if the rules that it is best to internalise or to try to internalise had been internalised will not have the same non-act mediated benefits associated with actually having internalised these rules. And acting in the required fashion cannot be justified on the grounds that it promises to bring about the internalisation of those rules either.

Here, as in the corresponding case with the second and third versions of local motive consequentialism there are three relevant points. The first is that acting as if you had internalised certain rules might not in itself help you to internalise the rules. The second is that if the right act is the act that having internalised certain rules would cause, then it is not clear why it is right for anyone to try to internalise them; the internalisation of those rules would not cause anyone, unnecessarily, to try to internalise them. And the third is that the rules that you would internalise by so acting might be manifestly inferior to others that you could have internalised by acting in some alternative way instead.

The second and third versions of local rule consequentialism cannot plausibly be said to deliver a more intuitive conception of right action either. Variations on the mad-scientist examples once again suggest that, in certain circumstances, it is far more intuitive to suppose that agents acts rightly when they maximise value. Consider the possible world in which there is a mad scientist who will make millions miserable if people haven't internalised callous rules of conduct here and now, and another possible world in which he will do so if they haven't internalised such rules in the future, but who couldn't care less how these people act here and now. Imagine further that people have not internalised the required callous rules of conduct here and now. It is surely quite counter-intuitive to suppose that they act rightly if they act as if they had internalised the callous rules here and now. For that will simply add to the misery that the mad scientist will produce without producing any clear benefit. It is far more intuitive to suppose that they act rightly if they act so as to maximise value; far more intuitive to suppose that the right thing for them to do is to internalise the callous rules, not to act as if they had already internalised them.

The situation is thus just as we said it would be at the outset. The very same pattern of objection that applies to the various versions of local motive conse-quentialism applies, as well, to the various versions of local rule consequentialism. We think that it is therefore reasonable to suppose that a similar pattern of objection would apply to all versions of local consequentialism. We readily admit that this requires an inductive leap, but the inductive leap required is, we think, hardly rationally resistible.

SECTION 7: CONCLUSION

Most philosophers now recognise that it is a mistake to think that right motives, right rules, and so on, are those that would promote right acts; they recognise that local act consequentialism, as we have called it, is unattractive. If the points we have made are sound, however, then they should also admit that it is equally unattractive to warp consequentialism in the manner illustrated by local motive or rule consequentialism. For going local in this latter way – defining right acts by reference to an independent account of right motives, right rules, or whatever – looks like it is always going to involve problems of the kind illustrated. There are many categories of evaluand: acts, sets of motives, sets of rules, as well as sets of such sets, and so on. If consequentialism is a sound strategy of evaluation in any one case, then it is hard to see why it should not represent a sound strategy in every case. Better, therefore, for consequentialists to go global; better for them to go the full monty.[14]

NOTES

1. The intuitive notion of rightness, as applied to acts, is thus just the idea of the act that it is right for someone to perform – as opposed, say, to the act that it is right for someone to forget. In the latter case the evaluand is forgettings, not acts.
2. Derek Parfit, *Reasons and Persons* (Oxford: Clarendon Press, 1984), pp. 24–5.
3. J. J. C. Smart appears to advocate a form of global consequentialism as well when he argues in favour of what he calls 'extreme utilitarianism'. See note 6 below.
4. R. M. Adams, 'Motive Consequentialism', *Journal of Philosophy*, 73 (1976), pp. 467–81.
5. 'An Outline of a System of Utilitarian Ethics', in J. J. C. Smart, and Bernard Williams, *Utilitarianism: For and Against* (Cambridge: Cambridge University Press, 1973), p. 9.
6. Immediately after the passage just quoted Smart of course goes on to argue against rule utilitarianism. Interestingly, in the earlier paper in which Smart argues in favour of a form of global consequentialism he also appears to argue against local consequentialism more generally, though he argues against it under the name 'restricted utilitarianism'. See his 1956 paper 'Extreme and Restricted Utilitarianism', reprinted in Philippa Foot (ed.), *Theories of Ethics* (Oxford: Oxford University Press, 1967).
7. Brad Hooker, *Ideal Code, Real World: A Rule-consequentialist Theory of Morality* (Oxford: Clarendon Press, 2000).
8. Adams, 'Motive Consequentialism', p. 479.
9. Simon Blackburn, *Oxford Dictionary of Philosophy* (Oxford: Oxford University Press, 1994), p. 388.
10. Adams, 'Motive Utilitarianism'; Peter Railton, 'Alienation, Consequentialism, and the Demands of Morality', *Philosophy and Public Affairs*, 13 (1984), pp. 134–71; Parfit, *Reasons and Persons*.
11. E.g., Adams, 'Motive Utilitarianism'.
12. Note that the restrictive form of consequentialism advocated by Pettit and Brennan is consistent with global consequentialism ('Restrictive Consequentialism', *Australasian Journal of Philosophy*, 64 (1986), pp. 438–55). According to restrictive consequentialism, even though the right act is that which maximises value, the right decision-making procedure – the procedure which maximises value – may not be to calculate case by case in an attempt to identify the act that maximises value. Rather, as Pettit and Brennan argue, it might instead be better to restrict one's calculation. 'Restrictive' in the sense of Pettit and Brennan is thus not synonymous with 'restricted' in the sense defined by Smart's 'Extreme and Restricted Utilitarianism'.
13. Fred Feldman, 'World Utilitarianism', in Keith Lehrer (ed.), *Analysis and Metaphysics* (Dordrecht: Reidel, 1975), pp. 255–71.
14. We would like to thank Lloyd Humberstone and Vera Koffman for their helpful remarks on an earlier version of this chapter.

7

Evaluative Focal Points

Shelly Kagan

Foundational consequentialists believe that justification in normative ethics is ultimately a matter of appealing to the goodness or badness of the consequences (in some suitably broad sense of 'consequences').[1] Famously, act consequentialists appeal to the consequences directly in evaluating any given act: an act is right just when the consequences of performing the act would be as good as those of any alternative act available to the agent. In contrast, rule consequentialists do not evaluate acts in this manner, that is, directly in terms of the good. Rather, they evaluate the given act in terms of a set of optimal rules, and it is only the rules that are themselves evaluated directly in terms of the good.

Acts and rules are two examples of what I will call *evaluative focal points* (other examples include motives, norms, character traits, decision procedures, and institutions). Act consequentialists and rule consequentialists share the foundational consequentialist thought that justification must be in terms of the good, but they differ in their choice of which evaluative focal point to make primary. The rule consequentialist makes the *rules* the primary evaluative focal point, evaluating the rules directly in terms of the good; she then evaluates the other focal points indirectly, in terms of the rules: thus, for example, acts are not evaluated directly in terms of the good, but only indirectly, via the rules. In contrast, the act consequentialist – as I will be understanding this position – makes the *act* the primary evaluative focal point, evaluating the act directly in terms of the good: other focal points, such as rules, are evaluated only indirectly. (This last claim is potentially misleading, involving, as it does, a bit of nonstandard stipulation; but we will return to it later.)

Since rule consequentialism evaluates the act in terms of the good only indirectly, rule consequentialism is an example of an 'indirect' consequentialist theory. There are other indirect consequentialist theories as well: thus, motive consequentialism takes motives to be the primary evaluative focal point, selecting the optimal motives directly in terms of the good, and then evaluating acts indirectly, in terms of the optimal motives; while decision procedure consequentialism holds that the primary evaluative focal point is the decision procedure, and evaluates acts indirectly, in terms of the optimal decision procedure; and so on. For simplicity, in the bulk of this paper I will be restricting my attention to act and rule consequentialism. But virtually everything I say carries over *mutatis mutandis* to these other consequentialisms as well.

Rule consequentialism has seemed to many to be open to the charge of 'rule worship'.[2] If the best act, as revealed via a direct appeal to the good, differs in some case from that prescribed by the rules, isn't it irrational to continue to insist on compliance with the rules? What is so special about *rules*? If what is of ultimate importance is good consequences, shouldn't we evaluate acts directly in terms of their consequences? (Similarly, motive consequentialism seems guilty of motive worship, norm consequentialism seems guilty of norm worship, and so on.)

Once we start thinking of all consequentialist theories as facing a choice between focal points, however, this charge seems stripped of some of its force. After all, act consequentialism (at least, as I have characterized it) makes its own choice of a primary evaluative focal point – acts – and evaluates the other focal points in terms of the primary one: the best rules, for example, might be those that direct us to perform the best acts. But this means that act consequentialism could with equal justice be viewed as an indirect consequentialist theory as well: the rules are not evaluated directly in terms of the good, but only indirectly, in terms of the best acts. Act consequentialism is admittedly a direct theory with regard to *acts*, but it is an *indirect* theory as far as the other focal points are concerned.

And having said this, we immediately see that rule consequentialism may indeed be an indirect theory as far as *acts* and other focal points are concerned, but it is a *direct* theory when it comes to rules. The language of direct and indirect consequentialism thus seems loaded in favor of act consequentialism: it is only if we are tacitly assuming that it is acts that somehow 'really' deserve to be the primary evaluative focal point that the standard labels will seem appropriate.

To put the same point another way: if rule consequentialism is guilty of rule worship, then act consequentialism is guilty of act worship. ('If the good is ultimately what it is all about, shouldn't rules be evaluated directly in terms of the good, rather than only indirectly, in terms of acts?')

That the two theories are in structurally similar boats can be seen quite easily if we diagram their structures, like this:

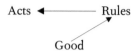

Figure 7.1 Rule consequentialism.

In Figure 7.1 we have a picture of rule consequentialism. I've placed the 'good' at the bottom of the diagram to represent the foundationally consequentialist view that justification in normative ethics is ultimately a matter of appealing to the goodness of the consequences. I've drawn the various evaluative focal points (here, acts and rules) above. The arrow going from the good to rules indicates that in rule consequentialism the rules are evaluated directly in terms of the good; while the arrow going from rules to acts indicates that acts are evaluated in terms of the best *rules*. Thus in rule consequentialism it is only the rules that are evaluated directly in terms of the good, while acts are evaluated only indirectly.

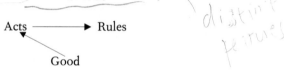

Figure 7.2 Act consequentialism.

In Figure 7.2 we have a picture of act consequentialism. Since it too is a foundationally consequentialist view, the good is again drawn at the bottom of the diagram. But now it is acts (rather than rules) that are evaluated directly in terms of the good, and rules (rather than acts) that are evaluated only indirectly.

Drawn this way, it seems clear that the choice between act and rule consequentialism turns on the question of what reasons there are to select one evaluative focal point over the other to be the primary evaluative focal point. Is there something about either acts or rules that makes them uniquely fit – or unfit – to be the primary evaluative focal point? (Alternatively, we might wonder whether we could somehow avoid elevating *any* focal point to the special status of being primary; this is a possibility I will consider below.)

I want to explore some aspects of this issue in what follows. Although I will be offering a number of arguments, some against rule consequentialism, some against act consequentialism, my primary concern is actually to try to illustrate and partially illuminate this general approach to the topic: I want to advocate thinking of moral theories in terms of the choices between evaluative focal points; and I want to get clearer about the indirect evaluation of secondary focal points in terms of the primary focal point.

Let's begin by focusing on rule consequentialism. The rules are evaluated directly in terms of the good. The optimal rules are those that would produce the most good, the best results overall. But rules – conceived as abstract linguistic items – don't generate results in and of themselves. Rather, they generate results only when they are concretely 'embedded' in some way: they generate results when they are thought about, taught, accepted, disdained, mentioned, mocked, acted upon, flouted, or what have you. So talk of selecting the rules that would have the best results is necessarily shorthand for talk of selecting the rules that would have the best results *if* they were embedded in some specified way. And the rules that are optimal relative to some set of embedding specifications might well not be optimal relative to some other embedding specifications.

Two basic types of specification seem worth thinking about: *ideal* embedding and *realistic* embedding. Ideal embedding is a matter of assuming perfect conformity to the rules. We would then be selecting the rules that would have the best results if they were perfectly conformed to. Here we are assuming that *everyone* conforms perfectly: thus, everyone is *motivated* to conform to the rules, everyone correctly *identifies* the act that is prescribed by the rules, and everyone flawlessly *executes* the identified act. As the name suggests, in assuming full and perfect conformity, ideal embedding makes a highly unrealistic, idealized specification.

Realistic embedding relaxes these assumptions in the direction of more accurately approximating a realistic scenario. It recognizes that for various possible rules, in any given case there may be some number of individuals that would lack the motivation to conform altogether; and some rules might be sufficiently complex or difficult to apply so that cognitive errors might arise in identifying the act that conforms to the rules, or performance errors might arise in executing the identified act. With realistic embedding, then, we do not assume perfect conformity; rather, we assume a more realistic level of conformity, with only imperfect or partial compliance. (Obviously, the rubric of 'realistic embedding' covers a family of distinct embeddings – depending on precisely how far one goes toward making the embedding approximate the current, actual embedding of the rules.[3] But for our purposes there will be no need to have more fine-grained distinctions.)

Among rule consequentialists we find advocates of both types of embeddings. And the choice here clearly matters, since the rules that would have best results if perfectly conformed to will quite likely differ from those that would have best results if we assume a more realistic level of conformity.

Now under rule consequentialism, *acts* are evaluated in terms of the optimal rules. But a further choice faces us when we specify how, exactly, the best or right act is to be identified. One familiar possibility is that the right act is the act that *conforms* to the optimal rules. Another way to view this is to see the right act as the act that would be performed if the optimal rules were ideally embedded, that is, under conditions of perfect conformity.

Given our previous distinction, however, this raises the possibility of a second way of identifying the right act: it is the act that would be performed if the optimal rules were realistically embedded. On this second approach, the right act is not necessarily the act that conforms to the rules, it is rather the act that *actually follows*, given a realistic embedding of the rules.

This second approach is less familiar in the context of rule consequentialism. But there are other moral theories where it is just this approach that seems to be accepted. For example, advocates of motive consequentialism often define the right act as the act that would in fact be performed by someone with the optimal set of motives. (Compare the theory that defines the right act as the act that would in fact be performed by the virtuous individual.) Here, the right act is not defined as the act that 'conforms' to the optimal motives; rather, it is the act that would actually be produced – the causal upshot – if one had the optimal motives.

Or consider one possible version of act consequentialism, which might hold that the best rules are those that would actually produce the best acts. (Under realistic embedding, these need not be the rules that simply direct the agent to perform the best acts.) Here, we are evaluating a secondary focal point (rules) that is causally 'further upstream' than the primary one (acts), and the suggestion is that the best rules are those which would, under realistic conditions, produce the best acts. But if the relation 'the Xs that would realistically produce the best Ys' can be used in evaluation going 'upstream' then it seems that the inverse relation – 'the Ys that would realistically be produced by the best Xs' – could be used when evaluating a secondary focal point that is causally 'downstream' of the primary focal point. It is just this, I have suggested, that is often done by motive consequentialism (and virtue consequentialism), and I see no reason why the same possibility should not be open to the rule consequentialist.

So when it comes to defining the right act in terms of the best rules, there are two possibilities: the right act is the act that *conforms* to the rules, or the right act is the act that would be the *upshot* of the rules (if realistically embedded). (Again, the act that would be the upshot under the assumption of ideal embedding would be the same as the act that conforms to the rules; so hereafter when I talk of the 'upshot' I mean upshot with realistic embedding.)

If there are two basic ways to specify the optimal rules, and two ways to identify the best act in terms of those rules, we have four basic versions of rule consequentialism. The right act is the act that:

1. *conforms* to *realistic* rules; [ideal/realistic]
2. is the *upshot* of *realistic* rules; [realistic/realistic]
3. *conforms* to *ideal* rules; [ideal/ideal]
4. is the *upshot* of *ideal* rules. [realistic/ideal]

What can be said for or against these various versions of rule consequentialism?

Consider, first, the version that defines the right act as the act that conforms to the realistic rules. I think such a theory is implausible. Indeed, I think there is an inherent implausibility in defining the right act in this way. To see this, it helps to notice an easily overlooked fact about how the optimal realistic rules may come to be optimal.

First, a complication. As I have already noted, until they are embedded, rules have – in and of themselves – no results at all, with which to be evaluated from a consequentialist perspective. However, once embedded, a variety of factors can affect the consequentialist 'score' that a rule (or a set of rules) receives. For example, once embedded, rules can have an impact on results that is independent of their impact on *acts*: it might be, say, that merely thinking about a set of rules reassures people, and so contributes to happiness. But for simplicity let us put aside such factors, and focus only on the impact that rules have by virtue of their effect on how we act.

Now when thinking about how it is that the optimal rules come to have the (relatively) high scores that they do, we are apt to focus on only one type of case – cases where as a result of the rules being embedded agents perform acts that conform to the rules, and those acts promote the overall good. But there is a second kind of case that may be relevant as well – cases of nonconformity.

The possibility of nonconformity obviously cannot be dismissed. Given realistic embedding, failures of motivation, identification, or execution can lead to imperfect conformity with any given rule. Given realistic embedding, even the optimal rules may sometimes yield acts of nonconformity. (To be sure, it is *possible* that the best rules would in fact have perfect compliance, but whether this is so is an open empirical question.)

No one is going to deny the possibility of nonconformity. But in thinking about nonconforming acts, we are typically inclined to assume that such acts will *lower* the score of the given rule: failure to conform to the rule will lead to worse results overall, and if the given rules are indeed optimal this is *despite* the 'losses' due to nonconforming acts. In fact, however, not all nonconforming acts need work to the detriment of the rules in this way: the fact that a rule produces a nonconforming act (when realistically embedded) can serve to *raise* the score of the rule. (One way this could happen is this: the rules are 'built' or 'designed' to take into account and match our various shortcomings – motivational, cognitive, and so on – so that we will end up violating them in just the ways that are actually preferable.)

Consider, then, the possibility of the following type of nonconformity case: under realistic embedding the agent would fail to conform to the rule, and this act of nonconformity actually produces *better* results than would be produced by an act conforming to the rule. (We might even throw in – for good measure – the possibility that it is the nonconforming act that strikes us intuitively as the right act to perform in this case.)

Such cases could play a significant role in helping to make it be the case that the optimal rules are indeed the rules with the best results under realistic embedding. In such cases of *desirable nonconformity*, part of the *virtue* of the rule from the perspective of rule consequentialism – part of the reason it gets a high score – will be the very fact that in cases of this sort, promulgation of the rules will produce *nonconformity* to those very rules. In short, one factor that might make a set of rules the optimal rules might be the very fact that in certain cases people will *violate* those rules, where this might be preferable both intuitively and in terms of promoting the good.

It is because of the possibility of such cases that it seems to me implausible to define the right act as the act that conforms to the optimal realistic rules. As just noted, the optimal rules might be optimal in part – indeed, perhaps in considerable part – because in certain cases they will be violated. In such cases, we *selected* the rules because of the fact that they would be violated. The acts of nonconformity are exactly what we are trying to produce – both intuitively and foundationally (that is, in terms of good results). In such cases it strikes me as simply bizarre to call the desired act *wrong*.

That is, it seems bizarre to insist that the right act, the morally preferable act, is the act that *conforms* to the rules – even though the optimal rules are optimal here by virtue of the very fact that they are going to be violated. It is, of course, an empirical question just how often such cases of desirable nonconformity arise for the optimal rules, and just how significant such cases are in determining the overall 'score' of the optimal rules; indeed it is a logical possibility that for the optimal rules such cases never actually arise at all. But to my mind this doesn't dampen the force of the criticism: if we are looking for the rules that would have the best results if realistically embedded, the possibility of such cases of desirable nonconformity is a live empirical one, and it simply seems bizarre to insist that the right act is the act that conforms to the rules – even when the rules may have been selected and designed in part so as to produce nonconforming acts, and it is one of these desirable nonconforming acts that we are evaluating.

In this light, the second version of rule consequentialism may seem more attractive. Here the right act is the act that would be the actual causal upshot of the optimal rules, where these rules are chosen relative to a realistic embedding. In cases of desirable nonconformity, where the agent violates the rules in a way that is both intuitively attractive and promotes the overall good, we will be able to classify the nonconforming act as the *right* act – since it will be the act that will actually be produced given the realistic embedding of the rules. (There is a natural harmony here between the embedding used to select the rules and the embedding used to evaluate the acts: we assume realistic embedding to evaluate the rules, and then continue with realistic embedding to evaluate the acts. In contrast, the first version of rule consequentialism gets into trouble by demanding perfect conformity to rules that were selected on the basis of their value under conditions of imperfect conformity.)

Unfortunately, this second version of rule consequentialism seems implausible in the face of the possibility of cases of *undesirable nonconformity*. What I have in mind are cases where the rules are violated, but the violation seem unattractive and unfortunate from the foundational consequentialist perspective – since the non-conforming act here fails to promote the good. (Once more, for good measure, we can throw in a reference to our intuitive judgment as well – this time the judgment that the nonconforming act is not the right act.) We would eliminate such acts of nonconformity if only we could. As it happens, we cannot realistically do so; and so such cases may be the inevitable undesirable fallout of our various shortcomings. Here the optimal rules are selected so as to minimize such acts of morally undesirable nonconformity. But to the extent that an ineliminable residue of such acts remains, it seems bizarre to assert that these acts are in fact the *right* acts to perform in the circumstances. Yet this is just what we must say if we define the right act as the act that would in fact be performed – the causal upshot – if the optimal rules were realistically embedded. So I take it that this second version of rule consequentialism should be rejected as well.

In short, if the rules are selected realistically, neither version of rule consequentialism is plausible. Realistic rules cannot provide a plausible standard for right acts.

(I believe that these results can be generalized, and would hold for other indirect consequentialist theories – theories that select some other focal point as primary, and evaluate acts in terms of the primary focal point – given that the primary focal point is selected on a realistic basis: if we define the right act as that which conforms to the optimal focal point, we overlook the possibility of morally desirable nonconformity; if we define the right act as that which would be the actual upshot of the optimal focal point, we overlook the possibility of undesirable nonconformity. Thus, realistically selected focal points cannot provide a plausible standard for right acts.)

What of our third and fourth versions of rule consequentialism, which evaluate acts in terms of *ideal* rules (that is, the rules that would have the best results if ideally conformed to)? The fourth version defines the right act as the act that would be the actual upshot of realistically embedding the ideal rules. The difficulty here is the same as that facing the second version, namely, cases of undesirable nonconformity. If we *realistically* embed the ideal rules, and ask what acts will actually be performed given this embedding, we have to face the possibility that the ideal rules will not themselves be perfectly conformed to, and some of these violations may well be *undesirable* – both intuitively and foundationally. It seems unacceptably bizarre to insist that such acts are right nonetheless. If anything, the objection seems even stronger here: the ideal rules were selected because of the results that they would have under conditions of perfect conformity; it would be bizarre to suggest that a *nonconforming* act that is intuitively unacceptable and that leads to bad results should, for all that, be classified as the right act to perform.

(Generalizing: indirect theories that define the right act as the realistic upshot of the optimal version of the primary evaluative focal point cannot provide a plausible standard for right acts – regardless of whether the primary evaluative focal point is selected on an ideal or a realistic basis.)

This leaves only the third version of rule consequentialism – where the right act is defined as the act that conforms to the ideal rules. Since the fourth version faced the same problem as the second – cases of undesirable nonconformity – we might well wonder whether the third will face the same problem as the first, that is, cases of desirable nonconformity. Do these also plague our final version of rule consequentialism? I believe so, although the problem does not arise in precisely the same way that it did for the first version of rule consequentialism. With the first version, we were dealing with realistic rules; that is, rules selected for the results they would have under realistic embedding: this opened the possibility that the optimal rules might be optimal in part because of situations in which they would be violated. But with our final version of rule consequentialism we are dealing with ideal rules; that is, rules selected for the results they would have under conditions of perfect conformity. Here it cannot be that the optimal rules are optimal in part because they would be violated, since we are selecting the optimal rules under the assumption that they will *not* be violated.

But for all that, I think there remains the possibility of cases where conformity to the optimal ideal rules is morally unattractive (from both a foundational and an intuitive point of view). If even the *ideal* rules can face cases where it is *nonconformity* that is desirable, then defining the right act to be the one that conforms to these rules – even in cases of this kind – seems problematic. Once more, to my mind at least, it seems bizarre to suggest that the right act, the morally preferable act, would be one that conforms to the rules, even though violating the rules would be better both intuitively and in terms of promoting the good.

However, this objection may seem less compelling than the earlier objections. Note that in all of the previous objections the use of realistic embedding – either at the level of selecting the rules, or at the level of evaluating the acts – introduced imperfect compliance, which in turn left cases of undesirable nonconformity and desirable nonconformity as live *empirical* possibilities. Even if the problem cases did not in fact arise for the optimal rules, this was mere 'luck' from the conceptual standpoint. They couldn't be ruled out, yet they led to unacceptably bizarre evaluative claims.

But when it comes to the current objection, it is far from obvious whether the possibility of desirable nonconformity is anything more than a verbally describable cubbyhole. Since our final version of rule consequentialism appeals to ideal conformity to ideal rules, unsettled empirical possibilities don't seem to arise. Given that the optimal ideal rules are those that have the best results when conformed to, can't we rule out a priori the possibility of desirable nonconformity? If so, then the rule consequentialist could admit that such cases – were they genuinely possible – would be problematic; but since they are not genuinely possible, they raise no serious difficulty.

To see whether cases of desirable nonconformity *can* be ruled out, we first need to consider the familiar question of whether rule consequentialism 'collapses' into act consequentialism.

It seems reasonably clear that for versions of rule consequentialism that appeal to realistic rules, the answer will be no. Given realistic embedding, it is not likely that the optimal rule will be a statement of act consequentialism, or some set of rules extensionally equivalent to it.

But what if we are dealing with *ideal* rule consequentialism? Here there is a plausible argument that suggests that the optimal rules *will* be extensionally equivalent to act consequentialism. Roughly, the idea is that if the purportedly optimal rules ever prescribed a nonoptimal act there would be some revised version of the rules that differed only in prescribing the optimal act; since the revised rules would have better results if conformed to, *they* would be the optimal rules (given the assumption of ideal embedding).

It seems to me, however, that this plausible argument is mistaken. Ideal rules are selected for the results they would have given ideal embedding – that is, within a world of ideal and full compliance. In such a full compliance world the directives of the optimal ideal rules will indeed never diverge from act consequentialism.[4] But will the optimal ideal rules contain clauses governing *imperfect* compliance worlds? It is far from obvious that there *will* be such clauses. After all, they would do no work under the assumption of ideal embedding – so why would they be added?

Of course, they will do no harm if added, since under the assumption of perfect compliance, clauses governing imperfect compliance will never be operative. So perhaps such clauses can be added after all. But since clauses governing imperfect compliance worlds will remain inoperative under the full compliance assumption, the perspective of a perfect compliance world offers no grounds for choosing between the alternative possible partial compliance clauses. Perhaps clauses will be added that are stupid and unattractive (whether intuitively, or foundationally). The full compliance world offers no *basis* for selecting plausible or attractive partial compliance rules.[5]

Perhaps this is too quick. Perhaps it will reassure the people in the full compliance world to have rules governing partial compliance situations. Yet why do these people need reassurance? Don't they realize that they are in a perfect compliance situation? (If not, then the rules that would be best for *their* world may need altering in light of that fact; and this moves us to a version of realistic embedding, with all its attending problems.) And at any rate, who says that the partial compliance rules that would be best suited for reassuring people (when inoperative, as under full compliance) would be best (intuitively, or foundationally) for governing *actual* situations of partial compliance? In short, there is no particular reason to think there *will* be rules governing partial compliance; and if there are any, there is no good reason to think that they will be attractive ones. If they are, this is really just a matter of luck.[6] The standpoint of perfect compliance is a poor choice for evaluating rules governing more realistic levels of conformity.

Since *act* consequentialism does entail directives governing partial compliance, directives that are at the very least attractive from the foundational perspective, the argument that rule consequentialism collapses into act consequentialism seems to me unsuccessful. But in the course of diagnosing where the argument fails I think we have established that cases of desirable nonconformity are indeed a live and pressing possibility. Since the ideal rules are those that would be optimal given perfect conformity, there is every reason to worry that the optimal ideal rules would sometimes offer no advice, or disastrous advice, in situations of partial compliance. In the light of this possibility, it seems implausible to *define* the right act as the act that conforms to the optimal ideal rules. (If no clauses explicitly govern partial compliance it will be just luck if applying the full compliance rules doesn't lead to unattractive results; if there are partial compliance rules, it will be just luck if they are attractive ones.)

This is an abstract and general statement of the 'disaster' objection to rule consequentialism: either there are no disaster clauses, or there is no good reason to think that there will be plausible disaster clauses. Of course *realistic* versions of rule consequentialism can easily answer this objection.[7] But – as we have seen – they face their own problems.

I conclude that rule consequentialism is an inherently implausible type of theory – in all four versions. Whether we appeal to ideal or to realistic rules, and whether we define the right act in terms of conformity to the rules or as the causal upshot of the rules, rule consequentialism cannot provide a plausible standard for evaluating right acts.[8]

Does this mean that we should become act consequentialists? No – for act consequentialism (at least, as I have characterized it) is itself an implausible view.

Here I can be somewhat more brief. Recall that act consequentialists evaluate acts directly, but rules only indirectly. Yet just as rule consequentialists cannot provide a plausible standard for evaluating the best acts in terms of the best rules, act consequentialists cannot provide a plausible standard for evaluating the best rules in terms of the best acts.

First, as to the evaluation of acts. Considered as abstract entities, act-types (like rules) cannot have results in and of themselves: they need an embedding. But any given act token will obviously come with a 'natural' embedding – the actual one – and so for simplicity I am going to restrict our attention here to versions of act consequentialism that evaluate acts in terms of this actual embedding. So the right act, or the best act, is the one that will in fact lead to the best results. (Other possible embeddings include the 'subjective' embedding – that is, a world in which the agent's beliefs are true – as well as other more exotic or idealized embeddings.)

Next, with regard to the evaluation of *rules*, the two most significant choices are the inverses of the two relations we have already discussed: conformity and upshot. Just as we can look for the act that conforms to a given rule, so we can look for the rule that enjoins or prescribes a given act. And just as we can look for the act that is the actual upshot of a given rule, so we can look for the rule that would actually produce the given act. Thus we have two versions of act consequentialism: the first says that the best rules are those that prescribe the right acts; the second says that the best rules are those that produce the right acts (given realistic embedding). (The first version is equivalent to one that says that the best rules are those that would produce the right acts given *ideal* embedding.)

Let's begin with the first view, according to which the best rules are those that prescribe the right acts. On this view, it should be noted, rules are not to be evaluated with an eye to their success in actually leading us to perform right acts. Indeed, questions about the actual causal upshot of the rules are simply irrelevant. Rather, the best rules are simply those that best enjoin or prescribe the right acts. Is this a plausible basis for evaluating rules?

I think not. To see this, consider the following rule: 'Do the right thing.' In terms of what this rule *says*, it is impeccable. If all agents were to conform to it perfectly, they would perform all the right acts.[9] The rule is completely correct in what it tells us to do, and it gives us correct advice in every conceivable situation. Thus, according to the version of act consequentialism we are currently considering, this rule is perfect; it is the best possible rule.

It is possible, I suppose, that there may be other rules (other than mere notational variants of this first one) that would be ranked just as highly in terms of prescribing all and only the right acts. Luckily, we need not pursue this question, for the point remains that as far as this first version of act consequentialism is concerned, the rule that tells us to do the right thing is *perfect*. It cannot conceivably be improved upon;

it is flawless. It is important to be clear on this point. This first version of act consequentialism holds that rules are to be evaluated solely in terms of the extent to which they enjoin right acts. The best rule, therefore, must be the one that enjoins us to perform all and only right acts. Thus, according to this version of act consequentialism, the simple rule 'Do the right thing' is as good a rule as one could possibly hope for: it is indeed perfect.

But this is an absurd view. Although the advice given by the rule is certainly correct, the rule is virtually useless if it is not supplemented by further rules, rules that help us to identify the right acts. In the eyes of the current version of act consequentialism, however, there is simply no need for such supplementation. Concerns about our *actual* ability to correctly identify right acts are simply beside the point, for in evaluating rules we are, in effect, entitled to assume perfect conformity. That is, in evaluating the rules, we are to assume a perfect ability to identify the acts enjoined by the rules. Thus the *only* relevant question is what rules enjoin the right acts. According to this first version of act consequentialism, then, the rule that tells us to do the right thing is complete in itself, perfect for every situation, every choice, every circumstance.

But this is, as I say, absurd. In evaluating rules we need to at least have open the *possibility* of taking into account our ability to use the rules correctly. No doubt, there may be some purposes for which it is indeed appropriate to assume an ideal ability to identify the particular acts enjoined by a given rule. But for many other purposes, obviously, we will want to make more realistic assumptions about our ability to use the particular act-identifying information provided by the rule. That is, in at least some cases we will want rules that can give us more substantive, concrete, realistically *usable* guidance. But this is a consideration that our first version of act consequentialism is necessarily oblivious to. I conclude, accordingly, that this first version of act consequentialism provides an inadequate basis for evaluating rules.

This suggests, however, that our second version of act consequentialism may be considerably more attractive. Here, we do not simply assume perfect conformity in evaluating the rules. Rather, we assume realistic embedding, and ask what the *actual* upshot of the rules would be. When rules are evaluated in this way, obviously enough, it will hardly be irrelevant to ask to what extent people are actually able to identify the specific acts enjoined by the rules. On this view, in effect, rules are not to be evaluated in terms of what they *tell* us to do, but rather in terms of how *successful* they would be in actually getting us to perform right acts.

According to this second version of act consequentialism, then, rules are evaluated in terms of their ability to actually produce right acts, given realistic embedding. In this way, the second version of act consequentialism escapes the objection that I have just raised against the first. It is important to remind ourselves, however, that this view is still a version of act consequentialism. It is only *acts* that are evaluated directly in terms of the good. Rules are evaluated only indirectly, in terms of their success in producing right acts. According to this second version of act consequentialism, then, the best rule is the one that would actually be *most* successful in producing right acts.

I imagine, however, that anyone who shares the foundational consequentialist thought will think that this concern with *right* acts per se is misplaced. What matters is not whether the right act is performed – what matters is whether the *good* is promoted.

Now this may seem a misplaced criticism. Since (from the perspective of act consequentialism) the right acts *are* the acts that promote the good, the way to promote the good *is* to perform right acts; and so evaluating the rules *in terms of* the right acts can hardly be misguided.

But the distinction is worth maintaining for all that, in light of the fact that under certain circumstances certain *kinds* of acts might be right more often than any other readily identifiable kinds, and yet performing acts of those kinds might do rather little good (as compared to alternatives). In such cases, concern for the *rightness* of the acts per se seems misguided. Accordingly, selecting *rules* on the basis of their success at actually causing us to perform right acts should strike us as misguided as well.

Here is a schematic case to bring out the point. Suppose that I must choose between two acts, A and B, but I cannot tell which of two scenarios I am in. Under the first scenario, if I perform act A, results improve by 1 unit; if I perform act B, there is neither improvement nor loss. Under the second scenario, if I perform A, disaster strikes and results deteriorate by one million units; while if I perform B, there is, again, neither gain nor loss. Finally, suppose that I must play ten times before learning the results of any one round, and I know that in exactly one round (but I can't tell which) I will be in the second scenario (see Table 7.1).[10]

Table 7.1 Schematic case representing acts A and B.

	Act A	Act B
Scenario 1	+1	0
Scenario 2	-1,000,000	0

What rule would be best for dealing with such a case? According to act consequentialism, rules are to be evaluated in terms of the best or right acts. And in particular, according to the version of act consequentialism we are currently examining, the best rule will be the one that is *most* successful in terms of actually causing us to perform right acts.

But what rule will this be? Recall that nine times out of ten I will be in the first scenario, and in this scenario the right act – the act with the best results – is act A. Perhaps, then, the best rule will simply tell me to pick A. Admittedly, when I am in the second scenario the right act is act B. But it is important to keep in mind that this second scenario arises only once every ten rounds. Thus A is the right act to perform *far* more often than B. Apparently, then, from the standpoint of our current version of act consequentialism the best rule will direct me to always choose A. Such a rule would result in my doing the right act nine times out of ten, and so do better in this regard than any other available rule.

This last claim might be disputed. After all, a rule that tells me to always pick A will only result in my doing the right act *nine* times out of ten, rather than all ten times. It will go wrong in the single case where it is B that is actually the right act (rather than A). Wouldn't the best rule be one that directs me to the right act in *all* cases?

But what would such a rule look like? What would it say? We can, of course, imagine rules that tell me to pick A, except when B would have better results, or to pick A, except when I am in the second scenario. But the trouble with such rules, obviously enough, is that I simply cannot tell when I am in the second scenario, so cannot tell when B would have better results. Given the stipulation that I have absolutely no way to tell when I am in the second scenario, rules of this sort will be of no particular use in helping me to perform the right act in all ten cases. Indeed, if a rule like this did ever lead me to pick B rather than A, the most likely result is that I would simply end up performing *fewer* right acts (I am nine times as likely to make a mistake, if I pick B, as I am to get it right).

Provided, then, that we are looking for the rule that would be most successful – given realistic embedding – in leading us to perform right acts, it seems that we must conclude that the *best* rule would simply direct me to always pick act A. This, I take it, is what our current version of act consequentialism must claim.

But this is absurd. It is absurd to suggest that the *best* rule tells me to always pick A, since following such a rule is guaranteed to lead to *disaster* (a net loss of 999,991 units). Admittedly, this rule does direct me to the right act more often than not, but it is obviously a complete failure with regard to the promotion of the overall good. In contrast, a rule that directed me instead to always pick B would be a very poor guide to right acts, getting it wrong nine times out of ten. Yet this would clearly be a preferable rule, since following this rule would lead to dramatically better results.

More abstractly put, the point is this: since we cannot always identify the right act, the rule that does best in this regard may be optimal by virtue of directing us to the right act in the 'unimportant' cases, and so do quite poorly in terms of promoting good results. But it is, accordingly, absurd to suggest that such a rule is indeed the best rule. Yet this is just what the current version of act consequentialism does, in so far as it evaluates the rules in terms of the best acts, rather than directly in terms of the good. In short, this version of act consequentialism does not provide a plausible standard for evaluating rules.

A natural objection to this argument suggests itself. I have assumed that when the act consequentialist asks which rule is best at promoting right acts, all right acts are to be counted *equally*. Thus, the relevant question is simply which rule actually produces the *most* right acts. It is only if this is the appropriate standard for evaluating acts that the act consequentialist must claim – unacceptably – that the rule directing me to always pick A is the best rule.

Perhaps, however, this is not quite the relevant standard. Perhaps we should look for the rule that does best in terms of producing right acts – but only when those acts are *weighted* with an eye to their *significance*. Thus, on the one hand, if a given right act would produce very little good (or avoid very little bad), it should only count slightly in favor of a given rule that it would actually cause us to perform that act. On the other hand, if a rule would cause us to perform a right act that would produce a great deal of good (or avoid a great deal of bad), this should count rather heavily in favor of the rule in question.

If the act consequentialist adopts this revised standard for evaluating rules, then he will no longer claim that the best rule will direct me to always pick A. Admittedly, such a rule will lead me to perform right acts in nine cases out of ten, but these will be – as we have already noted – unimportant cases, and so will count only slightly in favor of the rule; meanwhile, the fact that it will keep me from performing B (even in the case where this is the right thing to do) will count quite heavily against this rule. In contrast, a rule which directs me to always pick B will do much better: although it will cause me to perform *fewer* right acts, when the significance of these acts is factored in this rule will emerge as clearly preferable.

Apparently, then, act consequentialism *can* provide a plausible standard for evaluating rules in terms of producing right acts, provided that we remember to weigh the importance of the right acts with an eye to how much good they produce.

I believe, however, that to do this is tantamount to abandoning act consequentialism. For to embrace this alternative standard is simply to claim that rules should be evaluated *directly* in terms of the goodness of their consequences. And this is to abandon the distinctive claim of the act consequentialist – that it is only acts that are to be evaluated directly in terms of the good, and that rules are to be evaluated only indirectly, in terms of the best acts. Under the proposed revised standard, after all, the fact that a given rule produces *right* acts does no real work whatsoever. The rule is evaluated, rather, simply in terms of the goodness of its results.

This is not to say, of course, that it is implausible to evaluate rules directly in terms of the goodness of their results. It is simply to take seriously the idea that act consequentialists (as I have characterized them) do *not* evaluate rules directly, but only indirectly – only in terms of their connection to right acts. Thus, the revised standard does not represent a genuine version of act consequentialism at all; it is merely masquerading as one.

Apparently, then, the act consequentialist must stick to the original standard, and claim that the best rule is the one that produces the most right acts. This is, of course, an implausible standard for evaluating rules, but it is exactly what emerges from the act consequentialist's insistence that rules are to be evaluated only indirectly – in terms of the best acts. It is for this reason that I conclude that even the second version of act consequentialism does not provide a plausible standard for evaluating rules. And since I have already argued against the first version of act consequentialism, I conclude as well that neither version provides a plausible standard for evaluating rules.

(Generalizing: act consequentialism may provide an inadequate basis for evaluating other focal points as well. An ideal approach runs the danger that the secondary focal point may be unhelpfully specified simply in terms of the very phrase 'right acts', while a realistic approach may end up giving too much weight to right acts that are altogether unimportant.)

Let's review. Rule consequentialism was implausible in its attempts to evaluate acts indirectly – via a distinct focal point – rather than directly in terms of the good. Act consequentialism is itself implausible in its attempts to evaluate *rules* indirectly – via a distinct focal point – rather than directly in terms of the good. The conclusion to draw, I think, is this: if there is a plausible version of consequentialism, it will evaluate *both* focal points – acts *and* rules – directly. Neither focal point will be elevated to the status of primary evaluative focal point; neither focal point will be evaluated only indirectly. A theory that is direct with regard to *all* the focal points might be usefully labelled *everywhere direct* (in contrast to the earlier theories that are direct only with regard to a primary focal point). But for simplicity, let us just call such theories *direct* – reserving the label for this extreme case. My suggestion, then, is that consequentialists should be direct consequentialists.

I can now happily admit that many who have called themselves 'act consequentialists' have actually been direct consequentialists all along, rather than being act consequentialists in my technical sense of that term. Many others, I suspect, have failed to distinguish between direct and act consequentialism, and so may not have had a determinate position in mind at all. (Note, in this regard, that in so far as many who call themselves act consequentialists are simply wed to a standard for right acts – the right act being the act that best promotes the good – this position underdetermines the choice between what I have called act consequentialism and direct consequentialism.) But at any rate, my concern is not to criticize the real or imagined confusions of other self-designated act consequentialists; it is only to make clear that direct consequentialism is indeed a distinct theory from act consequentialism (in *my* sense of the term), and it is the former, not the latter, which consequentialists should embrace.

It is easy enough to illustrate the structure of direct consequentialism (see Figure 7.3):

Figure 7.3 Direct consequentialism (with acts and rules as focal points).

And once this is done it is obvious that this theory does indeed differ from act consequentialism (see Figure 7.4).

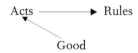

Figure 7.4 Act consequentialism.

Still, it is not at all obvious that direct consequentialism does not fall prey to difficulties of its own, difficulties that will be recognized as problematic even from the perspective of foundational consequentialism. I lack the space to do even a cursory job of addressing potential objections, but let me quickly clear up two points.

First of all, I have restricted our discussion to two focal points: acts and rules. But as I have already suggested, there are many other evaluative focal points that have been endorsed as *primary* focal points – such as motives, norms, institutions, and decision procedures. As I see it, the most plausible version of consequentialism will indeed be direct with regard to *all* of these. In fact, once we free ourselves from the thought that the evaluative focal points must be at least prima facie plausible candidates for the office of *primary* focal point, we realize that absolutely every kind of thing is a potential evaluative focal point (atoms, the weather, sewer systems, suns). So I believe that the most plausible version of consequentialism will be direct with regard to everything. Thus a more accurate illustration of the structure of direct consequentialism would actually look a lot like the sun (see Figure 7.5).

Figure 7.5 Direct consequentialism (with multiple focal points).

But then, second, what are we to say in cases of conflict? If the best rules direct us to different acts from the best motives, which in turn direct us to different acts from the best norms, and so on, what are we to do? Despite the appearance of difficulty, however, this question wears its answer on its own sleeve. If the question is what are we to *do* in the face of such conflicts, then the question is one about *acts*, and we already know the standard by which acts are to be evaluated: directly in terms of the good. Sometimes this means that the right thing to do will be to instill the best motive, and sometimes it will mean that the right thing to do is to promulgate some rule; sometimes we will have to choose between the two, and sometimes we will have to neglect both of them, for there will be something more pressing to attend to. But even if rightfully neglected, the best rule (say) is still the best rule for all that. So long as we remain clear about what *exactly* we are evaluating, the difficulty disappears.

I said at the outset that although I would be offering arguments against both rule consequentialism and act consequentialism, my primary concern was actually to try to illustrate the potential usefulness of thinking about moral theories in terms of their choices with regard to evaluative focal points. In the interests of this more methodological goal, let me make a few more general observations.

As I have already suggested, although only in passing, I believe that many of the arguments I have offered can generalize. Sometimes, perhaps, an issue turns on the specific nature of the focal point in question. But often it does not: I believe, for example, that the arguments I offered against rule consequentialism can be generalized to cover other versions of indirect consequentialism, versions that select some focal point other than rules to be primary.

But sometimes the arguments can be generalized even further. Little essential use was made in my arguments of the fact that we were working with foundational consequentialism. It seems to me that many of the arguments could have been stated in completely abstract terms ('if the given focal point is preferable from the standpoint of the given foundational theory . . .'). It would be helpful to know which of the arguments can be generalized in which ways. At the very least, this would save us the trouble of reinventing the wheel as we move from theory to theory. In short, I believe that evaluative focal points deserve study in their own right.[11]

Here is a quick final nod in that direction. As we have already seen, if we restrict our attention to two focal points, there are three basic types of theories available: two indirect and one direct. Here are the schematic diagrams (see Figure 7.6), abstracting away from the particular choice of foundational theory ('F') as well as the particular identities of the two focal points ('FP_1' and 'FP_2').

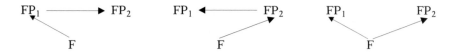

Figure 7.6 Possible theories with two focal points.

Obviously enough, if we introduce a greater number of focal points, the number of possibilities dramatically increases. Here are diagrams of some *sixteen* possible theories that arise once we have a mere *three* focal points (see Figure 7.7, overleaf).

Even here I have not given all the possibilities, since I have made the simplifying assumption that a given focal point is never evaluated on the basis of two other points; and both here and in the two focal point cases discussed above I have assumed that a focal point is never evaluated both directly *and* on the basis of another focal point.

Speaking personally, I have found it helpful to think about moral theories in terms of these structures.[12] I think it would be illuminating to see what kinds of structures are compatible with what types of moral foundations. It would be illuminating to see whether (and, if so, how) different foundational theories make different structures plausible, or whether – as I suspect, but certainly cannot prove – for any plausible foundational theory, the most plausible version of that theory will be a *direct* one.

I leave you, then, with three thoughts. First, if you share the belief in foundational consequentialism, you should be a direct consequentialist. Second, even if you prefer alternative moral foundations, you would still do well to consider seriously the merits of direct versions of those views. And finally, all of us – whether consequentialists or not – could profit from the study of evaluative focal points. This study I heartily commend to you.

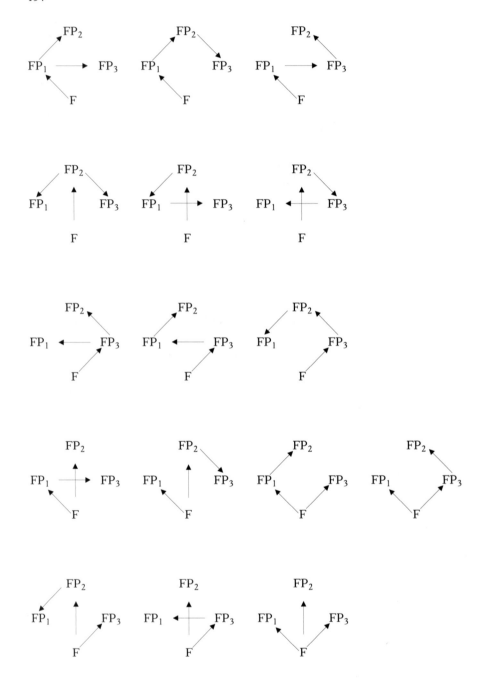

Figure 7.7   Possible theories with three focal points.

NOTES

1. I think we should distinguish between foundational consequentialism and *factoral* consequentialism – the view that consequences are the only factor relevant to determining the moral status of a given act. (I discuss this distinction in 'The Structure of Normative Ethics', *Philosophical Perspectives*, 6 (1992), pp. 223–42, and in *Normative Ethics* (Boulder, CO: Westview, 1998).) Rule consequentialists, for example, are typically only consequentialists at the foundational level, not at the factoral level. Act consequentialists, on the other hand, are typically factoral consequentialists as well (and I will assume so here; but see *Normative Ethics*, pp. 212–23, for discussion of this point).

2. The phrase, I believe, goes back to J. J. C. Smart.

3. At the limit, all rules have the same results under *completely* realistic embedding. Since that is the embedding that they all currently actually have, all rules have the same results – the actual results.

4. For a clear statement of the proof, see Donald Regan, *Utilitarianism and Cooperation* (Oxford: Clarendon Press, 1980). For simplicity, I've neglected the possibility that the rules might diverge from consequentialism by merely permitting rather than requiring the optimal act.

5. For a fuller discussion of this point, see *Normative Ethics*, pp. 228–35.

6. More precisely, the possibilities are these: (1) the ideal rules might be restricted in scope (whether explicitly or implicitly) to situations of ideal conformity, with none of the rules governing partial compliance situations; (2) the various ideal rules may be unrestricted in scope – governing both perfect and partial compliance situations; (3) some rules may govern perfect conformity situations, while other 'supplementary' rules govern partial conformity situations. If (1), rule consequentialism is either incoherent or incomplete. If (2) or (3), there is no reason to think that the rules – tested from the standpoint of perfect compliance – will provide suitable guidance for situations of imperfect compliance.

7. Though they may not be able to answer it adequately. See *Normative Ethics*, pp. 234–5.

8. I have been assuming, for simplicity, that under rule consequentialism the optimal rules are to be 'common' rules – that is, the same for everyone. What if we move to rule consequentialism with individualized rules? The same objections can still be generated – even the last (since ideal individualized rules might fail to provide plausible guidance given the realistic possibility of my past or future failure to conform). Only for a version that requires conformity to optimal ideal rules relativized to the *specific* choice situation can the 'disaster' objection be escaped: but at this point 'rule' consequentialism has indeed *collapsed* into act consequentialism (or, at least, into a theory that is like act consequentialism in evaluating acts directly in terms of the goodness of their consequences).

9. For simplicity, I put aside the possibility that in some cases two different acts might both be permissible, or right, even though we cannot – and need not – do both. In such cases, let us stipulate that 'do the right thing' is to be understood as requiring us to perform only one of the relevant right acts.

10. I owe this example to Joe Pabis.

11. I made this suggestion in 'The Structure of Normative Ethics' as well, using somewhat different examples.

12. For example, a contractarian theory that selects rules directly on the basis of the contract, and then uses these rules to evaluate both acts and institutions, is to be distinguished from a contractarian theory that selects *institutions* directly on the basis of the contract, uses the institutions to generate rules, and then evaluates acts in terms of the rules.

8

Hooker's Use and Abuse of Reflective Equilibrium

Dale E. Miller

A test of right and wrong must be the means, one would think, of ascertaining
what is right or wrong, and not a consequence of having already ascertained it.

(J. S. Mill, *Utilitarianism*)

INTRODUCTION

Anyone who intends to make a case for rule consequentialism must confront a
familiar dilemma. On the one hand, unless maximising value is the ultimate moral
goal there seems to be no reason for us to be consequentialists of any stripe. On the
other, if value-maximisation *is* the ultimate moral goal then it seems that a theory
which generates moral evaluations of actions ought to evaluate each action,
individually, on the basis of its contribution to the attainment of this goal. This
dilemma is captured by a question J. J. C. Smart poses (with a particular version of
rule consequentialism in view): 'the rule-utilitarian presumably advocates his
principle because he cares about human happiness; why then should he advocate
abiding by a rule when he knows it will not in the present case be most beneficial to
abide by it?'[1] In short, then, there is apparently an inconsistency, not within rule
consequentialism itself, but between the theory and what appears at first glance to be
a premise necessary to any argument in support of it.

In a recent series of articles, Brad Hooker has made a distinctive case for a version
of rule consequentialism. The unique strength of his case is that it is *not* premised on
the proposition that maximising value is the ultimate moral goal. But while his case
is not 'founded on an overarching commitment to the maximization of the good',[2] it
is founded on an overarching commitment to the conservation of moral judgements

which have currency within our moral community, and this approach is also problematic. In Section 1, I substantiate this description of his case, concluding that he employs the narrow reflective equilibrium method of moral theory selection. In Section 2, I present some familiar but still compelling reasons to believe that this method is in general inappropriate for moral philosophers – that, at the very least, it is inferior to one alternative, the method of wide reflective equilibrium – and I illustrate these points with reference to Hooker's work. There are at least two reasons why this undertaking should prove worthwhile. First, Hooker is now widely recognised as one of the leading defenders of rule consequentialism, and it is therefore important for his work to undergo thorough critical scrutiny. Yet while other writers have objected to his theory on various grounds, there has been little or no discussion of the basic methodology of his argument for it (and my criticisms here will be directed exclusively at the methodology; I will raise no objections to the theory itself).[3] Second, the question of what method of moral theory selection we should employ is a matter of the first importance, so it is crucial that we understand what can be said for or against the various candidates. Other philosophers have critiqued the method of narrow reflective equilibrium, but because examples of its use are scarce they were forced to keep their discussions at a fairly high level of abstraction. Studying Hooker's case for rule consequentialism – which is, so far as I am aware, the clearest example we have of this method's employment – should therefore give us a better understanding of its shortcomings.

SECTION I: HOOKER'S CASE FOR RULE CONSEQUENTIALISM

Hooker's version of rule consequentialism (hereafter HRC) says roughly that an action is morally wrong if and only if it would be forbidden by that moral code – that is, that set of moral rules – which could with the best consequences be inculcated into almost all of the members of the next generation.[4] In the same way, HRC says that an action is morally obligatory if it would be required by that code, and permissible if that code would permit it. Hooker's theory of the good, in light of which different sets of consequences are to be judged better or worse, maintains that both fairness and the well-being of sentient creatures are intrinsically valuable.[5] He argues for HRC by attempting to demonstrate its superiority to several rival theories – act utilitarianism, contractarianism, and 'Ross-style pluralism' – with respect to a set of desiderata, or theory virtues, for moral theories. These are (1) internal consistency; (2) fit or coherence with considered moral judgements which are widely shared among members of our moral community; (3) parsimony with respect to first principles; and (4) the ability to guide us in making moral decisions concerning issues about which our community has reached no confident consensus. The 'considered moral judgements' referred to in (2) are judgements about what actions are required, permissible, and/or forbidden in a particular set of circumstances, or about the acceptability of a more general moral rule (either absolute or pro tanto) that specifies what is required, permissible, and/or forbidden in a range of similar cases.[6] These judgements are not meant to be applications of any elaborate philosophical moral theory; perhaps all moral judgements are inevitably applications of at least a primitive, inchoate moral theory, but someone who already has adopted a sophisticated moral theory has no need for a method of theory selection. Hooker says that a pre-theoretical moral judgement is a considered judgement, for some individual, if she retains confidence in it 'after careful reflection . . . in light of our best theories in metaphysics, psychology, sociology, economics, etc'.[7] I will sometimes use the term 'ordinary morality' to refer collectively to those considered moral judgements which are widely shared in our moral community, although it would really be more accurate to say that these judgements make up that portion of our community's ordinary morality which most of us would reflectively endorse.

Hooker adjudges HRC superior to act utilitarianism because the latter is inconsistent with certain widely shared considered judgements. He focuses on two varieties of cases. First, there are circumstances in which act utilitarianism requires an action that ordinary morality forbids, such as breaking a promise or even killing or torturing an innocent person. While he acknowledges that ordinary morality permits promises to be broken in some circumstances, and that it might even judge the murder or torture of an innocent person to be acceptable if this were necessary to prevent catastrophically bad consequences,[8] Hooker believes there is a range of cases in which such actions maximise utility but are nevertheless judged to be wrong by virtually everyone.[9] He claims – quite plausibly, or so it seems to me – that HRC's implications fit this putative consensus rather closely; given the suffering inherent in any use of torture, for example, it would surely be optimific to inculcate in the members of the next generation a very stringent rule proscribing its employment, a prohibition attended with such strong moral feelings that it could only be violated in extreme circumstances. Second, there are circumstances in which requiring a great sacrifice on the part of some for the benefit of others maximises value; for example, at present act utilitarianism appears to demand tremendous sacrifices from a citizen of a first-world nation who knows full well that the vast majority of Westerners will make at most only very meager contributions toward fighting world poverty. Hooker supposes that most members of our moral community are as certain as he is that morality is not so demanding, and – while he has been challenged on this score – he contends that HRC closely fits common judgements about the demandingness of morality.[10] His argument against contractarianism proceeds along similar lines. This theory, at least in its most familiar forms, attaches no moral significance to the well-being of animals, and for this reason Hooker finds it inconsistent with common considered judgements about how they may be treated.[11] Because HRC endorses widely shared views about the treatment of animals it comes out ahead again.

By 'Ross-style pluralism' Hooker means the view that there is a plurality of moral first principles, that these may conflict, and that there is 'no strict order of priority' between them.[12] In arguing against this view he faces something of a quandary. He seems to have been beaten at his own game because, as he acknowledges:

> [d]epending on what general principles of duty the theory settles on, Ross-style pluralism can do an unbeatable job of cohering with the moral convictions that most of us share and have confidence in. Indeed it just lists the general principles to which we subscribe, and then very reasonably denies that there is any lexical order among them.[13]

Of course, Hooker does maintain that his is the superior theory. While HRC fits our considered judgements just as closely as pluralism does, he asserts, it has a single first principle and it gives us somewhat more guidance than pluralism in situations in which we lack firm shared convictions.[14] Now his final two desiderata have been brought into play, but he apparently considers them to be of secondary importance next to fit with common considered judgments; he feels that he has to assume the two theories 'tie' with respect to this desideratum before he can conclude that HRC wins the contest on other grounds.[15]

Hooker's claim that fairness is intrinsically valuable is also a product of his aspiration to find a moral theory which closely fits the ordinary morality of our moral community; he observes that if we assume fairness is valuable for its own sake then HRC will fit our shared considered moral judgements even more closely than it would were we to assume with the utilitarians that this is only true of welfare or happiness:

> Consider a rule which harms each member of a small group much more than it benefits each member of a much larger group . . . [rule utilitarians] would presumably endorse the rule. Yet most of us think such a rule would be unfair and therefore morally wrong (in at least many cases) . . . Worried by this possibility, I favour abandoning a purely utilitarian assessment of rules and accepting a broader kind of RC, one that assesses rules in terms of not only aggregate well-being but also fairness.[16]

To see why Hooker believes that these arguments are sufficient for his purposes we need to understand his philosophical methodology, which he identifies as the 'reflective equilibrium method of theory selection in ethics'.[17] Roughly put, the reflective equilibrium method is a means for finding or selecting moral principles such that the belief those principles ought to be followed coheres well with other beliefs one holds. Hooker observes that this methodology is available to, and in fact employed by, 'most contemporary moral philosophers – no matter what their views on the metaphysics, epistemology and language of ethics'.[18] Nevertheless, I will assume that those who employ the reflective equilibrium approach to moral theory selection are ethical cognitivists who construe judgements about whether actions are right or wrong as beliefs and whose aim is to find deontic principles which they are justified in believing ought to be followed. (This leaves open the question of whether or not they are moral realists who hold 'that there are moral facts and true moral claims whose existence and nature are independent of our beliefs about what is right and wrong'.[19])

As the reflective equilibrium method received its first formal statement and its name from John Rawls, when Hooker describes himself as a practitioner of this method he implies that his approach to theory selection is essentially the same as Rawls's. Yet this is not the case; there are reflective equilibria and then there are reflective equilibria. Rawls distinguishes between narrow and wide interpretations of the reflective equilibrium method,[20] and Norman Daniels has developed detailed accounts of each interpretation and of the differences between them. A narrow reflective equilibrium, Daniels writes,

> consists of an ordered pair of (a) a set of considered moral judgments acceptable to a given person P at a given time, and (b) a set of general moral principles that economically systematizes (a).[21]

The first step in the process by which an individual reaches this equilibrium, the method of narrow reflective equilibrium or, as I shall say, the 'narrow method', is that of generating a set of considered moral judgements. For Rawls and Daniels, this simply involves critically reflecting upon the pre-theoretical judgements one is disposed to make about specific cases or more general moral rules – these are one's 'initial moral judgements' – and eliminating judgements in which one has little confidence after reflection or which were made under conditions which might be conducive to error.[22] What remains are one's considered moral judgements, or, more accurately, 'pre-equilibrium considered moral judgements'. The next step is that of finding the most formally attractive set of principles that systematises these considered judgements, where formal attractiveness amounts to parsimony with respect to first principles and sufficiently wide applicability to have implications that go beyond the set of judgements.[23] Minor revisions may be made to the pre-equilibrium considered judgements if this will allow the selection of a more parsimonious and/or more widely applicable set of moral principles; revising a considered moral judgement might mean either arriving at a new considered judgement about that case/rule or simply no longer having one at all.[24] The end-product of applying this method will be a set of moral principles and a set of 'final considered judgements'.

A wide reflective equilibrium includes an element which is not present in a narrow equilibrium, a set of substantive background theories; equilibrium obtains only when the set of moral principles fits closely with both the judgements *and* the background theories. Any substantive considerations which are relevant to moral theory selection, which could favour or disfavour different sets of moral principles, would belong to this set. I will not attempt a general account of its contents; the most obvious possibilities are the sorts of views upon which most philosophers have traditionally based their arguments for moral theories – a category which I take to include metaphysical theories such as theories of the person, meta-ethical theories and very abstract moral views, theories of rationality, and theories in the social sciences – but the set of background theories might potentially include *any* substantive view or position other than moral judgements (whether or not the label 'theory' is warranted, strictly speaking). The first step of the 'wide method', as of the narrow method, is that of filtering one's initial moral judgements to arrive at a set of pre-equilibrium considered moral judgements. But the next step, for the practitioner of the wide method, is that of finding the set of moral principles which is most strongly favoured by the most compelling background theories; this will involve evaluating the philosophical arguments for and against different sets of principles which can be premised on the background theories. Some examples of the kinds of arguments I have in mind may be helpful here. Rawls argues against utilitarianism by suggesting this theory is incongruent with the metaphysical doctrine of the separateness of selves.[25] Derek Parfit, in turn, maintains that utilitarianism is not incongruent with the separateness of selves per se, but rather with the thesis that the divisions between selves are much deeper than those between the temporal segments of a single life; he rejects this thesis, and suggests that a better theory of the person may be congruent with some versions of consequentialism.[26] In *Morals by Agreement* David Gauthier argues for a contractarian moral theory from a maximising conception of practical rationality.[27] These are just a few illustrations, of course; I could just as easily have cited the arguments of any number of other historical or contemporary moral theorists.

Through the evaluation of arguments like these, the agent seeking wide reflective equilibrium determines that a particular set of principles is most favoured by the most compelling background theories. She must then determine how well these principles systematise her pre-equilibrium judgements, and presumably the fit will not be perfect; this means she will need to make changes somewhere. She may revise her pre-equilibrium judgements so that they conform to the principles, and in fact it is possible that she will revise most or even all of these judgments. While the narrow method only permits her to make minor revisions to her set of pre-equilibrium judgements the wide method does not impose the same limitation; the substantive background theories which initially appear most compelling may strongly favour principles that do not even come close to fitting her pre-equilibrium judgements, and in this case she may choose to eliminate the inconsistencies between them by making extensive revisions to the judgements. If she is extremely resistant to changing her mind about some judgement, however, then she may reject any principles which are inconsistent with it, and she may even revise whatever background theories favoured those principles as well.[28]

Rawls's method is that of wide reflective equilibrium; in *A Theory of Justice* he aims to show not only that his theory fits with the considered moral judgements in which we have the greatest confidence, but also that it is attractive in light of a set of substantive background theories which includes, as Daniels observes: 'a theory of the person, a theory of procedural justice, general social theory, and a theory of the role of morality in society'.[29] The only considerations favouring his theory to which Hooker refers, in contrast, other than its close fit with our considered moral judgements, are the formal desiderata of parsimony and generality, and this makes it appropriate to say that he employs the narrow method (although he himself makes no mention of the narrow/wide distinction, and refers only to reflective equilibrium *simpliciter*).[30] Of course, he does not, strictly speaking, employ the narrow method as I outlined it above, but then no one possibly could. We could never actually collect together all of our considered moral judgements, let alone formulate principles which fit those judgements perfectly. Clearly my description of the narrow method, like that of the wide method, was idealised. Practically speaking, all that one can do by way of implementing either method is to try to compare various salient sets of principles to see which seems to fit best on the whole with those classes of considerations that one's method picks out as germane to theory selection (and since the classes in question have so many members, one's arguments cannot possibly take account of all of them – one must try to pick out those considerations which are most telling).[31] But with this allowance made, Hooker's case for HRC appears to be virtually a textbook application of the narrow method as Rawls and Daniels describe it; when this method is employed the only considerations which influence moral theory selection are considered moral judgements and formal desiderata, and Hooker draws on these and only these in arguing for his theory.

Yet Hooker might protest here that he does in fact employ the wide method, or at least an essentially equivalent methodology. He agrees with advocates of the wide method that substantive background theories must play a role in theory selection, he might say, he simply brings them in at a slightly different point, namely the point where we winnow our initial set of moral convictions down to that subset which we are prepared to call considered judgements; recall that he defines a considered moral judgement as one which we remain confident about after reflection in light of the best scientific and metaphysical theories available. Now this proviso may not be entirely pointless; our best psychological theory might convince us that, for example, our moral convictions are very often subtly (or even unsubtly) influenced by our interests, and this may make us more willing to revise some of our own initial judgements (I raise this point again in the next section). But it is surely a mistake to think that we can bring the full range of background theories to bear on our moral judgements *prior* to giving any thought to selecting moral principles. How could any background theory – such as one, let us say, about the nature of personal identity – call into question my conviction that it is wrong for a surgeon to parcel out the organs of an unwilling donor to save the lives of a ward full of patients desperately needing transplants, except by bringing me to look more or less favourably upon moral principles that permit the well-being of some individuals to be sacrificed when this would substantially enhance the well-being of others? It is only through the mediating influence of moral theory that background theories can reach our moral judgements. So while Hooker gives substantive background theories some role in his methodology, this does not transform his approach into the wide method.

SECTION 2: IS HOOKER'S METHODOLOGY ADEQUATE?

On either of these interpretations, the reflective equilibrium methodology pre-supposes that an agent is justified in believing that a particular moral principle or set of such principles should be followed only if that belief is part of a highly coherent system of beliefs; this is the entire motivation for seeking principles which are in equilibrium with one's considered moral judgements and, on the wide method, with the background theories which one finds most compelling. While this methodology is commonly depicted as being grounded on a strictly coherentist theory of justification, according to which belonging to a highly coherent system of beliefs is both necessary and sufficient for a particular belief to be justified, Roger Ebertz has argued persuasively that it is in fact grounded on 'modest ethical foundation-alism'.[32] This epistemic view states that while membership in a coherent system of beliefs is necessary for a moral belief to be justified it is not sufficient; certain beliefs possess some limited degree of prima facie credibility or warrant which is independent of coherentist considerations, and a moral belief is justified just when it belongs to that highly coherent belief-system which coheres best, on the whole, with these modest foundations.[33] When the wide method is understood as being grounded on this account of moral justification both considered moral judgements and beliefs about what background theories are true, or 'background beliefs', are regarded as modest foundations. The notion of coherence is notoriously difficult to explicate, and I have nothing to contribute here myself, but Laurence Bonjour makes several important points:

> First, coherence is not to be equated with consistency. A coherent system must be consistent, but a consistent system need not be very coherent. Coherence

has to do with systematic connections between the components of a system, not just their failure to conflict. Second, coherence will obviously be a matter of degree . . . Third, coherence is closely connected with the concept of explanation.[34]

Similarly, Norman Daniels observes that 'Coherence involves more than simple logical consistency . . . [W]e often rely on inference to the best explanation and arguments about plausibility and simplicity to support some of our beliefs in terms of others.'[35] The degree to which the belief that a particular set of moral principles ought to be followed will cohere with a set of considered judgements depends on how closely those principles fit the judgements, that is, on the extent to which it is possible to see the principles as systematising the judgements (which is why many writers, including Hooker, refer simply to the degree of coherence between the judgements and the principles themselves).[36]

For an agent who has employed the (idealised) narrow method the belief that the moral principles he arrived at should be followed will cohere as well with his final considered judgements as any two sets of such moral beliefs can cohere, because the principles will systematise the judgements perfectly; if one of the judgements is that a particular action would be wrong in particular circumstances then one could deduce that the action would be wrong from the principles and a description of the circumstances.[37] But now we are in a position to see why the narrow method is inadequate. The reflective equilibrium methodology presupposes that whether the belief that a particular moral principle should or should not be obeyed is justified depends, wholly or at least in part, upon whether it is part of a highly coherent system of beliefs. If an agent employs the narrow method then each of his particular beliefs about which moral principles should be followed will certainly be part of a highly coherent *subsystem* of his total system of beliefs, a subsystem which comprises his other beliefs of this kind and his post-equilibrium moral judgements, but even if the remainder of his beliefs also forms a highly coherent subsystem the narrow method leaves the matter of the coherence of his total system of beliefs to chance. While the degree of coherence within each of the subsystems may be high, it may well be that the beliefs within one subsystem do not cohere well at all with those within the other; the narrow method does nothing to ensure coherence between them. If his belief-system lacks global coherence then the agent will not be justified in believing that the principles he arrived at ought to be followed, since if coherence matters at all to the justification of one's particular beliefs then what matters must surely be the coherence of one's total system of beliefs.[38] Things stand very differently with the wide method. So long as all of an agent's beliefs *except* her moral judgements and beliefs about moral principles form a highly coherent subsystem before she puts this method to use, her total system of beliefs will be highly coherent afterwards. This is true because the moral principles she arrives at will not only systematise her post-equilibrium moral judgements but will also fit or be favoured by the background theories she holds, and a background theory will favour a set of moral principles to the degree that the (background) belief that theory is true coheres with the belief that those principles ought to be followed in preference to others. Thus if the justification of particular moral beliefs indeed depends entirely upon their membership in a highly coherent system, the agent will be justified in believing that the principles she arrived at via the wide method should be obeyed. If the modest foundationalist theory of justification is correct then she will still be justified in this belief, so long as, in the course of attaining equilibrium between her beliefs, she was most willing to revise those beliefs with the least prima facie credibility.

To reiterate: my objection to the narrow method is that it is inferior to the wide method as a means of ensuring global coherence in the agent's belief-system; when an agent employs the narrow method we can expect the belief that the principles she settles on should be followed to cohere with *some* of her other beliefs, but we have no reason to expect it to cohere with *all* of them.[39] I have raised this objection against the idealised form of the narrow method, but clearly there is nothing in the practicable form of the method which Hooker employs that remedies this deficiency. If I am right, therefore, this means there is a critical lacuna in his case for rule consequentialism. The problem with his case is that he only concerns himself with how closely the different moral theories he considers fit our considered moral judgements; he does not advance any philosophical arguments to show that compelling substantive background theories favour HRC over rival moral views. Thus he gives us no reason to expect that our background beliefs will cohere well with the belief that HRC should be followed.[40]

There are three different routes which Hooker might take in responding to this objection, although of course my aim shall be to show that none of these responses succeed. The first is to claim that our considered moral judgements and beliefs about what moral principles ought to be followed form a sort of closed system. By 'closed system' I mean to suggest that the beliefs within this class are so entirely unrelated to the beliefs outside of it that no genuine coherence between the former and the latter is possible. If this is correct, and if coherentist considerations are relevant to the justification of the moral beliefs in this class, then it can only be their coherence with one another which is at issue. And *this* sort of coherence *can* be secured by the narrow method.

But this picture of the relation between our beliefs about moral principles and our other beliefs is not at all compelling. Earlier I gave examples of some attempts by Rawls, Parfit, and Gauthier to show that certain moral principles are more plausible or acceptable than others in light of particular background theories. These examples could have been multiplied endlessly; in fact, I take most of the work which has been done in the field of moral theory to consist of the presentation and evaluation of such attempts, and I think that – whatever one's estimation of the work of any given philosopher – we ought to be very reluctant to accept the view that all of this work has been fundamentally misconceived. It is rather staggering to ponder just how much of the history of moral philosophy, both distant and quite recent, is consigned to the intellectual rubbish bin by this defence of the narrow method. It is also significant that if, as one who takes this route claims, our substantive background views cannot favour or disfavour different sets of moral principles, then our moral explanations must end rather abruptly; we can answer the question of why, for example, contrariety to the set of rules the widespread acceptance of which would maximise value is a wrong-making property only by saying that it happens to be common to all those actions we think are wrong.

The second response Hooker might make draws on the idea that the reflective equilibrium method can be understood as being grounded on a modest foundationalist theory of justification; it is to assert that our considered moral judgements have so much more initial credibility than any of our background beliefs that, even if it is possible for our background beliefs to cohere with beliefs about what moral principles should be obeyed, we should select the principles which best fit our pre-equilibrium-considered moral judgements and then revise our background beliefs as necessary to maximise coherence. Following this route does, technically, mean conceding the inadequacy of the narrow method, since the narrow method makes no provision at all for revising our background beliefs, but it also means interpreting the wide method in a manner that brings it much closer in spirit to the narrow method than to the wide method as the latter is normally interpreted. This response might be one we would expect from someone who regards our considered moral judgements as moral intuitions which either are deliverances of some faculty of moral intuition or possess some degree of self-evidence. Hooker may well find this response congenial, for he comes very close to articulating it when he says that we ought to select our moral theory on the basis of the relevant considerations in which we have the most confidence and that these are our considered moral judgements.[41]

But I submit that critical reflection should evaporate most of our confidence in most of our pre-theoretical moral judgements. The suggestion that they are apprehended by some special faculty cannot be seriously entertained, and if we are inclined to maintain that they possess self-evidence we can reasonably ascribe only a very minimal amount of this property to most of them; we must acknowledge that their seeming self-evidence may be nothing more than a reflection of the combined influences of our families, schools, televisions, and so on, and we know perfectly well that these are not infallible sources of moral insight. When we take these points seriously and sincerely reflect on their implications we cannot maintain more than a modest level of confidence in most of these 'intuitions', especially where – given the human propensity for self-serving rationalisation – what we judge ought to be done conspicuously coincides with what would be in our interest or in the interest of those responsible for shaping our moral judgements, or where other individuals or moral communities, apparently no less intelligent or perceptive than ourselves, have reached moral judgements that differ sharply from our own. The proper conclusion for us to draw, I suggest, is that when we reflect critically and with an open mind we will probably lose all or nearly all confidence in many of our initial moral judgements; they will not qualify as considered moral judgements at all. And there will be at most only a very limited number of moral judgements about which we are so confident that we can conscientiously refuse to give them up come what may; these judgements can be described as 'fixed points'. We may have no more than a modest amount of confidence left in the rest of our considered moral judgements, no more than we have in many of our background beliefs.

Hooker will find himself facing this problem if he opts for this way of responding to my initial objection. Some of the moral judgements which are central to his case for rule consequentialism are ones in which we must lose a great deal of confidence upon reflection. How much confidence can I retain in my initial judgement that morality is not so demanding as to require Westerners to give up wearing designer clothes or buying compact discs when I take into account the human propensity for self-interested rationalisation and the fact that it is neither in my best interest, nor in the best interest of anyone who has been in a position to influence my moral intuitions, to believe that we must practise what Peter Singer preaches?[42] How much confidence can I retain in my initial judgement that the suffering of animals has significant moral weight when I know that other cultures judge it to be unimportant?[43] Certainly these judgements do not constitute fixed points. They will not even count as considered judgements unless our standards for conferring this status are quite low; that is, unless we are willing to regard a judgement in which we retain even a modicum of confidence after reflection as a considered one (and if they are not considered judgements then they can exert no influence on the process of theory selection). But even if we do regard them as considered judgements we cannot feel very confident about them, and, in so far as it is because of them that we are supposed to reject act utilitarianism and contractarianism, we cannot be very confident that we ought to give up on these theories (for which impressive philosophical arguments based on a wide range of substantive background theories have been given).

Hooker may be on somewhat firmer ground when he invokes act utilitarianism's apparent inconsistency with our sense of when promise-breaking, murder, torture, and so on are justified, but three points should be made here. First, while we may have considerable confidence in, say, the judgement that it is wrong to torture innocents in cases in which doing so would neither produce enormous benefits nor avert enormous harms, it may still be that on reflection we cannot be nearly so confident about the full range of ordinary morality's prohibitions on the use of torture. Second, it may be that a non-utilitarian act consequentialism could fit these intuitions as closely, or even more closely, than HRC; it is surprising that Hooker never considers such a possibility, given his explicit rejection of the utilitarian theory of the good.[44] And third, while act utilitarians believe, by definition, that an action is right just if it is utility-maximising, many also believe that agents should utilise some procedure for deciding what to do other than trying to calculate what possible action will maximise utility (or expected utility); they reason that, because agents with human limitations will frequently do a poor job of assessing actions' consequences, 'better results may come from people acting in accord with other principles, procedures, or motives than the basic utilitarian one'.[45] A variety of alternative decision procedures have been discussed, and in the course of these discussions the suggestion is frequently made, at least implicitly, that in terms of the actions they recommend the most promising procedures bear some considerable resemblance to ordinary morality.[46] Now suppose, for example, that an agent is considering whether to break a promise under circumstances in which ordinary morality declares the promise should be kept, even though breaking it will lead to the world containing slightly more happiness than would otherwise be the case (so that act utilitarianism declares the promise should be broken). Suppose further, however, that the best version of act utilitarianism holds that agents should follow a decision procedure which does not recommend breaking this promise. It is far from clear, at least to me, that we should treat our judgement that breaking the promise would be wrong as a reason to reject act utilitarianism. How far this point goes towards defusing Hooker's criticism of act utilitarianism will of course depend in part on just what decision procedure the best version of act utilitarianism does in fact recommend, and just how closely this procedure resembles ordinary morality; obviously I will not be able to explore this issue here. (Notice that even the wide method might have to be reformulated to take proper account of this final point.[47])

In claiming that few of our moral judgements constitute fixed points I do not mean to repudiate the modest foundationalist interpretation of the wide method (I think that much can be said in its favour, in fact, although I have tried to be neutral between it and the 'purely coherentist' interpretation here). First, I do not deny that some of these judgements may constitute fixed points, although I do deny that many of our moral judgements should be so regarded, and obviously I specifically deny this of some of the moral judgements to which Hooker appeals. Second, on a modest foundationalist interpretation of the wide method any considered judgement would count as a modest foundation, since all such judgements are treated as if they have a degree of prima facie credibility, not only those which we are extremely unwilling to revise (which is how I have defined 'fixed point').[48] I do want to insist that some of our background theories may have every bit as much right to be regarded as modest foundations as many of our considered moral judgements, however, at least so long as this depends upon the relevance of a consideration to moral theory selection and our confidence in it upon reflection. One might observe here that if we set our standards for the status of foundation high enough then only considered judgements will satisfy them, and one might believe that our standards *should* be set this high. But while it is probably true that we are more confident upon reflection about *some* of our moral judgements than about any of our background beliefs – those judgements that do qualify as fixed points, at least, and perhaps some others as well – I am sceptical about whether there are enough such judgements to serve as an adequate basis for the selection of moral principles, without any other considerations being taken into account. If one tries to employ the narrow method when one has only a handful of considered moral judgements then one may face a severe underdetermination problem; a number of salient sets of principles, of essentially equal formal elegance, may fit the judgements equally well. The fact that Hooker finds it necessary to rely upon judgements about which we cannot be very confident, upon reflection, in his arguments against act utilitarianism and contractarianism, seems to me to lend credence to this point.[49]

Hooker's third and final possible response is based on what, as far as I know, is the only explicit argument for the superiority of the narrow method over the wide one. While I will not recapitulate all of the reasoning with which she supports this claim, Margaret Holmgren contends that the narrow and wide methods should both be regarded as strategies which sophisticated moral intuitionists might employ in order to avoid arriving at moral principles by way of accidental generalisations from our considered moral judgements (Holmgren assumes that these judgements are the only potential moral intuitions).[50] She further contends that the narrow method will typically be a more successful strategy than the wide one. As she sees it, the narrow method aims to settle on some single moral principle which systematises all our considered moral judgements. According to Holmgren, the wide method aims at systematising all of our considered judgements not with a single principle but with a set of principles: the sought-after 'first-level' moral principle, which is analogous to the principle arrived at via the narrow method and is to be used in making moral evaluations of actions and rules, and a multiplicity of abstract background principles. The background principles serve to connect what I have been calling background views or beliefs with morality; Holmgren makes the important point that if I take, for example, my views about personal identity to favour some particular first-level moral principle over competing principles, then I must attach some credibility to the abstract conditional moral principle or proposition that if this theory of personal identity is true then this first-level principle should be followed (or some rival principle should not be).[51] On her account of the wide method the background moral principles necessarily draw all their credibility from their fit with considered moral judgements, but different judgements from those systematised by the first-level principle.

Holmgren's understanding of the wide method is influenced here by Daniels's proposal that the wide method should be governed by an 'independence constraint', which is a requirement that the background views should not merely reformulate the considered moral judgements which the first-level principle(s) are to systematise. The point of the independence constraint is to keep the wide method from collapsing into the narrow one. Translated slightly, so that Daniels's point fits into Holmgren's framework, this constraint says that if the credibility of the background moral principles is a product, to a significant degree, of their coherence with a set of considered moral judgements, then the judgements in question should be distinct from those which the first-level principle(s) are to systematise.[52] Daniels assumes that the segregation of moral judgements will not be arbitrary but will result from some difference in kind between them; he writes: '[T]he independence constraint may be satisfied if the background theories . . . incorporate different moral notions (say, fairness and certain claims about the nature of persons) from those (say, rights and entitlements) employed by the principles . . . and judgements [which they systematise] . . .'[53]

Why is the narrow method superior to the wide one? Holmgren reasons as follows. The single principle which one arrives at by following the narrow method 'derives its credibility from systematizing the *full* range of . . . [one's considered] judgements'.[54] The great explanatory power of this single principle is a powerful reason to deny that it constitutes an accidental generalisation from these judgements. In contrast, each of the moral principles one arrives at when one follows the wide method systematises only a portion of one's judgements; taken alone, none of these principles, including the first-level principle, is as secure against the charge of being an accidental generalisation as the principle on which the narrow method settles. While the support the background moral principles (in conjunction with our background theories) give the first-level principle does provide us with some reason to think that the latter is no mere accidental generalisation from the moral judgements it systematises, the amount of support the background principles can transmit to it is limited by the fact that we have real reason to worry that they might be accidental generalisations themselves. Even with the additional support they give to the first-level principle selected by the wide method, we still have better reason to believe that the principle the narrow method arrives at is no hasty generalisation. Ultimately, Holmgren maintains, the narrow method's single moral principle and the wide method's first-level principle both derive all their credibility from the same source, our pool of considered moral judgements, but the narrow method draws more support for its principle from this source than the wide method does; one might almost say that, according to her, it is a more efficient device for extracting support from that source.

Holmgren's analysis of the relative strengths and weaknesses of the narrow and wide methods is thought-provoking and deserves fuller treatment than I can give it at present, but I believe that it is flawed, and hence that there is no help for Hooker here. I will not take issue with Holmgren's assertion that the reflective equilibrium methodology, however interpreted, is of use only to intuitionists, for even if this is correct her argument for the superiority of the narrow method fails. She supposes that abstract background moral principles can have no credibility independently of their fit with some considered moral judgements, and that the considered moral judgements they systematise are enough like those which we are seeking to systematise via first-level moral principles that it would be possible to bring them all under such principles – even under one such principle – or at least that we should operate on this supposition unless and until our failure to find a suitable principle eventually forces us to concede defeat.[55] But although the abstract and schematic nature of her discussion tends to mask this to some degree, these suppositions are not very plausible. To see why, it will be helpful to have an example of an abstract background moral principle before us, such as the one Gauthier articulates at the beginning of *Morals by Agreement*: '[No] theory of morals serves any useful purpose, unless it can show that all the duties it recommends are also truly endorsed in each individual's reason.'[56] If we take this principle to be credible, and if we take it to express the proposition that we should reject any first-level moral principle which entails that an agent has a duty to do M in some set of circumstances in which it would not be rational for him to do M, then we will take theories of practical rationality to favour certain sets of first-level moral principles over others (as Gauthier takes the maximising conception of practical reason he endorses to favour the moral principles for which he argues). If this principle does derive its credibility from its fit with considered moral judgements, the judgements in question would have to be radically different from those relatively concrete ones which are typically offered as paradigmatic examples of the kind – think of the examples of possible considered moral judgements which I have given above, for example, the judgement that it is wrong to kill or torture an innocent person when doing so would neither produce enormous benefits nor avert enormous harms. If this is not obvious, then it may help to bear in mind that Gauthier's principle is meant to be logically prior to the question of what conception of practical rationality is best; it does not merely record that none of our moral duties require us to perform actions which are irrational according to a specific conception of practical reason, but instead places a constraint on moral principles which holds no matter what conception of practical reason turns out to be the best one. It is extremely hard to see how one principle could systematise such diverse judgements. So from what does the credibility of this principle derive? Different answers are possible. One is that its credibility derives from its fit with considered moral judgements, but judgements which – in conformity with Daniels's independence constraint – are very different in kind from the judgements which first-level moral principles would aim to systematise. A second answer, and to my mind a more satisfactory one, is that its credibility, if indeed it has any, is independent of its fit with any considered moral judgements whatsoever; I find this answer more satisfactory because I question whether anyone in fact has considered judgements of the kind which this principle, or other equally abstract principles, might systematise. While Holmgren does not allow for the possibility that background moral principles might have independent credibility, even an intuitionist could and should admit that this is possible. If we are disposed to take moral intuitionism at all seriously we have to acknowledge that intuitions come on different levels of abstraction, and that there is no justification for taking the more concrete ones more seriously than the abstract ones.[57] In fact, we might reasonably think that our more abstract convictions are less likely to be contaminated by bias or interest than the more concrete ones.[58]

In summary, then, it appears that the narrow method is deficient as a means of finding moral principles which we can justifiably believe ought to be followed. The very notion of reflective equilibrium presupposes that beliefs about moral principles must belong to a highly coherent belief-system if they are to be justified – that this is a necessary condition for their being justified, whether or not it is also a sufficient condition – and the narrow method is inadequate because there is no reason to expect that the belief that the principle or principles at which it arrives should be followed will cohere with all of the agent's other beliefs. While I have not claimed that the wide method is the best method of moral theory selection, I have shown that it is superior to the narrow method; so long as an agent's background beliefs cohere with each other before the method is employed, her total belief-system will be globally coherent afterwards. While the narrow method is therefore of little interest from a normative standpoint, it may be of some use for purposes of description. It is somewhat analogous to the method linguists employ in order to find principles which economically characterise a speaker's or a community's linguistic competence, which means, roughly, the utterances he/they are willing to count as grammatical. In a similar manner, the narrow method can be seen as a means for finding principles which characterise an individual's or a community's moral competence, and hence, as several writers have observed, it may be of some sociological or anthropological interest.[59]

CONCLUSION

The foregoing is (as of the time of writing) an up-to-date treatment of Hooker's published work. He has, however, taken the opportunity to respond to these criticisms verbally in commentaries on earlier versions of this chapter at the 1997 International Society for Utilitarian Studies conference and at the 1998 Eastern Meeting of the American Philosophical Association, and in papers of his own, read at the ISUS conference and the 1999 Keele University conference 'Re-evaluating Moral Intuitionism'.[60] I believe it is fair to say that he has agreed my criticisms have some force, and that he has modified his arguments in response to them. However, I don't believe that he has done enough, at least so far, to meet my objections adequately.

If I understand him accurately, Hooker now acknowledges the desirability in principle of employing the wide method, that is, the method of wide reflective equilibrium, as opposed to the narrow method. But he asserts that the *only* substantive background theories which can profitably be brought to bear on the problem of theory selection in ethics are abstract moral views (he may also intend to include metaethical theories under this heading); the reason, he maintains, is that the other background theories I have mentioned, such as theories of the person and of practical rationality, all cohere equally well with HRC and the best versions of the moral theories which are its most serious rivals (he has now expanded this list to include act consequentialism, particularism, and virtue ethics).[61] This claim may at least partly reflect a tendency on his part to conflate the notion of coherence with that of consistency; in the paper read at Keele, for example, he remarks that 'Wide reflective equilibrium is narrow reflective equilibrium *plus* consistency with "background conditions".'[62] In any case, he contends in addition that certain of our abstract moral convictions favour his theory over these competitors, particularly the convictions that 'the best code for general adoption by the group of which we are members [is] the one we should try to follow' and that the question 'What if everyone felt free to do what you are doing?' is morally significant.[63] He concedes, as of course he must, that his theory's rivals 'tap into other familiar and intuitively plausible ideas' about morality; contractarianism, for example, develops the 'very appealing general idea' that 'morality consists of rules to which everybody would consent under appropriate conditions'.[64] But rather than attempting to determine whether some of these theories develop ideas that are more compelling than others, or whether in some cases the development itself is more compelling than in others, he simply declares that the best versions of each of these theories tie in these respects, so that the choice between them ultimately has to rest on their degree of fit with our considered judgements.

I will not contest Hooker's assertion that the only substantive background theories which are pertinent to moral theory selection are abstract moral convictions here, although I do not agree with it. Far more worrisome is his claim that the best versions of all the leading moral theories are equally well supported by the relevant substantive background theories, whatever these should turn out to be. As I understand the history of moral theory to consist primarily of attempts to show that the most compelling substantive background theories favour one theory over others, this move seems far too quick to me; perhaps Hooker takes the lack of progress in moral theory to demonstrate the futility of arguing for moral theories in this way, and hence the need to try something else, but it is still early days for modern secular ethics – as several philosophers have recently observed – so such defeatism may be premature.[65]

NOTES

1. J. J. C. Smart, 'An Outline of a System of Utilitarian Ethics,' *Utilitarianism: For and Against* (Cambridge: Cambridge University Press, 1973), p. 10.

2. Brad Hooker, 'Rule-consequentialism, Incoherence, and Fairness', *Proceedings of the Aristotelian Society*, 95 (1995), p. 2.

3. But see Alan Thomas's contribution (ch. 9) to this volume.

4. This is a composite of Hoker, 'Rule-consequentialism, Incoherence, and Fairness', p. 20, and 'Ross-style Pluralism versus Rule-consequentialism', *Mind*, 105 (1996), p. 537.

5. Hooker, 'Ross-Style Pluralism', pp. 539–40.

6. Thomas Scanlon gives an interpretation of the reflective equilibrium methodology according to which considered moral judgements are not simply judgements about the rightness or wrongness of actions but judgements about what kinds of factors are relevant to rightness and wrongness; the principles which are sought via the wide method are to systematize these judgements, and to offer general statements about what factors count as moral reasons ('The Aims and Authority of Moral Theory', *Oxford Journal of Legal Studies*, 12 (1992), p. 9). I take this interpretation to be somewhat idiosyncratic, and whatever it has to recommend it I will not discuss it further here.

7. 'Ross-style Pluralism', p. 531.

8. Brad Hooker, 'Rule-Consequentialism', *Mind*, 99 (1990), pp. 74–5; 'Rule-consequentialism, Incoherence, and Fairness', pp. 24–7.

9. Hooker, 'Rule-Consequentialism', p. 69; 'Compromising with Convention', *American Philosophical Quarterly*, 31 (1994), p. 313.

10. Thomas L. Carson, 'A Note on Hooker's 'Rule Consequentialism', *Mind*, 100 (1991), pp. 117–21; Tim Mulgan, 'Rule Consequentialism and Famine', *Analysis*, 54 (1994), pp. 187–92; 'One False Virtue of Rule-consequentialism and One New Vice', *Pacific Philosophical Quarterly*, 77 (1996), pp. 362–73; Hooker, 'Rule-Consequentialism and Demandingness: Reply to Carson', *Mind*, 100 (991), pp. 270–6; 'Rule-Consequentialism and Obligations To the Needy', *Pacific Philosophical Quarterly*, 79 (1998), pp. 19–33.

11. Hooker, 'Rule-Consequentialism, Incoherence, and Fairness', pp. 20–4. For versions of contractarianism that *do* confer moral weight on the interests of animals see, for example, Brent A. Singer, 'An Extension of Rawls's Theory of Justice to Environmental Ethics', *Environmental Ethics*, 10 (1988), pp. 217–32; Robert Elliot, 'Rawlsian Justice and Non-Human Animals', *Journal of Applied Ethics*, 1 (1984), pp. 95–106; Donald Van DeVeer, 'Of Beasts, Persons, and the Original Position', *Monist*, 62 (1979), pp. 368–77.

12. Hooker, 'Ross-Style Pluralism', p. 534.

13. Ibid., p. 535.

14. Ibid., pp. 539–43.

15. Ibid., pp. 537–8.

16. Hooker, 'Rule-Consequentialism, Incoherence, and Fairness', pp. 30–1.

17. Hooker, 'Ross-Style Pluralism', p. 531.

18. Ibid., p. 533.

19. David Brink, *Moral Realism and the Foundations of Ethics* (New York: Cambridge University Press, 1989), p. 7. Rawls clearly believes that this method is available to constructivists as well as realists (see, e.g., *Political*

Liberalism (New York: Columbia University Press, 1993, pp. 95–7), as does Dworkin ('The Original Position', in Norman Daniels (ed.) *Reading Rawls*, (New York: Basic Books, 1975), pp. 16–52), but cf. Margaret Holmgren, 'Wide Reflective Equilibrium and Objective Moral Truth', *Metaphilosophy*, 18 (1987), pp. 116–24; and Roger Ebertz, 'Is Reflective Equilibrium a Coherentist Model?', *Canadian Journal of Philosophy*, 23 (1993), pp. 209–10.

20. Rawls, *A Theory of Justice*, 1971 Rawls, p. 49; (Cambridge MA: Belknap), 'The Independence of Moral Theory', *Proceedings and Addresses of the American Philosophical Association*, XLVII (1974/5), pp. 7–8.

21. Norman Daniels, 'On Some Methods in Linguistics and Ethics', *Justice and Justification: Reflective Equilibrium in Theory and Practice*, (New York: Cambridge University Press 1996, p. 67 (originally published in *Philosophical Studies*, 37 (1980), pp. 21–36).

22. Rawls, *A Theory of Justice*, p. 47; Daniels, 'Wide Reflective Equilibrium and Theory Acceptance in Ethics', *Justice and Justification*, 22 (originally published in *Journal of Philosophy*, LXXXVI (1979), pp. 256–82).

23. Daniels, 'Some Methods', p. 67.

24. Norman Daniels gives this account of the narrow method:

> The set of considered judgements (a) is pared down from a set of initial moral judgements in two stages. First it is pruned to eliminate judgements that *P* is not confident of, has made without adequate information about the situation, or has made in a state of mind conducive to error. Second, the resulting considered judgements are further adjusted to eliminate irregularities that may block fit with the most desired set of principles. Such principles not only must economically systematize the considered judgements that result from the first stage of pruning, but if possible should somewhat extend the set of acceptable considered judgements to include some about which the person was not so confident or found indeterminate. ('Some Methods', p. 67)

25. Rawls, *A Theory of Justice*, pp. 185–9.

26. Derek Parfit, 'Later Selves and Moral Principles', in Alan Montefiore (ed.), *Philosophy and Personal Relations* (Montreal: McGill-Queen's University Press, 1973) pp. 137–69; *Reasons and Persons* (Oxford: Clarendon Press, 1984), pp. 331–9; cf. Rawls, 'The Independence of Moral Theory', pp. 15–20.

27. David Gauthier, *Morals by Agreement* (Oxford: Clarendon Press, 1986). I mention Gauthier only to illustrate how someone who employs the wide method might understand a theory of practical reason to favour certain moral principles more than others. I do not mean to imply that Gauthier employs the wide method himself; in fact, he forcefully rejects the use of the reflective equilibrium methodology however interpreted:

> Trusting theory rather than intuition, we should advocate the view of social relationships sketched in this chapter without regard to the intellectual fashions of the moment. If the reader is tempted to object to some part of this view, on the ground that his moral intuitions are violated, then he should ask what weight such an objection can have, if morality is to fit within the domain of rational choice. We should emphasize the radical difference between our approach . . . [and] that of moral coherentists and defenders of 'reflective equilibrium', who allow initial weight to our considered moral judgements. (p. 269)

28 Daniels again, describing the wide method (and having just described the step where the initial set of judgements is pared down to that of pre-equilibrium considered judgements):

> We then propose alternative sets of moral principles that have varying degrees of 'fit' with the moral judgements. We do *not* simply settle for the best fit of principles with judgements, however, which would give us only a *narrow* equilibrium. Instead we advance philosophical arguments intended to bring out the relative strengths and weaknesses of the alternative sets of principles . . . Assume that some particular set of arguments wins and that the moral agent is persuaded that some set of principles is more acceptable than others (and, perhaps, than the conception that might have emerged in narrow equilibrium). We can imagine an agent working back and forth, making adjustments to his considered judgements, his moral principles, and his background theories. In this way he arrives at an equilibrium point . . . ('Wide Reflective Equilibrium', p. 22, emphasis in original)

29. Daniels, 'Wide Reflective Equilibrium', p. 23; Daniels, 'Reflective Equilibrium and Archimedean Points', *Justice and Justification*, pp. 50–9 (originally published in *Canadian Journal of Philosophy*, 10 (1980), pp. 83–103).

30. Hooker does also refer to the conviction that the 'moral point of view is ultimately impartial' ('Rule-consequentialism, Incoherence, and Fairness', p. 22) and an abstract moral conviction like this qualifies as a substantive background view. But he doesn't make any use of this consideration in his argument for HRC, and of course most if not all of HRC's leading rivals also give us an impartial moral point of view.

31. See Rawls, *A Theory of Justice*, p. 49. It is important to recognise that while the idealised descriptions of the reflective equilibrium methodology would suggest that when the narrow method is employed the principles selected will fit perfectly with the agent's post-equilibrium considered moral judgements, and that when the wide method is followed they will also perfectly fit his substantive background theories, the practical constraints on the employment of these methods may prevent this state of perfect equilibrium from being reached. For

example, the principles which fare best out of those the agent considers may still not fit perfectly with certain considered moral judgements he is unwilling to revise. So long as this is true then the agent will only be provisionally justified in holding those principles; there is always the possibility that even better principles may be discovered.

32. Ebertz, 'Is Reflective Equilibrium a Coherentist Model?' pp. 193–214; see also Laurence Bonjour, 'The Coherence Theory of Empirical Knowledge', in Paul K. Moser (ed.), *Empirical Knowledge: Readings in Contemporary Epistemology* (Totowa, NJ: Rowman and Allanheld, 1986), 118–19 (originally published in *Philosophical Studies*, 30 (1976), pp. 281–312).

33. If it is not possible to fit all of these modest foundations into one highly coherent belief-system then the highly coherent system which coheres with them best will be the one which preserves as much of their 'credibility mass' as possible (where the credibility mass of a group of beliefs is a function of their number and of the credibility of each).

34. Bonjour, 'The Coherence Theory', pp. 122–3.

35. Daniels, 'Introduction: Reflective Equilibrium in Theory and Practice', *Justice and Justification*, p. 2.

36. I am using 'moral judgement' in two different senses here; the difference is that between a belief and its content. What a moral principle fits is the moral acceptability or unacceptability of an action or rule, and what a belief about what moral principles should be followed coheres with is a belief about the moral status of an action or rule.

37. Actually the fit will be less than perfect in one respect, even on the idealised version of the narrow method, but this can be ignored here. An absolutely perfect fit between principles and judgements would, I take it, mean that the principles' deductive implications coincide exactly with the judgements. But this is essentially certain not to be the case with principles selecting via either the narrow or wide method; the principles' deductive implications will (as it is desired they should) extend beyond the set of judgements.

38. I will not argue for this claim here, but I will describe what one would need to do in order to refute it (in the hope that this will seem as difficult to everyone else as it does to me): one would need to articulate an account of why coherence matters at all for justification which entails that something less than global coherence is sufficient and which does not have the consequence that the coherence requirement – whether understood as a necessary or a necessary and sufficient condition for justification – becomes so easily satisfied as to be empty.

39. I am not aware of anyone else's having made precisely this point in precisely this way, but I claim no great originality for it; I take it to be implicit in the work of other critics of the narrow method, e.g., Daniels.

40. Some clarifying remarks are in order here. First, a reminder: the post-equilibrium considered moral judgements which we hold after employing the narrow method will almost certainly not be identical with those which we would have held if we had employed the wide method instead. Second, while our background beliefs will not change as a result of following the narrow method, since it makes no provision for revising these beliefs, the same is not true with respect to the wide method; even if our 'pre-equilibrium background beliefs' form a coherent subsystem we still may revise some of them in the course of employing this method.

41. Hooker, 'Ross-style Pluralism', pp. 533, 538. What he actually says is that we 'are more certain of some intuitions (moral verdicts) than we are of any theory' (p. 538), which I take to imply that we are more confident about these intuitions than we are of any other considerations that might lead us to favour one theory over another (while he says 'some' intuitions here it is clear from the context of the paragraph – not to mention the rest of the article, and the rest of his work on HRC – that Hooker believes there are a number of intuitions about which we are this confident).

42. I allude here to Singer's powerful argument for the existence of a moral obligation to aid those who are suffering (the most) until giving more would mean actually increasing the amount of suffering in the world. Peter Singer, 'Famine, Affluence, and Morality', *Philosophy and Public Affairs*, 1 (1972), pp. 229–43.

43. Richard Brandt, for example, writes:

> It is notorious that many peoples seem quite indifferent to the suffering of animals. We are informed that very often, in Latin America, a chicken is *plucked alive*, with the thought that it will be more succulent on the table . . . Or again, take the 'game' played by Indians of the Southwest (but learned from the Spaniards, apparently), called the 'chicken pull'. In this 'game', a chicken is buried in the sand, up to its neck. The contestants ride by on horseback, trying to grab the chicken by the neck and yank it from the sand. When someone succeeds in this, the idea is then for the other contestants to take away from him as much of the chicken as they can . . . The writer had the decided impression that the Hopis' disapproval of causing pain to animals is much milder than he would suppose typical in suburban Philadelphia . . . (*Ethical Theory: The Problems of Normative and Critical Ethics* (Englewood Cliffs, NJ: Prentice-Hall, 1959), pp. 102–3)

Brandt discusses the Hopis' attitudes towards cruelty to animals in greater detail in *Hopi Ethics: A Theoretical Analysis* (Chicago: University of Chicago Press, 1954), pp. 213–15.

44. For example, if we decide that it is intrinsically bad for an innocent person to be killed and that the magnitude of the evil of killing an innocent is greater than the magnitude of the good of a significant enhancement to the well-being of numerous individuals, then act consequentialism will not recommend murder in some possible cases where act utilitarianism will. Of course, it will still sometimes require us to kill some innocents when this is necessary to prevent even more innocents from being killed (and other things are equal). Hooker will presumably want to say that ordinary morality is more deontological than this, but it is not clear (to me, at least) that there is a confident consensus about this, and even he doesn't want to say it is deontological through and through because he acknowledges that it is sensitive to disastrous consequences.

45. William H. Shaw, *Contemporary Ethics: Taking Account of Utilitarianism* (Cambridge, MA: Blackwell Publisher, 1999), p. 144.

46. See, for example, John Stuart Mill, *Utilitarianism, Essays on Ethics, Religion, and Society: Collected Works of John Stuart Mill, Vol. 10*, ed. J. M. Robson (Toronto: University of Toronto Press, 1969), p. 22; Henry Sidgwick, *The Methods of Ethics*, 7th edn (Indianapolis: Hackett, 1981), pp. 475–95; G. E. Moore, *Principia Ethica* (Cambridge: Cambridge University Press, 1903), pp. 154–62; Smart, 'An Outline of a System of Utilitarian Ethics' pp. 42–4; R. M. Hare, *Moral Thinking: Its Levels, Method, and Point* (Oxford: Clarendon Press, 1981), pp. 48–9, 130–68; Shaw, *Contemporary Ethics*, pp. 151–8.

47. I owe this point to Ben Eggleston, although he informs me that he does not believe it is original to him.

48. Although Rawls uses the same term less restrictively (*A Theory of Justice*, p. 20).

49. I am grateful to Donald Bruckner for calling my attention to the importance of explicitly setting out the ideas in this paragraph.

50. Holmgren, 'Wide Reflective Equilibrium and objective Moral Truth,' pp. 56–9.

51. This assumes that it is not possible simply to derive, as Holmgren writes, 'a substantive moral conclusion from nonmoral premises' (p. 51). I tend to share her view that 'Most attempts to do so have been highly controversial and in my opinion implausible.'

52. If 'a set of considered *moral* judgements (a') plays a role in constraining the background theories in (c) . . . our *independence constraint* amounts to the requirement that (a') and (a) [the set of considered moral judgements to be systematised by the moral principles (b)] be to some significant degree disjoint'. (Daniels, 'Wide Reflective Equilibrium', p. 23, emphasis in quotation in original.)

53. Daniels, 'Two Approaches to Theory Acceptance in Ethics', *Justice and Justification*, p. 83 (originally published in David Copp and David Zimmerman (eds) *Morality, Reason, and Truth* (Totowa, NJ: Rowman and Allanheld, 1985), pp. 120–40).

54. Holmgren, 'Wide Reflective Equilibrium and objective Moral Truth', p. 59.

55. Holmgren, writes: It would be fundamentally bad methodology to abandon this search ['for a principle possessing the greatest possible degree of explanatory power'] unless we were quite certain that we could not move beyond a plurality of principles, each capturing only a limited range of our moral judgements. (Ibid., p. 59).

56. Gauthier, *Morals by Agreement*, p. 1.

57. Sidgwick, for example, famously claims there are several abstract 'rational intuitions' which rise to the level of 'self-evidence', e.g., that 'if a kind of conduct that is right (or wrong) for me is not right (or wrong) for some one else, it must be on the ground of some difference between the two cases, other than the fact that he and I are different persons', or that 'the good of one individual is of no more importance, from the point of view (if I may say so) of the Universe, than the good of any other' (*Methods*, pp. 379–82).

58. Note that even if Holmgren's presuppositions are in fact good ones moral realists would still presumably have an interest in abstract moral principles like that invoked by Gauthier. Some such principles could still presumably be true, after all, and well supported. Suppose that Gauthier's abstract principle is in fact true, but that the first-level principles for which he argues are false. This would mean (assuming the validity of his argument, and simplifying slightly) that his theory of practical rationality is false, an important result.

59. See for example Daniels, 'Some Methods'; Daniel Little, 'Reflective Equilibrium and Justification', *Southern Journal of Philosophy*, 22 (1984), pp. 377–9; and Hare, 'Rawls' Theory of Justice', in Norman Daniels (ed.), *Reading Rawls* (New York: Basic Books, 1975), p. 86. (Hare thinks the point applies to the wide method as well, and Little seems to arrive at nearly the same conclusion.)

60. Note that many of the claims which Hooker made on these occasions are incorporated into his chapter for this book.

61. Handout distributed (while serving as commentator on an earlier version of this paper) at the Eastern Division Meeting of the American Philosophical Association, Washington DC, 1998.

62. Hooker, 'Non-Inferentially Justified Moral Convictions, Moral Theorizing, and Contingency', paper presented at the conference 'Re-evaluating Moral Intuitionism', Keele University, June 1999 (the quotation is from a handout distributed at the talk).

63. Hooker, 'Why Rule-Utilitarianism is More Plausible than Act-Utilitarianism', paper presented at the International Society for Utilitarian Studies Conference, New Orleans, March 1997, p. 16.

64. Ibid., p. 17.

65. Parfit, *Reasons and Persons*, pp. 453–4; Michael Smith, 'Realism', in Peter Singer (ed.), *A Companion to Ethics* (Oxford: Blackwell Publishers, 1991), p. 409; on this lack of progress, see Kurt Baier, *The Rational and the Moral Order: The Social Roots of Reason and Morality* (La Salle, IL: Open Court, 1996), pp. 1–4. I would like to acknowledge the valuable comments and suggestions that I have received from Donald Bruckner, Jonathan Dancy, Jonathan Mandle, Andrew Mason, and Elinor Mason. Ben Eggleston has generously read and commented on numerous successive drafts. Brad Hooker has been exceptionally free with his help and encouragement.

9

Consequentialism and the Subversion of Pluralism

Alan Thomas

My aim in this chapter is to offer an account of moral pluralism which brings out some of its distinctive advantages over other normative ethical theories, but especially its advantages over consequentialism. The main stimulus to this paper has been the subtle and interesting challenge to pluralism presented by Brad Hooker's 'Ross-style Pluralism versus Rule-consequentialism'.[1] Hooker's paper raises the deepest questions about moral justification, about the grounds of moral judgement and about the nature of reflective equilibrium as a model for moral epistemology. I shall argue that Hooker is mistaken in his claim that the central rationale for pluralism, when fully thought through, leads one to a form of consequentialism.[2] In the course of offering some considerations against Hooker's argument I will develop an alternative view of pluralism and its commitments, which Hooker overlooks in his attempt to subvert the attractiveness of pluralism.

The plan of this chapter is as follows. Section 1 will offer an exposition of pluralism and its relation to 'methodological intuitionism'. Section 2 offers an exposition both of Hooker's argument and of an important objection to Hooker developed by Philip Stratton-Lake.[3] Section 3 considers different interpretations of the methodology of reflective equilibrium. Section 4 applies to the conclusions of Sections 2 and 3 to Hooker's argument raising in addition specific doubts about the feasibility of his proposal. Finally, Section 5 presents an alternative version of pluralism, which I argue is more resistant to Hooker's criticism.

Moral pluralism is the view that a correct account of the resources of moral thinking will find an irreducible plurality of principles of moral salience and basic ethical considerations.[4] I take basic ethical considerations to be the exemplification of values by situations, persons, and actions. These judgements will typically be conceptualised by drawing on a repertoire of 'thick' ethical concepts. Examples of such concepts would be the concepts of **treachery, brutality,** or **integrity**.[5] This class of judgements offers the basic class for the justification of other kinds of moral judgement. Thus, I regard 'thin' ethical concepts as ultimately grounded on evaluative judgements primarily deploying thick concepts. Examples of 'thin' ethical concepts would be **ought, right,** and **good**. Principles of moral salience dictate which reasons typically function to ground specific verdicts in particular cases; they are statements of the tendency of reasons to function as evidential considerations across a range of different contexts of judgement. The role of this class of judgements will be discussed further below.[6]

The constitutive features of pluralism which make it distinctive vis-à-vis other reflective accounts of morality have been expressed by Rawls:

> [Pluralist] theories, then, have two features: first, they consist of a plurality of first principles which may conflict to give contrary directives in particular types of cases; and second, they include no explicit method, no priority rules, for weighing these principles against one another: we are simply to strike a balance by intuition, by what seems to us most nearly right. Or if there are no priority rules, these are thought to be more or less trivial and of no substantial assistance in reaching a judgement.[7]

As we shall see, Rawls believes that the only means of rebutting moral pluralism, which he takes very seriously as a theory of moral judgement, is to construct a set of principles which can 'do better' from the point of view of developing lexically ordered priority rules.[8] In Rawls's account, the pluralist, on the contrary, does not believe such a lexical ordering can be discovered (or imposed).[9]

Two of the main advantages of pluralism are its close tie to moral phenomenology and its phenomenological plausibility. This directly relates pluralism to the more general theory of intuitionism. Following the seminal discussions of Rawls and Williams, it is now customary to draw a distinction between 'epistemological' and 'methodological' intuitionism. The former is usually understood as the epistemological thesis that certain moral truths are known via a faculty of rational intuition, comparable to the faculty of intuition that gives us knowledge of the a priori in the special sciences – though recent work has contested this standard view.[10] The latter is the view, held by Urmson and Williams, that the starting point of ethical enquiry should be a phenomenological description of the plural sources available in our ethical experience. Such an unprejudiced phenomenology will, it is argued, reveal a plurality of commitments both at the level of moral knowledge and at the level of principles.[11] Thus, the evidence of unprejudiced phenomenology, which is the starting point of methodological intuitionism, and the findings of the reflective account of morality, which is represented by pluralism, match precisely.

The claim that methodological intuitionism is phenomenologically plausible may not seem to be much of an advantage for the view on the grounds that since it simply redescribes our existing commitments; the pluralism it yields up does no more than reproduce a pluralism inherent in the original material.[12] If it does try to do more than this, moral pluralism runs into two problems: it confuses explanation with justification and it faces the problem that it may simply be reproducing a parochialism inherent in the original data.[13]

So let me refine the sense in which methodological intuitionism is phenomenologically plausible. It is plausible in that it takes up an internal perspective on our existing moral practices. I have argued elsewhere that any acceptable moral view must further undertake to entertain specific, grounded doubts about the deliverances of any moral phenomenology, without thereby being open to global doubts about our moral knowledge as a whole.[14] A reflective account of the ethical that is pluralist must thereby be open to correction from critical social theory. Its deliverances are thereby normative and do not merely reflect the de facto content of the ethical materials it seeks to describe.[15]

One way of understanding this position is in terms of the epistemological model of reflective equilibrium, a general reasonable procedure for adjusting moral principles to moral 'intuitions'. The version of reflective equilibrium involved would be wide, not narrow, to include the deliverances of background theories in the human sciences. I am going to discuss the model of reflective equilibrium at length in the next section, so at this point I offer only a brief characterisation of the reflective equilibrium method.

As canonically formulated by Norman Daniels, the method of reflective equilibrium begins by isolating a class of 'considered moral judgements'.[16] These judgements are moderately subject to reflection, in that they are filtered in the light of presuppositions about the appropriate contexts for reliable belief formation and are thereby shaped by a preliminary and moderately reflective theory of error. In Rawls's original formulation, these beliefs were marked by the subject's degree of confidence in them. The transition to narrow reflective equilibrium begins when these considered moral judgements are related to a set of principles which both justify and give insight into them; this involves a process of mutual adjustment which can involve the revision of either considered moral judgement or of general principle. The conclusion of this process is narrow reflective equilibrium; however, this is not the end of the process.

Further reflection draws on background theories in the human sciences relevant to the project at hand: theories of social stability drawn from sociology in the case of deliberations over social justice, or theories of the person or social and moral psychology in the case of moral deliberation. Rawls and Daniels accept that these background theories need not be 'value free' and may be significantly shaped by prior moral presuppositions. Daniels hopes that it is possible to disjoin those of our considered moral beliefs implicated in these background theories from the majority that are not so implicated. Only then, he believes, can the transition to wide reflective equilibrium uncover the full structure of reflective ethical justification without introducing a damaging circularity into the process.

I have elsewhere described how, in my view, the resources of pluralism have to be defended from the charge of parochialism or ideological distortion by drawing on the family of psychological and social theories known collectively as critical social theory.[17] This seems, on the face of it, similar to the proposal that pluralism, in narrow reflective equilibrium, must be embedded in background theories of self and society drawn upon in wide reflective equilibrium. However, adding the deliverances of critical social theory to ethical pluralism is not, in my opinion, best viewed in terms of the reflective equilibrium model. Building a filter on the admissibility of ethical options drawn from critical social theory into a model of moral knowledge is different in one crucial respect from the original proposal to move from narrow to wide reflective equilibrium. The content of the deliverances of critical social theory, besides being normative, is not sufficiently independent of morality to figure without circularity in wide reflective equilibrium. Critical social theories contain at the core of their research programmes a model of the emancipated human subject that expresses a conception of human flourishing; I do not see, pace Daniels, that a theory strong enough to supply an ideological critique of existing beliefs and institutions can have a content sufficiently disjoined from the majority of our considered moral beliefs, as Daniels hopes.[18]

SECTION 2

My aim in this section is to put into play Hooker's argument and an important discussion of it by Philip Stratton-Lake. Stratton-Lake's argument, it seems to me, both opens up interesting discussion in its own right, mainly about the correct interpretation of Ross, but also to lead on to a form of pluralism on which Hooker does not focus.

Hooker's argument proceeds as follows. He first motivates a 'four part methodology' for the assessment of moral theories: the requirement of internal coherence, the adoption of the methodology of wide reflective equilibrium, the requirement that 'Moral Theories should specify what (if anything) ties together our various general principles and justifies them' and the desideratum that such theories should 'help us deal with moral questions about which we are not confident, or do not agree'. After further motivating the first two requirements (the first of which does not require comment and the second of which I discuss in detail in the next section), Hooker turns to the crux of his argument. He describes a position he labels as 'Ross-style pluralism', defined by three claims:

> The first is that there is a plurality of first principles. The second is that these are capable of conflicting with one another. The third is that there is no strict order of priority for resolving conflicts between them, or at least none that eliminates the need for the exercise of judgement.[19]

This looks like a general definition of pluralism per se; Hooker adds that what justifies the qualifier 'Ross-style' is Hooker's interest in the claim that such a theory presents a list of 'general duties'. These duties constitute both a plurality of first principles and are 'prima facie' in the sense that 'none is absolute – that is, each is capable of being overridden by the others'.

Hooker then argues that there can be no presumption that a Ross-style pluralist's list of general duties is 'tied together' and 'justified' by a single first principle, but that as a brute contingency there is such a principle:

> [J]ust as we must not assume Ross-style pluralism is not the best theory, we must not assume it is the best theory. What could make some other theory better . . . ? For one thing, it might be just as good as Ross-style pluralism at matching our intuitions, but go further in finding some more basic principle that ties together and justifies our various general moral duties. Suppose we find such a basis . . . Such a theory would have everything Ross-style pluralism has, plus something extra.[20]

This contingent discovery offers both an intellectual insight, valuable in its own right, meeting the third desideratum for theory choice, and assistance with controversial moral questions, meeting the fourth desideratum. Hooker proposes that there is such a contingent single principle, a form of rule consequentialism he has elsewhere described in detail, which avoids an overarching commitment to maximising the good. The theory does, as Hooker concedes, contain a certain amount of internal plurality, but remains distinct from pluralism in its claim that there is a single principle for selecting general duties, even if that principle contains pluralist elements. It is also 'at least a little more helpful' in the solution of controversial moral problems.[21]

The remainder of Hooker's argument consists of defensive concessions to undermine the appeal of Ross-style pluralism. He considers two positive arguments given in favour of such a form of pluralism: first, that it is phenomenologically plausible and affords a realistic place to the ineliminable role of moral judgement. Second, one defence of pluralism claims that the theory affords a realistic description of the complex historical deposits of our inherited moral ideas. On the first point, Hooker argues that rule consequentialism must simply accept the point that such exercise of judgement is ineliminable, hence the two theories are on a par. Less impressed by the second argument, he contends that our method of theory appraisal should be wholly ahistorical and that claims to the contrary commit the genetic fallacy.

This is a challenging argument, not least because of its subversive methodology; the way it takes an established rationale for pluralism and suggests that if fully thought through, the rationale takes one to a different theory. However, there is some unclarity as to exactly which form of pluralism is undermined by the argument. To begin to address this issue, I will discuss an important criticism of it put forward by Philip Stratton-Lake.

Stratton-Lake's main focus is on Hooker's claim that the view he is attacking represents, historically, the work of W. D. Ross. Stratton-Lake argues that Hooker has misunderstood Ross, but his criticism goes beyond the purely historical issue. Stratton-Lake argues that Hooker is wrong to claim that his rule-consequentialist principle can justify a candidate list of prima facie principles:

> For if A is able to justify B (where B stands for some practical principle, or set of practical principles) A must satisfy the minimal formal requirement that it be able to answer the question: what reason do we have to deliberate and act in accordance with B? If A cannot fulfil this requirement, then it cannot justify B. Hooker appears to satisfy this requirement because he misunderstands Ross's concept of a prima facie duty.[22]

The misunderstanding alleged is this: that Hooker takes prima facie duties to be both prima facie/pro tanto and duties. In fact Ross's prima facie duties are neither prima facie in the ordinary sense nor duties. They are not prima facie in the sense Hooker, following Kagan, acknowledges by shifting to the term 'pro tanto' – they are real duties, not apparent duties. But neither are they duties; they are, rather, the *grounds* of duties:

> For Ross, prima facie duties do not describe general, but overridable duties, but the general features of actions in virtue of which they are right or wrong: that is, they describe the sort of general considerations which are salient to determining what one's duty is.[23]

Stratton-Lake suggests that the point is more clearly made in terms of Phillipa Foot's distinction between verdictive and evidential considerations.[24] Foot argued that it was important to distinguish between two ways in which moral considerations figure in moral deliberation: they can figure either as evidence in support of overall moral conclusions or as the overall 'all things considered' practical verdict that is the upshot of deliberation.[25]

Deploying Foot's distinction, Stratton-Lake argues that, 'prima facie duties are general evidential moral considerations on the basis of which we reach an overall moral verdict, that is, judge which verdictive moral consideration obtains'.[26] Stratton-Lake proposes the term 'principle of moral salience' as a replacement for Ross's terminology and I will present his own view using this terminology.

Stratton-Lake argues that Hooker's misunderstanding of Ross's list of prima facie duties as a list of general verdictive considerations is an error that leads directly to Hooker's subsequent argument for basing the list on a rule-consequentialist principle. For, if mistakenly interpreted as as a list of normatively basic verdictive judgements, the list requires no further backing by relevant evidence in the particular case. So, when Hooker presses for a further justification, his search for a further grounding of the list can only take him from verdictive considerations of the first order to verdictive considerations of the second order – hence the rule-consequentialist principle.

Positively, the revised account which Stratton-Lake attributes to Ross works as follows: the list of principles of moral salience expresses 'the basic types of evidential moral considerations on which any answer to the question "why should I do that?" will ultimately come to rest'. Citing reasons that form the content of the principles is to 'cite a basic (morally) reason giving consideration', functioning evidentially.

There is an ambiguity, which Stratton-Lake acknowledges, in the idea of a principle of moral salience, between whether it explains the functioning of basic reasons qua evidence and whether a consideration figures as evidence at all. The first issue – the extent of evidential support – is plausibly a matter of degree, the latter not. The point is important as it is crucial to Stratton-Lake's counter-argument that there is nothing to be said on the latter, criterial point. But Hooker's theory claims to address this issue; the rule-consequentialist principle allows one to determine not only the relevance of, for example, the fact that an act is a keeping of a promise to practical deliberation, but also the salience to deliberation of promise-keeping at all. The issue is the basicness of the class of basic reasons Ross identifies, which is not addressed by relating a list of general verdictive considerations to another general verdict. As an attempt to address the former issue, the rule-consequentialist principle must be question begging as it already assumes that well-being and fairness are salient to moral deliberation – the issue being addressed.

This important argument offers more than insight into the historical Ross. Taking Stratton-Lake's point into account, one can develop an alternative account of Ross's position. Ross is *primarily* an Aristotelian particularist. Verdictive judgements are always judgements about particular cases.[27] However, on the basis of this knowledge which is 'intuitive', one can on the basis of Aristotelian induction form principles of general evidential salience which are not verdictive.[28] They capture the element of generality in moral deliberation, the tendency of grounds to figure as the basis of practical verdicts. It is the commitment to Aristotelian induction which grounds Ross's separate view that the epistemic status of these grounds is necessary and known a priori.[29] This attractive package of views would allow one to steer between the pluralist claim that pluralists cannot be particularists because this position 'renders theory redundant' and the particularist claim that Ross's position should be rejected because of its generalism.[30] Further discussion of the merits of *particularism*, as opposed to pluralism, would go beyond the ambit of this paper, but suffice to say that there may be resources in Ross's account for a rapprochement between particularism and generalism.[31]

For my present purposes, the great interest of Stratton-Lake's proposal is that it suggests a distortion imposed on Hooker's entire argument by taking its subject matter to be the relationship between sets of general and verdictive considerations. I will suggest that Hooker's adoption of the reflective equilibrium methodology leads to the same problem by a different route.

SECTION 3

The question that Stratton-Lake has posed focuses on the relation Hooker envisages between a 'Ross-style' list of duties and a rule-consequentialist principle. I will examine this relation in due course, in Section 5, below. First, however, I want to ask a prior question: why does Hooker assume that a pluralist account of morality will take this form? Both he and Stratton-Lake assume that Ross's version of pluralism is the most defensible form of pluralist theory, an assumption that I will contest in Section 5. Pluralism is a reflective account of morality, but why does reflection lead to abstraction, in this case to a list of general duties couched primarily, if not exclusively, in terms of 'thin' ethical concepts?[32]

In addressing this question, I want to examine an understanding of the operations of the method of reflective equilibrium that could have led Hooker to the assumption that Ross-style pluralism was the strongest form of pluralist theory and the version most worthy of consideration. While the method of reflective equilibrium is common ground between Hooker and myself, the understanding of the method I will criticise is not.

Many different interpretations have been developed of the method of reflective equilibrium. A recurrent point of dispute between these competing interpretations was the degree of difference between the method and the epistemological intuitionism of Moore and Ross. Rawls's interpretations of the method shifted through time, but broadly speaking both Rawls and Daniels (whose formulation of the methodology has become canonical) put considerable distance between the method and the intuitionism they attributed to Moore and to Ross.[33] In particular, they emphasised that the initial class of 'considered moral judgements' do not possess even prima facie epistemic privilege. They argued that the status any class of judgements enjoys cannot be determined until the entire process of proceeding from narrow to wide reflective equilibrium has been completed.[34]

From the earliest reflections on the method a succession of critics have argued that this understanding of reflective equilibrium could not be sustained. Considered moral judgements must possess prima facie epistemic status for the methodology to make sense;[35] the contrast between narrow and wide reflective equilibrium has been overdrawn by Daniels;[36] some judgements must function relatively foundationally in the process of establishing reflective equilibrium, thus making the overall theory not a coherence theory at all.[37] I agree with these critics that reflective equilibrium is a supplement to established forms of moral epistemology, does not form a coherence theory of justification and is compatible with a 'modest' foundationalism (or contextualism). However, with particular regard to Hooker's argument I will focus on two more detailed points: first, that the method of reflective equilibrium should not be given a rationalist interpretation; second, that considered moral judgements can be of any degree of abstraction.

On the rationalist conception of how one applies reflective equilibrium to the data supplied by methodological intuitionism that I have in mind, the two accounts essentially complement each other, and when conjoined yield a coherence theory of moral knowledge.[38] Methodological intuitionism lists our plural moral commitments, assigning no rank order of epistemic priority to this list of commitments. Reflective equilibrium is an essential supplement in that it allows one to determine relations of epistemic priority amongst the items of the list and to render the list of commitments a coherent set.

The process is as follows. The concrete and specific materials yielded up by methodological intuitionism are described by a set of abstract principles, which takes us as far as narrow reflective equilibrium. We then hope that some of our initial considered judgements can be disjoined from the rest, so that they can offer non-circular support to those background theories of the person, of the role of morality in society and in the psychology of the individual that lead to further revisions as we enter into wide reflective equilibrium. The end point of the process is a list of concrete intuitions harmonised, systematised, and rendered coherent by the ideal set of abstract principles, in the light of established background theories in the human sciences. The conjunction of methodological intuitionism and reflective equilibrium thus yields a coherence theory of moral knowledge. Methodological intuitionism is here playing the role of a methodological preliminary to the full application of reflective equilibrium. Its plurality of principles and judgements are not violated by any attempt to reduce them to a single principle. They are rather, by application of the reflective equilibrium method, woven into a different kind of unity. This is the unity of a set of judgements standing in relations of mutual coherence, or standing in a certain kind of relation to any proposed addition to the overall set.[39] I regard this view of methodological intuitionism and reflective equilibrium as completely mistaken.

The line of argument I have sketched can in my view be diagnosed as both *rationalist* and *epistemologically realist*.[40] It brings to its discussion of moral knowledge the following crucial assumptions: in every body of knowledge there is an underlying 'epistemic order' of relations of epistemic priority and subordination. The postulation of such an underlying order explains why the subjective order of enquiry should align with this underlying objective order of reasons. In this overall process, degrees of concreteness and abstraction directly covary with classification of phenomena as 'data' and 'theoretical principle'; the concrete is equivalent to the evaluative and the contestable; the abstract is equivalent to principles of right and the foci of rational incontestability. These are all traditionally rationalist assumptions and if unchallenged they make the misunderstanding of the relations between methodological intuitionism and reflective equilibrium inevitable.

This rationalist picture misconceives the structure of methodological intuitionism in the following way. It takes the list of our commitments to be exhausted by 'concrete', conflict-ridden 'intuitions' which express an underlying theoretical order or unity awaiting discovery. These intuitions are evaluative and thereby essentially contested in the face of the kind of evaluative pluralism familiar in modern societies. Rationality in the face of conflict is restored by uncovering the underlying epistemic order of principles structuring the surface diversity of our plural commitments. The formulation of principles, the foci of rational agreement, assists in the practical task of problem solving and the formulation of moral advice.[41]

This interpretation of the reflective equilibrium method also overlooks a second point, emphasised by Scanlon, which is that considered judgements are picked out not by their relative 'concreteness', but *solely* by our degree of initial confidence in them.[42] They can be of any degree of 'abstractness' or 'concreteness'. Further, the class can be expanded to judgements as to the *relevance* of considerations for and against judgements. Both points lead Scanlon to emphasise that the relation between considered judgements and principles is not that of 'extensional fit', and hence that the role of principles in this model is to provide a fuller understanding of our initial reasons for making our considered judgements. Thus it is a misunderstanding to treat the relation of 'considered judgement' and 'principle' on the model of data and theory in a scientific theory:

> Such modification is not a matter of abandoning data points which are too far from the line . . . but rather a matter of coming to believe that we have misunderstood the reasons we had for accepting certain conclusions . . . The revisability of the class of considered judgements thus illustrates the fact that the search for Reflective Equilibrium is essentially a first person enterprise; if

the judgements in question were those of other people, treated as a kind of sociological fact, then they would not be susceptible to this particular kind of revision.[43]

The relevance of this point for my purposes is that it brings out the way in which Rawls's method fails to meet the rationalist conception of 'theory'. Reflective equilibrium does not look for underlying structures in a body of neutral data in the way that scientific enquiry seeks underlying explanatory structures. It offers insight into existing commitments from an internal perspective which takes our moral commitments as a going concern.[44] I will concede that reflective equilibrium does seek *generality*. However, as Scanlon notes, reflective equilibrium takes within its purview principles of evidential salience as well as principles of judgement and the modified Rossian theory suggests a role within such an account for a finding of generality. This point, that reflective equilibrium seeks generality but not abstraction, can be separated from the claim that reflective equilibrium should be viewed as a coherence theory of moral justification. It should, by my lights, be reinterpreted as offering a perspicuous surview of existing commitments rather than a 'theory' of them in the rationalist sense and as 'modestly foundational' (or contextualist).

To what extent does the reflective equilibrium methodology lend itself to such a rationalist and epistemologically realist interpretation? Admittedly, proponents of the method have frequently warned against interpreting it as exemplifying what Dworkin called the 'natural model', as akin to the formulation of scientific generalisations or laws from observational evidence.[45] My point, however, is that the rationalist/epistemologically realist understanding of the method can survive even when explicitly distanced from an overly scientistic understanding of the procedure. This mistaken understanding of reflective equilibrium will take the phenomenological data supplied by methodological intuitionism as input and yield a 'Ross-style' list of discursive abstract principles as output, modulo some standing background theory in the human sciences. Thus, we have at least *an* explanation of why Hooker takes pluralism to take the form he explicitly considers.

So much for how one should *not* view the relation between methodological intuitionism and reflective equilibrium. How ought one to see them as related? Here it seems to me important to emphasise that the reflective equilibrium method is in fact compatible with a degree of modest foundationalism, a point established by both DePaul and Ebertz.[46] DePaul argues that there are two ways of understanding the reflective equilibrium method, distinguished by whether it is possible completely to revise firm, considered initial judgements, a 'conservative' and a 'radical' interpretation. On the conservative interpretation, the grounds of such judgements may be further understood, but the judgements function themselves 'relatively' foundationally, vis-à-vis the other judgements in the course of reflection.[47]

Ebertz puts the case for 'modest foundationalism' as follows, 'some beliefs must be justified in virtue of some source or sources of direct prima facie justification'.[48] He then offers a two-pronged argument against the coherentist interpretation of reflective equilibrium which focuses on the role of considered moral judgements. First, on a 'conservative' understanding of the process of reflection, 'both considered judgements and common presuppositions *function as* foundational beliefs'.[49] They are based on an individual's moral capacity to make firm judgements, 'to respond evaluatively to situations around them'.[50] They are subjected to reflection, but this does not change their role:

> [T]hey have a prima facie privileged justificatory status in the structure, a status which is not derived merely from their relationship to other beliefs . . .
> they have prima facie direct justification . . . In the reflective process they may be defeated or thrown out. Nevertheless, if they do survive the process, we have no reason to believe they somehow lose their direct justification.[51]

However, this leaves open the possibility of 'global' replacement of such judgements in the more radical model of reflective equilibrium. I have already suggested that there is no reason to believe reflective equilibrium can be given such a radical interpretation, but even if it is Ebertz points out that *some* sets of judgements will play the role of considered moral judgements:

> [T]he fact that an individual's initial considered moral judgements are all rejected as she seeks reflective equilibrium does not entail that in the end there are no considered moral judgements in the system. In fact, it is crucial to Rawls's understanding of reflective equilibrium . . . that when reflective equilibrium is reached the resulting system of beliefs involves a balanced set of considered moral judgements and other moral and theoretical beliefs.[52]

So reflective equilibrium is compatible with a degree of 'modest foundationalism'.[53] Now, Hooker does not disagree with this first point; given that he takes reflective equilibrium and pluralism to be naturally compatible, and given that pluralism is a theory that can take a 'moderately' foundationalist form, he must at least accept the consistency of this combination. In my view the real interest arises when this claim is combined with a second point: initial judgements, which become 'firmly held' considered judgements in the course of reflection, can be concrete ethical judgements deploying thick concepts.

On this alternative understanding of reflective equilibrium, starting out as it does from a class of judgements which include concrete judgements deploying thick concepts, it proceeds as follows. Methodological intuitionism supplies a set of judgements which describes our moral experience. A degree of reflection on conditions of error leads us to revise this class into the class of considered moral judgements. These judgements vary from specific judgements which largely deploy thick concepts to more general judgements more reliant on thin vocabulary. We have to take this initial set of judgements to possess some degree of belief worthiness, some direct justification. We now seek on the basis of further reflection to determine if any further degree of generality (not abstraction) can be derived from reflection on the class of considered moral judgements. The course of reflection may lead us to dismiss some of this set of considered moral judgements, but it does not follow that those that remain have lost what direct justification they possessed (Ebertz).[54]

The pluralist believes that at this point, the discerning of further generality within this class of judgements will be limited. On Ross's view, we will only discern general principles of evidential salience. Now comes the transition from narrow reflective equilibrium to wide.

The first question that arises is what motivates this next stage. Holmgren, in her critique of Daniels, points out that the move to wide reflective equilibrium is justified by Daniels by one central argument: that wide reflective equilibrium is a superior strategy to narrow reflective equilibrium for ensuring that we do not 'accidentally generalise' over our considered moral judgements but are, rather, discerning theoretically insightful and explanatory structure in our moral beliefs. Holmgren points out that this justification is not wholly convincing.

We need to draw on moral background theories which are independent of the class of considered moral judgements in the sense that Daniels explained: independent, because supported by a disjoined subset of our considered moral judgements, not the set as a whole. So the general principles that narrow reflective equilibrium has drawn up now have two forms of sources of support: their relation to considered moral judgements and their relation to moral background theories. These sources are independent of each other. But even if this proposal is realisable – and I do not personally believe it is – why should this come as a surprise to the more orthodox intuitionist, disinclined to move beyond narrow reflective equilibrium? They can point out how much they have achieved by reaching narrow reflective equilibrium: considered moral judgements have been screened a theory of error and reflectively revised in the light of such general principles as are available. Holmgren argues:

> If wide reflective equilibrium differs from narrow reflective equilibrium only in the use of background moral theories, the proponent of wide reflective equilibrium must acknowledge, with the moral intuitionist, both that our considered moral judgements have a prima facie credibility and that moral theories derive their credibility from the fact that they systematize these judgements. In this case wide reflective equilibrium should be regarded simply

as a more sophisticated methodology to be adopted by the intuitionist rather than as a methodology that allows us to bypass moral intuitionism, along with whatever difficulties this position may entail.[55]

She adds that narrow reflective equilibrium has its own resource for avoiding accidental generalisation over considered moral judgements: seeking as small a number of judgements which are maximally explanatory. Whether this resource is preferable to drawing on the background theories cited in wide reflective equilibrium is, she argues, an open question.[56] The pluralist agrees that the question is open in principle, but is sceptical as to the degree of further generality discernible in our considered moral judgements and is similarly sceptical as to the required independence of background theories in the human sciences. The reflective equilibrium method is an addition to the armoury of the moral epistemologist, but its deployment is not guaranteed to take us much beyond an unsystematic pluralism which offers us deeper insight into our previous ethical commitments, akin to a Wittgensteinian 'perspicuous survey'.[57]

We have really been returned, I suggest, to Rawls's original modest proposal: that when we take methodological intuitionism as a starting point and apply the method of reflective equilibrium to this initial data the outcome is open. Both a comprehensive coherence theory or a pluralist theory are attempts at reflective explanations and justifications of the ethical phenomena and how far each view can realise its conflicting ideals is to be judged on the merits of particular proposals.

Now let me be quite clear that Hooker does not make the error of taking wide reflective equilibrium to be the launch pad of a coherence theory of moral justification; this is made clear by his remarks on the plausible combination of Ross-style pluralism with the wide reflective equilibrium method. Nevertheless, he does describe the wide reflective equilibrium model in such a way as to suggest that it relates 'concrete' data to abstract principle, with the aim of arriving at a set of discursive verdictive principles. Could Hooker have been led to the error Stratton-Lake accuses him of because of his assumption that the application of the reflective equilibrium method generates a set of discursively stated principles exhibiting a high degree of abstractness, functioning as practical verdicts? There is a further step to be taken from this assumption of the level of abstraction at which reflective equilibrium operates to the move from evidential to verdictive considerations. However, it is natural to take that step for the following reason: one could move from contrasting the concrete with the abstract, as in the rationalist understanding of the wide reflective equilibrium model, to contrasting the concrete with the general, as in Ross's model, and take these contrasts to align. I will suggest that they do not.

To focus the issue, let me relate these comments on the reflective equilibrium model as a whole to Hooker's use of the model. In some respects Hooker is clearly on the side of the angels. He explicitly deploys wide reflective equilibrium from an internal perspective. He claims that it leads naturally to pluralism and that there need be no further development of the theory towards the global systematisation characteristic of a coherence theory. He further, crucially, dropped epistemological realism – the claim that our ethical beliefs fall into epistemic classes or the claim that within a class our beliefs stand in determinate relations of epistemic priority or subordination. This is, in fact, the linchpin of his argument strategy.

It is tempting to misread Hooker in the following way: the pluralist's list of ethical commitments can be underwritten, unified, and justified by postulating an additional underlying principle, the rule-consequentialist principle. This is to discern epistemic structure within the pluralist's list, and a structure such that the more fundamental consideration – the rule-consequentialist principle – underwrites the epistemically derived items on the list. It can then fairly be objected that Hooker's argument begs the question: where does the underlying principle come from and how is it to be explained?

This argument has no force against Hooker as he renounces any such appeal to epistemological realism. To the claim that it would be a surprising contingency if our ethical beliefs all stemmed from a single normative principle, Hooker's reply is that it is indeed a surprising contingency.

I would like to focus, however, on the epistemic relationships between the list of general duties and the consequentialist selection principle. These relations are of two kinds, explanatory and justificatory. The justificatory relations are also of three kinds: the case where the list of general duties and consequentialist selection principle are symmetrically related and the two cases where they are asymmetrically related. The latter covers the two cases where the list of general duties is derived from the consequentialist selection principle, and vice versa. Since it is not part of Hooker's case to claim that the consequentialist selection principle is derived from the list of general duties – though a pluralist would be tempted to argue for this – I will focus on the two relevant cases from among those I have distinguished.

The case where there is an asymmetry in justification between the list of general duties and the consequentialist selection principle, with the former being 'derived' from the latter, is the tempting misreading of Hooker. For if this interpretation were correct, Hooker's advocacy of a rule-consequentialist model would rest on a fixed relation of epistemic priority with an underlying rule-consequentialist structure determining the list of plural principles. There are two problems with this interpretation. First, it is incompatible with the adoption of the wide reflective equilibrium methodology Hooker has assumed. The structure of reflective equilibrium, with its dialectical interplay between degrees of confidence in judgements and the considered judgements themselves, does not have rigid relations of epistemic priority. There could be dialectical interplay between the degree of initial confidence we have in the list of general duties and the degree of confidence we have in the consequentialist selection principle such that *the latter* could be revised. This possibility is eliminated if Hooker adopts the structure of orthodox rule-consequentialist models and takes the list of general duties to be derived from the consequentialist selection principle. But then we have the second problem with this interpretation of Hooker: his distinctive claim is lost. Hooker would be simply pressing the claims of rule consequentialism against our ordinary commitments as represented by the list of general duties. There may be a case to be made here, but it is a familiar one – to which there are equally familiar responses.

On the alternative reading, the list of general duties and the consequentialist selection principle are in a symmetrical relation of epistemic justification. Neither is prior to the other. The consequentialist selection principle has no more intellectual authority than the list of general duties from which it inherits such authority, but the converse is also true. On this interpretation Hooker's central argument explicitly renounces epistemological realism: the underlying consequentialist assumption is not epistemologically prior to that of the principles on the pluralist's list. It simply adds a degree of simplifying systematisation.

I argue that this causes three problems. First, the underlying consequentialist assumption stands in a symmetrical relation of mutual support to the principles of the list and thus both its normative content and its explanatory power must covary with that of the initial list. Thus, our desire to have the entailment of the list by the consequentialist principle explained must be unrealisable. Second, there is an internal tension between the claim that Hooker's position is equally explanatory to that of the pluralist and that the underlying consequentialist principle offers normative grounding for the list. Suppose the list is revised in the light of a change in moral phenomenology, to preserve its claim of explanatory adequacy. It is unclear whether Hooker's underlying principle can also change. If it does not, the account is no longer equally explanatory as pluralism; if it does, then the principle is the underlying normative ground of the list in a sense which makes it epistemically prior to it. This is a lapse into epistemological realism which Hooker explicitly renounces. The sense that Hooker wants to have his cake (explanatory adequacy no less than that of pluralism) and eat it (normative superiority to pluralism) seems well grounded.

There are also reasons, on the symmetrical interpretation, to ask why the consequentialist selection principle is a better guide to contentious moral issues than the list of general duties? Our current moral understanding is captured by the list of general duties and we need judgement to extend that understanding to new cases. How is this judgement assisted by being given 'a rule to interpret a rule', as the consequentialist selection principle must now be understood to do?

So Hooker has a response to those who take his project to be that of discerning underlying order in our ethical ideas: he can straightforwardly reply that this is no part of his aim. The problem, though, is that his appeal to a brute contingency seems to leave the aim of explanation unappeased. The pressing question this leads to is what motivates the enquiry. We were confronted by the pluralist's list of commitments and told that, surprisingly, this list could be systematised by a single principle. But the principle has not derived its epistemic legitimacy from the list (unless we are to lapse immediately into pluralism). Neither is it the underlying ground of the epistemic legitimacy of the list. We have a symmetrical relation of epistemic consistency and Hooker's extra rule-consequentialist principle is idling; it is doing no explanatory work in explaining any of the entailment relations to which we were already committed, nor is it doing any justificatory work as its justificatory potential is entirely inherited from the pluralist's existing list. What, besides a quasi-aesthetic preference for simplicity, would lead us to embrace such a principle? One could add that simplicity, as a theoretical desideratum, only applies to two theories which are in other respects equally explanatory.

So the force of Hooker's argument seems moot on its most charitable reading. However, the discussion of the previous section may have given grounds for more radical doubts. For if Hooker is tacitly working with a model in which we examine the epistemic relations that obtain between lists of abstract discursive principles, we already have reasons to reject Hooker's assumptions. The application of reflective equilibrium to the phenomenological data supportive of pluralism will yield a form of pluralism which combines concrete ethical judgements with a degree of reflective generality – not a list of abstract principles.

SECTION 5

Stratton-Lake's diagnosis was that Hooker had misrepresented Ross's notion of a prima facie duty by taking such duties both to be duties and to be verdictive rather than evidential considerations. I have added the suggestion that Hooker presents an optional way of understanding the methodology of reflective equilibrium itself. How would my proposal combine with Stratton-Lake's further to undermine Hooker's argument? In the following way: Stratton-Lake's proposal was that, given the way Hooker understands the idea of a prima facie duty as a verdictive consideration, the further question which arises about a 'Ross-style' list must be whether a further underlying verdictive consideration could be the basis of such a list. However, if a prima facie duty is understood correctly as a combination of rule of evidential salience and as a substantive piece of evidence, the only further question is whether the rule of salience is an acceptable rule or whether the evaluative considerations in play are indeed evidence. (Rawls's original model focuses on both of these points: the issue of salience and the issue of direct evidential force.)

My suggestion is that, properly understood, the model of reflective equilibrium does not force us to view the data that ethical experience offers to reflection to take the form of a set of raw data and abstract principles. It converges with Stratton-Lake's claim as to what we should take the material available to reflection to be: a range of evaluative considerations of differing degrees of concreteness/abstraction, plus principles of right action deploying a 'thin' deontic vocabulary.

The important point Stratton-Lake has emphasised is that pluralism should be a thesis about the *grounds* and not the *contents* of judgements. If Ross is interpreted as Stratton-Lake advises, as introducing a class of specific evaluative considerations which are the grounds of duties, then the way is open to develop an alternative case for pluralism which begins *from* the case for metaethical cognitivism. This is certainly the direction of argument I would recommend, being committed primarily to a form of metaethical cognitivism which in my view radically shapes our conception of moral judgement.[58] Hooker argues that his position can be assessed by those who hold a variety of metaethical views, but on this line of argument his eirenic position seems misguided.

Beginning from this alternative starting point, Williams, at least, holds a form of pluralism that does not fit Hooker's characterisation. This is a problem for a theory which recommends itself on the grounds of the elimination of alternatives, which is Hooker's strategic method. Williams's form of pluralism is to a significant degree historicised. Its account of moral phenomenology takes that phenomenology to reflect the historical development of different sets of ethical ideas, which have to various degrees fused or remained incommensurable with each other. Furthermore, the degree to which the social reality described has proceeded along a path of typically modern reflection will determine the extent to which participants in sets of ethical arrangements deploy thick or thin concepts in describing their experience. [59]

Nevertheless, one can expect that the description of this phenomenology will deliver judgement of any degree of abstraction or concreteness, including the concrete deliverances of specific evaluations as well as 'thinner' vocabulary, which comes in degrees. All of these form the starting point for reflection and Williams further argues that the outcome of reflection will be a non-prioritist pluralism and a particularist account of judgement. The grounds for his particularism is the ubiquity of judgements of 'importance':

> Judgements of importance are ubiquitous, and are central to practical life and
> to reflection at a more general level about the considerations that go into

practical decision . . . It may be obvious that in general one kind of consideration is more important than another . . . but it is a matter of judgement whether in one particular set of circumstances that priority is preserved: other factors alter the balance, or it may be a very weak example of the consideration that generally wins. Last, there is no reason to believe that there is one currency in terms of which all relations of comparative importance can be represented . . . [For] any such currency . . . it will make sense to ask whether, on a given occasion or more generally, it is more important than something else.[60]

As a concession to Hooker, let's add to this position a commitment to the use of reflective equilibrium as an epistemological model, so that Hooker cannot simply object that this form of pluralism does not share a neutral starting point with his argument. As I have shown in Section 3, this addition does nothing materially to change the outcome. For reflective equilibrium, applied to the phenomenological materials Williams invokes, applies to beliefs whose contents is of any degree of concreteness and abstraction and does not automatically form an ascent from the 'thick' to the 'thin'. My argument has been that applying reflective equilibrium in this way will find generality and a degree of system in principles of moral salience, but (as Rawls allows) will leave pluralism intact as both the most plausible reflective account of morality and as compatible with particularism as the best theory of ethical judgement.[61] Reflective equilibrium is not particularly at the service of coherentist or abstracting theory, but is better viewed in Wittgensteinian terms as offering a 'perspicuous surview' of our existing ethical commitments, offering insight into the reasons we already hold.

The ubiquity of importance and the need for judgement figure in the explanation of why the reflective equilibrium method can have no implications for the degree of abstractness/concreteness of the content of the belief. Any plausible phenomenological description of the various evaluative beliefs we would reflectively endorse will find those beliefs range from a wide variety of judgements deploying 'thick' ethical concepts which we can confidently take to express moral knowledge, to other evidential or verdictive judgements employing thinner deontic vocabulary. All of this vocabulary can figure in judgements of any degree of abstractness or concreteness.

These beliefs are functioning 'modestly foundationally', that is, as initial considered judgements possessing a direct justification as exemplifications of moral knowledge, further buttressed by reflection which does not overturn the direct justification of the beliefs but deepens their ground or status as 'firm' beliefs for the subject. They may be couched in 'thick' or 'thin' concepts: a belief in an abstract principle of right may yield to a vivid appreciation of a betrayal of a friend.

Conversely, an appreciation of suffering caused may have to be outweighed by a commitment of principle, such as the need to avoid negotiation with evil doers in coercive crises. The need for 'importance' and judgement reflects the multidimensionality of such judgements. This feature of the reflective equilibrium method makes it implausible to assume that the product of wide reflective equilibrium will be a set of abstract principles. This is another assumption to which Hooker is not entitled, in addition to his assumption that pluralism is a thesis about verdictive judgements.

My argument is that whatever the merits of Hooker's proposal for tying together and systematising a list of discursive, abstract, and very general duties by a single discursive, abstract principle for selecting duties, it seems very implausible to see the more realistic form of pluralism I have described as awaiting systematisation by a single principle. This alternative form of pluralism does not take the form of a list of principles of a parallel degree of abstraction, even allowing for the application of the reflective equilibrium method. By adding the modifier 'Ross-style' to the term 'pluralism' Hooker made the case for the subversion of pluralism look more straightforward than it in fact is; it restricted pluralism to a thesis which has already taken the phenomenological data and reduced it to a list of abstract discursive principles primarily couched in thin vocabulary.[62] Hooker may, as Stratton-Lake alleges, make the further error of viewing these principles as functioning verdictively, but from the pluralist's perspective the seeds of this error were sown earlier in an unjustified assumption about the form a pluralist theory would take. Certainly Hooker's claim to have refuted a representative form of pluralism can be resisted even if one conceded the success of his argument against 'Ross-style pluralism'.

SECTION 6

In conclusion, I have attempted in this chapter to rebut Hooker's subversion of the arguments for pluralism in three ways. First, I have sought an explanation of why the pluralism he discusses takes the form of a list of abstract discursive principles; I have suggested that Hooker's adoption of the methodology of reflective equilibrium incorporates an optional, rationalist assumption about how such a model functions that makes this apparently neutral assumption contentious from a pluralist perspective. Assuming that reflective equilibrium seeks abstraction and ascent from thick ethical judgements to the thin leads to the fundamental error in Hooker's position: assuming that pluralism takes the form of a list of discursive principles. This offers a deeper grounding for Stratton-Lake's complementary criticism that Hooker takes the list to be functioning verdictively, rather than evidentially. Second, I have offered direct criticisms of Hooker's argument in order to suggest that it is unworkable in its own terms. Third, I have described a form of pluralism to which Hooker's argument does not apply and which undermines his claim that rule consequentialism has eliminated the other available conceptions of normative ethical judgement. In my view pluralism has remained resistant to attempted subversion.[63]

NOTES

1. Brad Hooker, 'Ross-style Pluralism versus Rule-consequentialism', *Mind*, 105 (1996), pp. 531–52
2. The form defended by Hooker in, inter alia, 'Rule Consequentialism', *Mind*, 99 (1990), pp. 67–77; 'Rule-Consequentialism, Incoherence, Fairness', *Proceedings of the Aristotelian Society*, 95 (1995), pp. 19–35. See also R. B. Brandt, 'Some Merits of One Form of Rule-Utilitarianism', reprinted in *Morality, Utilitarianism and Rights* (New York: Cambridge University Press, 1992).
3. Stratton-Lake, 'Can Brad Hooker's Rule-Consequentialist Principle Justify Ross's Prima Facie Duties?', *Mind* 106 (1997), pp. 751–8.
4. Pluralism has been defended by W. D. Ross, whose work will be discussed in detail, and in contemporary moral philosophy by Davidson, Nagel, Williams, Berlin, Taylor, and Gaut. Berys Gaut, 'Moral Pluralism', *Philosophical Papers*, 22 (1993), pp. 17–40, contains further bibliographic references.
5. I have adopted the typographical convention of referring to concepts in bold typeface.
6. Foot's distinction between evidential and verdictive considerations will also be important in what follows, but I take this to be a distinction between ways in which reasons can function, rather than as forming a classification of types of reasons.
7. Rawls, *A Theory of Justice* (Cambridge, MA: Harvard University Press, 1971), p. 34. Strictly this is a definition of 'non-prioritist pluralism', as Urmson, Swanton, Williams, and Gaut note, but I will drop the qualification taking it that all subsequent uses of the term 'pluralism' in this chapter refer to the non-prioritist variant. (But see footnote 9, below.) See especially Christine Swanton, 'The Rationality of Ethical Intuitionism', *Australasian Journal of Philosophy*, 65 (1987), pp. 172–81, note 3 on p. 172.
8. Rawls has in addition a series of 'in principle' arguments against pluralism, well dealt with by Christine Swanton and Berys Gaut in their respective papers: Christine Swanton, 'The Rationality of Ethical Intuitionism'; Berys Gaut, 'Moral Pluralism'.
9. Philip Stratton-Lake has pointed out to me that this claim of Rawls's is false: the pluralist could, for example, assign lexical priority to perfect over imperfect duties. Furthermore, not every priority claim need be as strong as lexical ordering.
10. Robert Audi, 'Intuitionism, Pluralism and the Foundations of Ethics', in W. Sinnott-Armstrong and M. Timmons (eds.), *Moral Knowledge* (New York: Oxford University Press, 1996), pp. 101–36.
11. J. O. Urmson, 'A Defence of Intuitionism', *Proceedings of the Aristotelian Society* (1975), pp. 111–19; Bernard Williams, 'What Does Intuitionism Imply?' in *Making Sense of Humanity* (Cambridge: Cambridge University Press, 1995).
12. I take the first line of objection from those critics of Rawlsian reflective equilibrium who objected to what they took to be the lingering intuitionism of Rawls's commitment to starting from 'our' considered moral judgements: R. M. Hare, 'Rawls's Theory of Justice', reprinted in N. Daniels (ed.), *Reading Rawls* (New York: Basic Books, 1975); Peter Singer, 'Sidgwick and Reflective Equilibrium', *Monist* 58 (1974), pp. 493–4. It should be clear from what follows that my sympathies lie with Rawls, not his critics, and that this line of objection seems to conflate the requirement that we should be able critically to challenge any claim to moral knowledge with the claim that we must be able critically to challenge all such claims. Hooker is not committed in this way to global scepticism about our considered judgements, nor to defending consequentialism in such a form that it would evade such a global form of scepticism.
13. I take the charge that pluralism conflates justification and explanation to be implied by Hooker's remarks on the 'genetic fallacy'; Hooker, 'Ross-style Pluralism', pp. 546–7.
14. In *Value and Context* (Oxford University Press, forthcoming), especially chs 5, 6 and 7.
15. Gaut's 'Moral Pluralism' similarly emphasises that any defensible pluralism must build into itself safeguards against the distortion of moral thought by power and interests. Gaut builds into his theory the quasi-contractualist idea of 'generative reflection'. There are similarities between this idea and the constraints I invoke in *Value and Context*. The main point of difference is that Gaut's theory is not sensitive to history, either in its conception of the problem to be solved or of the solution. Gaut assumes that there is single unitary 'common sense morality', which Ross definitively described making the latter's theory phenomenologically accurate. I am not convinced, on historical grounds, that anyone is entitled to this assumption.
16. The papers by Daniels now form Part I of *Justice and Justification: Reflective Equilibrium in Theory and Practice* (Cambridge: Cambridge University Press, 1996).
17. *Value and Context*, ch 7.

18. For a conception of how social theory can be modelled as a Lakatosian research programme with a core model of the human subject as its basis, see Terence Ball, 'From Paradigms to Research Programs: Towards a Post-Kuhnian Political Science', *American Journal of Political Science*, 20 (1976), pp. 151–77; J. Donald Moon, 'Values and Political Theory: A Modest Defence of a Qualified Cognitivism', *Journal of Politics*, 39 (1977), p. 900.

19. Hooker, 'Ross-style Pluralism', p. 534.

20. Ibid., p. 536.

21. Ibid., Section 6.

22. Stratton-Lake, 'Can Brad Hooker's Rule-consequentialist Principle Justify Ross's Prima Facie Duties?', p. 752.

23. Ibid., pp. 752-3.

24. Phillipa Foot, 'Are Moral Considerations Overriding?', *Virtues and Vices* (Oxford: Basil Blackwell Publisher, 1985), pp. 181–8, especially p. 182.

25. 'That a promise is being broken, or a man killed or injured, is an evidential moral consideration; that something immoral is being done is a verdictive moral consideration.' (Foot, 'Are Moral Considerations Overriding?' p. 182.)

26. Stratton-Lake, 'Can Brad Hooker's Rule-consequentialist Principle Justify Ross's Prima Facie Duties?', p. x.

27. Ross wrote: 'We apprehend prima facie rightness to belong to the nature of any fulfilment of a promise. From this we come by reflection to apprehend the self-evident prima facie rightness of an individual act of a particular type . . . But no act is ever, in virtue of falling under some general description, necessarily actually right; its rightness depends on its whole nature and not on any element in it.' *The Right and the Good*, p. 33.

28. 'Intuitive', in the limited sense Audi clarifies in 'Intuitionism, Pluralism and the Foundations of Ethics'. Among the misconceptions of intuitionism that Audi rebuts are the claims that Ross believed we possessed a special faculty of intuition, that the deliverances of such a faculty are indefeasible and that such propositions cannot be known to be true without the judger also knowing the epistemic status of the judgement (for example, that it is self-evident).

29. This is, immediately, an instance where Audi's reminder that one can know a proposition to be true without knowing its epistemic status is useful for defenders of Ross's position.

30. On the first point, it can be argued that the list of principles of moral salience is not verdictive and hence is not in competition with particularism about how one forms all things considered verdictive judgements in particular cases. The two accounts have different objects. On the latter point, it can be argued that Ross's generalism is solely at the level of evidential considerations and does not impact directly on his espousal of particularism, which he seems to hold for many of the reasons that have moved contemporary particularists such as Williams and Dancy. Dancy especially bases his case for particularism and his rejection of Ross on the 'holistic' nature of reasons, but Ross's remark concerning the 'rightness' of an act as depending on its 'whole nature' would seem to anticipate Dancy's point.

31. Philip Stratton-Lake, in personal correspondence, has put to me the case for resisting such a description of Ross as an Aristotelian particularist. While Ross is a particularist about particular verdictive judgements and universal verdictive principles, he does believe, as I have described, that there are exceptionless moral principles, basic evidential moral principles. On that ground alone Stratton-Lake finds the term 'particularist' misleading, but notes that this registers a terminological preference. Audi notes that, '[Ross] holds the view that ethical generalizations do not *independently* carry evidential weight in such conflicts [between duties]. One should not, e.g. appeal to a second order generalization that duties of justice are stronger than duties of fidelity. Rather, one should focus on the specific facts and, in that light, determine what one's duty is.' 'Intuitionism, Pluralism and the Foundations of Ethics', p. 105.

32. As Brad Hooker reminded me, the kind of discursive principle he assumes will be on a Ross-style pluralist's list will include both thick and thin ethical concepts: an example would be 'it is pro tanto wrong to be dishonest'. But I would interpret such a principle in the light of my supervenience claim that thin ethical concepts supervene on thick ethical concepts. It is the thick concept in such a principle that is doing all the justificatory work.

33. The major point of difference between Rawls and Daniels is that while both see the method of reflective equilibrium as a form of coherence theory, in Rawls's eyes this allows one to construct ethical truth, whereas Daniels leaves open the combination of a coherentist epistemology with a form of realism in the manner of Boyd and Brink.

34. This is particularly emphasised by Daniels in 'Wide Reflective Equilibrium and Theory Acceptance in Ethics', reprinted in *Justice and Justification*, pp. 21–46.

35. Stefan Sencerz, 'Moral Intuitions and Justification in Ethics', *Philosophical Studies*, 50 (1986), pp. 77–95; Margaret Holmgren, 'Wide Reflective Equilibrium and Objective Moral Truth', *Metaphilosophy*, 18 (1987), pp. 108–25.

36. Margaret Holmgren, 'The Wide and Narrow of Reflective Equilibrium', *Canadian Journal of Philosophy*, 19 (1989), pp. 43–60.

37. Michael DePaul, 'Two Conceptions of Coherence Methods in Ethics', *Mind*, 96 (1987), pp. 463–1; 'Reflective Equilibrium and Foundationalism', *American Philosophical Quarterly*, 23 (1986), pp. 59–69; Roger Ebertz, 'Is Reflective Equilibrium a Coherentist Model?', *Canadian Journal of Philosophy*, 23 (1993), pp. 193–214.

38. A position explicitly defended by Kai Nielsen in 'Reflective Equilibrium and the Transformation of Philosophy', *Metaphilosophy*, 20 (1989), pp. 235–46, in addition to the construal of reflective equilibrium as leading to a coherence theory of justification combinable with an independently motivated realism cited in note 33 above.

39. A distinction explained by Michael Williams in *Unnatural Doubts: Epistemological Realism and the Basis of Scepticism* (Oxford: Basil Blackwell, 1991), p. 276: 'Although officially "coherence" designates a property of our belief system taken as a whole, it often gets treated as the name of a relation that a candidate belief may or may not bear to some antecedently given system . . . We may call the two versions of coherence "systematic" and "relational".'

40. I take these terms from the excellent discussion of these issues in Williams, *Unnatural Doubts*.

41. Why do rationalism and epistemological realism of this form survive in moral and political philosophy when they are on the retreat elsewhere – save, interestingly, the philosophy of mathematics? One plausible historical diagnosis invokes the seventeenth-century trope of 'Maker's Knowledge', the theme that just as divine insight into reality is underpinned by reality being a divine construction, so moral and political knowledge offers certainty as it is insight into a moral and political order we have constructed. I discuss this issue further in *Value and Context*, ch. 7.

42. Rawls's earliest presentation of the reflective equilibrium method restricted considered judgements to judgements about particular cases; it was generality that was allowed into the method later. For the earlier version, see 'Outline for a Decision Procedure for Ethics', *Philosophical Review*, 60 (1951). The point that in the mature theory considered moral judgements can be of any degree of generality is emphasised in the valuable discussion of Thomas Scanlon, 'The Aims and Authority of Moral Theory', *Oxford Journal of Legal Studies*, 12 (1992), pp. 1–23.

43. Scanlon, 'The Aims and Authority of Moral Theory', pp. 9–10.

44. Scanlon now describes the aim of 'Philosophical Enquiry' into morality as 'explain[ing] more clearly the kind of reasons those who accept morality have for doing so', in ibid, pp. 1–23.

45. Ronald Dworkin, 'The Original Position', reprinted in N. Daniels (ed.), *Reading Rawls*, pp. 16–52. The disanalogy between the adjustment of considered judgement to principle and the adjustment of observational evidence to covering law in a scientific context was stressed by Daniels in Section 3B of 'Wide Reflective Equilibrium and Theory Acceptance in Ethics'.

46. DePaul, 'Two Conceptions of Coherence Methods in Ethics'; Ebertz, 'Is Reflective Equilibrium a Coherentist Model?'

47. As Ebertz notes, this distinction is connected to the 'wide'/'narrow' reflective equilibrium distinction, 'Is Reflective Equilibrium a Coherentist Model?', note 11. 'Wide' reflective equilibrium seems to give one greater leverage on initial considered moral judgements. Thus one would need to establish that the distinction between 'wide' and 'narrow' was overdrawn by Daniels as is argued by Holmgren, 'The Wide and Narrow of Reflective Equilibrium'.

48. Ebertz, 'Is Reflective Equilibrium a Coherentist Model?', p. 201.

49. Ibid., p. 204. My italics, to emphasise the contextualist reading of this remark, which would highlight how beliefs can function foundationally within a context.

50. I interpolate the term 'firm' into Ebertz's theory, taken from Audi's 'Intuitionism, Pluralism and the Foundations of Ethics', pp. 109–10.

51. Ebertz, 'Is Reflective Equilibrium a Coherentist Model?', p. 202.

52. Ibid., p. 203.

53. I would, like Mark Timmons, in fact interpret Ebertz's conclusion differently, as an argument for contextualism. I discuss contextualism at length in *Value and Context* and it is not my direct concern here.

54. Holmgren further notes, 'In attributing prima facie credibility to our considered moral judgements, we need not claim that any of them are in principle immune to revision. We need only claim that they must be regarded as credible unless we have good reason to revise or discard them', 'The Wide and Narrow of Reflective Equilibrium', p. 46, n. 8.

55. Ibid., p. 57.

56. On the basis of her interesting argument on pp. 58–9 that if a single principle in narrow reflective equilibrium, P, captures a wide range of considered moral judgements which is captured by a plurality of background theories Q,R,S,T in wide reflective equilibrium, the latter must be more internally complex because of the independence

constraint. So a theory which was based on P would be preferable to the theory based on Q,R,S,T. Holmgren concludes that 'the strategy narrow reflective equilibrium embodies for avoiding accidental generalisation is in fact more basic . . . than the strategy embodied in wide reflective equilibrium. However, [the latter] is clearly workable . . . it seems appropriate for the sophisticated moral intuitionist to regard these two strategies as complementary rather than competing techniques.' 'The Wide and Narrow of Reflective Equilibrium', p. 59.

57. How could it? It is, after all, only a methodological proposal. It cannot be expected to yield a coherence theory of moral justification; this would have to be a (surprising) upshot of deploying the method.

58. See *Value and Context*, chs 1 to 7.

59. Williams also claims that this process can be continued to destroy the ethical knowledge that particular groups have; for doubts about that extra step in the argument see *Value and Context*.

60. *Making Sense of Humanity*, p. 190. Williams elsewhere rejects 'the general additive model of moral considerations or reasons in terms of the resolution of forces: if a type of consideration . . . ever in itself exerts an influence, then it always exerts an influence, and the method of agreement and difference can be used to isolate the influence it exerts. I see no necessity to accept this idea; there are surely many examples of non-moral practical reasoning, and also of aesthetic judgement, that tell against it' ('Acts and Omissions, Doing and Not Doing', reprinted in *Making Sense of Humanity*, p. 57). For parallel arguments see Dancy, *Moral Reasons*, pp. 82–4.

61. Rawls does, after all, envisage reflective equilibrum as applying to principles of the evidential salience of reasons as well as to reasons themselves.

62. For the rider 'primarily' see note 20.

63. I am grateful for help with this paper to Kathryn Brown, Roger Crisp, Brad Hooker, Martin Stone, and Philip Stratton-Lake.

10

Why Rule Consequentialism is not Superior to Ross-style Pluralism

Phillip Montague

In its standard form, act consequentialism can be considered monistic, since it implies that an action's possessing a certain single feature (that of maximising aggregate value) is necessary and sufficient for that action to be morally required. Thought of in these terms, rule consequentialism is pluralistic – as are deontological theories of the sort espoused by W. D. Ross.[1] In view of the notoriously serious difficulties associated with act consequentialism and other forms of moral monism, pluralistic theories are certainly worth considering; and the question naturally arises of whether some basis exists for determining which of these theories to accept. In particular, is there any basis for choosing between rule consequentialism and Ross-style pluralism?

Brad Hooker has proposed such a basis in the form of four adequacy criteria for moral theories.[2] He maintains, moreover, that rule consequentialism satisfies all four criteria, but that Ross-style pluralism fails to satisfy one of them. According to Hooker, then, rule consequentialism has all the advantages of Ross-style pluralism, together with an additional advantage that is important enough to render the former superior to the latter as a moral theory. I will argue here, however, that Hooker too easily assumes that rule consequentialism satisfies all of his criteria. I will also suggest that rule consequentialism has a disadvantage not possessed by Ross-style pluralism. Since the disadvantage to which I refer is not obviously a failure to satisfy any of Hooker's four adequacy criteria, these criteria might need supplementation, or at least modification in certain ways. Although my discussion focuses on certain of Hooker's views, much of what I say is applicable to the general problem of formulating and defending rule consequentialism.

Hooker states his criteria as follows:

(1) Moral theories must be internally coherent.

(2) Moral theories must have implications that cohere with the moral convictions we share and have confidence in, after careful reflection and in the light of our best theories in metaphysics, psychology, sociology, economics, etc.

(3) Moral theories should specify what (if anything) ties together our various general principles and justifies them.

(4) Moral Theories should help us deal with moral questions about which we are not confident, or do not agree.[3]

Hooker claims that, whereas rule consequentialism satisfies all four of these criteria, Ross-style pluralism fails to satisfy condition (3).

As interpreted by Hooker, rule consequentialism is the view that actions are determined to be permissible, obligatory, and so on by rules belonging to 'codes' that have a certain status; and whether some code has the requisite status is determined by whether its

> inculcation in the overwhelming majority of the next generation could reasonably be expected to result in as good consequences (aggregate well-being and fairness) as could reasonably be expected to result from any other identifiable code.[4]

Rule consequentialism therefore exemplifies a general type of double-level theory of which rule egoism, contractualism, and 'rule' versions of divine command theories are also examples.

Although Hooker formulates rule consequentialism as concerned with sets of rules, for simplicity's sake I will pretend that his formulation refers to individual rules rather than to entire codes.[5] In addition, I will use 'maximises value' as an abbreviation for the maximisation condition stipulated in the quoted passage. In light of these simplifying assumptions, rule consequentialism can be stated as follows:

> (R) An action is morally obligatory if and only if its being obligatory follows from a rule that maximises value.

If Hooker is correct in claiming that rule consequentialism satisfies (2), then it has implications that match certain 'moral convictions'. Presumably, these implications include the rules of Ross-style pluralism, rules that I will call 'Rossian'.

If rule consequentialism is interpreted according to R, however, then it does not imply the Rossian rules – or any other rules for that matter. Moreover, R is not a particularly perspicuous formulation of rule consequentialism since it obscures the double-level character of the theory. Both these problems are solved if R is replaced by

> (R1) An action is morally obligatory if and only if its being obligatory follows from a rule that is true, and rules are true if they maximise value,

and if R1 is conjoined with this proposition:

> (R2) The Rossian rules maximise value.

The conjunction of R1 with R2 implies that the Rossian rules are true. In other words, rule consequentialism (interpreted according to R1) implies the Rossian rules if R2 is true; and, in fact, Hooker takes R2 for granted.

But even though Ross-style pluralists tend to be cognitivists and to regard their rules (or, better perhaps, their *principles*) as true, Hooker adopts a position of neutrality on the question of whether there are such things as moral truths and falsehoods. If this neutrality is to be respected, then R1 will not do as a formulation of rule consequentialism. The question remains, then, of how to interpret rule consequentialism so that it implies the Rossian rules (in a manner that reveals its double-level structure, and on the assumption that R2 is true); and here are two possible alternatives to R1 that might appear to do the trick:

> (R3) An action is morally obligatory if and only if its being obligatory follows from a rule with which people are morally obligated to comply, and people are morally obligated to comply with rules that maximize value.
>
> (R4) An action is morally obligatory if and only if its being obligatory follows from a rule that is morally justified, and rules are morally justified if they maximize value.

Even if R2 is true, however, neither R3 nor R4 implies the Rossian rules. Rather, they respectively imply that people are obligated to comply with the Rossian rules, and that the Rossian rules are morally justified. Are these implications sufficient to satisfy Hooker's criterion (2)? While the answer to this question might appear to depend on whether (2) is construed so that it does not require theories to imply the Rossian rules per se, R3 and R4 are in fact open to interpretations under which (given R2) they *do* seem to imply the Rossian rules.

Note first of all that R3 and R4 are equivalent if 'Rule r is morally justified' is equivalent to 'People are morally obligated to comply with r'; and, in fact, it is hard to see how else the notion of a morally justified rule might be interpreted.[6] Suppose now that the rule that promise-keeping is morally obligatory is morally justified.

Then people are morally obligated to comply with the rule that promise-keeping is morally obligatory. But 'People are morally obligated to comply with the rule that promise-keeping is morally obligatory' is equivalent to 'Promise-keeping is morally obligatory.' Hence, given R2 and either R3 or R4, the rule that promise-keeping is morally obligatory is morally justified, which implies that promise-keeping is morally obligatory.

Ross-style pluralists are almost certain to insist, however, that their rules are concerned with prima facie obligations, and hence that rule consequentialism implies the Rossian rules only if it can accommodate the distinction between obligations that are prima facie on the one hand, and obligations that are strict (*sans phrase*, actual) on the other.[7] In considering whether rule consequentialism can satisfy this condition, it will be convenient to focus on the following formulation of the theory:

> (R5) An action is morally obligatory if and only if it is of a kind K such that acts of kind K are morally obligatory; and acts of kind K are morally obligatory if the rule 'Acts of kind K are morally obligatory' maximises value.

Suppose now that rule consequentialism is supposed to deliver conclusions about the strict obligatoriness of actions. Then if moral rules are interpreted in the standard Rossian way, the first occurrence of 'obligatory' in R5 refers to a strict obligation and the other occurrences refer to prima facie obligations. Then R5 implies that an action is strictly obligatory if it is of a kind such that acts of that kind are prima facie obligatory, and this implication is simply false. R5 is therefore false if it is made to accommodate the Rossian distinction between prima facie and strict obligations in the manner just suggested.[8]

Certain modifications of R5 might seem to improve its chances of success. For example, the first component of R5 might be replaced by 'An action is (strictly) morally obligatory if and only if it is of a kind K' such that actions of kind K' are (prima facie) morally obligatory *and the action is not of a kind K' such that refraining from acts that are K' is (prima facie) morally obligatory*. Unfortunately, R5 would again be false if modified in this way. Another possibility would consist in stipulating that all occurrences of 'obligatory' in R5 refer to prima facie obligations. While R5 might be true under this interpretation, however, rule consequentialism would then imply nothing about the strict obligatoriness of particular actions and might therefore be incomplete.[9]

If the problems just described centre on the relation between prima facie and strict obligations, then they will plague Ross-style pluralism no less than rule consequentialism. In fact, however, the problems in question arise not from the prima facie–strict distinction, but rather from the fact that rule consequentialism purports to provide conditions that are necessary and sufficient for an action to be (strictly) obligatory; and Ross-style pluralism need not (and I think should not) purport to provide any such conditions.

My purpose here is not to foist an unworkable or otherwise inadequate formulation of rule consequentialism on its proponents, but rather to emphasise the importance of providing a really clear and defensible statement of the theory. I strongly suspect, moreover, that the barriers to producing a satisfactory formulation of rule consequentialism are quite formidable, and that surmounting them would require more that merely tinkering with wording. The barriers to which I refer are particularly prominent if Hooker is right in claiming that rule consequentialism must imply the Rossian rules, and if the rules are assigned their standard Rossian interpretations.

To be sure, rule consequentialism can imply the Rossian rules – and hence satisfy Hooker's criterion (2) – even if it is false (as long as R2 is true). Although rule consequentialism need not be true for it to satisfy Hooker's criterion (2), however, the theory satisfies criterion (3) only if it is true.[10]

In making this last statement, I have in mind the requirement that moral theories *justify* the Rossian rules. Criterion (3) also requires that moral theories tie rules together, and this requirement seems open to interpretations under which it can be satisfied by rule consequentialism even if the theory is false. To simplify matters, I will assume that rule consequentialism ties the Rossian rules together by attributing moral significance to a feature (namely, that of maximising value) that is possessed by all the Rossian rules. Then rule consequentialism ties the Rossian rules together only if R2 is true (that is, only if the Rossian rules maximise value), but perhaps even if the theory itself is false.

In stating his criterion (3), Hooker does not distinguish between moral and epistemic justification. Although I strongly suspect that Hooker's concern is with the latter, some brief comments on moral justification might serve to eliminate certain potentially annoying difficulties.

I introduced the notion of moral justification in considering R4 as a possible statement of rule consequentialism, and suggested that 'Rule r is morally justified' is equivalent to 'Complying with r is morally obligatory.' I also noted that, if r has the form 'Acts of kind K are morally obligatory,' then 'Complying with r is morally obligatory' is equivalent to r itself – which implies that 'r is morally justified' is equivalent to r. Now, if rule consequentialism (interpreted according to R4 or R5) is true, and if R2 is also true, then rule consequentialism morally justifies the Rossian rules. But since 'Rule r is morally justified' is equivalent to r, 'Rule consequentialism morally justifies the Rossian rules' is equivalent to 'Rule consequentialism *implies* the Rossian rules and rule consequentialism is true'. Likewise, since Ross-style pluralism trivially implies the Rossian rules, it *morally* justifies the Rossian rules if it is true. If, therefore, Hooker's criterion (3) is construed as referring to moral justification, then Ross-style pluralism is no worse off than rule consequentialism with respect to satisfying that criterion.

The concept of moral justification can now be set aside, and in the remainder of this discussion I will be concerned only with epistemic justification.

It seems clear enough that rule consequentialism justifies the Rossian rules only if it is true, and can therefore imply the Rossian rules without justifying them. This necessary condition for justification is not sufficient, however. The point being made here is commonly brought to bear against certain versions of the divine command theory by way of the familiar Socratic distinction between, on the one hand, an action's being obligatory because God commands that it be performed and, on the other, God's commanding that an action be performed because it is obligatory. The proposition that all actions commanded by God are obligatory is completely compatible with the proposition that no actions are obligatory *because* God commands them. This becomes clear on noting that God might command actions to be performed because they are obligatory – from which it follows that actions are not obligatory because God commands them. Analogously, a type of action might be obligatory if the rule affirming that the act type is obligatory maximises value; and yet the act type might not be obligatory *because* it maximises value.[11]

The upshot, then, is that rule consequentialism justifies the Rossian rules only if something like the following is true:

> (R7) Complying with a Rossian rule is morally obligatory *because the rule maximises value.*

If, for example, rule consequentialism justifies the rule that promise-keeping is obligatory, then promise-keeping is obligatory because the rule 'Promise-keeping is obligatory' maximises value.[12] Merely to stipulate R7 would be objectionably ad hoc, however; and a simple thought experiment can be used to undermine R7.

Thus, suppose that the rule that promise-keeping is morally *forbidden* would maximise value. Then, according to R7, promise-keeping would be morally forbidden. Three options now present themselves: either (i) reject R7; or (ii) deny that the rule that promise-keeping is forbidden could maximise value; or (iii) acknowledge that, if the rule that promise-keeping is morally forbidden did turn out to maximise value, then promise-keeping would be morally forbidden. To select (i), however, would amount to rejecting rule consequentialism (or at least to abandoning Hooker's criterion (3), thereby depriving him of his primary reason for preferring rule consequentialism to Ross-style pluralism). As for (ii), some reason is clearly required for denying that the rule that promise-keeping is forbidden could maximise value; and perhaps the most plausible basis for this denial is the claim that so counter-intuitive a rule could not possibly maximise value. This claim would imply that moral rules are not justified in virtue of their maximising value, however. In the absence of some alternative basis on which to select option (ii), it – like (i) – is incompatible with rule consequentialism as a theory that justifies the Rossian rules.

We are therefore left with option (iii): bite the proverbial bullet and say that if the rule that promise-keeping is morally forbidden did turn out to maximise value, then promise-keeping would indeed be morally forbidden. This option is incompatible with Hooker's approach to moral theorising as reflected throughout his article and in a particularly clear and concise fashion in this passage:

> I am looking for a theory that matches and makes sense of our considered convictions (or 'intuitions' in some metaphysically and epistemologically neutral sense of the term). I furthermore admit that we are more certain of our intuitions (moral verdicts) that we are of any theory. So I admit that in moral theorizing our confident shared intuitions are fundamental.[13]

The clear message here is that moral theories are tested against the Rossian rules, that the Rossian rules are more basic than any theory, and that if a choice must be made between a Rossian rule and some theory (rule consequentialism, say), then the theory should be jettisoned.

Hooker's view that moral theories must accommodate what might be called 'moral data' strikes me as eminently plausible. After all, theories of other sorts are commonly regarded as having to satisfy an analogous condition: scientific theories must accommodate observational data, and the method of counter-examples is a standard approach to assessing philosophical theories.[14] Having claimed that moral theories must accommodate the data, however, Hooker cannot then insist that moral theories *justify* the data against which they are tested. So, having acknowledged that 'shared intuitions' are more fundamental than moral theories, Hooker cannot then require that these intuitions be justified by moral theories.[15]

To be sure, discovering that all the Rossian rules have some feature in common (a feature not possessed by clearly unacceptable rules) could be useful. If, say, all the Rossian rules maximised value, then the fact that some controversial rule maximises value would provide some reason for accepting that rule. I see little cause for optimism, however, regarding the possibility of demonstrating that the Rossian rules have any such feature in common. In particular, I doubt that Hooker could establish the assumption (to which I referred earlier) that the Rossian rules maximise value.

Having offered reasons for doubting Hooker's claim that rule consequentialism satisfies his third criterion (and is thereby superior to Ross-style pluralism), I will now explain my earlier suggestion that Ross-style pluralism has a certain advantage over rule consequentialism. I refer to the fact that, if rule consequentialism is true (and given some extremely plausible assumptions about what is possible), then the Rossian rules – if true at all – are only contingently so; and that, in contrast, Ross-style pluralism can allow that the Rossian rules are necessarily true. Indeed, rule consequentialism implies that the features of actions to which the Rossian rules attribute moral significance are only contingently significant, whereas on Ross-style pluralism those features can have necessary moral significance. That is, rule consequentialism attributes necessary moral significance to only one feature of actions, namely, that of being in conformity with a rule that maximises value; while Ross-style pluralism can accommodate attributions of necessary moral significance to an action's being an instance of promise-keeping, to its being an instance of causing pain to others, and so on.

Why does this difference count in favour of Ross-style pluralism? In large measure because of how extremely implausible the view is that being in conformity with a rule that maximises value is the one and only feature of actions with necessary moral significance.[16] On this view, there are possible worlds in which the fact that, say, an action involves causing pain to an innocent person, or is an instance of promise-breaking, or an act of vandalism has no bearing at all on the action's moral status. In the absence of any good reason to regard such implications as acceptable, the fact that they follow from rule consequentialism but not from Ross-style pluralism counts heavily in favour of the latter and against the former.[17]

NOTES

1. In W. D. Ross, *The Right and the Good* (Oxford: The Clarendon Press, 1930).

2. Brad Hooker, 'Ross-style Pluralism versus Rule-consequentialism', *Mind*, 105 (1996), pp. 531–50.

3. Ibid., 531.

4. Ibid., 537.

5. I do not mean to imply that there is no great difference between interpreting rule consequentialism as applicable to sets of rules on the one hand, and interpreting it as applicable to individual rules on the other. The differences between these two interpretations are not important here, however.

6. Hooker's reference to the 'acceptability' of rules (Hooker, 'Ross-style Pluralism', p. 541) might also be understood as a reference to the obligatoriness of conforming to rules. In any case, an explanation of the reference would be helpful.

7. Hooker's statement that 'the general duties are pro tanto, not absolute' (Ibid., 545) indicates that he accepts a distinction that at least closely resembles the Rossian distinction between prima facie and strict obligations.

8. As I noted above, Hooker wishes his discussion to remain neutral on the question of whether 'moral convictions' (including those that concern moral rules) are capable of being true or false. I am nevertheless assuming that R5 can be true or false, which in turn probably implies that rule consequentialism (or formulations of rule consequentialism, at any rate) can be true or false. I don't know whether Hooker wants his neutrality on the matter of whether moral convictions can be true extended to moral theories; and I suppose that I could frame my discussion so that it does not presuppose that moral theories can be true or false, but doing so would surely not be worth the effort. Hence, I will continue to assume that moral theories (and components of moral theories like R5) can be true.

9. I should add that matters are not improved by dropping the pretence that rule consequentialism is concerned with individual rules rather than with sets of rules. Thus, consider this reformulation of R5:

   (R6) An action is morally obligatory if and only if it is of kind K1, or K2, or . . . , such that acts of kind K1 are morally obligatory and acts of kind K2 are morally obligatory and . . . ; and acts of kind K1 are morally obligatory and acts of kind K2 are morally obligatory and . . . if the set of rules consisting of 'Acts of kind K1 are morally obligatory', and 'Acts of kind K2 are morally obligatory', and . . . maximises value.

   R6 is problematic for the same reasons as R5 if interpreted in light of the Rossian distinction between prima facie and strict obligations. In particular, R6 is false if the first occurrence of 'obligatory' equated with 'strictly obligatory' and the rest with 'prima facie obligatory'.

10. More accurately, perhaps, rule consequentialism justifies the Rossian rules only if R2 is itself *justified*. I have framed my discussion in terms of the requirement that R2 be true for stylistic reasons: to avoid a confusing plethora of occurrences of 'justify', 'justified', and so on. The points at issue in my remarks would not be affected if references to the truth of R2 were replaced by references to R2's being justified.

11. The point here is more easily made in terms of claims about true moral rules. That is: 'All true moral rules maximise value' is compatible with 'Moral rules maximise value because they are true.' It would not be surprising if inculcating moral truths into the overwhelming majority of the next generation would produce more good than would the inculcation of falsehoods, and this *because* holding true beliefs is better than holding false ones.

12. I am relying here on the fact that 'Complying with the rule "Promise-keeping is obligatory" is obligatory' is equivalent to 'Promise-keeping is obligatory'.

13. Hooker, 'Ross-style Pluralism', p. 538.

14. For example, theories that equate propositional knowledge with justified true belief are rejected on the ground that they cannot accommodate the epistemic data reflected in 'Gettier cases'.

One who denies that the method of counterexamples applies to moral theorising and who opts for a revisionistic approach in this area is faced with the problem of providing plausible adequacy criteria for revisionistic moral theories. Much of what Shelly Kagan says suggests that he, for one, is engaged in revisionistic moral theorising; and he proposes adequacy criteria for moral theories. (Shelly Kagan, *The Limits of Morality* (New York: Oxford University Press, 1989), pp. 11–15.) Whether Kagan's criteria are up to the task for which they are intended is impossible to determine from his discussion, however. For example, Kagan claims that moral theories must explain and justify 'the moral realm'. Neither the nature of the moral realm nor whether a theory can both explain and justify it is at all clear, however.

15. A similar point can be made in connection with Hooker's claims about reflective equilibrium (Hooker, 'Ross-style Pluralism', pp. 532–4). As I understand reflective equilibrium, the terms of the relation are end-products of a process that begins with provisional acceptance of items of sorts that those terms instantiate. If (as Hooker claims) reflective equilibrium relates rules and something else (theories or convictions about particular cases), then certain rules are provisionally accepted at the outset, and they are examined in the light of provisionally accepted items of some other kind. But Hooker also claims that there are rules whose acceptance is not (and has never been) provisional – rules 'that no "external" perspective could really get us to give up' (Ibid., p. 533). These presumably include the Rossian rules, but certainly the rule 'that it is wrong to torture innocent people for fun' (Ibid., p. 533).

16. Rule consequentialists should be sympathetic to this point, since a major reason for preferring rule consequentialism to act consequentialism is that the latter cannot account for the necessary moral significance of certain features of actions.

17. I am very grateful to Brad Hooker, Frances Howard-Snyder, and Hud Hudson for helping me to improve earlier drafts of this chapter.

11

Ruling Out Rule Consequentialism

Tim Mulgan

Act consequentialism claims that the right thing to do in any situation is the act with the best consequences. One familiar objection is that this approach leaves the agent too little room (time, resources, energy) for her own projects or interests. For instance, under act consequentialism, a well-off member of a contemporary first-world society should donate (virtually) all of her income to reputable international aid organisations. As this may seem unreasonably harsh, many consequentialists have attempted to develop less demanding alternatives. One popular alternative is rule consequentialism, which can be characterised as follows: an act is morally right if and only if it is called for by the set of desires and dispositions the having of which by everyone would result in at least as good consequences judged impartially as any other. A relatively small percentage of the combined income of the well-off should be enough to feed the world. Rule consequentialism would thus make reasonable demands on the affluent.[1]

Rule consequentialism has considerable intuitive appeal. It is natural to see moral philosophy as the search for the optimal set of moral rules, and to expect those rules to be those which produce the best consequences.

Many objections have been raised against rule consequentialism: that it requires agents to blindly follow certain rules even in situations where it is disastrous to do so (for instance, if the optimal rule is to drive on the right, then followers of that rule will wreck havoc in a country where everyone else drives on the left); that it collapses into act consequentialism (as the best rules will be those which lead you to produce the best possible outcome in your particular situation); and that it cannot cope with situations of partial compliance (for instance, the optimal set of rules will not tell us how to deal with criminals, as an ideal society would contain no crime).

To meet these (and other) objections, rule consequentialists introduce various epicycles into their theory. Two common epicycles, introduced by Richard Brandt, are the Exception Clause and the Complexity Constraint. Given the initial plausibility of rule consequentialism, it is worth exploring the more sophisticated rule consequentialism which results, to see whether it constitutes a more plausible moral theory than the original. In this chapter, I argue that, in the end, neither epicycle is acceptable, as each creates new problems for rule consequentialism.

SECTION I: BRANDTIAN EXCEPTION CLAUSES

In a recent article, Hooker defines rule consequentialism as follows:

> An act is morally permissible if and only if allowed by the code of rules whose universal predominance could reasonably be expected to result in as good consequences (impartially considered) as would result from any other code identifiable at the time.[2]

He then goes on to say that:

> by the 'universal predominance' of rules, I mean their acceptance by everyone except young children, the mentally impaired, and a small but indeterminate proportion of 'normal' adults.

The last clause is adapted from Richard Brandt,[3] and as Hooker explains that 'we need rules for dealing with problems created by the non-compliance of adults'.[4] I shall now argue that Brandt's exception clause is unacceptable as it causes rule consequentialism to collapse into act consequentialism in cases where a disaster, such as a famine, results from (near) universal failure to act.

To begin with, consider five simple hypothetical cases:

> *Famine Just Happens:* through no action or inaction or fault of any particular person or group of people some people face starvation or famine. For instance, a large and adequate store of grain may have been destroyed by an unpreventable (or unforeseeable) act of God.

> *The Brigands' Famine:* there is plenty of grain in the country, but the soldiers of one side in a civil war burn all the crops in the territory of the other side.

> *The Hoarders' Famine:* famine arises because those who own the grain decide to hoard it. They refuse to sell it or give it to those who require it (or, at least, they refuse to sell it to the latter at a price which they can possibly afford).

The Ignorers' Famine: famine results (in part) from the collective inactivity, or inaction of developed countries.

The Capitalist Famine: in a regime of pure international capitalism, a famine results from the mysterious interactions of the global market.

In Famine Just Happens, we don't have to exclude anyone from the domain of collective acceptance, as no one's wrong-doing or action brings about the undesirable situation. In the Brigands' Famine we must exclude from our domain of collective acceptance the people who are responsible for burning or destroying the grain. This is because their collective acceptance of desirable moral rules would have been inconsistent with the existence of the problem under discussion. In the Hoarders' Famine, the problem we're discussing would not arise without the behaviour of the grain hoarders. Therefore, we must look at rules whose collective acceptance includes everyone except the grain hoarders. Note that the grain hoarders cause the famine as a result of inaction. The grain is not destroyed. Nothing is done to it. It is just not delivered to the people who need it. We would thus be excluding people from the domain of collective acceptance on the basis of what they do not do, as well as what they do.

Our second-last tale, the Ignorers' Famine, is similar to a case Hooker himself describes elsewhere.[5] An appropriate response from developed countries would remove the famine. The behaviour of ordinary citizens in the developed West is necessary for the continued existence of the problem under discussion. Therefore, they must be excluded from the domain of collective acceptance.

In our final tale, the Capitalist Famine, it is hard to see how we can avoid excluding everyone in the world from the domain of collective acceptance, as they would all be participants (to some degree) in the global capitalist system. It will be almost impossible to isolate some subset of market participants whose behaviour can be said to have caused the famine in question.

But now our rule consequentialism is hardly collective at all, for to decide what I should do, I must look at all possible sets of rules and examine their collective acceptance by everybody except brigands, grain hoarders, citizens of the developed West, and participants in the global economy. Our universal acceptance is now a (near) universal rejection.[6]

Excluding virtually everyone in the developed West greatly reduces the appeal of rule consequentialism. In particular, it weakens Hooker's claim that his theory is less demanding than act consequentialism. When deciding how much money I should give to OXFAM, I should ask what amount of money would be sufficient if given by all those people in the West who are already giving significant amounts to OXFAM. Clearly, my share of the burden of relieving famine will be far greater in this case than in Hooker's original version, where I ask instead what amount of money would be sufficient if given by everyone in the West, including the vast majority who are not currently giving significant amounts to charity.

It may seem possible for rule consequentialists to avoid this objection by drawing a distinction between action and inaction. However reasonable it may seem, this move is not really available to the Consequentialist. A major plank of the Consequentialist's position has traditionally been the claim that there is no moral difference between doing and allowing. A version of rule consequentialism which survives only by smuggling such a distinction into a Brandtian exception clause would be unacceptable.[7] It is also not clear how such a move would enable us to deal with a situation such as the Capitalist Famine, in which it is very hard to draw a line between market participants who have contributed to the disaster by their actions and those who have contributed to it by their inactions.

Another problem with an over-exclusionary Brandtian exception clause is that it would require different sets of moral rules for almost every particular problem situation. Many current problems only exist or persist because of the inaction of some group of people. For instance, environmental problems are often exacerbated by the inaction or ignorance of the majority of people in the developed West. So those people would need to be excluded from the domain of collective acceptance.[8]

Rule consequentialists may reply with an appeal to the distinction between following a rule and accepting a rule. They may argue that, in a case such as the Ignorers' Famine, the majority of people *accept* a moral rule which, if everyone followed it, would alleviate the problem. They simply don't *follow* that rule. However, this move would seem to strain the notion of 'accepting' a moral rule. As I acknowledged above, we certainly should allow that people can accept a rule which they don't quite live up to. But do we really want to say that a rule may be accepted within a given community even if almost no one even makes any serious attempt to follow it? Also, this response would be incompatible with Hooker's overall strategy in two key ways. First, if a rule has been accepted without being followed at all, then we will have little reason to accept Hooker's claim that very demanding rules cannot be accepted. If acceptance requires little more than lip service, then such rules will be demanding to follow, but not to accept. Second, Hooker's theory gives great weight to the consequences of a rule's being accepted. If a rule can be accepted without anyone attempting to follow it, then it's not clear either what the consequences of acceptance will be, or why we should be particularly interested in them. The significance of the acceptance of a rule presumably lies in the fact that it makes it more likely (though not inevitable) that the rule will be followed.

SECTION 2: BRANDTIAN COMPLEXITY CONSTRAINTS

It is often objected to rule consequentialism that it requires agents to blindly follow certain rules even in situations where it is disastrous to do so. It is also objected that rule consequentialism collapses into act consequentialism, as the best rules will be those which lead you to produce the best possible outcome in your particular situation. Rule consequentialism tries to meet both these objections with a more sophisticated account of moral rules. On the one hand, a rule can include clauses telling agents how to deal with situations of partial compliance with that rule. In the driving example, the optimal rule might be: drive on the right except when others are more likely to be driving on the left, in which case drive on the left. On the other hand, we should limit ourselves to rules which could be taught to a human population at non-prohibitive social cost. The infinitely adaptable rules which lead to the collapse into act consequentialism are thus ruled out.[9]

The next step for rule consequentialism is to tease out these constraints on the complexity of a moral code. One such constraint is the following:

> *The Teachability Constraint*: We should consider only those rules or dispositions which our current institutions would be capable of teaching to an ordinary human being. Also, the cost of teaching the rule or disposition (which will presumably increase in proportion to its complexity) must be borne in mind when assessing possible societies, especially if we are assuming that the total resources available within any given society are more or less fixed.

Versions of this constraint have been advocated by (among others) Richard Brandt and Brad Hooker.[10] One problem with this approach is that teachability is a function, inter alia, of time. As Brandt notes with approval, what is teachable in future generations may not be teachable now. The limits of teachability are fluid. Altering the moral code of a society will itself alter or expand the set of moral codes which could be taught to the next generation. The moral code of a society affects and is affected by the social institutions, behavioural dispositions, and educational practices that are current in that society. The question for those who adopt the teachability constraint is thus 'Teachability when?' Are we interested in what is teachable in the first generation, or what is teachable in the second, or . . . ? There seem to be two basic options: long-term teachability and short-term teachability.

Teachability in the Long Term

Brandt's own teachability constraint construes the notion of teachability as applying in the long term.[11] We are interested not in rules which could be taught to human beings now, but in rules which could be taught in the long term in a society which sought to have good maximising rules. For instance, assume that we are trying to maximise the amount of good in our society. We decide that, other things being equal, there will be more good if people are more altruistic. We then set out at each generation to make the next generation more altruistic. Assume also that at each stage future improvements in altruism will only be chosen if these seem to produce an increase in goodness. Increases in altruism which are too costly to inculcate or produce will not be chosen. We can then measure the degree of altruism in such a society at any point in time. We then say that the optimal degree of altruism, given that we are limiting our attention to rules which could be taught in the long term, will be the degree of altruism which is present in the long term in this society.

We now have three questions for rule consequentialism, a positive answer to any of which will undermine its claim to be not unreasonably demanding:

1. Is the optimal level of altruism greater than the maximum degree of altruism which it would be reasonable for any moral theory to demand?
2. Is the optimal level of altruism greater than the maximum degree of altruism which is psychologically possible for (current) human beings?[12]
3. Is the optimal level of altruism greater than (or equal to) the degree of altruism demanded by act consequentialism?[13]

We must now ask if the rule consequentialist can give adequate (that is, negative) answers to these questions? Any such answers will naturally be extremely speculative. Even if we assume that there is a limit to the degree of altruism which is teachable in the long term, it would be extremely difficult to locate that limit. In particular, we need to determine which cultural, social, technological, or biological changes will be admitted into our consideration of possible future societies, and which will not. For instance, should we countenance the possibility of a society in which people are made much more altruistic from one generation to the next by means of genetic engineering? If so, then the optimal level of altruism seems very likely to be high. If not, why not?

I do not propose to answer these questions in any detail. Instead, I want to make some general comments. The questions that rule consequentialism must answer are extremely complex and involved. It seems possible that many of them may not even admit of any precise formulation. However, without reasonably specific answers to these questions, the rule consequentialist cannot assure us that she will be able to answer our three principal questions in the negative. Without such assurance, the rule consequentialist cannot show that her theory is an acceptable alternative to act consequentialism. Finally, whatever their success in answering them, the very fact that rule consequentialists must pose these complicated questions raises serious doubts about their theories. Intricate speculation about the possible future course of biotechnological and socio-cultural evolution simply should not bear so strongly on the question of how we, in the actual world at present, ought to respond to pressing moral problems. If rule consequentialism requires us to answer these questions, then it is surely misguided.[14]

Teachability in the Short Term

Given the problems which surround any form of rule consequentialism based on teachability in the long term, it seems reasonable to explore the possibility of teachability in the short term. On this view, rule consequentialists will limit themselves to the consideration of those rules which could become widely accepted within our society in the near future. Two questions, in particular, arise. The first is how short is the 'short term'? Are we interested in those sets of rules which could be taught to us, or to our children, or to our children's children, or . . . ? If we choose to stop at the n-th generation (where n is between 1 and infinity), then we will need some compelling reason for not choosing n-1 or n+1. The second question is what do we keep constant, and what do we vary, when we're asking what is teachable? Are we asking what is teachable given the exact institutions we have, given institutions of the general form we have, or given possible institutions which might grow in the next two or three generations out of the institutions we have, given the institutional dynamics we have? Are we talking about our own particular psychology, or idealised human psychology, or general human psychology? About our own culture, or any possible culture, or a culture somewhat like our own, or one somewhat like what our culture will or might turn into? Who will do the teaching? Are we looking for rules which we could teach, for rules which could be taught by someone in our society (teachers, educationalists, moral philosophers, politicians), or for rules which could only be taught by perfect teachers? If the short-term teachability theorist is to have a reasonably definite theory, then these and other questions need to be given relatively definite answers.

On the face of it, it seems as if the short term teachability theorist faces a choice between three basic options:

1. A theory which is dependent on current institutions, current psychology, and current social practices. For instance, we might say that a set of rules only counts as teachable if it is one which we could actually teach to our children. Here the teachability theorist faces a dilemma. On the one hand, a theory which is too closely tied to current institutions and practices will be unable to criticise those institutions or practices. On the other hand, we have no guarantee that a theory which is only loosely based on such institutions will not be significantly more demanding than they are (and, hence, no guarantee that it will not be unreasonably demanding).

2. A theory which is dependent on some specific idealisation, some particular utopian vision of what is teachable. The problem would then be to justify this specific idealisation in all its complexity, as opposed to every other specific idealisation. Once again, we have no guarantee that such a theory won't be unreasonably demanding.

3. A theory which is vague, indeterminate, or impossibly difficult to cash out. For instance, if we limit ourselves to those sets of rules which human beings are psychologically capable of learning, then, even if there is a definite answer to the question of where those limits lie, it seems very unlikely, given our reluctance or inability to perform the relevant and necessary experiments, that we would ever determine that answer with sufficient accuracy to know whether or not our theory was too demanding.

This is not of course to say that short-term teachability cannot be made to work, merely that there is no particular reason to believe that it can. Unfortunately, most rule consequentialists merely sketch their accounts of teachability. The questions and difficulties I raise are more often noted or glossed over than addressed. Nowhere, to my knowledge, are we given a detailed account of how such a theory would be worked through in practice. Of course, a perfectly detailed account would be impossible to construct. Some degree of abstract hand waving is inevitable. However, without a good deal more detail than has as yet been forthcoming, we have no particular reason to believe that a viable account of short-term teachability is even a coherent possibility. It is thus reasonable to be sceptical of the weight which some theorists seek to place on the notion of teachability.

Faced with such difficulties, rule consequentialists might be tempted to replace teachability with another constraint on the complexity of moral rules. Initially, there seems no reason why another such constraint might not be available. However, if we accept the plausible view that the notion of a rule, particularly the notion of a moral rule, is necessarily tied up to its being capable of being learnt by human beings, then it is not so clear that we could have a constraint on the complexity of such rules which was completely independent of the notion of teachability. Any constraint must appeal to psychological features of human beings, not merely to formal features of rules. Yet any such psychological constraint will face the same problems as the teachability constraint. It is likely to be either too closely tied to existing behaviour to permit it to criticise that behaviour, or too demanding to be acceptable, or too vague to be of any use.

SECTION 3: CONCLUSION

Hooker attempts to rehabilitate rule consequentialism by introducing two Brandtian epicycles into the theory. I have shown that neither of these epicycles is acceptable, as each would make our obligations, under rule consequentialism, depend upon inappropriate, and impenetrable, empirical questions. If rule consequentialism is to survive, it would do better to dispense with Brandt's additions, if it can.

NOTES

1. See Richard Brandt, 'Some Merits of One Form of Rule-Utilitarianism' and 'Fairness to Indirect Optimific Theories in Ethics', in his *Morality, Utilitarianism and Rights* (Cambridge: Cambridge University Press, 1992) and Brad Hooker, 'Rule-consequentialism', *Mind* 99 (1990), pp. 67–77 and 'Rule-Consequentialism, Incoherence, and Fairness', *Proceedings of the Aristotelian Society*, 95 (1994), pp. 19–35, for representative statements of rule consequentialism. I have argued against rule consequentialism on other grounds elsewhere. (See Tim Mulgan, 'Rule Consequentialism and Famine', *Analysis*, 54 (1994), pp. 187–92 and 'One false virtue of Rule Consequentialism and One New Vice', *Pacific Philosophical Quarterly*, 77 (1996), pp. 362–73.) For a response to some of those criticisms, see Brad Hooker, 'Rule Consequentialism and Obligations Towards the Needy', *Pacific Philosophical Quarterly*, 79 (1998), pp. 19–33. Some of the material in this chapter is drawn from Tim Mulgan, *The Demands of Consequentialism* (in progress).
2. Hooker, 'Rule-Consequentialism, Incoherence, Fairness', p. 20.
3. See Brandt, 'Some Merits of One Form of Rule-Utilitarianism'; and Brandt, 'Fairness to Indirect Optimific Theories in Ethics'.
4. Hooker, 'Rule-consequentialism, Incoherence, Fairness', p. 20.
5. Hooker, 'Rule-consequentialism'.
6. Note that if we exclude all those whose inaction is a necessary part of describing the problem situation, then we may end up with something like Donald Regan's cooperative consequentialism (see Don Regan, *Utilitarianism and Co-operation* (Oxford: Clarendon Press, 1980)). Regan's cooperative consequentialism is fairly complicated, but it consists essentially of recommending the following decision procedure to moral agents.
    Step 1: identify all potential cooperators.
    Step 2: predict the likely responses of non-cooperators to various patterns of behaviour by potential cooperators. Treat those responses as given.
    Step 3: play my role in the optimum cooperative strategy.
    Such a procedure is almost identical to that which would be followed by someone seeking to find the appropriate rule-consequentialist response to a disaster, if they were factoring out the behaviour of those whose actions contributed to that disaster (that is, the non-cooperators). We should also note that, in practice, Regan's cooperative consequentialism seems perilously close to an act consequentialism which cautions me to take account of the effects my actions are likely to have on potentially sympathetic others. A full discussion of Regan's theory is beyond the scope of this chapter. However, the possible collapse from Hooker's collective consequentialism through Regan's cooperative consequentialism to traditional act consequentialism serves to highlight the precarious nature of the rule consequentialist's search for an acceptable response to problems caused by non-compliance.
7. It is worth noting that building a distinction between doing and allowing into the foundations of rule consequentialism is very different from the claim that the optimal rule set will include some distinction between doing and allowing.
8. Similarly, if our problem were poverty in the USA, we might need to exclude from the domain of collective acceptance all those people (whether affluent or not) who are in the habit of voting for the current government, as the combination of their action in electing a government which is unwilling to use public funds to adequately relieve poverty, combined with their collective inaction in not providing sufficient charitable donations, may be a significant cause of the existing poverty.
9. Brandt, 'Some Merits of One Form of Rule-Utilitarianism'; Hooker, 'Rule consequentialism'.
10. See Brandt, 'Some Merits of One Form of Rule-Utilitarianism' and 'Fairness to Indirect Optimific Theories in Ethics' and Hooker, 'Rule Consequentialism' and 'Rule-consequentialism, Incoherence, and Fairness'.
11. Brandt, 'Some Merits of One Form of Rule-Utilitarianism', p. 125.
12. We should note that the maximum degree of altruism which it would be reasonable for any moral theory to demand and the maximum degree of altruism which is psychologically possible for human beings are unlikely to be identical. In fact, the former should be significantly less than the latter. The demands which we regard as reasonable for morality to make will be less than the limits of our psychology. There must be some limit beyond which we are not required to go, even though we could. Without such a limit, there will be no room for supererogation or moral choice, no breathing space in the moral life. The possibility that the optimal level of altruism is greater than the maximum degree of altruism which is psychologically possible for (current) human beings is thus the greater threat to rule consequentialism.
13. This will most clearly be the case if the optimal level of altruism occurs when everyone treats their own interests exactly on a par with the interests of everyone else. In such a society, everyone will effectively be an act

consequentialist. As rule consequentialism is usually put forward as an alternative, in particular a less demanding alternative, to act consequentialism, the possibility that the optimal level of altruism is no less than the degree of altruism demanded by act consequentialism is a serious threat to rule consequentialism.

14. My discussion of long-term teachability owes much to Sidgwick's criticism of Spencer's views concerning the relationship between evolution and morality. (On which, see Sidgwick, *Lectures of the Ethics of T. H. Green, H. Spencer and J. Martineau* (London: Macmillan, 1886); 'Critical Notice of Spencer, H., *Justice: Being Part of IV of the Principles of Ethics*', *Mind* 1 (1892); *The Methods of Ethics*, 1907 edition (Indianapolis: Hackett Publishing Company, 1981), p. 470.)

12

Reflective Equilibrium and Rule Consequentialism

Brad Hooker

At the beginning of this chapter, I set out what I think are the two main ways of arguing for rule consequentialism. As I go on to explain briefly, there are compelling objections to one way of arguing for rule consequentialism. I then consider the other way of arguing for rule consequentialism. The rest of the chapter develops this argument and considers some objections to it.

SECTION I: TWO WAYS OF ARGUING FOR RULE CONSEQUENTIALISM

One way of arguing for rule consequentialism stresses that focusing on the benefits of communal acceptance of rules will in fact produce better consequences than focusing directly on acts. This way of arguing for rule consequentialism begins with a pre-commitment to the thesis that what yields the best consequences is morally best.

A quite different way of arguing for rule consequentialism contends that rule consequentialism does a better job of according with our considered moral convictions, at all levels of generality, than any other moral theory. This second way of arguing for rule consequentialism does not begin from a pre-commitment to a consequentialist framework.

Both of these ways of arguing for rule consequentialism have been assailed by impressive attacks. But this chapter will concentrate on the argument that rule consequentialism does a better job of according with our considered moral convictions, at all levels of generality, than any other moral theory. For I believe the argument about considered convictions is more promising than any argument for rule consequentialism that begins from a pre-commitment to a consequentialist framework.

There is a familiar objection to arguing for *rule* consequentialism from consequentialist premises. This objection starts by acknowledging that agents should decide how to act by appeal to certain rules. Examples are: don't physically attack others, don't steal, don't break your promises, pay special attention to the needs of your family and friends, be generally helpful to others. Beyond question, there is a role for such rules in our moral thinking. But, according to many philosophers, these rules merely constitute a *procedure for making moral decisions*. The thought, in other words, is that these rules play a central role in guiding moral decisions but no role in determining whether an act really is right or wrong, that is no part in the *criterion of moral rightness*. In short, there is a consequentialist argument for having rules as part of the decision procedure, but, if there is a distinction between the appropriate decision procedure and the criterion of rightness, then there is no consequentialist argument for having rules in the criterion of rightness.

As I indicated, this is familiar objection against an argument for rule consequentialism from consequentialist premises. But the objection is by no means unassailable. One way of attacking it is to challenge the distinction between the criterion of moral rightness and what morally good agents should be considering when they decide what to do. However, I shall not say more about this line of attack, because there is a far more obvious problem with arguing for rule consequentialism from a pre-commitment to some sort of foundational consequentialism.

The problem is that this pre-commitment itself needs justification. For there are other proposed foundations for morality that compete with any proposed consequentialist foundation. No one of these proposed foundations, whether consequentialist or non-consequentialist, is so clearly superior to its rivals that it can triumph without the aid of further justification.

Let me explain why I refer here to 'further' justification. Each putatively foundational moral belief – or at least each of the familiar ones – seems intuitively attractive independently of its consistency with our other moral ideas. These beliefs already possess what we can call *independent credibility*, or non-inferential justification. An independently credible belief seems right on its own. Of course independently credible beliefs are not necessarily true.[1] But their independent credibility provides some reason to believe them.

If an independently credible belief about the foundation of our other moral beliefs does indeed fit with them, this is a *further* reason to believe it. Indeed, we would naturally ask whether one view about the foundation of morality, together with all that follows from that view, accords better with our considered moral beliefs than any rival view about the foundation of morality.

SECTION 2: FORMULATING CONSEQUENTIALISM AND RULE CONSEQUENTIALISM

Of course, whether rule consequentialism fits with our considered convictions depends not only on what these convictions are but also on which version of rule consequentialism is used. There are many versions of rule consequentialism. The version I favour is as follows:

> Rule Consequentialism: An act is wrong if and only if it is forbidden by the code of rules whose internalisation by the overwhelming majority (say, 90 per cent) of everyone everywhere in each new generation[2] has the highest expected value, where a code's expected value includes all costs of getting the code internalised.

Note that this form of rule consequentialism refers to the expected value of codes. Tim Mulgan and others persuaded me that wrongness cannot be determined by the code that would *actually* have the greatest value (except in the unlikely case where this is the same code as the one with the highest expected value). For figuring out which code would actually have the greatest value is beyond virtually everyone. The truth about what is wrong cannot be so inaccessible. But the *expected* value of various possible codes is accessible, though often not obvious.

Admittedly, thinking about the expected value of the internalisation of a code involves a great deal of speculation about natural facts. To take but one element, Mulgan's chapter in the present volume (see Chapter 11) rightly points to the speculative nature of our views about the relative costs involved in getting this or that code internalised. Calculating these costs would be speculative even if the internalisation were to be by just one generation. Calculating the internalisation costs is even more speculative when a code is to be internalized by generation after generation.

I admit that such speculation is practically difficult and theoretically worrying. We *may* disagree about what rule consequentialism requires because our empirical speculations are different. But I believe that rule consequentialism's sensitivity to empirical information is one of its virtues. I will come back to this in a later section.

Rule consequentialism is here formulated as holding that the moral permissibility of an act depends on which code is such that its internalisation has the highest expected value. Even act consequentialists admit that widespread internalisation of merely the one rule 'maximise the good' does not have high expected value. The rules whose widespread internalisation has the highest expected value will be limited in terms of complexity (because of our cognitive limitations) and in terms of demandingness (mainly because of the high costs associated with teaching very demanding rules to generation after generation). The upshot of this is that rule consequentialism will not collapse back into extensional equivalence with act consequentialism. In other words, the rules whose widespread internalisation has the highest expected value will sometimes call for acts which in fact will not maximise expected value.[3]

But if rule consequentialism sometimes endorses acts that do not have the highest expected value, can rule consequentialism really be considered consequentialist? Mustn't a *consequentialist* theory always say that the possible action with the best consequences should be performed?

I indicated in Section 1 above that I think the argument to rule consequentialism from consequentialist premises is unpromising. The route to rule consequentialism does not rightly start from consequentialist premises. Furthermore, rule consequentialism certainly conflicts with the idea (often associated with consequentialism) that every act is to be assessed only by comparing its actual or expected consequences with the consequences of alternative acts. In the end, we should not be bothered by the question of whether 'consequentialism' is defined in such a way that rule consequentialism turns out not to be a form of consequentialism. What matters most, after all, is whether the theory going under the name 'rule consequentialism' is plausible, not whether the theory's name is misleading. Nevertheless, there is a way to define 'consequentialism' so that rule consequentialism is aptly named. We can say that a theory is consequentialist if and only if it assesses acts and/or rules (or motives, social codes, virtues, or ways of life) in terms solely of the production of agent-neutral, that is, impersonal, value.[4]

SECTION 3: THE PLACE OF FOUNDATIONAL BELIEFS

In a 1996 article,[5] I summarised what I took to be the mainstream (and correct) view:

(1) Moral theories must be internally coherent.
(2) Moral theories must have implications that cohere with the moral convictions we share and have confidence in, after careful reflection and in the light of our best theories in metaphysics, psychology, sociology, economics, etc.
(3) Moral theories should specify what (if anything) ties together our various moral principles and justifies them.
(4) Moral theories should help us deal with moral questions about which we are not confident, or do not agree.

I need to clarify (2) and add a specification to (3). But, before doing so, I want to acknowledge that, even with these improvements, my list (1)–(4) was inadequate. As I have learned from Dale Miller, I should have added:

(5) Moral theories should start from attractive general beliefs about morality.

The reason (5) is needed is as follows. Suppose some moral theory fulfilled perfectly criteria (1)–(4). This theory would nevertheless be suspect if it offered a seemingly alien account of right and wrong. Certainly, if there were two rival theories that did equally well in terms of the other four criteria, but only one of these theories offered an account that starts from familiar and attractive ideas about morality, this theory would seem clearly superior. Hence the necessity of supplementing (1)–(4) with (5).

Now, does rule consequentialism have what (5) requires? Yes, rule consequentialism invokes the familiar idea that we should try to live by the moral code whose communal acceptance would, as far as we can tell, have the best consequences, impartially considered. When wondering about the morality of some conduct, we ask, 'what would the consequences be if everyone felt free to do that?' This is a question it seems natural to interpret as suggesting rule consequentialism.

While for completeness (5) needs to be mentioned, it doesn't really cut any ice. This is because rule consequentialism's main rivals likewise begin with attractive general ideas about morality. This is true of act utilitarianism, contractualism (of both Hobbesian and Kantian kinds), and other of rule consequentialism's rivals. Since each of these theories arises from and develops attractive general ideas about morality, we need some other ground for deciding which theory is best.

SECTION 4: IMPLICATIONS AND IMPARTIALITY

I now believe that my 1996 article stated (2) poorly. What I meant was merely that, to be plausible, a moral theory must *endorse* the moral convictions we have after careful reflection on everything relevant. I meant (2) as such to leave open that there is vanishingly little system in our considered convictions.

In the limiting case, there is nothing general but instead only judgements about particular situations. This is the view taken by moral particularism. I did not mean for (2) as such to condemn either particularism or any other deeply pluralistic moral theory. (2) was *not* meant to *insist* that a moral theory find system in our moral convictions, or to identify some small set of our moral convictions that could explain all the others. Particularism is condemned by the conjunction of (2) with the virtually irresistible view that at least some of our moral convictions take the form of general principles. Note that what condemns particularism is this conjunction, not (2) all by itself.[6]

Other deeply pluralistic theories – such as a Ross-style pluralism – oppose particularism, since they embrace general principles. The problem with these deeply pluralistic theories concerns not (2), nor (2) conjoined with the view that at least some of our moral convictions take the form of general principles. The problem with these deeply pluralistic theories concerns other criteria, a point to which I shall return.

Many philosophers take coherence to require that every proposition of a coherent theory be explained, or even entailed, by all the rest.[7] This requirement would condemn deeply pluralistic moral theories as incoherent. I believe such theories are not incoherent *as the word 'incoherent' is used in ordinary language*. Still, I regret using a term in a way different from the way it is used in much contemporary philosophy. I should have used 'entail' in (2) where I used 'cohere with'.

What are often called moral pluralists deny that there *is* a moral theory that both has intuitively plausible implications and manages to identify a foundational principle that explains why all other moral truths hold. In defence of their view, moral pluralists often claim that we have no reason to assume there must be some first principle from which the rest of morality derives.[8] I agree with them about that. But I think they should (and usually do) agree that, other things being at least roughly equal, a principle that unites and explains the rest of morality is desirable. The question is not whether a moral theory with both a foundational principle and wholly attractive implications would be desirable. The question is whether there is such a theory available.

I did mean (3) to express the desirability of finding a general principle that united all the various more specific moral convictions and explained why they hold. This is indeed how my (3) has been interpreted. But, as I warned above, I need to augment (3). It should have been formulated as:

> (3) Moral theories should identify a fundamental principle that both explains why all our more specific considered moral convictions are correct and justifies them from an impartial point of view.

So I have now added that we are looking for *impartial* justification.

But what is 'impartial justification'? There is a very minimal degree of impartial justification if a rule applies to everyone, or at least to everyone in relevantly similar circumstances, and is then impartially (fairly, justly) applied. We might say that an impartial rule must be one that requires everyone to be treated in the same way except where differences between them, or their circumstances, are relevant. Rules themselves pick out differences. The rule that we must keep our promises distinguishes between those to whom we have made promises and those to whom we have not. When rules pick out differences and are then impartially applied, there is a minimal degree of impartial justification. But it is minimal, since rules that are themselves very unfair can be impartially applied.[9] A rule that everyone must be the slave of the tallest person could be impartially applied.

Clearly, what is most germane in the evaluation of possible moral principles is whether they themselves pick out differences between people that really are morally relevant. Now what makes some differences morally relevant and others not? We might hope that this question could be answered impartially. The hope would be that, when we look at the matter impartially, we can see that some differences matter and others do not.

Now what is impartial evaluation of principles and the differences between individuals that these principles say are relevant? The most obvious conception of impartiality holds that the well-being of each has equal importance. And the most obvious conception of this is the utilitarian one: benefits and harms to any individual matter exactly the same as do the same size benefits and harms to any other individual.

Another prominent conception of impartiality is the contractualist idea of seeking the rational or reasonable consent of *every* individual. Of course, often agents find themselves faced with a set of alternatives no one of which everyone consents to. There must be some way of determining what to do in such situations.

One idea with particular appeal is that a set of rules should be evaluated in terms of whether those left worst off by the alternative could *reasonably* reject it. But as against this idea, it seems too strong to give the worst off an absolute veto on any proposal. First, such a veto would be paralysing where the individuals who would be worst off under one arrangement were not the same individuals as those who would be the worst off under a different arrangement. Second, suppose we faced a choice between a new rule that would produce huge benefits for a middle-class majority and an alternative rule that would produce the tiniest of benefits for a small minority of people who are worst off. In this case, it would seem unreasonable for the worst off to insist on the code better for them when this would benefit them only a tiny amount whereas the other rule would benefit the better off hugely.[10]

No matter how high a priority contractualism puts on benefitting the worst off, consequentialism *can* match it. For example, one form of rule consequentialism would evaluate codes *solely* in terms of maximising the welfare of the worst off. There are other distribution-sensitive forms of consequentialism that give less priority to the worst off. Such views agree that the worst off should have some priority. What these views deny is that even small benefits to the worst off are more important morally than huge benefits to the better off.

Any form of consequentialism giving some degree of priority to the worst off arguably departs from the most natural understanding of impartiality. Suppose we are comparing two sets of rules, set A and set B. Suppose that, although B would produce more aggregate well-being than A, we think A better than B because A would leave no one as badly off as B would. Then, in some sense, we are not being purely impartial; we are giving priority to, being partial towards, the worst off.

Another doubt about the place of impartiality comes from the thought that a completely impartial morality is highly counter-intuitive. Certainly, everyday moral thinking seems correct to leave room for some considerable degree of bias (a) towards yourself and (b) towards your family, friends, benefactors, and so on. Yet this is not necessarily to reject the idea that the fundamental level of moral justification is impartial. For example, a moral theory might provide for a wholly impartial selection of moral rules that in turn allow or even require partiality to dominate much of our day-to-day decision-making.[11]

I accept that we may not be able to find a moral theory that both is fundamentally impartial and has no severely counter-intuitive implications. For example, perhaps any moral theory that gives no priority to the worst off will fail. On the other hand, perhaps we can understand impartiality broadly enough so that it can accommodate priority for the worst off. In either case, we can make a claim about the status of fundamental impartiality where other things are roughly equal. This is the claim that, other things roughly equal, a moral theory that is fundamentally impartial seems to have a decisive advantage over its rivals.

Suppose we are comparing two moral theories. Suppose both have intuitively plausible implications. But suppose one of these theories provides an impartial foundation for its principles and the other doesn't. The one with the impartial foundation seems better.

SECTION 5: REFLECTIVE EQUILIBRIUM NARROW AND WIDE

My 1996 article's criteria for selecting a moral theory were meant to affirm the so-called reflective equilibrium methodology. But my discussion in that article paid little attention to the distinction between narrow and wide reflective equilibrium.[12] Was this a mistake?

Narrow equilibrium is obtained when we find a set of principles that economically systematises our considered moral convictions. My earlier article defended the search for this sort of equilibrium. Given that evaluations of moral views have to start from *some evaluative* perspective, the appropriate one to start from is constituted by the moral evaluations in which we have most confidence.

But many moral philosophers say that narrow reflective equilibrium is hardly enough.[13] They think we should search for wide reflective equilibrium. Wide reflective equilibrium is narrow reflective equilibrium *plus* consistency with 'background conditions'. So wide reflective equilibrium adds the requirement that moral theories be:

(i) consistent with the best theories of rationality;[14]
(ii) consistent with the best scientific theories;
(iii) consistent with the best metaphysical theory of personal identity;[15]
(iv) consistent with the best accounts of human flourishing.

Of course I agree moral theories should be consistent with our best theories of other areas. They should be consistent with our best theories of rationality, consistent with the best scientific theories, consistent with the best theories of personal identity, and consistent with the best accounts of human flourishing.

But thinking about these background conditions will not be much help when we are trying to decide which is the best moral theory from among the best versions of the main contenders.

Consider first (i). The problem here is that when views about rationality are put forward as premises in arguments supporting one of these normative moral theories over its rivals, the views about rationality are controversial and even questionable.[16] So they do not ground a *compelling* argument in favour of any one normative moral theory. I mean that conclusion as a normative claim. But let me add a sociological observation: few philosophers are convinced that *all* moral theories except one are disqualified on grounds of irrationality. I myself think *none* of the main normative moral theories is clearly irrational.[17]

Turn now to (ii). The problem here is that all the best versions of the main normative moral theories are consistent with the best scientific theories. Or at least they could fairly easily be reformulated so as to be consistent with the best scientific theories.

Much the same can be said about (iii). The best versions of all the leading normative moral theories are, or can be made, consistent with the best metaphysical theory of personal identity.

Again, with respect to (iv), the best versions of all the leading normative moral theories will be able to pass this test. They are, or can be made, consistent with the best accounts of human flourishing.

I can put this another way. In his contribution to this volume (see Chapter 8), Miller notes that narrow reflective equilibrium is constituted by coherence within the subsystem of overtly moral beliefs but does nothing to guarantee that there will be coherence between that subsystem and other subsystems. He is certainly right that moral beliefs need to be consistent with all other subsystems of beliefs – that is, with beliefs about other things. Wide reflective equilibrium is important. But I believe the best versions of all the main moral theories *are* consistent with the most plausible systems of beliefs about other things.

The hard part is *not* finding a moral theory consistent with compelling theories of rationality and human flourishing, and with the best scientific theories and theories of personal identity. Nor is the hard part finding a theory that coheres with our considered moral convictions. As I indicated, the hard part is finding a moral theory that, in addition to satisfying (2), articulates an underlying principle supporting all the other principles, ideally from an impartial point of view (that is, satisfies my (3)). Achieving narrow reflective equilibrium is the hard part.

In the final two sections of this chapter, I shall discuss what seem to me the best objections to rule consequentialism. These are both objections that presume that a moral theory is inadequate if it conflicts too sharply with our considered convictions. Both of the objections I shall consider are effectively arguments that rule consequentialism does in fact conflict with our considered convictions – either about what would be right in other possible worlds, or about what would be right in the actual world.

SECTION 6: CONTINGENCY

Montague, in Chapter 10, quotes me as stating, 'we are more certain of our intuitions (moral verdicts) than we are of any theory'. The intuitions in play here are such familiar rules as 'Don't kill or physically harm the innocent', 'Don't steal', 'Keep your promises', 'Be loyal to your friends and family', 'Do good for others', and so on. Montague understandably refers to some such set of rules as the 'Russian rules'. He then comments, 'The clear message here is that moral theories are tested against the Russian rules, that the Russian rules are more basic than any theory, and that if a choice must be made between a Russian rule and some theory (rule consequentialism, say), then the theory should be jettisoned.'

I admit that what we are most confident about in ethics are, I believe, certain Ross-style rules specifying pro tanto duties.[18] But *it is a mistake to suppose that what we are most confident about is also what is most basic.* Our most confident beliefs in the empirical realm are about 'ordinary mid-sized dry goods'. Yet clearly facts about such objects supervene upon more basic facts about molecules and atoms. Likewise, in ethics the normative propositions in which we have most confidence could be ones that turn out to be based upon, that is, derivable from, more basic propositions.

Montague notes:

> To be sure, discovering that all the Russian rules have some feature in common (a feature not possessed by clearly unacceptable rules) could be useful. If, say, all the Russian rules maximised value, then the fact that some controversial rule maximised value would provide some reason for accepting it.

The question, then, is whether all the rules that seem intuitively most attractive do fit with rule consequentialism. In other words, are rule consequentialism's implications about what morality requires plausible, or do they conflict with moral convictions in which we have greater confidence?

We can divide this question into one about what is right in the world as we know it, and one about what would be right in a different possible world. Someone might then say that, even if rule consequentialism endorses intuitively attractive rules for the world as we know it, rule consequentialism makes the correctness of these rules *merely contingent.* This might be thought to be shown by the fact that rule consequentialism endorses different rules for other worlds that are sufficiently different. But is it true that rule consequentialism construes as contingent what really is not?

I take it that rule consequentialism, like most versions of Ross-style pluralism, holds that whether one should follow a particular rule on a particular occasion depends on what opposing considerations there are. I should keep my promises, but not at the cost of innocent lives. In this sense, the rightness of my keeping my promises is contingent. This is not, however, a form of contingency that clearly condemns rule consequentialism. On the contrary, it seems intuitively right to set aside normally binding rules when necessary to protect the innocent from serious harm. Rule consequentialism will agree with this, I believe, since it will endorse rules about avoiding disasters.

The particular problem about contingency is not a problem about what to do when rules conflict, and in particular not one about what to do when acting on a rule would produce disaster.[19] The problem about contingency is about the standing of the rules themselves. Does rule consequentialism *wrongly* hold that the moral goodness of certain dispositions is contingent on the value resulting from the widespread internalisation of these dispositions?

Consider the level of altruistic concern you consider virtuous in this world. Refer to that level of virtuous altruism as VA. Now imagine a world where people are fantastically good at taking care of themselves but are poor at ascertaining what would benefit others. If people in that world had the level of altruism that would be best in our world, the level we are calling VA, then they would very often try to help others but most of these actions would misfire and make others worse off. They would be like well-intentioned but meddlesome neighbours. In addition, the extra altruistic concern would cause them to worry so much about others that this psychological cost would regularly outweigh whatever extra good they were able to do for others. (This is not unrealistic: we've all seen parents worry themselves sick over what really is of trivial significance to their children.)

So in that other world, the level of altruistic concern that would result in the greatest aggregate well-being would be less than VA. Call the level of altruistic concern that would, in that world, result in the greatest aggregate well-being VA^-. I am not supposing that people in that world should have no altruism. VA^- does not equal zero. Nevertheless, VA^- is less than VA. If people in that world had the *extra* altruism that VA adds to VA^-, things would go worse – both for the intended beneficiaries and for the intended benefactors.

In this example, what is normally and paradigmatically a virtue, a certain level of altruistic concern, becomes counter-productive. Here what is normally a virtue is no longer valuable. Perhaps we should say that it is no longer a virtue. If we say this, we can admit that virtue per se is intrinsically and necessarily valuable, but that a disposition that is a virtue in one world might not be in another.

Indeed, we can go so far as to say that, given the rule-consequentialist principle for selecting rules and virtues, and given a complete set of empirical facts, it is a *necessary* truth which rules are morally justified and which dispositions are virtues.[20] In a different world, one with relevantly different empirical facts, the rule-consequentialist principle could endorse a different set of rules and dispositions. In short, the rule-consequentialist principle itself would apply universally, but the rules it endorses would be relative to the empirical facts of that world.[21]

However, do certain Rossian pro tanto duties seem applicable no matter what empirical facts obtain? How could there be a possible world where there isn't a pro tanto duty not to harm the innocent, or one not to help the innocent avoid harm? The problem with this question is that it is extremely hard to imagine a world in which the widespread internalization of a pro tanto duty not to harm the innocent, and of a pro tanto duty to help the innocent avoid harm, wouldn't produce good consequences on the whole.

Yet, maybe we can imagine a world in which no one could physically harm or help others. Concerning physical harm, Hart wrote,

> [Men] are both occasionally prone to, and normally vulnerable to, bodily attack. Yet though this is a truism it is not a necessary truth; for things might have been, and might one day be, otherwise. There are species of animals whose physical structure (including exoskeletons or a carapace) renders them virtually immune from attack by other members of their species and animals who have no organs enabling them to attack. If men were to lose their vulnerability to each other there would vanish one obvious reason for the most characteristic provision of law and morals: *Thou shalt not kill.*[22]

Let us go beyond Hart's example and consider possible worlds where people not only cannot physically harm one another but also cannot benefit one another. And suppose that in each of these possible worlds there is always a cost associated with people's internalising a rule – if only just the cost of learning and remembering the rule. Such a cost needs to be outweighed by benefits from internalising the rule. If in a given possible world there would be *no* benefit from people's internalising certain rules, then a cost–benefit analysis would indeed condemn those rules for that world.

Would the internalisation of rules enjoining beneficence and forbidding maleficence yield any benefits in the possible worlds under consideration? We need to make a distinction here between two possible worlds, both of which fit our description so far. In one of these possible worlds, people would get the benefit of knowing that others would help them if they could, and that they wouldn't harm them even if they could. In the other, such benefits would not be available.

Consider the possible world where there would be some benefit from people's internalising certain rules even if they would never have an opportunity to act upon those rules. For that world, the internalisation of those rules seems desirable. Now consider the possible world where there would be no benefit from people's internalising rules they could not act upon. For that world, the internalisation of those rules does not seem desirable.

If these are our considered intuitions about these possible worlds, then our intuitions about what duties would exist or what dispositions would be virtues vary as our hypotheses about the empirical facts in different worlds vary. If our intuitions do vary in this way, then this seems an argument against some of rule consequentialism's critics. In particular, it is an argument against defenders of Ross-style pluralism. For they seem committed to the thesis that which dispositions and rules are morally desirable does not vary across worlds. Or at least it is mysterious to me how that commitment is not a presupposition of their criticising rule consequentialism for making the goodness of a rule or disposition contingent on features of the world.

But it is not yet an argument in favour of rule consequentialism. This is because some other theory, for example contractualism, might give a more compelling account of how the desirability of various possible rules varies between different possible worlds. I cannot take up here the huge task of arguing that rule consequentialism gives the most plausible account of appropriate variation between different possible worlds.

SECTION 7: COMPLIANCE

Instead, I shall address a related objection to rule consequentialism. The previous section considered the objection that rule consequentialism makes rightness *too* contingent. This final section will consider an objection that rule consequentialism makes rightness *not contingent enough*.

This is an objection having to do with levels of *compliance*. The objection is that rule consequentialism makes moral rightness depend on what would happen in an ideal world of full compliance with the rules, whereas actually moral rightness should be contingent on features of the real world, including the degree of non-compliance therein.

Of course, one thing that can vary is the extent to which people accept and conform with any particular set of rules. At one end of a spectrum of possible worlds, there are worlds in which every single person accepts the rules and always succeeds in identifying the right act and doing it. At the other end of the spectrum, no one except you is at all motivated to follow these rules. When we are evaluating a set of rules, should we consider the consequences of acceptance and conformity by 100 per cent of the population, or less? If less, how much less?

In a 1998 reply to earlier papers by Tim Mulgan, I explained why I think we should not imagine complete acceptance by 100 per cent of the population.[23] If we imagine complete acceptance by 100 per cent of the population, we have simply imagined problems of non-compliance out of existence. In other words, we would be evaluating rules by their consequences in idealised worlds where everyone is trying to be good. A very crude form of such thinking is the pacifist's 'In a perfect world, people never fight; so I won't fight even when people in this very imperfect world are attacking me.' But a perfect world is hardly an adequate model for how to deal with real-world problems.

On the other hand, rule consequentialism is conspicuously committed to some degree of idealisation. Rule consequentialism maintains that the right way to evaluate rules is by the consequences of their internalisation by the general population, even if not by every last person.[24] This leaves us with the question of how much idealisation is appropriate. Again, how widely should we imagine the rules would be internalised?

My 1998 reply to Mulgan put forward the following two-part answer. First, the desirability of some rules does not depend on precisely how widely they are internalised. This is true of rules against attacking innocent others, theft, and promise-breaking, for example.

In the case of other rules, however, the desirability of the rules *does* depend on how widely they are internalised. I admit that there is no precise level that is obviously more reasonable to imagine than every other. Nevertheless, we can make a defensible choice of a percentage. We should hypothesise a percentage close enough to 100 per cent to hold on to the idea that moral rules are for acceptance *by the whole society of human beings*. Yet, we should pick a percentage far enough short of 100 per cent to *make salient the problems about recalcitrant non-compliers*. In the face of these conflicting considerations, I humbly propose we take internalisation by 90 per cent of each new generation as the figure to use in our calculations.

Let me add that I am assuming perfect compliance with the rules by the 90 per cent of the population who internalised the rules. On this model, we do a cost–benefit analysis on internalisation-plus-compliance by 90 per cent of the population. We do not have to set standards high in order to counterbalance most people's coming up short of whatever standards are set.

An analogy from the law might be helpful here. On the rule-consequentialist model I am advocating, if it would be best for people to drive under sixty miles per hour, then the rule should be that people drive under sixty. On other models, ones that hypothesise a gap between internalised rules and behaviour, the best rule might be that the speed limit should be fifty, since most people will exceed whatever limit by some margin. Like Kagan, I find counter-intuitive any version of rule con-sequentialism that aims to have people do one thing (for example, drive under sixty), has rules telling them to do something else (for example, drive under fifty), and then has these rules determine right and wrong. I agree that rightness should be determined by the rules, but the rules should not be stricter than needed given internalisation-plus-compliance by 90 per cent of the population.

Now let me stress that it is no part of this proposal that the 10 per cent who are imagined not to have internalised the rules are required or allowed not to follow the rules that everyone else is required to follow. There is no suggestion here that non-compliance with the rules is desirable. *The rules are ones everyone should follow*, though we assume not everyone will.

Now, if this version of rule consequentialism requires everyone to comply with the best rules, does it find itself advocating what Kagan might call 'undesirable conformity'? Certainly, there can be instances of conformity with a rule that do not maximise the good. So, *from an act-consequentialist point of view*, these instances of conformity are undesirable. But 'undesirable from an act-consequentialist point of view' is hardly the kiss of death. Perhaps these instances of conformity with rules are desirable *from the point of view of ordinary moral intuitions*.

But we must ask whether all instances of conformity with the best rules are desirable from the point of view of ordinary moral intuitions. Sometimes, for example, keeping a promise *is* undesirable from this point of view. Suppose keeping a small promise prevents you from rescuing someone's life. But rule consequentialism does not require conformity with a rule about keeping small promises when this prevents you from saving a life. As I indicated, rule consequentialism endorses a 'prevent disaster' rule, and this comes into play in such cases. More generally, conformity with this 'prevent disaster' rule will serve to prevent intuitively undesirable conformity with other rules.

Kagan, however, has another objection to rule consequentialism. Let me generalise and paraphrase from a point made in his note 6 (see Chapter 7). Whatever level of general internalisation we imagine for a code of rules, there is no reason to think that the rules – tested from the standpoint of *that* level of internalisation – will provide suitable guidance for cases where the level of internalisation is quite different. Suppose you conform to idealised rules, such as ones whose internalisation by 90 per cent of the population would produce the best consequences. But suppose also that in the real world far fewer than 90 per cent of the population accept or comply with those rules. Then your following these rules in the real world will often fail to maximise the good.

However, it perhaps remains to be seen whether it is counter-intuitive to claim that these are the rules you should follow. We may well find that there is some degree of idealisation, and in particular some sort of generalisation test, stubbornly embedded in our conception of morality. If so, then, when you follow these rules, you may not be maximising the good, but you may be doing what morality requires.[25]

NOTES

1. So here is a difference between independent credibility and W. D. Ross's concept of self-evidence. Ross wrote that a self-evident belief is 'evident without any need of proof, or of evidence beyond itself' (*The Right and the Good* (Oxford: Clarendon Press, 1930), p. 29). But Ross defined 'self-evident' such that any belief that really is self-evident must be *true* (see Robert Audi, 'Intuitionism, Pluralism, and the Foundations of Ethics', in W.

Sinnott-Armstrong and M. Timmons (eds), *Moral Knowledge?* (New York: Oxford University Press, 1996), pp. 101–36, at pp. 107–8, 131).

2. For the sake of avoiding some complexities, assume that improvements in genetic makeup are sufficiently minor to leave intact the claim 'human nature hasn't changed'.

3. My *Ideal Code, Real World: A Rule-consequentialist Theory of Morality* (Oxford: Clarendon Press, 2000) discusses these points at length.

4. I first made this point in 'Is Rule-consequentialism a Rubber Duck?', *Analysis*, 54 (1994), pp. 92–7.

5. 'Ross-style Pluralism versus Rule-consequentialism', *Mind*, 105 (1996), pp. 531–52.

6. I discuss particularism more fully in 'Moral Particularism – Wrong and Bad', in M. Little and B. Hooker (eds) *Moral Particularism* (Oxford: Oxford University Press, 2000).

7. For some accounts of coherence, see F. H. Bradley, *Essays on Truth and Reality* (Oxford: Oxford University Press, 1914), pp. 202–3; Brand Blanshard, *The Nature of Thought* (London: Allen and Unwin, 1939) vol. 2, pp. 265–6; Wilfred Sellars, 'Givenness and Explanatory Coherence', *Journal of Philosophy*, 70 (1973), pp. 612–82; Keith Lehrer, *Knowledge* (Oxford: Clarendon Press, 1974); Jonathan Dancy, *Contemporary Epistemology* (Oxford: Blackwell, 1985), ch. 8; Geoffrey Sayre-McCord 'Coherence and Models for Moral Theorizing', *Pacific Philosophical Quarterly*, 18 (1986), pp. 170–90; 'Coherentist Epistemology and Moral Theory', in W. Sinnott-Armstrong and M. Timmons (eds), *Moral Knowledge?* (New York: Oxford University Press, 1996), pp. 137–59.

8. Ross, *The Right and the Good*, p. 23, is again an example. See also E. F. Carritt, *Ethical and Political Thinking* (Oxford: Clarendon Press, 1947), p. 11; H. Joseph, *Some Problems in Ethics* (Oxford: Clarendon Press, 1931), p. 67.

9. H. L. A. Hart, *The Concept of Law* (Oxford: Clarendon Press, 1961), p. 157.

10. See James Griffin, *Well-Being: Its Meaning, Measurement and Moral Importance* (Oxford: Clarendon Press, 1986), pp. 170–83:

11. For some non-consequentialist discussions of this, see Thomas E. Hill, Jr, 'The Importance of Autonomy', in Eva Kittay and D. Meyers (eds), *Women and Moral Theory* (Totowa, NJ: Rowman and Allanheld, 1987); Marcia Baron, 'Impartiality and Friendship', *Ethics* 101 (1991), pp. 836–57; Brian Barry, *Justice as Impartiality* (Oxford: Oxford University Press, 1995), chs 8, 9; and T. M. Scanlon, *What We Owe Each Other* (Cambridge, MA: Harvard University Press, 1998), p. 225: 'Quite impartial reasoning about the rejectability of principles leads to the conclusion that we are not required to be impartial in each actual decision we make.'

12. For influential discussions of this distinction, see John Rawls, *A Theory of Justice* (Cambridge, MA: Harvard University Press, 1971), p. 49; 'The Independence of Moral Theory', *Proceedings and Addresses of the American Philosophical Association*, 48 (1974/5), pp. 5–22, at pp. 7–8; Norman Daniels, 'Wide Reflective Equilibrium and Theory Acceptance in Ethics', *Journal of Philosophy*, 76 (1979), pp. 256–82; 'Reflective Equilibrium and Archimedean Points', *Canadian Journal of Philosophy*, 10 (1980), pp. 83–110; 'Two Approaches to Theory Acceptance in Ethics', in D. Copp and D. Zimmerman (eds), *Morality, Reason and Truth* (Totowa, NJ: Rowman and Littlefield, 1985), pp. 120–40.

13. In the present volume, the discussions by Dale Miller (ch. 8) and Alan Thomas (ch. 9) take up these matters.

14. Cf. David Gauthier, *Morals By Agreement* (Oxford: Clarendon Press, 1986), p. 1; Samuel Scheffler, *The Rejection of Consequentialism* (Oxford: Clarendon Press, 1982), ch. 4; 'Agent-Centred Restrictions, Rationality, and the Virtues', *Mind*, 94 (1985) , pp. 409–19.

15. Cf. Rawls, *A Theory of Justice*, pp. 185–9; 'The Independence of Moral Theory', pp. 15–20; Derek Parfit, *Reasons and Persons* (Oxford: Clarendon Press, 1984), pp. 331–9.

16. I am influenced here by Griffin, *Well-Being*, pp. 141–2, 153–5, 173–5.

17. Again, a theory often accused of irrationality, or incoherence, is rule consequentialism. In my 'Rule-consequentialism, Incoherence, Fairness', *Proceedings of the Aristotelian Society*, 95 (1995), pp. 19–35, and in my *Ideal Code, Real World*, I have shown that a certain form of rule consequentialism is innocent of this accusation.

18. I explore this in 'Intuitions and Moral Theorizing', in P. Stratton-Lake (ed.), *Moral Intuitionism* (Oxford: Clarendon Press, 2001).

19. There *are* problems about these things, but I explore them in my *Ideal Code, Real World* and will not do so again here.

20. H. L. A. Hart suggested that rules protecting persons, property, and promises have a 'natural necessity' as long as certain basic *contingent* truths about human beings and the world they live in remain the same (*Concept of Law*, p. 195).

21. Of his own moral theory, David Copp writes, 'It is a contingent matter whether a given moral standard is justified. This is a virtue of the theory, because it is what makes it possible for the theory to explain why

standards are justified, when they are justified, on the basis of contingent facts about human nature and the nature of societies.' (David Copp, *Morality, Normativity, and Society* (New York: Oxford University Press, 1995), p. 214).

22. Hart, *Concept of Law*, p. 190.

23. See my 'Rule-consequentialism and Obligations to the Needy', *Pacific Philosophical Quarterly*, 79 (1998), pp. 19–33.

24. If we instead focus on the level of likely actual compliance, and if this is low, then I think we have abandoned the idealisation that a moral code should be appropriate for internalisation by the whole. For a very carefully worked out theory that does abandon this idealisation, see Donald Regan's *Co-operative Utilitarianism* (Oxford: Clarendon Press, 1980).

25. I am grateful to Elinor Mason and Dale Miller for very helpful comments on an earlier draft of this chapter.

13

Rule Consequentialism and the Value of Friendship

Madison Powers

SECTION I: INTRODUCTION

A familiar objection to consequentialism is that it cannot provide a plausible account of the value of goods such as friendship.[1] The complaint is that consequentialism's commitment to maximising impersonal value cannot be reconciled with the importance agents attach to friendship and the dispositions to care specially for those with whom they are intimately related. The motives, dispositions, and beliefs required by an agent's acceptance of a consequentialist moral theory are said to be incompatible with her experience of friendship as valuable for its own sake.

One line of reply to this objection is that consequentialism requires only that agents *have* whatever motives, dispositions, or beliefs best achieve the aims of the theory. Thus, on consequentialist grounds, it claims that agents need not have any awareness of the aims and requirements of a theory if, in fact, the absence of such awareness best promotes that theory's conception of good consequences.[2] Hence, consequentialism can bypass worries about an agent's moral phenomenology as long as it does not instruct anyone to believe that the theory is true, correct, or justified, to have dispositions to comply with the theory, or to believe that the theory supplies the justification for the agent's dispositions. However, I wish to explore the prospects for defending consequentialism as a moral theory which an agent can consciously accept without succumbing to the objections to the way consequentialist agents are thought to view friendship.

A successful defence would have to address at least four distinguishable objections that have evolved and sharpened in response to consequentialist counterarguments. These objections include complaints which focus on: (1) the divergence

between the requirements of action recommended by consequentialist theories and
the kind of motivations and dispositions that sustain the existence of friendship; (2)
the tension between the motivations and dispositions associated with a commitment
to consequentialism and the motivations which give rise to friendship; (3) the agent's
inability to reconcile the dispositions involved in judging friendship as valuable for
its own sake and the beliefs consequentialists must have about the justification for
those dispositions; and (4) the logical incompatibility of the beliefs required by an
acceptance of consequentialism and the beliefs involved in treating friendship as
intrinsically valuable.

While consequentialists have offered persuasive replies to versions of the
motivational arguments, many who are sympathetic to consequentialism appear
doubtful that a defence against objections that focus on an agent's beliefs can
succeed.[3] However, I argue that a version of rule consequentialism can meet these
objections, and I conclude with a brief reflection on how a successful account of
consequentialism brings it closer to a contractualist moral view.

SECTION 2: MOTIVATIONAL OBJECTIONS   INTEGRITY AND ALIENATION

Bernard Williams claims that because consequentialism is committed to imperson-
ally good consequences as the ultimate source of all value, the acceptance of a
consequentialist moral theory alienates the agent from his actions and the motivations for his action and undermines his integrity.[4] His argument assumes that an
agent who accepts a consequentialist moral view has a 'general project of bringing
about maximally desirable outcomes'.[5] This higher-order commitment makes an
agent's projects depend upon 'what projects and what potential satisfactions there
are within calculable reach of the causal levers near which he finds himself'.[6] Such a
theory is said to ignore the fact that agents also have first-order projects, things they
care about for their own sakes.[7] A commitment to producing maximally good
outcomes is incompatible with the fact that an agent's actions must flow from the
'projects and attitudes which in some cases he takes seriously at the deepest level, as
what his life is about'.[8] A commitment to consequentialism as a higher-order project,
therefore, seems to expose an agent to demands that he act routinely in ways that
substantially diverge from his deepest value commitments. The consequentialist life
would lack the direction and stability that comes from the agent's actions being
guided by his fundamental values.

The acceptance of a consequentialist moral theory seems to render an agent
incapable of properly appreciating both the importance of the values that accounted
for his undertaking of those projects in the first place, and the firmness of certain
dispositions that sustain them. As Samuel Scheffler observes, consequentialism gives
the wrong account of how an agent's projects are generated and sustained.[9] The first
worry is that when agents undertake projects, or make commitments, they normally

are motivated by concerns other than a desire to promote the aims of a con-sequentialist moral theory. The second worry is that having the general project of bringing about maximally good outcomes interferes with an agent's ability to sustain personal commitments that are fundamentally characteristic of human agency.

A reply suggested by Gabriele Taylor can provide a partial defence against the criticism that consequentialism undermines the sustainability of an agent's first-order projects. She argues that whatever interest agents have in living lives of moral integrity, they need not be viewed as demanding lives in which their deepest values, and the actions required by their moral theory, never diverge. In exceptional, often tragic cases agents might act contrary to well-established value commitments, and yet they can remain persons of integrity.[10] However, what agents cannot do, consistent with the value of moral integrity, is live their lives in ways in which their values and actions routinely, or even very often, diverge.

Accordingly, a minimally adequate refinement of consequentialism would pre-scribe that agents should inculcate, and maintain within themselves, firm disposi-tions to act for the benefit of friends, and that agents also should foster a strong tendency to feel guilt (or disapproval) when they (or others) fail to act consistent with those deeply entrenched dispositions.[11] Indeed, the aversion to certain types of action may be so deep that it may be exceedingly difficult for agents to bring themselves to act contrary to settled dispositions, even if they believed that doing so would produce better consequences.[12] Consequentialist agents having this sort of motivational structure can maintain projects and commitments that give value to a life without the felt need for continuous behavioural adjustment. Such a theory therefore would escape the charge of unsustainability, and the consequentialist agent's moral integrity would be secure from the threat of constant erosion.

A critic may still object that consequentialism provides the wrong account of how projects and commitments are generated, even if it can show how they can be sustained. The objection is that a higher-order commitment to maximising the good ensures that an agent's moral consciousness will be characterised by two kinds of primary dispositions which inevitably pull in opposing directions. Our moral theory seems to tell us that we must be disposed to care for and act for the sake of maximising the overall good; and yet, friendship requires that we have, and act upon, a special concern for the well-being of a friend for her own sake with no further end in mind. Hence, the point of the alienation objection is not just that a commitment to consequentialist morality can lead to an unsustainable divergence between the requirements for action and the specific values and dispositions an agent has cultivated. It also embodies dispositions in constant tension with one another from the inception of an agent's projects, and it offers an implausible account of how those projects originated as projects agents think worth pursuing for their own sake. Our deepest projects are thus said to emanate from an irreducibly personal point of view, not from an impartial perspective that picks out those things worth doing.

Peter Railton's well-known response to the alienation objection proceeds in two steps. The first step is to spell out the consequentialist's value theory. Objective list theories enumerate a plurality of distinct elements of the good that the theory directs the agent to realise. An agent who embraces an objective list theory which includes friendship as a separate and distinct element of the good does not view friendship as valuable simply because it is a means to some further substantive, all inclusive value, such as pleasure or happiness. To be sure, pleasure and happiness may be goods included on the list as well, and friendship often brings pleasure and happiness, but goods such as friendship are seen as valuable in themselves, even if their realisation does not bring pleasure or happiness to the agent. Such a view allows the agent to see each element of the good as intrinsically valuable and hence the source of independently motivating force.

It is not enough, however, for a consequentialist to argue for the independently motivating force of friendship. The co-existing consequentialist motivations must be compatible with a motivational stance directly responsive to the intrinsic value of friendship. The second component of Railton's strategy is addressed to this concern. He describes a sophisticated act-consequentialist agent as someone whose motivational structure meets a counterfactual test: although he does not ordinarily do what he does for the sake of doing what is right, he would lead a different sort of life if it were not compatible with leading an objectively consequentialist life.[13] This account allows him to distinguish being committed to something for its own sake and an agent's having an overriding commitment. The dispositions associated with each intrinsically valuable good on the objective list direct the agent's action in the first instance, and only if having such dispositions did not maximise the good would the sophisticated consequentialist agent be motivated to change them. Accordingly, Railton's strategy seeks to reduce the potential for alienation, not to eliminate it entirely. Moreover, his argument is that no plausible moral theory should eliminate completely the tension between the motivational demands of a moral theory and the agent's personal projects and commitments.

SECTION 3: NORMATIVE INCOHERENCE

A third criticism is that Railton's attempt to reconcile two seemingly incompatible kinds of disposition does not respond to what is fundamentally objectionable about the consequentialist account of moral agency. Williams, in some places, also argues that the incompatibility involves a conflict between an agent's dispositions and beliefs. He claims that it is not possible to combine all kinds of reflection with all kinds of disposition, and that consequentialist beliefs about the dispositions one ought to have are not 'stable under reflection'.[14]

Neera Kapur develops an example of the third version of the objection as a conflict involving an agent's beliefs about friendship. She argues that beliefs required by a commitment to consequentialism are deeply incompatible with the 'necessary irreplaceability' of friendship: 'to love a friend as an end is to place a special value on her – to *believe* that her value is not outweighed, say, simply by the greater needs of others or the needs of a greater number of others'.[15] Because consequentialist reflection can lead an agent to believe that he ought to have different dispositions than the ones he has, consequentialism represents an implausibly weak form of attachment to friends. A proper appreciation of the value of friendship requires that we remain disposed to act for the welfare of our friends, and that we believe that we ought not to change our dispositions whenever a calculation of the overall good leads us to believe that such dispositions are less than optimal.

William Wilcox makes the argument more pointedly. He argues that Railton's compatibilist solution is inadequate, for an overriding commitment to consequentialism means that an agent should view *any* increase in overall good as requiring him to abandon what we ordinarily take to be essential to a commitment to a friend, and even perhaps, to make an effort to rid ourselves of our dispositions to care specially for our friends.[16] Wilcox describes this tension as a *normative incoherence*. His complaint is not that consequentialism admits that agents sometimes may be required by morality to choose against the welfare of a friend for the sake of some weightier good. Such a view of friendship in which such tragic choices are not possible Wilcox sees as overly romantic.[17] The problem is that an overriding commitment to consequentialism is 'so pervasive' that it leaves too little room left over for the special concern for a friend to have much 'practical effect'. For the agent must think that he ought to redirect his energies and concerns whenever he believes any *slight* increase in the overall good will result. Such beliefs are said to be incompatible with true friendship.

I argue that a version of rule consequentialism is especially well suited to meet the normative incoherence objection. However, there are two preliminary replies an act consequentialist might make, and it is instructive to see why these replies are helpful but not yet adequate.

The first reply is that a different picture of a consequentialist's belief structure and processes of belief formation can reduce the significance of these criticisms. Even if consequentialism does require agents to form beliefs about the consequences of having and maintaining certain dispositions, it does not require them to adopt lenient evidentiary standards for belief formation. In matters that are highly complex and speculative, one need not change one's beliefs about the dispositions one ought to have towards one's friends based on the slightest shift in the balance of currently available evidence. To borrow a legal expression, there is no rationale for demanding that consequentialist agents reach conclusions about likely consequences of alternative sets of dispositions on the basis of the mere preponderance of available evidence. It is entirely reasonable, on purely consequentialist grounds, to demand at least clear and convincing evidence, or the satisfaction of a more stringent standard of proof, before concluding that one's attitudes towards friendship ought to be revised.

Second, if an agent has a particular understanding of the way the goods on an objective list are related to one another, it is less likely that she will believe that the best constellation of human goods will be one in which friendship is readily interchangeable with or replaceable by other goods. She may embrace what James Griffin calls a weak incommensurability thesis which supposes that some goods are such that, at a given level of fulfilment, *no additional amount of some other competing goods can outweigh them.*[18] A life without friendship, or a life in which friendship cannot be sustained, will not be judged a prudentially valuable life on this kind of value theory, even if that life is rich in many other respects. A world in which lives lack sustainable friendships would be judged to be a worse world than one in which friendship flourishes, even if friendship prevents some other goods on the objective list from being realised. An agent's belief in a weak incommensurability thesis thus puts some further limits on what the agent *can believe* regarding possible trade-offs among goods and still count as the constellation of goods believed to be maximally good in an individual life; and a proper concern for the overall good summed across lives cannot ignore what the consequentialist's own value theory supposes as the kinds of lives most likely to realise his theory's aims.

If we combine a stringent epistemic requirement for change of belief about well-settled, considered judgements about the value of friendship with the weak incommensurability thesis, the following picture of the agent's beliefs about friendship emerges. An agent would not be epistemically disposed to believing that she ought to change her dispositions without compelling reasons to do so, and even if she believes that some improvement in some other goods that make life worthwhile could be obtained by such a change in belief, the change would have to be considerable before it rises to the level of a threat to how she appreciates the value of friendship. For the holder of the weak incommensurability thesis would believe that the contribution friendship makes to the total good within a life is such that even very large increments of other goods will not compensate for even slight decreases in the good to be derived from friendship. Thus the kinds of lives consequentialists favour mirror the kinds of lives many of its critics charge them with repudiating.

However, the combination of a belief about the appropriate epistemic standards of belief formation and a belief in a weak incommensurability thesis will not be enough. Critics can argue that, although a world in which lives generally lack sustainable friendships will be a worse world than one in which friendship flourishes, a consequentialist may still believe that *he* ought to change *his* dispositions towards his friends, and that he ought to forgo the benefits of friendship *himself,* whenever he believes that doing so will produce more good generally, including, for example, a greater good obtained from ensuring that others can form and sustain friendships. Therefore, consequentialism's account of friendship is said to be too demanding in so far as it treats the value of one's own friendship as a mere instantiation of the agent-neutral moral value of friendship generally. If a consequentialist agent's overriding commitment is to realising the agent-neutral value of friendship, then the agent must believe that her friendships may be sacrificed in favour of a state of affairs in which there is more agent-neutral value produced by the existence of more lives benefitting from friendship. The value of friendship is thus seen as fully interchangeable across lives, and the agent who accepts a consequentialist moral theory must believe that his own friendships are readily dispensable, even if friendship is believed to be a weakly incommensurable good and his standards of justified belief formation make such beliefs about the value of his own friendships more resistant to revision. Thus, a reflective consequentialist agent finds no respite from the incipient demands for self-sacrifice when it comes to friendship.

The problem of how an agent can believe that his own friendships are sustainable under pressure to maximise agent-neutral value of friendship, however, can be addressed if we adopt a form of consequentialist assessment that moves in the direction of rule consequentialism. The rationale for that shift is twofold.

First, a plausible form of consequentialist assessment must permit an assessment of the kinds of lives as a whole that are best on consequentialist grounds. Friendship is the kind of good that has value only if sustainable over whole lives or significant stretches of time. Assessment of its value cannot be made on an occurrent basis, estimating the consequences of retaining one's dispositions moment by moment, act by act. The consequentialist who believes that friendship is an ingredient in the best form of life for individuals therefore will understand the value of friendship as a good whose value can be realised only when certain dispositions reliably guide and shape the particular decisions and choices of an agent over the course of a long duration. Otherwise, consequentialism lacks a plausible framework for assessment which can take account of goods which have value only in their durability.

The implication of the global account of how some kinds of values are realised is that act consequentialism, at least for some types of goods, provides the wrong unit for consequentialist assessment. While some suppose that the move from act to some other form of 'indirect' assessment is a powerful concession to consequentialism's critics, the shift need not be construed as a mere strategic retreat. If a consequentialist is committed to the realisation of the best overall consequences – the best total history of the world, as Derek Parfit puts it – then the consequentialist should adopt as its object of consequentialist assessment whatever method best captures the truth about how goods of various sorts are realised in the world. If some goods are realised only globally, then the consequentialist method of assessment would be remiss in not taking that fact into account. Rather than being merely an opportunistic manoeuvre, attention to the differing ways the various goods within its value theory contribute to the overall best consequences is a requirement of a consistent consequentialism.

The first move offers one rationale for favouring some form of rule consequentialism, but by itself it still does not avoid the problem of agents having beliefs that lead them to sacrifice their own friendships too readily. A successful response to critics must show how it is possible for a consequentialist agent to appreciate the value of friendship realised in the life of each individual agent, not just for agents in general. One way of making this shift is to move to a rule-acceptance consequentialist (RAC) theory. On the RAC account, the right action is not the one which brings about the best consequences, as in Railton's sophisticated act consequentialism. RAC treats individual acts as right if they are in conformity with the moral rules the *universal acceptance of which* would bring about as much good as any other alternative set of accepted rules.[19]

To make clear how RAC immunises beliefs about one's own dispositions from the self-sacrifice objection, we need to see how dispositions figure in RAC's account of consequentialist assessment. The answer lies in the fact that, while this brand of consequentialism appears to retain a central place for the notion of moral rules, the actual object of consequentialist assessment is not the set of moral rules or norms in existence in society, but the dispositions involved in their universal acceptance. Some rule consequentialists argue that accepting rules is largely a matter of 'having a certain character and conscience'.[20] R. B. Brandt makes this point when he claims that morality is a system of intrinsic aversions to types of actions, with a corresponding tendency to feel guilt or disapproval when such actions are performed, and a belief that these attitudes are justified.[21] Acceptance of the rules or requirements of a morality therefore is a matter of having a set of standing dispositions to act in ways that are consistent with the achievement of the fundamental aims of that morality in one's own life, throughout the course of that life.

Universal acceptance of some account of the value of friendship, for example, involves the universal having of certain dispositions towards one's own friends. RAC therefore is concerned not with maximising the sum of agent-neutral value of friendship but rather with the set of dispositions towards friends, the having of which by everyone would bring about the greatest overall good.

The combination of a long-term account of how friendship is realised within a single life and an RAC commitment to the universal possession of the dispositions essential to friendship changes the nature of the kinds of beliefs a consequentialist agent has about friendship. An RAC theory, which contains among its universally accepted set of rules the requirement that all agents be disposed to act for the sake of their friends, does not require an agent to believe that *she* ought to change *her* dispositions towards her friends whenever she believes that doing so will produce the greatest overall good. The RAC agent has a different kind of belief: she believes that she is morally justified in having and acting on dispositions the universal possession of which brings about the greatest overall good.

To be sure, consequentialist reflection can have radical implications for the beliefs one has regarding friendship. After reflection on the long-term consequences of certain social practices, institutional arrangements, or forms of social interaction, an RAC agent may conclude that all of us ought to renounce certain types of commitments or to eliminate or modify the dispositions associated with them. (For example, some feminists urge not only a change in attitudes towards one's own spouse, but a change in our assessment of the value of traditional marriage itself.) But such reflection, although radically revisionist in its potential, does not involve the pervasive and insidious erosion of dispositions envisioned by the normative incoherence objection. Reflection on consequences does not advise some of us to forego the good of friendship so that others may have more of that good. Nor does a consequentialist assessment of the value of friendship involve a calculation of its net agent-neutral value to determine what dispositions one is justified in having. The agent who accepts RAC believes that the motives and dispositions she is justified in having depend on what motives and dispositions she believes all other agents are justified in having. The level of self-sacrifice of one's friendships, while not rendered impermissible, is not a necessary consequence of a RAC theorist's beliefs.

SECTION 4: LOGICAL INCOHERENCE

A fourth version of the friendship objection points to an alleged logical conflict between beliefs possessed by agents who accept a consequentialist moral theory. On this view, the problem is a conflict between two incompatible modes of justification. A consequentialist account of the justification of friendship and its characteristic dispositions is said to conflict with the way agents ordinarily view the justificatory basis for the things they believe intrinsically valuable, or valuable independently of any assessment of their contribution to the overall good. Kapur, for example, claims that 'friendship that is an end in itself is characterized by activities that are done not solely, or even primarily, for the sake of any end beyond itself'.[22] Yet acceptance of a consequentialist criterion of right action demands that agents view such goods as valuable only instrumentally, as valuable only as a means to the realization of some further moral end. A consequentialist is said to believe that 'I place special value on you so long, but only so long, as valuing you thus promotes the overall good.'[23]

The heart of the logical incoherence objection is that the agent has to believe two incompatible things, namely (1) that her dispositions to care specially about friends are justified intrinsically, or non-instrumentally, apart from any contribution they make to the overall good; and (2) that such dispositions are justified only instrumentally.[24] The logical incompatibility objection, therefore, explicitly denies that the two forms of justification for one's dispositions are compatible on the assumption that, for a consequentialist, the instrumental value of friendship provides its *sole* moral justification. Kapur contends that consequentialism 'sees the moral worth of friendship as *entirely dependent* on its total consequences, with no independent moral weight assigned to its worth for the individuals involved'.[25]

It's unclear, however, why the consequentialist must accept Kapur's character-isation. I consider three versions of this claim, which supposes that consequentialism permits only an instrumental justification of friendship.

The first version is that consequentialism makes the value of all goods such as friendship solely dependent upon their contribution to the best overall consequences obtainable.[26] Consequentialists are said to believe friendship valuable only because of and in so far as it is a part of the constellation of goods that make up the best consequences. Yet agents normally value friendship more directly, as valuable for its own sake, not simply valuable under the description 'a contribution to the best overall consequences obtainable'.

The consequentialist has a readily available response to this first version of the logical incoherence objection. There is no reason why a consequentialist agent must be saddled with the belief that friendship, or any other good on her list of prudentially valuable goods, cannot be valued under two compatible descriptions, valuable as 'a contribution to human well-being', and valuable as 'a contribution to the best overall consequences obtainable'. Consequentialists can be described as believing that friendship is prudentially valuable as an end in itself and valuable also as a means to the moral good embodied in their commitments to realising the overall good. The distinction between the prudential ends that matter morally to an agent and the ultimate moral ends of an agent's moral theory permits consequentialists to claim without contradiction that agents can believe that friendship is justified both intrinsically and instrumentally.[27]

A second version of the logical incoherence objection denies that the distinction between prudential and moral value is a sufficient rejoinder. It holds that what the consequentialist theory fails to explain is the sense in which agents view friendship as having *intrinsic moral value*. It suggests that the distinction between prudential and moral ends does not get at the root of the problem. One way of putting the point is that, phenomenologically, it's not just a practical loss but a moral loss which is felt when an agent makes a trade-off involving friendship and some weightier good.[28] The complaint is that consequentialism can't adequately account for the sense of moral guilt or moral regret felt when friendship is sacrificed. Kapur follows

Scheffler, who argues that for a consequentialist, the moral significance of friendship is exhausted once a consequentialist assessment is made.[29] On this view, the motivational structure and emotions of a consequentialist agent and a non-consequentialist agent look very different. Both agents will acknowledge the loss of something of intrinsic value, but only the non-consequentialist agent can feel a genuine moral loss and not just a loss to her own or to some agent's well-being.[30]

The claim underlying this last objection is that the agent must believe these two logically incompatible things: that friendship is morally valuable for its own sake (as evidenced by the deep sense of regret she feels) and that friendship, while prudentially valuable (to her or to her friend) for its own sake, is only instrumentally morally valuable (according to the moral theory she accepts). Consequentialists then face a dilemma: they lack either a moral emotion that they ought to have, or else they have the proper emotional response to the trade-off of a morally important good, but they cannot justify having it, and cannot reconcile having it with the other beliefs they have about what emotions they are justified in having.

One perhaps not very satisfying reply is an error theory: the consequentialist may admit that the critic has the right account of the moral phenomenology but deny that it is anything more than a deeply entrenched and widely shared illusion. Shelly Kagan, for example, questions whether the widely accepted idea that the willingness to favour persons with whom we feel a special attachment is essential to love or friendship.[31] The upshot of Kagan's approach is that an agent is not required to believe the conjunction of two incompatible things: (1) that his emotions are a product of a systematically induced false but beneficial belief, and (2) that an unwillingness to favour a friend involves a genuine moral loss. Kagan's strategy seems to come down on the side of abandoning the latter belief. This move, of course, will not satisfy the critic who insists that friendship really does carry its own moral justification independent of what a consequentialist moral theory has to say about it, but we are at a stalemate: the consequentialist insisting that moral value is calculable only after being processed through the filter of a moral theory and the opponent insisting on attaching moral value to friendship pre-theoretically.

A different sort of reply can take the critic's charge seriously and for the sake of argument admit that friendship has moral value prior to the deliverances of any consequentialist calculation. It begins with the claim that agents have two kinds of moral ends, prima facie ends and all-things-considered ends. Sanford Levy makes this kind of case for promise-keeping.[32] He supposes that we understand the kind of moral commitment involved with promise-keeping in the following way. We morally value promise-keeping in that we believe that we ought to have dispositions to keep promises and that we ought to feel moral regret when we do not keep promises. We believe that the moral basis, both for our beliefs and feelings, lies in the primary justification supplied by their contribution to overall good consequences, but agents also have a prima facie moral commitment to promise-keeping for its own sake if promise-keeping is an element of the good recognised within our moral theory.

This two-tiered account of moral justification explains the seemingly deep sense of moral regret that agents feel when promises are breached, and why it is not irrational, on consequentialist grounds, to have dispositions to honour promises and to have feelings of regret when they are broken. It is rationally justified for the consequentialist to have a belief in the prima facie wrongness of certain actions because such actions are normally associated with predictable harms to well-being that flow from their performance, but it is only in virtue of consequentialist considerations that we can say that not keeping promises is in fact wrong, all things considered. Levy's strategy thus allows the consequentialist to claim that the two beliefs about justification are beliefs of differing kinds and hence, not in logical conflict.

Levy's proposed solution, however, does not address another important aspect of the objection. As long as a breach of promise is seen merely as an action normally associated with predictable harms to well-being, then the consequentialist does not have what the critic might call a reason of the right kind for feeling moral regret. Her reasons for feeling moral loss with the breach of a promise may not be irrational in consequentialist terms, but that feeling is explained entirely by the consequentialist justification for the dispositions it is rational to have, given her moral aim of maximising the good. The defence of a genuinely compatibilist solution which would satisfy the critic has to show why the agent would feel a moral loss for additional, purely non-instrumental moral reasons. The disposition to keep promises would continue to appear to be only instrumentally valuable as a means to the promotion of maximal well-being, not something that the agent genuinely believes to be morally valuable for its own sake. Thus, a distinction between prima facie and all-things-considered wrongness cannot show that there is a moral reason to care about promise-keeping that is both independent of its role within a maximising conception of morality *and* not logically incompatible with a consequentialist justification.

The same objection can made against the RAC theorist's defence of the dispositions to favour friends differentially. The charge is that such dispositions are valued only instrumentally (just as dispositions to keep promises are valued), and that the justification for the regret one feels when one acts contrary to deep dispositions lies solely in the role regret plays in a maximising conception of morality.[33] The criticism therefore is that, if an agent does not believe her dispositions independently justified, the consequentialist account of friendship will not cohere well with ordinary moral phenomenology.

Once again, of course, the proponent of an error theory might claim that the demand for an independent moral reason to care about promise-keeping or friendship apart from its role within a maximising conception of morality begs the question against the consequentialist view of justification. However, I shall pursue a different line of thought aimed at meeting the critic's objection on his own terms. I shall consider two ways an RAC theorist might defend the non-instrumental moral value of friendship and its associated dispositions.

On the first account, the consequentialist's belief structure, properly spelled out, is that (1) only well-being matters morally, and (2) that it is rational to prefer more good to less. She, no less than a non-consequentialist, believes that any diminution of any of the goods which constitute an essential aspect of an agent's well-being is a morally regrettable event. Because a consequentialist approach to justification rests fundamentally on the central idea that all that matters morally is that lives go well, any loss to an aspect of well-being, even if outweighed by other gains, has moral significance. Its moral significance, contrary to Scheffler's famous characterisation of consequentialism, is not exhausted by the consequentialist calculus. That some trade-offs are believed to be justified, according to the principle of rationality they also accept, does not signal any lack of felt moral significance attached to the foregone alternative. A sacrifice of any basic element of the good that forms an integral part of the aim of a moral theory, even if a sacrifice is believed to be morally justified all things considered, is always a moral loss, and thus an occasion for genuine moral regret. As Wayne Sumner rhetorically asks, 'What else could morality be *for*?'[34] Indeed, the consequentialist's single-minded commitment to the production of well-being would be unintelligible if we were to think that she is incapable of attaching moral value directly to the various elements of well-being for herself, her friends, and others. Contrary to the order of moral justification the critics of consequentialism suppose, it is thought rational to prefer more good to less good *only* because consequentialists have certain threshold beliefs about what goods matter morally, and they care about the promotion of those goods for their own sake.

A further refinement in the account of an RAC theorist's beliefs should be even more convincing to critics. Call this the egalitarian consequentialist view. The egalitarian consequentialist account of an agent's belief structure, properly spelled out, is that (1) only well-being matters morally, and (2) that it matters equally that all lives go well. As Will Kymlicka points out, not all consequentialists defend maximisation on the assumption that rational social choice mirrors a widely accepted model of rationality for individual choice.[35] Some consequentialists, including James Griffin and John Harsanyi (and according to Kymlicka, Bentham), argue for the superiority of their moral view on grounds that it provides a better account of equal moral consideration than some of its deontological competitors.[36]

Although some consequentialists defend the account of equality embodied in various forms of act consequentialism, egalitarian consequentialists who adopt a universal rule-acceptance theory have specific beliefs about equality that form part of the rationale for accepting a consequentialist account of moral justification. Like the first defender of rule consequentialism's view of the moral value of friendship, she is motivated by the belief that well-being is what matters morally, and that it matters morally even when outweighed by other morally weightier concerns. Unlike the first defender, however, she believes in a view of equality in which only those rules universally accepted and universally applied to agents are justified, and thus, she does not think that friendship or any other element of what makes lives go well matters morally *only* because it is a contribution to maximal goodness. It also matters that the goods her theory seeks to realise are realised as part of the optimal set of rules, dispositions, and beliefs universally accepted.

Now one might object to this egalitarian version of RAC on the grounds that we have done great damage to consequentialism's claim to be a single-principle moral theory, one which takes the maximisation of the good to be sole criterion of rightness. This criticism, however, seems misplaced even as applied to consequentialists such as Sidgwick. For his defence of consequentialism also rested on twin pillars: (1) that rationality requires maximisation of the good; and (2) that my good is no more important than the good of any other. The latter claim is a claim about equality. Where Sidgwick and the egalitarian RAC consequentialist differ is in their interpretations of the consequentialist's commitment to equality, not in the latter's going beyond the consequentialist's allegedly single-principle rationale supporting his moral theory.

SECTION 5: CONCLUSION

We have seen that an RAC theory can provide solutions to both versions of the motivational objection, the normative incoherence argument, and the various forms of the logical incompatibility objections. The essential elements of this moral theory include: (1) the acceptance of certain universally applicable rules; (2) the acceptance required is universal, not individualised; (3) the acceptance of rules is a matter of having certain dispositions and beliefs which reliably shape and guide action in conformity with the rules over complete lives or at least long durations; and (4) the object of a morality made up of a universally accepted, universally applicable set of rules is both the production of the best overall consequences and its conformity to some conception of fairness or moral equality.

The consequentialist thus avoids a family of friendship objections by shifting away from act consequentialism to a rule-acceptance account. However, the shift raises some thorny questions about the rationale for remaining in the consequentialist fold. With the possible exception of (4), the elements of the RAC moral theory are identical to some contractualist conceptions of morality. Both take seriously the importance of friendship in the lives of separate persons; both depend upon a notion of universal acceptance of moral rules; and both view acceptance as involving deep dispositions and elements of an agent's character, not just a cognitive, detached appreciation of the rules.

Although rule consequentialists and contractualists typically disagree about the object of morality, we see that consequentialists themselves may differ in what they take to be the rationale or object of morality. Egalitarian consequentialists have been shown to embrace a notion of moral equality strikingly similar to one many contractualists would defend. Moreover, nothing in the account offered here prevents a contractualist from laying claim to maximisation of the good as part of his own account of morality's object as long as the commitment to equality is maintained.

The contest for the best account of impartial morality, therefore, will likely depend upon the most plausible account of its object, but it seems that less divides the contenders than many assume.[37]

NOTES

1. Bernard Williams, 'A Critique of Utilitarianism', in J. J. C. Smart and Bernard Williams, *Utilitarianism: For and Against* (Cambridge: Cambridge University Press, 1973), p. 83; and Neera Badhwar Kapur, 'Why It is Wrong to Be Always Guided By the Best: Consequentialism and Friendship', *Ethics*, 101 (1991), p. 485.
2. Derek Parfit, *Reasons and Persons* (Oxford: Oxford University Press, 1984).
3. James Griffin, 'On the Winding Road from Good to Right', *Value, Welfare, and Morality*, R. G. Frey and C. Morris (eds), (Cambridge: Cambridge University Press, 1993), pp. 158–79.
4. Williams, 'Critique', pp. 116–17.
5. Ibid., p. 110.
6. Ibid., p. 115.
7. Such commitments take a variety of forms, such as 'a person, a cause, an institution, a career, one's own genius, or the pursuit of danger' (ibid., p. 112).
8. Ibid., p. 116.
9. Samuel Scheffler, The Rejection of Consequentialism (Oxford: Oxford University Press, 1982), p. 14.
10. Gabriele Taylor, *Pride, Shame, and Guilt: Emotions of Self-Assessment* (Oxford: Clarendon Press, 1985), pp. 123–6.
11. Peter Railton, 'Alienation, Consequentialism, and the Demands of Morality', *Philosophy and Public Affairs*, 13 (1984), pp. 153–4, 157–9.
12. R. B. Brandt, 'Morality and Its Critics', *American Philosophical Quarterly*, 26 (1989), p. 91.
13. Railton, 'Allienation', pp. 113–14; Elinor Mason, 'Can an Indirect Consequentialist be a Real Friend?', *Ethics*, 108 (1998), pp. 386–93.
14. Bernard Williams, 'The Structure of Hare's Theory', *Hare and Critics*, Douglas Seanor and N. Fotion (eds), (Oxford: Clarendon Press, 1990), pp. 189–90.
15. Kapur, 'Why It is Wrong', p. 484, emphasis mine.
16. W. Wilcox, 'Egoists, Consequentialists, and their Friends', *Philosophy and Public Affairs* 16 (1987), pp. 73–84, especially 78–9.
17. See also, Kapur, 'Why It is Wrong', p. 485.
18. James Griffin, *Well-Being* (Oxford: Clarendon Press, 1986).
19. Brad Hooker, 'Rule-consequentialism', *Mind*, 99 (1990), pp. 67–77. But for a revised account, see Hooker, 'Rule-consequentialism, Incoherence, and Fairness', *Proceedings of the Aristotelian Society*, 95 (1994), pp. 19–35.
20. Hooker, 'Rule-consequentialism, Incoherence, and Fairness', p. 21.
21. Brandt, 'Morality and Its Critics', p. 91.
22. Kapur, 'Why It is Wrong', p. 491.
23. Ibid., p. 493.

24. Ibid., pp. 491–4.
25. Ibid., p. 498.
26. Ibid., p. 485.
27. James Grunebaum, 'Friendship, Morality, and Special Obligation', *American Philosophical Quarterly*, 30 (1993), p. 57; and Madison Powers, 'Contractualist Impartiality and Personal Commitments', *American Philosophical Quarterly*, 30 (1993), pp. 62–71.
28. Kapur, 'Why It is Wrong', p. 503
29. Ibid., pp. 492–3.
30. Ibid., p. 499.
31. Shelly Kagan, *The Limits of Morality* (Oxford: Clarendon Press, 1989), pp. 367–9.
32. Sanford Levy, 'The Coherence of Two-Level Utilitarianism: Hare vs. Williams', *Utilitas*, 6 (1994): especially pp. 306–9.
33. Kapur, 'Why It is Wrong', p. 494.
34. L. W. Sumner, 'Two Theories of the Good', in Ellen Frankel Paul, Fred Miller, and Jeffrey Paul (eds), *The Good Life and the Human Good*, (Cambridge: Cambridge University Press, 1992), p. 1.
35. Will Kymlicka, 'Rawls on Teleology and Deontology', *Philosophy and Public Affairs*, 17 (1988), pp. 173–90.
36. See James Griffin, *Well-Being*, especially, pp. 167–70, 208–15, 239–42, and 295–301. (Page references to Griffin are from Kymlicka, 'Rawls on Teleology and Deontology', p. 117, n. 8.)
37. I have benefitted from comments on an earlier draft from Brad Hooker, Whitley Kaufman, and Eran Klein. Responsibility for errors remains my own.

Notes on Contributors

D. W. HASLETT is Professor of Philosophy at the University of Delaware. His books include *Equal Consideration* (University of Delaware Press/Associated University Presses, 1987) and *Capitalism with Morality* (Clarendon Press, 1994).

BRAD HOOKER is in the Philosophy Department at the University of Reading, UK. He is the author of *Ideal Code, Real World: A Rule-consequentialist Theory of Morality* (Clarendon Press, 2000).

SHELLY KAGAN teaches moral philosophy at Yale University. He received his Ph.D. from Princeton, and has previously taught at the University of Pittsburgh and the University of Illinois at Chicago. He is the author of *The Limits of Morality* (Clarendon Press, 1989) and *Normative Ethics* (Westview, 1998), and is currently working on a project on *The Geometry of Desert*.

SANFORD S. LEVY is Associate Professor of Philosophy at Montana State University. His most recent publications are 'Utilitarian Alternatives to Act Utilitarianism' and 'Thomas Reid's Defense of Conscience'. His current research includes a study of the logic of moral supervenience and an examination of character-utilitarianism, its role as a tool for moral conversion, and its use in defending an ecocentric environmental ethic.

DAVID LYONS is Professor of Law and Professor of Philosophy at Boston University, as well as Susan Linn Sage Professor of Philosophy emeritus and Professor of Law emeritus at Cornell University. His books include *Forms and Limits of Utilitarianism* (Oxford University Press, 1965), *In the Interest of the Governed* (Oxford University Press, 1973), *Ethics and the Rule of Law* (Cambridge University Press, 1984), *Moral Aspects of Legal Theory* (Cambridge University Press, 1983), and *Rights, Welfare, and Mill's Moral Theory* (Oxford University Press, 1994).

ELINOR MASON is an Assistant Professor of Philosophy at Arizona State University. Her Ph.D. is from the University of Reading. She works primarily on the topics of consequentialism and friendship, and she has published articles in the journals *Ethics* and *Ethical Theory and Moral Practice*.

DALE E. MILLER is an Assistant Professor of Philosophy at Old Dominion University. He received his Ph.D. from the University of Pittsburgh, and has previously held positions at the University of Minnesota Duluth and the University of Florida. He has published articles on Mill's moral psychology and political philosophy in *Utilitas* and *History of Political Thought*, and he is currently working on a book on Mill, which is to be published by Polity Press.

PHILLIP MONTAGUE is in the philosophy department at Western Washington University. He is the author of *In The Interests of Others* (Kluwer, 1992) and *Punishment as Societal Defense* (Rowman and

Littlefield, 1995). He has also published articles on ethics in a number of journals including *Philosophy and Public Affairs*, *Philosophical Studies*, *Nous*, and *American Philosophical Quarterly*.

TIM MULGAN is in the Philosophy Department at the University of Auckland and is the author of *The Demands of Consequentialism* (in progress) and of several articles on moral and political theory which have appeared in *Philosophy and Public Affairs*, *Analysis*, *The Journal of Political Philosophy*, *Ratio*, and *Utilitas*.

PHILIP PETTIT is Professor of Social and Political Theory at the Australian National University and a regular Visiting Professor at Columbia University, New York. Among his recent books are *The Common Mind: An Essay on Psychology, Society and Politics* (Oxford University Press, 1993, 1996); *Republicanism: A Theory of Freedom and Government* (1997, 1999); and (with Marcia Baron and Michael Slote) *Three Methods of Ethics: A Debate* (Blackwell, 1997).

MADISON POWERS is Associate Professor of Philosophy and Senior Research Scholar at the Kennedy Institute of Ethics, Georgetown University. He is completing a book entitled *Morals, Markets, and Medicine* with co-author Ruth Faden.

JONATHAN RILEY is a Professor jointly in the Murphy Institute of Political Economy and the Department of Political Science at Tulane University. His most recent books are the *Routledge Philosophy GuideBook to Mill on Liberty* (Routledge, 1998), *Mill's Radical Liberalism* (Routledge, 2000) and a co-edited volume (with John Ferejohn and Jack Rakove) on *Constitutional Culture and Democratic Rule* (Cambridge University Press, 2000). He is currently working on *Maximizing Security: A Liberal Utilitarian Theory of Justice and Rights* (forthcoming in the Oxford Political Theory series).

WILLIAM H. SHAW is Professor of Philosophy and chair of the Philosophy Department at San Jose State University. He is the author of several books including *Moore on Right and Wrong: The Normative Ethics of G.E. Moore* (Kluwer, 1995) and *Contemporary Ethics: Taking Account of Utilitarianism* (Blackwell, 1999).

MICHAEL SMITH is Professor of Philosophy at the Research School of Social Sciences, Institute of Advanced Studies, Australian National University. He is the author of *The Moral Problem* (Blackwell, 1995) and the editor of *Meta-Ethics* (Dartmouth, 1995).

ALAN THOMAS is a lecturer in philosophy at the University of Kent at Canterbury. He is the author of *Value and Context* (forthcoming from Oxford University Press).

Index